The Naked President

By the same author

The Hard Road to Market
The Priest Who Had to Die
(with John Moody)

ROGER BOYES

The Naked President

A POLITICAL LIFE OF LECH WALESA

Secker & Warburg
London

First published in England 1994
by Martin Secker & Warburg Limited
Michelin House, 81 Fulham Road, London sw3 6rb

Copyright © 1994 by Roger Boyes
The author has asserted his moral rights

A CIP catalogue record for this book
is available from the British Library
isbn 0 436 20055 4

Phototypeset in 11pt Garamond by Intype, London
Printed in Great Britain
by Clays Ltd, St Ives PLC

For Farida Kuligowska

Behind Walesa's study in the Belvedere Palace
there is a small corridor leading to a shower room.
One day Walesa heard the telephone ringing
on his desk and burst into the room,
dripping water on the carpet.
His secretary entered at that moment,
bringing him his afternoon tea and biscuits.
She gawped at the wet, hairy figure.
"What's the matter?" he barked.
"Have you never seen a naked president before?"

Acknowledgments

Everybody in Poland has a view on Lech Walesa; many have insights and morsels of information that enrich a portrait of the man. After a decade in Poland it would be impossible to repay every debt. Those named below are just a few who helped to keep the picture in focus. Jerzy Borowczak, Stefan Bratkowski, Bishop Jerzy Dabrowski, Wanda Falkowska, Wojciech Gielzynski, Andrzej Gwiazda, Joanna Duda-Gwiazda, Father Henryk Jankowski, Michal Komar, Krzysztof Leski, Wojciech Lamentowicz, Adam Michnik, Piotr Nowina-Konopka, Wladyslaw Sila-Nowicki, Radek Sikorski, Edmund Szczesiak, Tadeusz Wozniak.

The biggest single contribution was made by Malgorzata Kuczynska, who researched, organised and transcribed thousands of pages of material. Gill Coleridge sold the idea, bought time and gently prodded me on. Judy Cooper broke speed-typing records. *The Times* (especially Peter Stothard, Martin Ivens and Richard Owen) encouraged the book, gave me time and kept me in Poland even when it became a "normal" country.

My biggest debt is of course to my wife Farida Kuligowska, to whom this book is dedicated.

Contents

To the royal castle

There were mirrors everywhere. The tall one showed the cut of his long black overcoat. His trousers were the correct length. That was very important. Vaclav Havel, on his inauguration day, had hitched up his trousers and flashed his socks as he strolled in the presidential manner past the *gard du corps* in the courtyard of Prague castle. The Czechs had smiled affectionately. In years to come they would judge Havel more harshly but then, on that special day, the slightly comic figure of the president struck a chord; he was an intellectual, his mind was elsewhere, on Thomas Masaryk perhaps, or some new parody of power. Neither Walesa nor his advisers saw any charm in Havel's unworldliness. Walesa had been brought up to believe that dressing sloppily was a mark of disrespect. That was the code of the Polish countryside where jackets, ties and shoes were worn on Sundays. A fashionable Polish designer had been engaged and she had brought to Gdansk her own designs as well as imported German and Italian suits, and an array of hats for Walesa's wife Danuta. Walesa joked about the fuss, but he took the choice seriously. He was determined, said his advisers, to fit into the mould of an institutional politician. That reading was slightly askew. Walesa wanted to *look* like a statesman for he understood, better than most, the power of illusion in politics. He might dress like George Bush, but he would lead as he always led: in touch with the crowd, intuitive, human, pragmatic. That, at any rate, was the plan.

The smaller mirror in the government villa in Klonowa Street would have shown Walesa's 1990 face: the crags and billows of flesh around his jaw and cheeks, a carefully trimmed grey moustache. The features of the lean, fox-like worker, who had led the Gdansk strikes a decade earlier had all but disappeared. An army barber had compounded the change, cutting back the hair so that Walesa's head now resembled a squashed rugby ball. Did Walesa, as he stared at his reflection, recognise those changes, acknow-

1

ledge how he had aged since 1980? The passages had been remarkable. From worker rebel to grudging revolutionary; from sought-after hero of the Western media to prisoner in virtually solitary confinement; from political non-person to power broker with the Communist authorities; from behind-the-scenes tactician to head of state. All this had taken its toll. "I've simply grown up," he would say later. But there was never anything simple about Walesa.

Lenin, who knew about such things, used to declare that the critical part of a revolution was only reached when there had been a physical, tangible handover of power. The Solidarity revolution, according to this formula, was not complete when the union won the June 1989 elections, nor when Tadeusz Mazowiecki took over as premier (for there were still Communists in his cabinet). It was complete only on inauguration day when Walesa received the insignia of office. Certainly it seemed to Poles as if the wheel had turned its full span. The Polish president-in-exile Ryszard Kaczorowski – whose "government" had been meeting in London for over 40 years to show that Poles would never accept Communist rule – formally resigned. "Today when moral and political authority have become united I believe that the centuries-long effort of Polish émigrés and exiles will bear fruit." *Moral* and political authority? Walesa swore his oath in front of parliament (the Sejm) – "I swear that the good of my country and that the welfare of its citizens will always constitute for me a dictate of the highest order" and then added, "So help me God!" The religious reference was not a casual afterthought. It stated that Walesa was going to tap a tradition of Christian rule that stretched back to King Mieszko in the year 966. For a thousand years, the Church, the Pope, the saints and the talisman have been part of the magic of kingship in Poland. In 973, when Mieszko's son Boleslaw had to be left behind in Germany (supposedly a hostage), the king sent locks of his child's hair to the Pope and sought his protection. Mieszko symbolically subordinated his country to the will of the Pope. Centuries later King Jan Kazimierz thanked the Virgin Mary for her part in defeating the Swedish siege of Jasna Gora monastery in 1655 and declared the so-called Black Madonna to be the spiritual protectress of Poland. Thus was state power wedded with the Church. All the elected kings of the eighteenth century were committed Catholics. Only the post-war Communists had tried to rule against the Church. When this failed the Communists tried to secure the Church's political neutrality. But even from the sidelines the Church was able to make plain its ruling preferences. In August 1956 – a few months before the "October Spring" and the takeover of party chief Wladyslaw

Gomulka – a million Poles spontaneously trekked on a pilgrimage to the Jasna Gora monastery in Czestechowa. The power of the crowd, and of the Church, became obvious to the Communist rulers. By the time a Polish pope ascended the Throne of St Peter in 1978 it was clear that the Church could decisively influence the Polish political scene, without directly participating in it. The Gdansk strikers pinned to the fence of the Lenin shipyard in 1980 the slogan "The Madonna is striking with us." By introducing a religious element to the presidential oath, by wearing a badge of the Black Madonna in his lapel, Walesa wanted to underline that the era of Communist regents was over.

Talking to aides some weeks before the ceremony Walesa mentioned how diplomatically awkward the presence of General Wojciech Jaruzelski would be for the president-in-exile, indeed for all the participants. The aides took this as an instruction to bump Jaruzelski, the outgoing president, off the invitation list. Later Walesa would try to pin the blame elsewhere and play down the decision, but there was little doubt that the snub was more than clumsy protocol; it was a calculated political gesture. In parliament Walesa proclaimed a "Third Republic" of Poland, the successor of the independent Second Republic that had existed between the two World Wars. The point was clear. Power was not being handed over to Solidarity from the Communists – since the Communists and their Peoples Republic never ruled legitimately – but rather from the pre-war regime. Jammed into parliament for the speech there were 400 deputies (including the ex-dissident Jacek Kuron in denim jeans) but also the daughters of Josef Pilsudski, the formidable leader of inter-war Poland. The word "Communist" did not appear in Walesa's speech and when he expressed the wish for good neighbourly relations he mentioned Ukraine, Belorussia and Lithuania – but not the Soviet Union. It was as if the almost five decades of Communism were no more than a bad tooth to be extracted as cleanly and as painlessly as possible. Remove the tooth and Poland could resume its rudely interrupted history, picking up the strands of the first modern independent Polish state.

Yet the rubble of Communism needed to be carefully sifted and understood. Poles had a duty to review the immediate past even if that meant breaking a few idols, discarding some myths or staring bravely into the mirror. Had Walesa addressed the matter, inauguration day could have been a defining moment for the new Polish state. But Walesa dodged it. By rejecting Jaruzelski – architect of martial law though far from being a universal figure of hate – Walesa was rejecting part of himself. What did the new Poland stand for? Merely ignoring the Communist era was not enough, least of all for Walesa, who was so patently moulded by the system. Would Walesa take on the mantle of Pilsudski, who had saved the country's independence but who also rode roughshod over parliament? Or would Walesa develop the ideas of the frustrated ultra-nationalist Roman Dmowski, who had so coloured the politics of pre-war Poland? Walesa offered no vision, for he had none. There was to be a market economy, of course, but by late 1990 there was no dispute about this in Poland; even the former Communists preached the wonders of the social market. Democracy? Well, yes. But Walesa was soon to make clear that like Pilsudski, or for that matter the old Communist chief Edward Gierek, he had scant respect for parliamentary debate.

The original English use of the word "Revolution" suggests a turning back, a rotation, the return of a wheel to its earlier position. Poland's revolution may have been just such a shift, as conservative as it was radical. By 1994 Poland was incomparably better than Poland in 1984. Important liberties had been won, democratic institutions were gaining strength and the shops were full. But the huge effort, the hard slog of systemic transformation had taken over from the initial fever of change. Special leadership qualities were needed and were demanded of Walesa.

The time for improvised street politics had passed; the nation was not a crowd. Charismatic leadership is based on an emotional relationship between leader and led. The people must believe that their leader will overcome all obstacles, solve all problems. When the belief crumbles, the charismatic leader is lost. He must either make way for others, or reinvent himself as an institutional politician. Walesa's long road from the barricades of Gdansk to the Belvedere Palace represents precisely that kind of personal transformation. It is an intriguing story of a fallible hero, often infuriating, capable of real personal courage and unpredictable flights of political imagination.

After Walesa's speech parliament applauded the new president. Contrary to the Polish news reports it was not a rousing tribute. Left-wing deputies did no more than stand up dutifully while others clapped but refused to sing the traditional song "May he live a hundred years". Walesa, they rightly suspected, would not be an easy partner. The president left the building, half blinded by the flashlights and for the first time settled into the official limousine of the head of state. It was a black armour-plated Volvo 740, rarely used by his predecessor because the general could not sit upright without removing his peaked cap. "To the royal castle!" Walesa barked to the chauffeur, and for the first time that day his face broke into a broad smile.

4

CHAPTER ONE

Absent fathers

The study was familiar terrain for veteran readers of the *New Yorker*. One wall was plastered with framed diplomas, all copperplate and red-wax seals. There was a tall potted rubber plant in the corner behind Doctor Z's black Swedish desk. In the waiting-room piped Brahms was calming the patients; in the study only the sound of the radiator, gurgling like a happy infant, interrupted Dr Z's long professional silences. Thurber would have insisted on a couch. Doctor Z preferred leather armchairs so deep that patients invariably lost their small change.

Doctor Z was a Freudian, and one of the first psychoanalysts to set up in private practice in Poland. The early post-Communist years were a boom time for analysts. Poles were rendered giddy by their new individual responsibilities; the collapse of the collective spirit had forced them to sort out priorities. It was a time of great personal anxiety. For the neurotically rich, or the richly neurotic, Doctor Z offered his counsel. Since professional ethics discouraged advertising, analysts were dependent on word-of-mouth recommendation. A discreet plug in a London newspaper would do Dr Z no harm at all. Over the telephone he had purred his acceptance; he would be delighted to help.

"It's about an acquaintance, a politician," I said as Doctor Z nodded and gave a slight, knowing smile. He was in his late 40s, unbearded, Brooklyn-trained.

"A Pole, of course?"

"Of course. A war baby. His father died when he was still in nappies. Later his mother – whom he loved dearly – married his father's brother. The boy and the stepfather couldn't stand each other. The boy became unruly, verbally aggressive, bit of a bully."

"Not uncommon." Dr Z was cleaning out his pipe. A pen lay ready.

"Well," I continued, "he starts what we might call a political career and

5

odd things happen. He seems to hate authority but at crucial moments he caves in to it. After a while nobody was quite sure whether he was playing the game of the authorities or was pitted against them. It's not really clear whether he knows himself. Ordinary people say he is unpredictable, unstable. None of which would matter much except that he has suddenly become rather important."

"And you want me to work this through with you, to see how an Oedipal relationship affects a politician's future behaviour?"

"That's about it."

"Then I need to have more data. We should start with his name."

"Lech Walesa."

Doctor Z's expression did not change. He did not clench his fist or break a pencil. He poked his pipe again. After a while he pulled out a drawer and removed a Polish Filofax.

"I think," he said, without lifting his eyes from the pages of the book, "that my usefulness has come to an end. I shall try to find some colleagues who might be of more help." Within two minutes I had been courteously shown out of the room.

So much for the pursuit of psycho-biography. Dr Z's colleagues, keen enough to bluster at cocktail parties, became strangely reticent when Walesa's name was raised. This reaction was based on more than clinical discretion. It was a recognition of a powerful taboo by a group whose professional claim was to be beyond taboos. Similar reactions came from many other Poles. The myth of Lech Walesa as the revolutionary who broke the spine of Communism had to be kept intact. Few Poles believed, in the 1990s, that Walesa would survive a closer look at how or why he became a revolutionary, and at how or why he made the transition to statesman. And if Walesa's statue were to be toppled, if he were to join the other broken idols, what would remain of peoples' lives, of their personal histories? Lech Walesa and Solidarity had defined a generation. The Solidarity movement had splintered. What would survive if Walesa went too? Better, then, to be silent. Or to grumble at Walesa's defective grammar and his political gaffes while leaving his biography untouched: he was the man who jumped over the Gdansk shipyard fence in 1980, the plucky electrician who walked like Charlie Chaplin. That is how he should remain. There were those, on the political fringes, who tried to re-write the legend. Walesa, they claimed, had been a secret agent for the Communists in the 1970s and had not clearly distanced himself from the security police since then. His closest adviser as President was a man who had sinister gaps in his *curriculum vitae*. Too often, they said, Walesa had brokered deals that came out in the Communists' favour. Yet the conspiracy theories which sought to explain away the paradoxes, the bullying and the submissiveness, never quite held water. For one thing Walesa had publicly acknowledged, in the first volume of his autobiography, that he had signed some papers at the behest of the secret police: hardly an act of a man with a guilty secret. If Walesa was a puppet, who was the puppet-master?

To accept the conspiracy view of Walesa you had to believe that a secret-police mastermind decided in the 1980s that Communism was bound to collapse and selected Walesa as the man most capable of steering Poland towards a peaceful power-sharing deal which would allow the Communists to keep or to make their fortunes. That kind of speculation led nowhere except deeper into the dark labyrinth, perhaps to bedlam itself. The debate about Walesa's past flared up in 1992 and 1993 and came to no conclusion. Remarkably, Poles after twelve years of contact with Walesa could not reach a judgment on whether he was a hero, villain or buffoon. The reason was that few Poles dared to excavate the past.

Walesa's motivation in times of crisis – in 1970, 1980, 1982 and 1989 – has been allowed to remain a mystery; his choice of friends and enemies is regarded merely as eccentric or the product of a whim. The depiction of Walesa as a secret agent was almost certainly misplaced, but it did raise questions: why *did* Walesa behave so strangely, sometimes with genius, sometimes surrendering important political positions? Walesa's life provides a key to understanding the collapse of Communism in the East and a way of unravelling the riddles of the post-Communist world – its latent violence, its most profound fears. But until now, his life has been examined only by hagiographers and disgruntled courtiers.

The starting point must surely be the gritty dirt road to Popowo.

In the winter, a grey mixture of mud and slush sprays against the horse-drawn carts and trucks of the farmers as they bump over the potholes. No bus comes this way. The postman avoids the place. When the snow melts, the khaki streaks of the field peep out, adding colour to the buckled landscape. There are more colours in the spring and you can even romance about the village with its ten shabby farmsteads; call it Chopin country, watch out for storks, admire the strength of the trees as they resist the wind. But in truth it is a desolate corner, on the outer edge of history. It has not figured on a map since 1918.

7

Lech Walesa was happy to escape Popowo and the Dobrzyn county, to call himself a worker and not the son of an impoverished farmer. It is hard country that drives people – including many of Walesa's ancestors and recent relatives – to emigrate. Walesa usually returns only once a year, on All Saints Day to visit the family graves. He comes in a high-powered Volvo, flanked by bodyguards, a gaudy riot of sirens and flashing lights. He leaves quickly, for Popowo shows him, more profoundly than any other of his presidential pitstops, how little he has changed Poland and how close he is to failure.

There are several villages in Poland called Popowo, and it is easy to pick the wrong one. Cautious visitors seek regular reassurance from peasants at the roadside, lumpy flushed men in stained jackets. Many of them are drunk. The harvest is in, the crop sold and it is time for *bimber*, the home-brewed vodka. They may stagger and slur their words like the reeling characters from Wyspianski's epic *Wesele*, but they know the road well enough. "The old Walesa house? That ruin? Waste of time! Straight on, turn right – don't look back!"

Nobody really knows why Mateusz Walesa bought 400 acres here at the beginning of the nineteenth century. He appears to have left France in a hurry. In any case he was a shrewd lord of the manor, renting out packets of land and setting up in the roadside inn a Jewish publican who served as an informal banker for the peasant community. Other Walesas saw little future in the Popowo lands. After the death of Mateusz, his estate had to be divided between three sons. Two ended up in Siberia after participating in the 1863 insurrection against the Russians. The third, Jan, headed for France where he discovered the intriguing world of gaming-houses. He returned to Poland infrequently, mainly to sell off woodland and the more fertile fields to pay off his debts. This became a pattern for two generations. His eldest son, also called Jan, found the casinos of French spa-towns more congenial than bleak Popowo. This Jan was the last of the "grand" Walesas, the last to have a library, to have a servant, the last to pretend to be a gentleman landowner. He frittered away his land.

Kazimierz Pawlowski, one of the oldest inhabitants of Popowo, recalled: "Jan was well read and educated – but he was also a violent man. He used to gamble at cards and drank a lot in the Chalin inn. That's why he had to keep selling off land. His sons were different though." Boleslaw (Lech's father) was left with a kerchief-sized plot, enough for potatoes and chickens.

Locals were rather contemptuous of the Walesas, for their poor husbandry and fickle habits. But the contemporary Walesas – Lech, his sister Izabella and assorted cousins – speak with some pride of the last Jan. He was a rogue, boasting of his early love affairs in France and of dubious acts of wartime heroism, but he was an important link with the past in a dismal present. By the time Lech Walesa was old enough to listen and learn, Jan's world had disappeared: the Jews who had played such an important part in this stretch of Dobrzyn county had been wiped out by the Germans in the Second World War, the Czarist police had been replaced by a Communist-controlled militia. France was far away, an "imperialist, capitalist tool" of the Americans. The old order had collapsed and all that remained of Jan's universe was the boggy land – and even that no longer belonged to the Walesas.

For children brought up in the political stasis of Stalinist Poland, Jan's stories told of bewildering and exciting change: the collapse of the Austro-Hungarian and Czarist empires, the First World War, the Russian Revolution, the 1918 independence of Poland, the military campaign against the Bolsheviks in 1920 led by Marshal Josef Pilsudski.

All this action, at cinematic pace. Yet the Polish countryside followed its own rhythms, even at a time of political upheaval. Betrothals and christenings, saints' days, the sewing and the harvesting and the bartering on market day: these set the pattern of Lech Walesa's early life, just as they had governed the daily lives of his ancestors. The nineteenth-century uprisings against the Russians had claimed some menfolk, so too had the campaign against the Bolsheviks. The men would travel by cart or on horseback to the nearest barracks, blessed first by the priest from nearby Sobowo. Most would return a few months or years later and in the meantime the women kept the farms alive, the children and the animals fed.

The returning soldiers brought war stories that later became the dominant, most lively part of the children's education. Jan Walesa, a member of Pilsudski's Legions, claimed for example to have saved his leader from marauding Cossacks by dressing him up in women's clothes. Not even grandson Lech fully believed that story, but it made the point: Popowo was a place to hide, not to fight. The battlefields were elsewhere.

The German occupation, after Hitler's 1939 invasion, did however fundamentally change the life of Popowo. In Polish cities food was rationed but farmers and their city go-betweens set up an effective if highly-priced supply of black-market meat. The Germans, convinced that black marketeers also had contacts with Polish partisans, tried their hardest to stop this traffic. There was a strict ban on the slaughtering of livestock and the brewing of alcohol. The police made spot checks at night. Boleslaw Walesa, Lech's father, also traded meat – there was no other way of clothing the family – and narrowly escaped arrest.

Attempting to slaughter a pig one night, he botched the job and merely stunned it. Killing a pig was not easy. Some neighbours with pitchforks formed a circle while Boleslaw (known as Bolek) rushed the scared animal. The pig slipped away despite the desperate stabbings of the peasants and Bolek had to lunge at it with a knife. The wounded animal escaped and left an incriminating trail of blood out of the farm. The next day the police pounced on the Walesa farm but Lech's mother persuaded, perhaps bribed, the police to drop the investigation. The pig was confiscated.

Bolek and his brother Stanislaw had both fought in the short, early campaign against the German invaders in September 1939 but came back to Popowo after the rapid German victory. Edward Walesa, one of Lech's older brothers, remembers it as a time of elaborate hide-and-seek. "My uncle Stanislaw, later to be my stepfather, took part in the 1939 war and was taken prisoner near Mlawa. He managed to escape from the train taking him to a prisoner-of-war camp. Then he found his way to us and hid in our house. Iza (Lech's sister) and myself acted as sentries – we ran back and knocked at the door as soon as we saw someone approaching the farm. But somebody must have denounced him. The Germans came and made him show where we were hiding a barrel full of meat. They were torturing him – I saw it with my own eyes." As Hitler swept through Poland into Russia, the lot of the Poles deteriorated. The farm was not enough to keep the family, which by 1943 included three children. Bolek survived on carpentry work and though his pre-war building gang – which had put up barns and even churches – could not function under German rule, there was no shortage of odd jobs.

When the tide of battle changed so too did the life of Popowo and the Walesa family. The war in the east began to go badly for Hitler. The Polish partisan armies were becoming more confident and the Walesa children willingly carried toy buckets full of food and drink to the nearby woods where the Polish soldiers occasionally went to ground. The large number of Wehrmacht deserters passing along the fringes of the village – also fed by the Walesa children – was a clear indication that the Germans were in trouble. Yet this military reversal also brought misery for the Walesa family. The Germans, now desperate for manpower, rounded up Poles to build defensive fortifications along the Vistula and Drweca rivers. Early one morning the Germans caught Boleslaw.

The Polish prisoners were taken first to Chalin, to the former country house of the Zielinski family. After the war the Communists converted the modest house into a school and Lech Walesa attended class there, but in 1943 it was merely a convenient staging-post for the Germans. The prisoners were beaten up regularly. Lech Walesa recalled seeing bloodstains on the walls many years later.

Boleslaw Walesa was moved to a labour camp in Mlyniec, near Torun. According to Edward it was there that Lech was conceived. "Towards the end of 1942, when I was six, my mother received permission from the Germans to visit him in the camp. She took me with her. We walked for two days because the Germans wouldn't let us go by bus or even by cart. We arrived at Mlyniec in the morning. She was so happy, when she came out, so changed. They made love that night and after nine months, on 29 September 1943, Leszek was born. That is how the president of Poland was conceived."

Boleslaw's health deteriorated in the camp. The dormitories were unheated and in the winter the frost was so intense that the hair of the prisoners froze to the wall at night. There was little food, and even less for those registered as sick. By the time he returned to his farm in Popowo, there was not much left of Lech Walesa's father. After two months at home, coughing blood in his bedroom, he died.

In Poland the war created a fatherless generation. They were, in the words of the German psycho-analyst Volker Pilgrim, Mother-sons, *Muttersöhne*. Certainly Lech, 18 months old when his father died, became his mother's favourite. She was in her mid-20s and had been deeply in love with Boleslaw. As a 17-year-old girl Feliksa Kaminska had defied her family by marrying a Walesa. The Kaminskis shared the local assessment of the Walesas as careless spendthrifts. In particular the mother of Feliksa – an ambitious, well-educated and well-travelled woman – had higher hopes for her daughter. The families however were eventually reconciled. Boleslaw (called Bolek by all the Walesas) was a transparently honest man with none of the blarney of his father and with a sound sense of commerce. But Bolek's death in June 1945 devastated Feliksa. She had four children to bring up, a small time-consuming farm to run. In 1945–46, as the Communists manoeuvred their way into power, ordinary Poles were becoming aware of the poverty of their country. Popowo had no electricity and was not to be linked up until 1967. In winter, night fell before four o'clock and Feliksa Walesa would light up the kerosene lamp. But since kerosene was difficult to buy – indeed all the most basic goods were unavailable – the day effectively came to an end at dusk.

Lech Walesa was brought up in a world without books; there was no light and no time for reading. There was barely a book in the village apart from the family bible and home-made scrapbooks. The priest in Sobowo did have books and access to information; that was part of his power over the community. A few ancient radios brought news to the village and some morsels, often only half-understood, would be passed on by the menfolk. Various attempts were made to set up a library in the 1950s, but the demand was low. A farmer allowing his house to be used as a library had to take on irksome bureaucratic tasks, including keeping a record of all books borrowed. He was also required to set aside one well-lit room throughout the year and heat it in the winter. With coal scarce that was ample deterrent. Popowo in the late 1940s and the early 1950s was a netherworld, cut off from the big political currents. All energy was concentrated on survival.

Feliksa had only one rational way out of her personal crisis: to marry her brother-in-law. Two days before war broke out in August 1939, Stanislaw had travelled by cart to Sobowo with Bolek and Feliksa. Stanislaw had pledged on the church bible that he would look after Feliksa should Bolek fall in battle. This was a common pledge in the nervous weeks before the outbreak of war. Since the parish priest had a written record of the pledge, he was able to marry Feliksa and Stanislaw. Under more usual circumstances the Church would have objected since the family tie was too close. Feliksa, it seems, was not particularly attracted to Stanislaw. But her own mother had been twice married and twice widowed, and so the idea of taking a new husband was not particularly repulsive or shocking. Married to Stanislaw, some money would come into the household, the roof of the small cottage could be repaired, the animals slaughtered and the children given some firm paternal discipline.

Stanislaw was more flamboyant than his brother Bolek, sharper with money and market trading. He had never planned to settle in Popowo – he, more than his unfortunate brother, had inherited the Walesa restlessness – but he could see the merits of taking on Feliksa. Poland had been shattered by the war; most city-dwellers were leading very hard lives, reconstructing smashed houses on low wages and poor rations. Life in the country was tough too, but at least farmers lived close to food. If things became worse in the towns, farmers would still have the ultimate bargaining chips: chickens, eggs, milk. The farms of Poland, unlike other East European countries, were still in private hands. There was though, in those early post-war years, a definite policy of discrimination against private farms to cajole young peasants to work in the new state factories and leave elderly farmers

12

without heirs. Since the state controlled the supply of vital goods, from fertiliser to nails, the Communists had a formidable lever. But the Polish peasantry battened down, learned to improvise and concentrated on producing enough food for immediate family needs and a small surplus for barter, or for sale. Had Stanislaw gone to the city to work he would have got more cash but he would certainly not have had a flat to live in. And so he chose to stay. Feliksa was still pretty, perhaps life would improve. When it did not, Stanislaw became increasingly brutal to his children and to his stepchildren.

Stanislaw had a strange war. He had been captured a second time, in late 1942, with Bolek. They were jailed together in Chalin. But while Bolek was sent to the camp near Torun, Stanislaw was transported to Germany as part of a forced labour detachment.

On the way to Dachau concentration camp, he escaped from the convoy and survived by holing up with a German girl who fed and sheltered him for over a year. That at any rate is the story he told to the Walesa children. In 1945 when he returned to Poland he was spotted in a German uniform which he said later was merely a disguise. There is something odd about this tale. The only corroboration for Stanislaw's account of his time in Hitler Germany would be from the German woman, and she has not been traced. It is not at all clear why the Germans should have been taking him to Dachau. But there were many Poles in Dachau, and war does produce unusual, incomplete episodes, so Stanislaw's version should stand. It would surprise nobody, though, if it were to emerge that Stanislaw had added a few imaginative flourishes to the story – he had been brought up, after all, listening to the epic love affairs and war adventures of Jan, his father.

After a year helping Feliksa on the farm for a while, Stanislaw married his sister-in-law. This caused real dismay among the Walesa children. Izabella, the eldest child, developed a hatred of her stepfather. Lech Walesa remembers Izabella leading her brothers and sisters into the woods to hide from Stanislaw. It was Izabella who first took Lech, then four or five years old, to see the grave of their father and it was only then that he understood that Bolek, and not Stanislaw, was his real father.

Tadeusz Walesa, Lech's first stepbrother, born in 1948, watched as one half of the family turned against the other. "Iza was the first to leave the family home. She studied at a school in Plock and lived in a dormitory there – she seldom visited us. She could never forgive my mother for remarrying. The other two brothers left and so of Bolek's children only Leszek stayed. He addressed my father – that is Lech's stepfather – as Daddy

13

until he was about ten years old. Later, under the influence of his elder sister and brothers, he began to call him Uncle. For them, my father was just that – an uncle. In fact I think he treated his three natural sons much more harshly than his late brother's kids. Frankly, he was tough on all of us. He would say something once, then repeat it – but there would be no third time. He would reach straight for his leather belt. We all got our share of that."

There was a great deal of violence in the household but it was broadly accepted by the children. It was the norm for country children in Poland. Lech's passionate dislike of his stepfather was rooted rather in the feeling that Stanislaw was a usurper, that he was the man who stole his mother and his mother's love.

Bolek's children discussed the death of their father over and over again. "It was a burden that cast a shadow over my whole childhood," recalls Walesa. Izabella in particular had a clear memory of her father and depicted him as a solid, saintly figure. Stanislaw, by contrast, was regarded as almost wicked. Their grandmother, the wife of their admired Jan Walesa, had died in childbirth – while giving birth to Stanislaw. Bolek had been killed by the war, and was a kind of hero, while their stepfather had not only survived, but had come back in a German uniform. This resentment carried on into adulthood.

It was Stanislaw who persuaded Feliksa to emigrate to the United States in 1973, where she died. He did not return to Poland for her funeral. Interviewed by Oriana Fallaci in 1980, Walesa was still contemptuous of his stepfather, whom he said had become a money-grubber. As they grew older all four of Bolek's children began to challenge their mother: "Why did you marry this man?"

Tadeusz, Stanislaw's first child, was born exactly one year after the death of Lech's father. For Iza that was the final straw. She had wanted to lay flowers on her father's grave. Instead she had to be on hand in the house as her first stepbrother was born. That was hardly Stanislaw's fault, but from then on, 15 June became a marker date for the Walesa family. One half celebrated the birth of Tadeusz, the other mourned the death of Bolek. The family was bound to disintegrate anyway, Tadeusz Walesa believes. "My sister Iza is fourteen years my senior. Because of the large age gap between us the ties between us were not strong. We were all leaving home one by one and our parents did not object." As Edward Walesa remembers it, the family quickly lost any cohesion. "It was only Christmas Eve, that was the only day when we were a true family – though without the true father.

Even then, when we grew up we went our own way. As soon as we started our own families we never met at the Christmas table."

The mistrustful elements of Lech Walesa's character probably originated in this uneasy, fractious childhood. There were some parallels with the early childhood of Lenin and other revolutionaries. Erik Erikson (in *Childhood and Society*, 1963) suggests that basic attitudes of trust and mistrust are formed in the early oral phase at childhood. Lenin, perhaps because of an absent father or the birth of a sister, became a very suspicious child. Like Lenin, Walesa was difficult to befriend – and difficult to betray, since nobody was allowed to stay close for long. Nowadays critics of Walesa say that power, the jump from revolutionary to statesman, has made him a lonely man. In fact, Walesa was also a lonely child, competing for his mother's love and time.

Walesa's life was bound by school, church and farm. The school – the manor house which had imprisoned his father – was 4 kilometres in one direction, the church in Sobowo 6 kilometres in the other. In school he was a mediocre pupil in a mediocre class. Above average in mathematics, below average in Polish.

Today the school is a ruin. It was closed down in 1984 because of fears that the ceiling might collapse and since then the place has run to seed. In Walesa's time the setting was quite grand. Since then bricks and timber have been stolen from the estate, the park is overgrown with weeds and is used as a dumping-ground for bulky rubbish. Behind the mansion is the field where Walesa played football – he preferred to be goalkeeper since, with his short legs, he could not keep pace with the other boys. The lake where he and his brothers used to swim is heavily polluted; tin cans and discarded condoms bob on the surface. After returning from school Walesa had various farm jobs – chopping up straw, tending the livestock. It was the normal existence of a Polish peasant boy but Walesa felt it to be drudgery. Only the Church provided some break from the daily routine. Above all it bonded him closely to his profoundly religious mother.

"I sucked religion from my mother's breast," says Walesa (later the Israeli premier Yitzhak Shamir, angered at apparently anti-Jewish comments made by Walesa, would declare: "Poles suck in anti-Semitism with their mothers' milk"). Feliksa, with a clutch of young children, sometimes found it impossible to make the long walk to church and Lech Walesa, with the elder children, would then feel particularly proud as if they were their mother's emissaries. Since their father was buried in the Sobowo graveyard it was also a way of maintaining family solidarity, part of the great emotional struggle with Stanislaw.

The local church was not, in the 1950s, a crucible of opposition. There were no great pulpit appeals on behalf of the imprisoned Cardinal Stefan Wyszynski, though the local chaplain usually managed to make a reference of some kind to the Primate. But in those days any church building had some political significance. The mere survival of the Church as an institution during the long periods when Poland had been deprived of its independence – between 1794 and 1919, and again under the Nazi occupation – had helped to create a specific blend of Catholicism and Polish patriotism. In the second half of the nineteenth century the church played an active part in building national sentiment in the countryside. By the 1950s the peasantry, deeply suspicious about the motives and future plans of the Communists, saw the Church as natural protector. When Wladyslaw Gomulka took over the Communist leadership in 1956, the tension between Church and state eased somewhat and the new freedom eventually percolated through to the pulpit in Sobowo where the sermons became slightly more daring. Walesa was thirteen at the time and for the first time he began to listen more intently to the words. Walesa was not particularly devout as an adolescent. He stresses that he was always a believer – apart from a drifting period between the ages of 17 and 19 – but he tended to be rather pragmatic in his attitude to the Church. "What's the point of going to confession if you have nothing to confess?" he joked with a schoolmate. In one interview in the early 1980s, Walesa claimed that he wanted to be a priest but no one can recall him stating this ambition as a child or teenager. To his friends in class he said he wanted to be a pilot.

The Sobowo church did however play some part in the rough education of Walesa. It was, for one thing, the only place where Walesa was exposed to a well-spoken, grammatically correct version of the Polish language. Neither his mother nor his stepfather had mastered the various cases and even the teachers in Chalin, hastily trained and far from enthusiastic, stumbled over their words.

The Sobowo church was a home away from home, in a practical as well as a spiritual sense – it was a legitimate way of ducking out of tedious work on the farm. As he entered his teens Walesa became more and more resentful of labouring on the farm. Stanislaw, by 1951, had three sons of his own – Tadeusz, Zygmunt and Wojciech. Among Bolek's children he was obviously the last in the pecking order, after Edward, born in 1937, and Stanislaw, born in 1938. There was not the slightest chance that he would inherit a significant amount of land. Walesa, with no clear idea of his future, became an unruly teenager. One local remembers the Walesa brothers – with Lech, the youngest, as gang-leader – walking to church fairs. "They would rip off pieces of wooden fencing on the way, to use them later in fights. That's why we called him *sztacheciarz* (the fencer)." The fairs celebrated church holidays but they usually ended in brawls and carousing. Unlike his brothers Lech never got drunk: his stepfather would have thrashed him hard. The Walesa brothers would attend the traditional Saturday dances at the fire station in Sobowo. Sobowo is a relatively big village strung out along a narrow asphalt road which eventually leads to Dobrzyn-on-the-Vistula. The fire station is at one end, the church – on a steep hill – at the other. A middle-aged woman who has spent her whole life in Sobowo remembered how the fire-station dances would end when the Walesa brothers let themselves go. "I often met him and his gang at the dances in those days. My memory of him is that he was quarrelsome and aggressive. If there was a brawl going on you could be sure that he had something to do with it. They grabbed anything close at hand. Stones, sticks, anything. There were plenty of black eyes and bloody noses . . . although he had a rather poor physique Walesa usually got the upper hand – I think that was because of his determination. There was some anger inside him."

From his stepfather, Lech Walesa learned to hate the countryside. "Work hard at school," Stanislaw would advise all the children, "make as much money as you can – don't end up like me." Then he would motion around the family kitchen as if it were a prison. Walesa freely admits his distaste for Popowo and the rituals of farming life. But it is also, he says, his "network", his future code of behaviour. "That stayed with me – the attachment to tradition, the stability, the respect for elders, priests and religion." But in the post-war years the countryside was also synonymous with poverty and impotence. "What I couldn't stand," writes Walesa, "was the helplessness of the peasants; that I had to walk seven kilometres to church and five to school and didn't even have a bicycle; that I drowned in snowdrifts and choked on the dust." Walesa's poverty may be overstated. The original Walesa line that he had to walk barefoot to school and church has been somewhat modified over time. In fact he often took off his shoes because they pinched and he was under parental orders not to scuff them. Even so, a visit to Walesa's birthplace shows how tough life must have been. It is little more than a shack: a wooden roof, brick and timber beginning to splinter. There are two rooms – barely 30 square metres in total – a peeling

17

green-painted front door. Life for the seven children and the two adults must have been intolerably cramped.

The only Walesas still living in Popowo by the 1990s were the farmer Stefan Walesa and his son, Jaroslaw. Stefan's father, Jan, was the brother of Bolek and Stanislaw – Stefan is, in other words, the cousin of Lech Walesa. Stefan now owns Bolek and Stanislaw's land (about fifteen acres) and it is on his fields that Lech Walesa's birthplace nestles among the bracken. Stefan's father worked in a steelworks in the United States and signed up for the US Army during the war, seeing action against Japan. That earned him an army pension which for a time made his family rich, in Polish terms. The result is plain to see: Stefan's farm is the most modern in Popowo. He even had a small combine harvester. Jaroslaw has been hesitating whether to take over the farm from his father. It is the same debate, phrased in almost the same terms, as the Popowo Walesas have been engaging in for the past century or more.

"There's nobody else to take over," muses Jaroslaw, "and maybe it's not sensible to move to town when townfolk are losing their jobs. I suppose it's difficult to imagine Popowo without Walesas." For Jarek, and other waverers, the decisive element would be if there were a surge of public investment in the village. Lech Walesa's hut could become a museum, then bus services would have to be started. A motel could be built on the site of the old Popowo inn, established by Mateusz Walesa in the early nineteenth century. Maybe a road could be built. "When the thaw comes it is difficult to reach Popowo even by tractor," grumbles Jaroslaw. And the other farms join in with the complaints of farmers throughout Eastern Europe. Crops are sold cheaply, but machines and equipment are priced at Western levels. "A litre of milk should cost the same as a litre of diesel oil," says young Jaroslaw.

In Popowo there is great bitterness about Lech Walesa. In the presidential elections in the autumn of 1990, he secured only 156 votes in the Chalin district, barely ahead of the obscure Polish-Canadian émigré Stanislaw Tyminski who picked up 124 votes. Walesa's divorce from the countryside rankles. And the old local prejudice about the Walesa family – that they were a clan of weak gamblers and poor farmers – has been replaced by the myth of Walesa as a rich miser, punishing Popowo for his own unhappy childhood. Every contact that Walesa has had with his home village in recent years has sparked off new resentment. When Popowo complained that the Polish president had not visited his birthplace, Walesa was determined to show he was not ashamed of his roots. He arranged to meet the local farmers in the old Sobowo fire house to hear their complaints. A new back door was cut into the wall of the fire station to allow his many bodyguards to enter; a respectable crowd, not jubilant but merely curious, gathered in the main hall waiting for the local-boy-made-good. But the meeting was delayed — the farmers had refused to let the presidential helicopter land on their fields. When Walesa's mother, and then later his stepfather, died in the United States, Walesa received a small inheritance. He made this over to the Sobowo parish priest, Father Jan Placiszewski, as a tribute to the church that had figured so strongly in his childhood. The cash was used to build a chapel at the cemetery, to extend and modernise the vicarage. The priest never entered the donation in his account books because under the Communists he would have had to pay a hefty sixty per cent tax and might have attracted the attentions of the secret police. As far as Walesa was concerned the money just seemed to evaporate. There was a tacit understanding between the priest and Walesa that a Walesa museum would be set up in a small house on the church grounds. Walesa found some old pipes, family pictures, the huge ball-point pen with which he signed the Gdansk agreements in 1980 and handed them over. But no museum has been established. Walesa's home village is as neglected as it was in the 1940s and the 1950s. The grudges from those days have survived too; there are still many in Popowo, Chalin and Sobowo who refuse to talk to Walesa for some past slight or imagined insult. Walesa, questioned about the bad blood, raises his hands in despair. There could be no more powerful motive for fleeing from the countryside to the anonymity of Gdansk.

CHAPTER TWO

Look what they're doing to our children

Lech Walesa took the train to Gdansk in 1967, and there he stayed. By chance he met a friend who suggested signing up at the shipyards; in the rush to build one of the world's biggest shipbuilding industries, the yard management was desperate for electricians. Walesa was not fresh to work. During school holidays he and his brothers had worked at a brick factory near Popowo. And, at the age of 16, he had enrolled at a vocational school in Lipno, the largest town in the area. The idea of the school was to train mechanics for future employment in a POM, Panstwowy Osrodek Maszynowy, depots that serviced the vehicles and machines of the farmers. POMs were part of the new socialist vision, halfway houses between factory and farm, a useful support in the drive to collectivisation. Actually by the time Walesa started at the school, in 1959, all the political steam had left the Communist collectivisers. Polish agriculture was to stay firmly in private hands. But with little investment in the countryside, farmers stuck mainly to the old methods – horse-drawn ploughs, harvesting by scythe. When their few machines broke down, they had only a scant notion of how to repair them. POMs also rented machines to farmers. And so POMs still had a mission. The vocational school was also supposed to teach the pupils, who lived in strictly run dormitories, some rudimentary academic subjects. Walesa proved to be adept at the mechanical side of the course, and scored above average grades in mathematics, sport and, to everyone's surprise, behaviour. He was constantly being reprimanded for smoking, or for stuffing his cap in his pocket, or for cheekiness. But he was something of a gang leader in the dormitory and managed to keep the place in order. That appears to have compensated for his occasional flashes of rebellion.

Contemporaries remember a small, bustling, energetic character with a wise-cracking manner. It seems that he was happy in Lipno, away from home for the first time, from the stifling discipline of his stepfather and the slog of farm work. At the Lipno school, history was his weakest subject and in conversation, since he was elected head of state, he has always expressed amazement at his own weak grasp of the subject. Yet in the context of the Stalinist and immediately post-Stalinist 1950s there was nothing very shaming about this. The sense of civil society in Poland was built precisely on the rejection of the official version of history. For Walesa, history was the scrapbook tracing the family line from Mateusz Walesa – an album that was unfortunately burnt by his stepfather before emigrating to America – and the adulation of Josef Pilsudski as a military conqueror of the Bolsheviks and leader of the first modern independent Poland in the 1920s and 1930s. History was the sermonising of the parish priest that dwelt on the Catholic heritage of Poland. History was the shared, if blurred, village memory of generous landowners and of those who had emigrated to seek their fortune. It was an eclectic, and not always accurate, collection of facts that stood in stark contrast to the schoolroom accounts of class warfare, friendly Soviet assistance, the decadence of the West, the clumsy impenetrable jargon of the Cold War.

The result of this collision in world views was more than a few failing grades on his report. He started his working career with a mixture of ideas: Catholic, instinctively anti-Soviet, sceptical of official propaganda. Yet at the same time he was an elemental socialist. As a peasant anxious to become a worker and to rise on the social ladder, he accepted without question the routine drumbeat about the primacy of the working class. Nor did he question the daily newspaper warnings about German revanchism, the rise of fascism, the military ambitions of Bundeswehr: he remembered how his father had died. He was, in short, typical of the younger workers at the shipyards in the 1960s: sensitive to inequities at the workplace, but no revolutionary.

The shipyard was run along rigid hierarchical lines. There were the top departments – engine fitting – and the lower ranking, such as the health-destroying paint section. The pecking order ran from engineers to tea-women, and within the individual crews from foreman to the newest worker. Old-timers claimed certain privileges – the best holiday dates, the extra overtime – and the younger or temporary workers had to put up with it. Walesa fitted well enough into this order not because of his experience at the POM, where he had a great deal of independence and could earn additional pocket-money by fixing motor bikes on the side, but because of his army service. After the end of his Lipno schooling he was drafted into the signals regiment, had developed his talents as an electrical repairman

21

and risen to the rank of corporal. His commanding officer was quite impressed with his competence in organising his section and had proposed that he sign up as a professional soldier. He refused, partly it seems out of concern for his mother and partly because the army was notoriously underpaid. Even so, he came to the yards with the knowledge that he could both give and take orders.

Gdansk in the 1960s was a teeming ant-heap. It had been sixty per cent destroyed in the war – as the German-dominated Free City of Danzig it was a natural strategic target for Allied bombing. In 1939 250,000 people had lived there but by the end of the war the population had dwindled to 117,000, sapped not only by battle casualties but also by the forced expulsion of the German residents. The massive reconstruction work stretched over decades. The old city centre was to be meticulously reconstructed, chiefly to assert the essential Polishness of the city. At the same time the port was to be developed, and a shipbuilding industry established more or less from scratch. That in turn needed workers, sucked in from the surrounding countryside. By the time Walesa arrived in Gdansk the population had ballooned to almost 300,000. Housing estates and hostels were slapped up quickly to house first building workers and then the workers from the yards. The result was a complete reshuffling of the social cards.

When Lech Walesa began work at the Stocznia Gdanska there were 16,000 employees – about one-third of them under the age of 25 and most of them, like Walesa, separated from their country roots. The odd anonymity of the place is best captured in a story told by Walesa himself. He met an attractive girl with the exotic name of Lala soon after arriving in Gdansk. Since he wanted to impress her, he concealed the fact that he was working in the yards in the rather modest function of cable-layer. He made himself out to be a successful businessman and, though it was rather an improbable persona, the affair flourished. One morning he saw the exotic Lala at her true place of work – for she had kept it mysterious – delivering crates of milk. He approached her and confessed everything. They were both from the country, determined to remould themselves as workers, both had been play-acting. The affair ended.

Walesa lived in lodgings and though the accommodation was cramped, shared with two other workers, it offered far more freedom than Popowo. He did not plunge into the destructive hard drinking of his workmates, but he carefully studied the role of worker and it turned out to be not at all like the clean-cut poster images. "I had no idea of the world of working-class values before. Getting to know them – the tricks of the trade, the different mafias – meant getting involved with it, experiencing it all. You had to pay the entry fee." And so he went out on the town, flirted with girls, watched television (still a novelty), went to football matches. The impression Walesa gives now is that he was not very comfortable in these pursuits.

A schoolfriend from Chalin visited Walesa in Gdansk and was struck by how much he had changed. "He swore like a trooper – fruity swear-words that he had picked up in the army – and he did not seem to have the time for church. If Stanislaw, his stepfather, had heard it he would have beaten him, that's for sure." Walesa claims to have drifted away from the Church only in his late teens and to have returned after a bitter experience with a girl. He also says he was drunk only twice in his life, once in Lipno and once in the army. But witnesses report that he was drunk quite often in the early days, though not in the manic road-to-oblivion manner of his worker contemporaries. And Walesa took many years to find his way back to the Catholicism of his mother. In the Polish army, under Communist rule, there was no question of attending church or wearing crucifixes, and little chance to pray privately. The move to Gdansk also broke the regular church-going habits he had learned in the countryside. But he was always conscious of the gap and felt guilty about it. "His faith was being tested," says Father Henryk Jankowski, who was the shipyard priest in 1980. Walesa started to read religious pamphlets and to work his way back to the Church. By his mid-20s he was attending church again; it answered his loneliness and helped him to overcome his self-doubt.

The work in the shipyards was tough. Poland had little experience of shipbuilding, it had no trained craftsmen, no designers, not even the subcontractors needed by every shipbuilder. Yet by 1960 Poland was fifth in the world in terms of the numbers of ships completed. The yards had started after the war with tramp steamers, small cargo ships and trawlers. By 1955 they had built their first ten-thousand-tonner. And by the time Walesa signed up the yard was turning our huge ships for the Soviet Union and successfully selling smaller vessels to the West, including traditional shipbuilders like Britain and Norway.

The price of this success was paid by the workers. The management was constantly working out ways of keeping down production costs. Work norms were adjusted so that a welder, for example, had to complete almost twice the previous work for the same money. The piecework system held most of the workers in thrall. The day began at six o'clock and since many workers had to commute a considerable distance, few had time for breakfast.

23

There was only one fifteen-minute break for food and the tea-and-sandwich stand could only feed a fraction of the yard in that time. The result was that workers either had to lose money – piecework waits for no man – or go hungry. Czeslaw Wisniewski, who was a temporary worker at the yards in the 1960s, recalls: "It was like working in a coal mine, only for less money. Being inside the bowels of a ship is not much different from being underground. It was dirty work, yet there were no showers, the toilets were so far away that you could lose an hour's wages just by going for a slash. When it rained your overalls got stinking wet but there were no proper lockers – certainly not for temps – and so the next morning you had to put on the same soaking clothes, like a compress. People were ill all the time but you couldn't afford to take time off. You saw a forty-year-old welder or painter in those days and he looked sixty."

At first the misery was offset by the relatively high wages – even under the oppressive piecework rates the workers in the yard could make more than teachers, or civil servants – and by the propaganda that hailed the Gdansk yards as an essential part of the triad that also took in the Nowa Huta steelworks and the Silesian coal mines. These were the new aristocrats, the cream of the proletariat. The shipyard had a great modernising mission; the vocational school attached to the yards was turning out the future industrial élite and a simple welder, trained in the yards, could find a job anywhere.

The turning point, the incident that spotlighted the differences between the propaganda vision of the era and the grim daily reality, was an accident on the hull of the *Konopnicka* in 1967. As usual, the yard management had agreed to an unrealistically early delivery date in order to secure a contract. The result was that some two thousand workers were labouring round the clock inside the hull of the ship. Normal safety standards, in any case very lax, were ignored. The tired workers began to make mistakes. A pipe was cut too short, fuel leaked and, probably sparked by a welder's torch, there was an explosion, fire running fast through the separate corridors. The escape exits had been sealed and so holes had to be cut through the hull to reach the trapped workers, but 22 were burned alive. There were furious discussions after the accident and Walesa was at the heart of them: "We're being driven like horses! And even horses are watered and fed and not left to burn in their stables!" The management put up the wages and hoped that the workers would forget, but they did not..

The mood of the workers was shifting throughout Poland and Walesa was proving to be a sensitive barometer. The "Bread and Freedom" riots in

24

Poznan had erupted in 1956 when Walesa was barely 13. But the workers in the yard were still very much under the influence of those demonstrations over a decade later. They had shown what could be achieved, and what could be taken away. Poznan had much stronger working-class traditions than Gdansk, and a tradition too of resistance to the nineteenth-century Prussian occupation. The Cegielki engineering plant had been saddled with new, unrealistic production targets and a wrongly applied taxation system in effect cut the wages of the workers. On 26 June they were marched to the city centre and, hearing rumours that there had been mass arrests, they stormed the police armoury. Bloody street fighting spilled onto the streets and over fifty people were killed. The shock of the brief revolt accelerated the process of de-Stalinisation. Wladyslaw Gomulka – who had been jailed for political deviations in 1951 – re-entered the political game and emerged in October as the new Communist Party chief. Poland began to enjoy new freedoms. Censorship was relaxed, the security police were purged: moves were begun to free Cardinal Stefan Wyszynski and to regulate relations between Church and state. Each new concession led to pressure for others. The outspoken *Po Prostu* weekly campaigned heavily on behalf of worker councils, to introduce some measure of shopfloor democracy. Gomulka, who was always opposed to rapid collectivisation, gave some protection to private farmers. He removed some taxes from private craftsmen. Economic reform was back on the agenda. Poland had thus avoided the dreadful spectacle of Hungary – Soviet tanks squashing all hopes of reform for over a decade – thanks to the "common sense" of the workers who accepted the new ordering of affairs. The worker reforms however were quickly scratched back. Within two years the worker councils established in only a few factories had been replaced by worker self-government, a device that allowed the Party to retain its control on the factory floor. But the brief Gomulka "thaw" had taught the working class a fundamental lesson: that it was no longer a matter of marching with the Party, it was necessary also to make demands on the Party.

Leszek Gozdik was an assembly line worker at Warsaw's FSO car factory in 1956. In April – that is, some months before the Poznan riots – he stood up at a party meeting and demanded more democracy, the end of censorship, more communication between leaders and led. He was local party secretary at the time and would under more usual circumstances have been sacked. But these were fluid times; Gozdik was protected, he survived and, when Gomulka took over, briefly flourished as the national hero of the workers' councils. "Those councils were our panacea. They were supposed to be the

25

real masters at the factory, to help to draw up a realistic production plan, monitor the management, correct wage levels . . . and all that had to be explained to people without forgetting what had happened only months earlier in Poznan."

For a while Gozdik became a model worker-hero. The authorities saw him as a way of siphoning discontent, as part of a control operation; Gozdik saw himself as an early Walesa. "Of course we looked different – we wore ties and ironed shirts in those days, not beards and sweaters – but we were fighting for something similar." By the end of 1956 Gozdik – photographed a dozen times with Gomulka – was complaining that workers' councils were being given no real powers, that they were a sham. By 1957 Gozdik had lost his job as party secretary; by 1970 he was out of the Party altogether. The socialist state chewed up its heroes.

The bitterness of Gomulka's betrayal lingered on in the great industrial strongholds of Gdansk, Poznan and Warsaw. Communism had promised much to the workers, and to a limited extent had delivered. There was full employment, the landed estates and large pre-war industrial plants had been nationalised. There were, it was true, income differentials between blue- and white-collar workers but these were balanced out by a national health system, kindergartens and crèches. That is how Communist apologists argued and the workers of the immediate post-war years accepted the logic; there was, after all, very little choice. But by the mid-1950s the mythology of a worker and peasant state was already beginning to crumble. Workers were edged out of decision-making. At the top of the Party, a professional governing class was already in place. The workers in the Politburo and the Central Committee were by and large tokens; soon enough they came to be regarded as Uncle Toms. In the factories, workers responded by slowing down. When salaries-plus-overtime were introduced in place of piecework, the workers idled away the normal hours, saving their energy for the better-paid after-hours labour. There were scores of short, unreported stoppages to press management into re-drawing holiday schedules or altering shifts. The balance of advantage was still overwhelmingly with the state managers, but gradually in the 1960s the workers began to capture ground.

Nor were the workers entirely concerned with earning more money, or redeeming the privileged position promised by the Communists. The type of work, its pace and the poor housing all added to a general demoralis-ation of the workers. Most of all they were conscious of living the lie so well described by the young poet Adam Wazyk in 1955:

26

They ran to us shouting,
"Under socialism
A cut finger does not hurt."
But they felt pain.
They lost faith . . .
. . . there are boys forced to lie,
there are girls forced to lie . . .
There are people waiting for justice,
there are people who have been waiting for a long time.

The surprising feature of the worker revolt in Poland is that it took so long to crystallise. All the complaints and grudges that poured out in August 1980 were part of the daily grumbling in the 1960s. Walesa's genius was to grasp that these moans were actually a political statement, part of what Herbert Marcuse calls the Great Refusal. Why then did the Gdansk workers not come out in support of the rebellious students in March 1968? Why did some workers even allow themselves to be used as shock-troops – honest proletarians giving a good beating to idle youth? The student revolt in 1968 began when Gomulka ordered a Warsaw theatre to stop showing *Dziady* by the great Romantic Adam Miskiewicz. The play is full of comments about Russian oppression of Poles – "Polish history is conducted in a prison cell", "We Poles have sold our soul to Moscow for silver roubles" – each of which earned thunderous applause from the young, intellectual audience. The closure of the play triggered student protests in every major Polish city including Gdansk, and the slogans plainly showed that the young generation wanted a Prague Spring, socialism with a human face. Since the military leadership of the Warsaw Pact was already working on plans for an invasion of Czechoslovakia, the Polish leadership panicked. The former partisan and Interior Minister, General Mieczyslaw Moczar, made his bid for power by spinning the rebellion into a broader crisis of confidence in Gomulka's leadership. The student rebels, he said, were "tools of Zionism", not true Poles. Since some of the student leaders were indeed the children of high-ranking Communists of Jewish origin, the ground was laid for a sweeping purge of Jews and liberal thinkers.

It was a shameful and for many workers, including Walesa, a confusing time. There was no great love for the engineering students in Gdansk and when they shouted "come with us" most workers merely shrugged. First the students did not seem to be addressing their problems. And the students had no grasp of the work-sleep-work drudgery, the sensation of being a rat

27

on a treadmill. Demonstrating for free speech, even demonstrating against the Russians, appeared to be missing the point. Or to be the result of some skilful puppet-mastery. That is why it was more sensible to stay at work or, for a few hard-hats, an excuse to go out and crack some skulls.

Walesa understood intuitively that the workers and students were being artificially divided and set against each other, and that they shared some common goals. Changing for work one day he saw the bruises on the back of an apprentice lashed by truncheons. Together with a few other workers, mainly electricians, he paraded around the yards with the boy shouting: "Look what they're doing to our children!" It was obvious whom he meant by "they" – the secret police based in Okopowa Street. "They" were defining the rules of the 1968 events and in pursuit of power they could destroy lives. Unlike East Germany, where the Stasi burrowed deep into every second family, Polish workers generally knew who the informers were in their factory and yard; they were avoided, or treated with frosty correctness, never befriended. But even so they were feared. It did not take much to push a worker down from the satisfying, well-paid engine department to smearing lead paint on the stomach of a ship. Walesa knew that he had to banish that fear, push it to the margins. Only then would workers win.

That initial courage came from an early marriage to a strong unpretentious woman. Miroslawa Golos was a dark-haired, dark-eyed, frail-looking girl barely out of her teens when Walesa first met her. She was working in a flower shop and Walesa quickly grasped that she was no "Lala". She did not speak much – a contrast to his quick patter – but when she did the words were measured and without guile.

Her roots were similar to those of Walesa. She came from the hamlet of Krypy – little more than three farmsteads – and had been brought up strictly in a blackened wooden hut near a pigsty. Like Walesa she came from a big family. Her brothers were in and out of trouble, picked up by the police for drunkenness and brawling. Miroslawa's teacher, Janina Zaledowska, remembers her as a mouse-like, lonely girl, frequently absent from school because she had to help on the farm. Within days of their first date Walesa had pressed her to use her second name – Danuta, or Danka for short – and abandon the name she had been known by for the previous 20 years. They were married in 1969, Danuta wearing her sister's old wedding dress, in the parish church of Wegrow near Krypy. Danuta, it quickly emerged, was more devout than Walesa and there was no question of sleeping together before marriage. The Swinging Sixties were not merely a Western phenomenon – students in Gdansk and Warsaw were leading hectic sexual lives – but workers from Catholic country backgrounds were more restrained. Lech Walesa and Danuta Golos rushed towards marriage, though Walesa rarely confided his political thoughts to his young wife. A weekend together would take in a drink or two, a walk through town, shopping, bed, a fishing expedition, a visit to church – but no great political debate. Yet Danuta, like Walesa, intuitively understood that there was something wrong: farmers were working poor land for poor pay, factory workers were putting in exhausting shifts, food was disappearing from the shops, a modest apartment – with room for a baby – seemed an impossible dream. When they were at school the hard times were explained away as the need to rebuild a country devastated by the Germans. By the late 1960s this was wearing thin. Neither Danuta nor Walesa knew much about the West but they certainly grasped that life was much better there, and that life could be improved in Poland. It was perhaps a question of the leaders listening to the people, to the ordinary workers.

But first the workers had to find a voice.

CHAPTER THREE

Will you help me?

Walesa used to keep a grainy newspaper photograph pinned above his desk. In the middle of the picture there is the tall figure of Edward Gierek, a long oval face, crew-cut hair, his mouth set in the careful pose of a listening politician. To his left, there is a young fresh-faced worker; hair swept up and probably stuck in place with grease. No moustache – but it is unmistakably Lech Walesa. The photograph, at least in its touched-up version, shows an open, trusting face. "That's correct," says Walesa, "that was me exactly. The picture did not lie." Yet a few weeks earlier, on 16 December 1970, Polish workers had been gunned down in the streets of Gdansk by the Polish authorities.

Three days before the shooting the government had announced that the price of most cuts of meat and many other basic products would be pushed up. In the shipyards of Gdansk and Szczecin, the mood reached boiling-point. It was the shopping week before Christmas, the time when families stocked up with meat. The queues were already long, and angry, the quality of the meat poor. Some kinds of meat were virtually unobtainable – notably ham, usually offered to guests, veal that is ground up into meat pâté, cheese and turkey. It might take hours to reach the front of the queue, by which time only scraps were available. But at least the meat was cheap. Suddenly, it was not.

The centrally planned economy was crippled by bureaucratic arthritis. The emphasis on building up heavy industry had not been abandoned by Gomulka and the result was a neglect of housing construction, consumer industry and private farming. As long as the workers had money in their pockets, the families could live with shortages: many still had relatives in the countryside who could provide at least eggs and some pork. Housing was cramped. Walesa recalls living briefly in a hostel after his marriage to Danuta, a bathroom and lavatory at the end of a corridor, drunks thundering on the door every Friday night; but that was the accepted form of city life for a migrant from the even more neglected countryside. By the middle of 1970, however, even the shipyard employees were feeling the squeeze.

Work norms had been raised, and it was becoming more and more difficult to keep wages at the old level. In those last Gomulka years, real income for the Polish worker rose only 1.8 per cent. The price rises far outstripped the slender wage increases. The timing and the transparently clumsy manner in which the authorities tried to soften the blow – the prices of 40 types of consumer goods were cut but these included hopelessly over-priced television sets, unsellable plastic shoes and chalky end-of-the-line toothpaste – struck at the pride as well as the pockets of the workers in what was now known as the Lenin shipyards. On Monday, the first working day after the rises were announced, a few thousand shipyard workers marched on the district Communist Party headquarters and then split into different groups, one moving towards the northern shipyards and factories to drum up support there, others to the Polytechnic to summon the students. The workers publicly apologised for letting down the students in 1968 and now, in an echo of the student marches, chanted, "Come with us." For the most part however the students did not come out on the streets. Many were about to start their Christmas holidays; others did not feel badly hurt by the meat price rises, since they were single and were cushioned by subsidised canteens. Police threw a cordon around the Party headquarters and though some workers managed to break through there was no major onslaught. Walesa says that he spent this Monday buying a pram for his first child, Bogdan. His electricians' team had a free day, since they had just finished wiring up one vessel. Even so, it was odd that Walesa did not join the crowds of colleagues who were marching through the city centre. Both in 1970 and 1980, Walesa was not responsible for the initial protest; he arrived late, followed the mood. On Tuesday, when Walesa went to the shipyards the mood was still relatively light-hearted. The management certainly thought that the worst had been weathered. A few dozen workers had disappeared after Monday's scuffles and it was assumed that they had been arrested.

The first priority for Walesa and the other more outspoken workers – it was still too early to speak of him as a leader – was to free their detained colleagues and squash the food price increases. The yard management could do neither. The first was in the hands of the Interior Ministry, the second a matter for the government. Walesa, in the manager's office, snatched a loudspeaker and passed on the manager's refusal to the crowd outside. "What do we do now?" asked Walesa, and the workers shouted that they

31

should march again on Party headquarters. As Walesa tried to leave, the manager grabbed his arm and offered him a large pay rise if he calmed the crowd down. Walesa shrugged himself free and took his place at the head of the crowd. They thronged to the Party building, a first line of militiamen scurrying for cover as the workers linked arms and started to bellow their demands. The Communist headquarters was barricaded from inside and armed soldiers could be seen peeping through the windows. And so the crowd headed for the main police office where, it was assumed, their workmates were being held. Walesa pushed his way inside, ran up three flights of stairs to the commander's office and offered a deal: if the workers were freed immediately, the police station would not be stormed. Walesa says the police commander agreed to this arrangement. Walesa was given a megaphone and he started to address the crowd. But the younger shipyard men had already begun hurling cobblestones and bricks at the windows. As Walesa spoke, militiamen armed, as it soon emerged, with live ammunition, were pouring out of the building from all sides, bracketing the crowd. It was plain to the protestors that the militia had no intention of freeing anybody and were ready for action. "Traitor," shouted some of them to Walesa, "son of a bitch." Walesa slipped out of the building, aware that he had played his cards poorly.

"After Walesa saved the militia headquarters," remembers Andrzej Gwiazda, "the workers got really mad and, hungry for action, they marched along Kalinokowski Street. As they passed the offices of the WRZZ, the official trade unions, somebody shouted, 'Screw the unions.' A couple of minutes later the building was demolished. And then later they attacked the Party committee."

There were to be several assaults on that day. The Party headquarters was set ablaze and soldiers inside shot at the demonstrators. Armoured vehicles moved around the railway station and fired short bursts into the demonstration. By Wednesday there were tanks in the streets of Gdansk and Gdynia. Walesa returned to the militia headquarters after the crowd had gone and, as he remembers it, proposed that the police hold off if workers elect delegates to negotiate with the authorities. There was by then no doubt that the police were preparing for brutal action: large boxes of live ammunition were being distributed to the different units along the Baltic coast. In the shipyard, there was complete confusion with some wanting revenge, others inclined to give up for the time being and stage an occupation strike after Christmas. Walesa's proposal to elect delegates seemed like a reasonable compromise; above all, it postponed the need to make decisions. But, as the secret police officer had calculated, it also gave the authorities time to move into position. The police strategy, it was plain in hindsight, was to contain all the workers in their yards, in Gdansk and Gdynia, and prevent the demonstrations spreading throughout the cities. The workforce elected a three-man strike committee, including Walesa. The workers camped out for the night – a novel experience in 1970 that was to become a standard feature of protest in the 1980s. Early on Wednesday morning, before daybreak, Walesa and the strike committee were warned that the army and the police had encircled the yards. If the workers left the yard, the managers warned, they would be gunned down. Most, including Walesa, regarded this as bluff. A few score of workers meanwhile had been pushing against one of the main gates, questioning and taunting the soldiers. A rumour was spreading that they were Russians in Polish uniforms and so the workers were demanding that every soldier say something in Polish. Suddenly the commander ordered his troops to fire. From a distance, the strikers saw the smoke, heard the crackle of guns and then after an eerie silence the wailing of the wounded. Walesa, in common with the rest of the workforce, panicked. Nobody had known the limits of strike action but it was always a reasonable assumption that the Workers' State would not use force against the workers who gave it legitimacy. Years later, the writer Jakub Karpinski would comment wryly: "It is difficult to determine whether the use of the police and the army against workers has been more common under socialism or under nineteenth-century capitalism." But then, even after the memory of the Poznan shootings, the use of guns was profoundly shocking; it was to make a revolutionary out of Walesa. For the time being, though, Walesa still had to learn the basic skills of crowd control. The strike committee had collapsed amidst much squabbling within a few hours of being set up. Walesa was *de facto* a strike leader, but not everybody respected his authority. The management threatened that the tanks would break the gates down by noon, that there would be a massacre unless the strikers gave up. All grievances would be duly noted. To Walesa the choice was: to fight, or to withdraw with dignity. Although some workers had already prepared a battery of Molotov cocktails and tank traps, the majority wanted to give up. This was Walesa's view too, and they marched out of the front gate, past the troops.

Walesa was sharply criticised for his leadership and there are strike organisers from that time who believe that he was manipulated by the security services. Certainly his habit of going ahead of the crowd and seeking talks with police commanders aroused suspicion.

Critics like Andrzej Gwiazda say that Walesa throughout his career, first as an agitator then as a union leader, was too keen to clinch deals with the authorities. There is a germ of truth in Gwiazda's judgment. But it ignores the need for subtlety, for nuance and gamesmanship in leading a rebellion against a police state. Gwiazda, concentrating on the moral imperative, failed as a revolutionary leader. Walesa regarded December 1970 as a personal slight as well as a blow to the Polish workers. He came, though, to understand that there was only seldom a clear-cut choice between fighting and surrender. His mistake, he came to realise, was that he should have negotiated a higher price for giving up demands; that was the difference between defeat and tactical retreat. By 1980, and especially by 1988 – when he ended the shipyard strike in return for a risky but credible promise of Round Table talks – he had learned the lesson. One important opportunity slipped past Walesa amid the gunsmoke and the bafflement of that winter rebellion. On 17 December, the day after the Gdansk shootings, the Warski yards in Szczecin came out on strike. As in Gdansk and Gdynia, the troops opened fire. But the strike, more intelligently led, created a political platform that was to become the basis for the dismantling of the Communist state: the abolition of the Communist-dominated council of trades unions, which, said the strikers, "has never represented the interests of the working class", and the establishment of autonomous unions "which would be controlled by the working class". The Szczecin agreement reached with the local party chief Stanislaw Rychlicka on 20 December committed the government to a thorough purge of the Communist unions. Naturally these political promises were not honoured, but it was Szczecin not Gdansk that had set the opposition agenda for the next decade.

The failure to follow through on the strikes can be put down to Walesa's inexperience – he was 27 – rather than the conspiracies favoured by Gwiazda and other critics. Andrzej Kolodziej, a rebel worker of the 1980s, even claimed to have seen Walesa consorting with the police in December 1970 – yet Kolodziej must have been about 11 years old at the time.

Walesa's actions were always open to interpretation. He came to realise in the 1980s that his power as a worker leader rested in his ability to end rather than begin a strike; it was this quality that forced the Communist authorities to recognise his authority and the independent status of the workers. In Gwiazda's eyes, however, Walesa became a strike-breaker, the man who stifled legitimate worker protests in pursuit of his own, often obscure political claims. In 1970 Walesa's actions were more transparent. He thought, like his workmates, in socialist categories. Something was going wrong with socialism – the bosses were amassing privileges, the workers were being stripped of their special status – and Poland needed real socialists in charge. After the troops opened fire in Gdansk there was a serious proposal from the strikers to use the yard radio transmitter and appeal to the Soviet Union for help, in support of the workers.

For Walesa, the underlying problem seemed to have been solved when, on 29 December, the Communist Politburo replaced Gomulka with Edward Gierek, a Silesian who had worked as a coal miner. Gierek first visited Szczecin – which had gone on strike again and insisted on a visit by the new leadership – and then went on to Gdansk. The workers bombarded him with complaints. "Every second worker on our ships is blind, deaf, rheumatic or has some lung disease . . . so much suffering for so little money . . . the directors live in luxury while others can barely make enough for bread . . . we demand that the guilty be punished . . ." But Gierek disarmed the workers. Yes, he said, he had been on the Politburo when the shooting was discussed. But what could he do? He considered resigning but if he had done, one faction or another would probably have tried to pin the blame on him. He was a worker (hands raised up high to show the old calluses) and understood them. The mood in the yards swung towards him: "We must give Comrade Gierek a chance, just as we gave Gomulka at the beginning. Give him a year or two." Gierek's skill was to make the workers, smarting from their December wounds, feel powerful again. The workers had brought Gomulka to power in 1956, and now they had toppled him. There was blood on the snow, but it had been worth it. Now Gierek, playing the same rhetorical trick in Szczecin and Gdansk, stood up and asked, "Will you help me?" And the workers, grudgingly at first and then with enthusiasm, bellowed: *We will help you!* Walesa was among them, shouting until his lungs ached.

It does not need a commitment to the psychobabble school of biography to see that Gierek filled an emotional need in Walesa. His brittle relationship with his stepfather had two clear effects: it gave him an ambiguous relationship to authority, part rebel, part conformist. And it encouraged Walesa to look for father-substitutes. Gierek, a towering, impressive man, met the bill. Not perhaps for long but for a critical period in which Walesa started to shape both his political and family life. Even in the 1990s, a decade after being the single biggest cause of Gierek's overthrow, Walesa found himself mimicking Gierek in personal gestures and in political tactics.

Gierek appeared to give the workers at least part of what they wanted in terms of wages and prices, and so the workers turned inwards, away from politics into private life; they had more time, more money, there were more goods in the shops – imported oranges, fruit juices, meat – and more lively television. For Walesa too it was a time of shifting priorities.

Danuta, the slight young woman from the flower shop, had borne Walesa's first child, Bogdan. Walesa was immensely proud and ready to take on parental responsibilities. For the first time since the war it was not difficult to obtain fruit juice for babies, prams and clothes. Walesa stood in pharmacy queues, changed nappies, fed Bogdan. Danuta's rugged country background was not so very different from Walesa's and he felt more at ease with her brothers (two of whom landed in jail for assault) and sisters than with his own half-brothers. His stepfather still cast a shadow over the Popowo home so he preferred instead to visit Danuta's mother, show off the baby, do the electrical repairs on the modest farm and fish thigh-deep in the nearby river. Walesa was still in love. He liked Danuta's lack of pretence; Walesa was ill-suited to courtship and Danuta accepted him as he was, saw through his bluster and occasional deceit. Perhaps it was the awareness of baby Bogdan that restrained Walesa in December 1970, that made him try to snatch a quick compromise out of the crisis. The birth of his many children punctu-ated his career and indeed seemed to coincide with critical points in the history of the 1970s and 1980s. He was arrested while Danuta was delivering a daughter, interned when he should have been attending the christening of another.

Both family and political events however conspired to change Walesa, stopped him slipping into a complacent paterfamilias more or less happy with his lot. Just when he had been hoping to build a new bridge to his mother – Walesa could picture her as an indulgent but sensible grandmother – she left for the United States. That was in 1973. Two years later, exhausted and still far away across the Atlantic, she died. There was no longer anything binding Walesa to Popowo – apart from bitter memories about his stepfather who had persuaded his mother to leave. This sense of betrayal was com-pounded by Gierek. The economy had improved. In five years the party chief appeared to have crafted an economic miracle. Industrial output rose by over 70 per cent between 1971 and 1975. Some factories were completely modernised thanks to equipment bought from the West. Real wages were rising by eight per cent a year, five times more than under Gomulka, consumer products mainly bought from the West filled the shops. Not only was there full employment, but three million young people were absorbed into the economy. Gierek imagined that this improvement was part of a process that might be termed imported growth. Liberalised trade with the

West = higher standard of living = higher productivity = higher growth. But Gierek was amassing debts that would drag the economy down in the second half of the decade. The oil price shock and inflation in the West meant that imports were increasingly expensive. The miracle was a mirage. The oranges began to disappear from the shops. Walesa knew that real incomes were going up only because there was immense pressure to work overtime. The shipbuilding industry was in deep recession and Poland could only compete by undercutting West European yards. It was a familiar story. And the promises to improve worker democracy were quietly forgotten. One of the Gdansk strike leaders from 1970 was framed and fired. Edward Nowicki was accused of faking his timesheet so he could pocket extra wages, and photographs – actually montages cooked up by the secret police – showing him in pornographic poses were circulated around the yard and sent to his family. In Szczecin, the youngest member of the 1970 strike committee, Bogdan Goloszewski, died in August 1971 after a mysterious gas leak in his apartment. Adam Ufik, deputy strike leader, survived a gas attack by secret police, was arrested on trumped-up charges and released only after strike threats. Even so he was barred from working at the yards and died a sudden death in February 1976. Another strike leader, Edmund Baluka, had to flee abroad. It was becoming clear that "helping" Gierek was no easy matter. Walesa himself managed to stay on in the yards, though he was denied promotion. For a short time he was elected works inspector but all of his recommendations on improving safety or working conditions were thrown out. Still he continued to press hard. By the mid-1970s he had come to two conclusions. The first was that workers should start organising their own democratic groups – call them councils or committees or self-governments – that would continually embarrass the official-manipulated unions and shame them into action. The second was that Gierek should be reminded of his broken promises by keeping alive the memory of December 1970. With an influx of new workers and rigid censorship, the December shootings were being forgotten and had lost their shock value. Walesa though was deeply troubled by December. It had been his first public political action, his début, and at the same time it was in many ways a personal failure. And there was the shame of investing his trust in Gierek. If even half the stories from Warsaw were true – of corrupt manoeuvrings in the foreign trade ministry, extravagant lifestyles of Gierek's barons from Katowice – it was obvious that Gierek, the surrogate father, had let him down. At a union meeting in February 1976, his patience broke. Gierek had betrayed the workers, he said, the unions were at best incompetent and needed a complete overhaul. It was a passionate, almost hysterical speech that won immediate applause from those in the hall. But the following week he was dismissed. There was no popular uprising at this obviously political sacking; it was simply the price to be paid. By the time that Walesa clambered over the shipyard fence in August 1980 many workers had forgotten about the existence of Walesa. He soon found a job as an engine mechanic with the ZREMB works and by moonlighting, fixing up old cars, he made quite a handsome living. But the yards were the top of the heap; to be sacked from there, even for political reasons, was to fall from grace. Walesa felt hurt and vengeful.

Perhaps the management had sensed the trouble ahead. To wriggle out of its economic bind, Gierek had given the go-ahead for a set of price rises. Meat products were to rise by 69 per cent, sugar by 100 per cent and other foodstuffs by up to 50 per cent. Even according to the official calculation that would raise the cost of living by some 16 per cent. The move was better prepared than in 1970 – a series of wage rises and compensation payments was promised, farmers were to receive higher purchase prices – but was as clumsily implemented. In the arms factory in Radom, a smoky city in central Poland, the workers demanded negotiations with the management over wage increases. The management and the Communist authorities refused and the result was intense street fighting with some 17 killed and at least 2,000 arrested. At the same time in the Ursus tractor factory, in the suburbs of Warsaw, the management also refused to discuss the rises. As in Radom, the workers went on strike and took their protest outside the factory, blocking the Moscow–Paris express. Dozens of lower-key protests erupted around Poland. In the Gdansk shipyards there was a modest protest, for the events of December 1970 had seared the souls of the workers. They trod carefully. And, from the outside, a frustrated Walesa had to watch.

The Gierek leadership had learned at least one thing from 1970. As soon as the protests turned violent they withdrew the price rises. But they covered up this retreat with a particularly virulent crackdown. Thousands were sacked for political reasons, choreographed rallies attacked the strikers, and courts, acting on instructions, passed harsh jail sentences on worker-organisers. The attempt to persuade Polish workers that the strikers of Radom and Ursus were anti-socialist mavericks failed. It was clear to everybody, even Party members in the Gdansk shipyards, that Gierek had turned against the workers, had betrayed their trust. Everything that followed, and above all the glossy television reports of broadcasting chief Maciej Szczepanski, was regarded as part of the Bigger Lie. Radom and Ursus spelled the end

38

of the illusion that the Communists could, under the right circumstances, be spokesmen for worker interests. A British commentator writing shortly after the unrest put it well: "five years earlier . . . the working class had struggled alone against a party-led leadership that could count on the passivity of the students and intellectuals, the support of the church, the neutrality of the peasants and the vigorous solidarity of Moscow." Now it could count on none of these pillars. The tide had turned.

Instead a broad group of intellectuals promptly sided with the persecuted workers, redressing the wrongs of 1970. KOR, the Committee for the Self-Defence of the Workers, was founded in September 1976 by an odd hybrid comprising prominent pre-war social democrats such as the economic reformer, Professor Edward Lipinski, some prominent wartime resistance fighters and thinkers including Jan Jozef Lipski, and a large group of student leaders from 1968, including Adam Michnik. Some, such as Jacek Kuron, had been Communist Party members, other such as Antoni Macierewicz were even further on the left and had only recently abandoned their Mao badges. (Macierewicz subsequently jumped through many ideological hoops and by the 1990s was regarded as a militant right-wing Catholic.) Although dominated by intellectuals from the democratic Left, KOR did attract the following of some devout young Catholic activists. Initially KOR, printing in Samizdat, reported on persecution and passed to the West graphic accounts of police brutality. But its brief expanded, it lobbied parliament on behalf of jailed workers, raised money for worker families and eventually became a clearing house for human rights abuses throughout Poland. It hung on because of a simple subterfuge – calling itself a social rather than a political organisation and so removing itself from head-on confrontation with the Communists. Eventually KOR members started to suffer the same kind of treatment handed out to the people they were trying to defend. Even this backfired on the authorities. When a Cracow student, Stanislaw Pyjas, an active KOR supporter, was found dead, masses were said throughout Poland and a large candlelight procession marched throughout Cracow.

George Orwell, in *The Road to Wigan Pier*, captures the critical moment very well. Talking to a British miner in the 1930s, he asks him when he first became aware of the housing shortage. "He answered, 'When we were told about it,' meaning that till recently people's standards were so low that they took almost any degree of overcrowding for granted." A similar Rubicon had been crossed in Poland. Walesa felt it too. He had been bottling up his anger. Now it started to spill out. Jerzy Borowczak, a shipyard worker who had retained his contacts with Walesa, remembers how aggression bubbled out of him. "His attitude towards the Communist authorities was anything but peaceful. I remember that whenever some of our people got beaten up somewhere, or jailed, Lech would say, 'Remember for every one of us picked up – two grenades must land in a police station!' " That was probably just wind – though Walesa's critics would say that they were the classic utterances of an *agent provocateur* – and what actually happened was much milder. Borowczak recalls: "We once burnt a large banner in Gdansk saying 'The Party is the Leading Force of the Nation', or something similar. It was Lech's idea to burn it. We simply poured a line of petrol, put a large rag like this" – Borowczak held up a tea towel – "over the banner, stepped back ten paces and Poof! Everything erupted."

CHAPTER FOUR

Half an eye

Historians, both in the West and in the post-Communist states, are rightly puzzled by the evolution of the opposition in the 1970s. How did a small group of dissidents numbering at most a few hundred manage to keep alive the idea of a civil society for so long, under such intense pressure? The secret police had agents and informers in almost every crevice of society. Censorship ensured that the views of nonconformists were not published or broadcast. Above all the compartmentalisation of society, not merely the wedges driven between workers and intellectuals or town and country but the physical and emotional separation of workers themselves, gave the Communists an important and highly effective instrument of control. When Lech Walesa was sacked from the shipyards, his colleagues barely noticed. Gdansk was full of people resembling Walesa: good mechanics and craftsmen, fresh from the country, looking for a stable job in a big plant that could provide not only a decent wage but also subsidised holidays at rest homes, help with finding an apartment, a measure of protection and prestige. If somebody risked all this by sticking his nose out politically, well, it was sad, but life went on. As for the intellectual opposition, Adam Michnik and Jacek Kuron of KOR were certainly the best known. Yet their names meant little even to politically curious workers, still less to farmers. True, Western radio stations were keeping their names in play, much as advertisers jostle for brand recognition. An information network was also shaping up. Books were being produced on émigré and Samizdat presses and KOR was turning out a newsletter cunningly named after a wartime resistance journal, the *Biuletin Informacyny*. But the circulation of these publications was limited geographically (Warsaw and Cracow being the main target areas) and in terms of readership. Very few dissident broadsheets were making it into the industrial fortresses.

Lech Walesa, a popular worker at ZREMB, the state-run workshops needed to patch up ageing factory machinery, was edging towards the idea of free trade unions. He was not inspired by any underground text or dissident declaration. It was simply something he was cobbling together himself, much as in Lipno he would shun mechanical textbooks and dismantle machines to find out how they worked and why they were going wrong.

It is difficult to find friends from this period, 1976–77, but one colleague from ZREMB recalled that Walesa never attacked the regime or shouted about the Communists. "Leszek just said workers had rights and that these rights did not come from the top from Gierek or anybody, they just belonged to us like our noses or our ears. They couldn't be taken away except by force and they couldn't be cut off. Whoever heard of a man with half an eye?" Walesa, it seemed, was still proceeding from the assumption that the Party could not be overthrown. Hungary 1956, Prague 1968 and December 1970 all showed in their different ways that Communists were ready to kill to stay in power. But short of this direct challenge, everything else was up for negotiation. It was obvious from the behaviour of the Party bosses that very few believed in socialism, only in power. Gierek in 1971 appeared to distance himself from the official trade unions. Very soon he forgot about his promises but he had shown that the Party and the unions need not be identical. Walesa was sure that if driven hard enough the Party could accept other forms of worker representation. KOR pointed to one way forward: it was breaking the monopoly on information from the factories and publicising abuses on workers. Free trade unions seemed to Walesa to be a natural extension of KOR activities. He understood the frailty of the worker in this system and knew of waitresses fired for complaining about managers who cheated, fitters who had fallen to their death because of faulty safety harnesses. When these people were sacked or crippled in industrial accidents, they slipped into a kind of oblivion. They had been taught to identify themselves with their workplace, to treat it as a second family. Yet when they were propelled outside the factory gates, it was as if they had been pushed into the darkness beyond the gates of Eden. Walesa knew this all too well – by the end of 1978 he was ejected from ZREMB because the company, advised by the secret police, had discovered that it no longer needed an electrical maintenance man in its transport section. In the interests of productivity it was better if he sought work elsewhere. The real reason was that Walesa had been elected to be ZREMB transport section's representative to a conference on worker self-government. This was essentially a stooge body that had been set up in 1958 to replace the spontaneous worker

42

councils. By 1978 they were hollow vessels making little noise. Walesa, the police must have calculated, was trying to penetrate them and make them into a fighting instrument.

They were right. Walesa had made his first contact with the grandly named but minuscule Association of Free Trades Unions in the summer of 1978. He had found the name and address of the association's organisers, the electrical engineer Andrzej Gwiazda and his wife Joanna Duda-Gwiazda, printed on the bottom of an illegal newspaper, *Robotnik Wybrzeza*, (The Coastal Worker). The journal was a Baltic variant of KOR's Warsaw paper, *Robotnik*, edited by the mathematics don Jan Litynski. Walesa was not sure whether it was a provocation, the universal idiom for a stunt by the secret police to flush out dissidents. But he went along anyway. It spoke directly to his needs. He knew that despite the rhetoric of the Communists about the unity of the working class, workers were alone, separated from each other. This isolation was the very essence of the totalitarian system. Much later East Germans were to discover how deep this totalitarian approach could soak into society: it led to husbands betraying wives, soccer players betraying team mates, doctors betraying patients, schoolteachers their pupils. In Poland it had never reached this pitch. There were limits on the reach of state control – agriculture was private, the strength of the Church put paid to any hopes of Marxism becoming a secular religion – and these gaps had to be exploited. The first step was to make workers feel less alone. There were only two ways: to infiltrate existing worker organisations and make them less of a sham, or to set up alternatives. The first possibility, Walesa was now convinced, was impossible. The police were setting the limits of direct, legal participation in union work. The second option was presented by the Gwiazda couple, by the young historian Bogdan Borusewicz and by the brothers Blagoje and Krzysztof Wyszkowski who were the backbone – indeed the majority of members – of the free union association. For Walesa the most appealing aspect of *Robotnik*, apart from its obvious aim of connecting workers from different factories along the coast, was that it openly named its organisers. It was part of the conspiratorial culture, but at the same time open, saying in effect: here we are, come and get us! Walesa approved. The only way to do battle with the secret police was to abolish secrecy.

The Gwiazdas were happy to see Walesa in their narrow, crowded apartment in Wejhera Street. "To be honest," said Gwiazda, a tightly-coiled man with a flinty humour, "we were not being flooded with applications. Everybody was welcome, we took them as they came." And, Joanna Gwiazda chipped in, the free unions needed a worker to declare himself, to set an example to the others. Despite KOR's conscious attempts to build a bridge with workers, the Polish opposition of the 1970s had very little comprehension of the working class and little idea of how it would fit into a broader opposition movement. The Gwiazdas at least realised that no opposition group could flourish without the proletariat. The aim was no longer to lobby for reform within the Communist Party but to generate support from below. Nobody had a very clear idea how to do this; it was the Communists who were the masters of mobilising the masses. The free trade union banner was first hoisted by Kazimierz Switon in Katowice but, as Gwiazda says, he did so from a very slender organisational base. "Its members did not even work in big factories, which are always adept at providing some kind of support to jailed colleagues," recalls Gwiazda. "So whenever the secret police got to them KOR was forced to throw its whole weight into defending them. Leaflets were printed in Warsaw and taken to Silesia. But in nine cases out of ten the KOR couriers were arrested." When KOR found out that the Gwiazdas were going to set up a free trade union association in Gdansk they did their best to dissuade them. "But the situation in Gdansk was different, although there were only a few of us too. The Gdansk population was much richer, it had its memories of December 1970 to draw on." Walesa compared the opposition movement with a series of tiny streams that eventually converged to form a huge river. The image is quite good but the streams never lost their separate identity when they merged. The early history of the opposition shows that Solidarity was always doomed to be a temporary coalition.

The Gwiazdas' involvement in the free union movement began when they wrote a public letter of support to KOR at the end of 1976. The letter was quoted by the Munich-based Radio Free Europe and the secret police started to take notice. In January 1977 the Gwiazdas were denied the right to a passport. By Easter of that year Bogdan Borusewicz had joined the group. In May 1977 a student self-defence committee – later to call itself the Young Poland Movement – was set up in Gdansk.

And then from the germs of the Glos group the Movement for the Defence of Human and Civil Rights (ROPCIO) began to operate. Like KOR it was made up of pre-war activists – like the leader of the former Christian Democrats, Stefan Kaczorowski – and younger dissidents. But they were much further to the right than KOR, much less inclined to play within the Communist rules, inclined towards nationalist postures. Initially its leading light was Leszek Moczulski who left in 1978 and soon afterwards set up the ultra-nationalist Confederation for an Independent Poland (KPN). The splits that were later to break up Solidarity and produce a plethora of small political parties in the 1990s were already apparent twenty years earlier. But as Gwiazda remembers, the general right–left split in the opposition did not cause any major friction, chiefly because so few people were involved. "We still met together and the whole milieu closed ranks." The free trade unionists, according to Gwiazda's plan, should not be a hierarchically organised group. Each activist had to be responsible for himself; there were to be no cells or team leaders.

And the philosophical aim was clear: it was no longer a matter of intellectuals defending workers. Workers had to be taught how to defend themselves. The intellectuals were giving clandestine lectures to workers – Borusewicz on the true history of Polish–Soviet relations, Lech Kaczynski on how to exploit the labour law – but the workers themselves had to take over their own political education.

"We told Walesa, in fact all newcomers, what the free trade unions were all about and what repercussions he could expect for even contacting us. And we told him straight away that he should not count on us bailing him out if he was in trouble." Unlike the Young Poland Movement, which was pressing for an annual commemoration of those killed in December 1970, and Moczulski's group, which celebrated every suitable anti-Soviet anniversary, the free trade unionists were not keen to stage events. Nor did they seek the shelter of the Church – distributing leaflets in the pews was one of the safest ways of spreading information. They favoured instead poster campaigns inside factories and quiet recruitment.

Walesa approved of the tactics and joined the poster teams. A typical Sunday afternoon would see Walesa pushing the pram of one of his children and stopping at convenient walls and pasting up: "Free Trade Unions Now!" Gwiazda gave him books on sociology and economics but he later regretted the move: "a wasted gesture. He never read them and I never did get them back."

Edmund Szczesniak, who followed Walesa's career from the 1970s, saw the Gwiazda–Walesa tension as one of those important yet transitional relationships that emerge in every revolution. "It was a conflict between a people's tribune, with the gift of attracting people and making them follow him (a gift that Walesa lost when he became a professional politician) and a man who looked good at close-quarters. Gwiazda's voice is feeble, he had no charisma. He was good on private occasions, or at the negotiating table."

The few workers drawn to the Association of Free Trades Unions quickly spotted Walesa as a potential leader, though technically Gwiazda was supposed to be the guiding force. Borowczak recalled: "Some of us were drawn to Stogi [the suburb where Walesa lived] and some to Gdansk [to the Gwiazdas]. Walesa simply suited our needs better – he was smart and quick, spoke in a straightforward way. Still I can't say Gwiazda was bad – his lectures were excellent. But more than Gwiazda, Walesa gave the impression that he knew what he was after."

Opposition was growing. By 1978, the KOR journal *Robotnik* and its Gdansk affiliate had been joined by two major student journals, *Bratniak* (Fraternity) and *Indeks* (Index). *Gospodarz* (The Farmer) opposed any return to collectivisation, fighting for fair pensions and compensation for farmers. A further 13 literary-political Samizdat periodicals including *Zapis* (The Record) and *Puls* (Pulse) were in circulation. The secret police launched occasional raids but on the whole did not use their full potential to crush this underground culture. It appears to have been regarded as a safety valve by the Gierek leadership: as long as the intellectuals spent their time and energy grumbling among themselves, the state was safe. As soon as an underground magazine pitched itself, in simple language, at workers rather than theology students or structural philosophers, the police pounced.

From the debates in these magazines one can trace the path that led to Solidarity, but also untangle the roots of the political class that was to emerge at the end of the 1980s. *Glos* for example was started in 1977 under the protective wing of KOR. But it soon broke away from its protector. The editor Antoni Macierewicz refused to publish an article by Adam Michnik since it suggested that Communism was not all bad. That marked an important divorce. *Glos* contributors – including Piotr Naimski, Marcin Gugulski, Jerzy Kropownicki and Jan Olszewski – started to articulate the views of a nationalist right-wing opposition that by 1992 became the core of the Olszewski government. Kropownicki became labour minister, Naimski head of the secret police and Gugulski was premier Olszewski's spokesman. Their deep distrust of Michnik survived for almost two decades. It was plain that 1968 and not 1970 was regarded as the main turning-point for the intelligentsia. Those who were students at the time, such as Adam Michnik and Jan Litynski, understood that the unleashing of an anti-Semitic national-Communist campaign was part of an internal political manoeuvre which would spell the end of the "revisionist" illusion. The thought that the Party could improve itself – under pressure, of course – and transform Communism into a more liberal, modern and just form of government now seemed hopelessly naive. Jacek Kuron used to say: "I don't believe in a liberal wing of the Party, only in the pragmatism of the people in power." This was still quite some way from wanting to oust the Communists. During a study trip abroad, Michnik was asked what reforms the Party could concede without losing its grip. He ticked off: an end to censorship, free trade unions, independent youth organisations, an end to religious discrimination. From the perspective of the 1990s these seemed rather modest demands from a man who was already being branded by the Communist press as a fanatical anti-Communist. Where for example was the demand for a parliamentary democracy? But his checklist was inconsistent with the evolving thoughts about how to wriggle out from underneath the boulder of authoritarian government.

Leszek Kolakowski, digesting the lessons of 1968, had charted the intellectual basis for change. Since open revolution on the periphery of the Soviet empire would lead to an invasion and bloodshed, and since the Party was not able to initiate reform, change should come from below, from partial but structural reforms that would reconstruct independent social life. The ambition to impose totalitarian rule in Eastern Europe was deeply flawed and nowhere more so than in Poland where the contradictions were all too apparent: the practical irrelevance of ideology clashed with the need for ideological continuity, the need for technical development clashed with the need for political control. These contradictions could be the launching-pad for a popular movement. Michnik seized this idea and converted it into an action programme. The pressure from below had to be organised if there was to be some form of social contract – Will You Help Me? – but the partners were not equal, since one was organised, and one was not. None of this required a uniform opposition programme. Instead a pluralistic opposition could best create a foundation of a pluralistic independent culture. It was a form of anticipatory democracy, acting in the present in the way one would like to act, legally, in the future. Kuron, in his earthy manner, defined freedom as knowing that the secret police were everywhere but behaving as if they were not.

The 1968 generation identified with these views and they became the credo of the new political class. It was this class that immediately jumped onto the worker cause in the Gdansk strikes of 1980, they who advised Walesa, they who were interned and led the opposition through martial law, they who sensed the weakness of the authorities and pushed for Round Table power-sharing arrangements. And it was they who made up the backbone of the first two Solidarity governments.

Not everybody, however, had drawn the same conclusions from 1968 and

1970. Within the Communist Party, some reformers continued to believe in a tolerant, but socialist Poland. Members of the Experience and Future group, with supporters both in and outside the Party, drew up a devastating account of the state of the economy and the need for reform. Within the Politburo and the Central Committee there were those who believed that Gierek had squandered his opportunities. General Wojciech Jaruzelski in particular was aware of a political drift. He had been defence minister in 1968 and was shocked by the anti-Semitic purges of March 1968, the naked scramble for power, and was even more deeply affected by his own role in helping to plan the Warsaw Pact invasion of Czechoslovakia. These events, crowded into a few months, had made a politician out of a soldier: they had shown him simultaneously the need for, and the limits of, reform. He, and sympathisers like *Polityka* editor Mieczyslaw Rakowski, came to believe that the Party should return to the ideals of October 1956 when economic reform was on the agenda, the arts were allowed to flower, censorship was lax and the workers were given a say.

The ideological gap between the 1968 dissident generation and the reformers was huge – the Party men were after all trying to devise new ways of clinging on to power – but the practical differences were not unbridgeable. That is why both sides eventually managed to devise the then unique formula of a round table.

The political equations worked out by Michnik and his colleagues had an attractive symmetry about them and seemed both to describe the current discontent – simmering workers, frustrated writers – and prescribe a cure. But a great deal was also left out of the calculations. What about farmers and their rights, and how to ease the strain between urban centres and the desperately poor, undermechanised countryside? Michnik had tried to overcome the traditional leftist antipathy towards the Catholic Church in an essay entitled "The Church, the Left, a Dialogue", which redefined the Church as, above all, a defender of human rights. That certainly helped to overcome some of the doubts felt by the bishops about the different blossoming opposition groups. But it did not actually set out the role of the Church in any future alignment. Could it be that the dissidents were aiming for a second secular Poland, more democratic, perhaps more generous to the Church, but still far away from Polish religious roots? Were the dissidents not ignoring the real hub of the problem, the Soviet Union? And, crucially, what about the workers? Perhaps the workers were really not ripe for revolt, perhaps they would be happy with any arrangement that guaranteed them full shops, reasonably low prices and a decent wage? If that were the case, the 1968 thinkers were missing the point. They should be concentrating on devising economic reform strategies, lobbying the Party leadership, and not rejecting out of hand the possibility of change coming from within the Party. The fact was that very few intellectuals knew anything at all about the workers. This introspective phase might well have continued for five years or more, a fretting debate that would have filled the years until the Soviet Union itself showed signs of changing, had not a Pole been elevated to the throne of St Peter. Karol Wojtyla was well remembered in Cracow and known to philosophers, playwrights and other intellectuals elsewhere in Poland. As a Church politician he was naturally overshadowed by the Primate, Cardinal Stefan Wyszynski. His elevation in October 1978 was therefore a matter of great national pride but it was not initially interpreted as a fatal blow to Gierek, or to Communism. Indeed, in a strange way Gierek seemed to gain in popularity from the sudden presence of a Polish Pope. It was obvious for example that he would have to concede more to the Catholic Church, that his ideologically bankrupt regime would have to dress up in national-patriotic garb. At the same time Leonid Brezhnev was very determined that the Pope should not interfere in Polish politics.

Not everyone shared the *Kulturpessimismus* of underground writer Marek Turbacz, but there seemed no doubt that the opposition was in for a long haul: "We are not able to free ourselves from the domination of Russia . . . Poland, which is its most important satellite located in its road to Western Europe, cannot regain sovereignty as long as the Russian empire exists . . . The restoration of Poland's sovereignty and a basic change of the present system would be possible only if preceded by a fundamental change in Russia itself, or a drastic shift in the constellation of forces in the world at large. For this we may have to wait as long as a quarter of a century."

And then, quite suddenly, the terms of the equation changed: a Pole was Pope. The Catholic Church in Poland had supported Gierek in 1970–71, if only to avoid further bloodshed. But when the Party leadership tried – successfully at first – to buy popularity with consumer imports, the Church changed gear. The Second Vatican Council had already set in train important changes: the intellectual training of priests was at a much higher level, the number of young clerics was rising fast and Church publishing had become a major venture. All these new tools were deployed as the Church swung against Gierek's consumerism and the associated corruption of everyday life. Most Poles, Walesa included, were being driven to the black market for goods that, by the late 1970s, were no longer in such ample supply. There was a smell of sickness in the air. Why should the citizens of an avowedly

49

socialist country have to break the law and change their earnings into dollars to buy Western medicines, or even coffee? The Church sensed that workers were feeling both cheapened and cheated. It had worked hard – Wojtyla in Cracow more than most – to sow the seeds of a religious revival, to rescue the lost spirituality of the workers. The Church was helped by the sloppiness of the Communist propaganda machine, which had assumed that Poland would be secularised in step with the process of urbanisation. This had not happened, but only a few in the Communist hierarchy had noticed, or cared: since 1971, the Church had become marginal to the Politburo.

Wojtyla's elevation changed that but only at the most superficial level. The true political significance of a Polish Pope, of *this* Polish Pope, was discovered by the opposition after some months of digging into his early writings. The Pope, who had done forced labour under the Germans, understood workers! More, he grasped how a dispirited workforce could be manipulated, how their lives could become empty shells. His central idea – that workers should be the subject of labour and not the object – was to be spelled out in the 1980 encyclical *Laborem Exercens*, virtually the spiritual charter of Solidarity. But his early poems, eagerly studied in Poland in 1978–79, showed the pattern of his thinking.

In "The Car Factory Worker", he asks:

> What makes you think that man
> can tip the balance on the scales of the world?

And in "The Armaments Factory Worker", the worker ponders:

> I cannot influence the fate of the globe
> Do I start wars? How can I know
> Whether I'm for or against?
> . . .
> Though what I create is all wrong,
> the world's evil is none of my doing.
> But is that enough?

Not surprisingly, all the opposition groupings were enthusiastic about Pope John Paul II. Even the most left-leaning dissidents accepted the Pope's diagnosis: the Communist system had reversed normal human priorities by enmeshing the worker, making him into a labour drudge whose horizons were limited to the piece-rate slog, commuting, sleeping and queuing.

50

Naturally the Pope, in talking about the passive status of workers, was also thinking about capitalist companies. But this was quietly set aside. The opposition had a platform of sorts: to fight for the spiritual needs and the basic (that is God-given) human rights of the workers. On this, all factions could agree.

The Vatican immediately started negotiations for a papal trip to his homeland. Gierek was not initially enthusiastic and the first response of his leadership was to put up tripwires. But in the end he accepted that to deny the Pope access to his Poland would be more damaging than a carefully controlled and censored tour. It was fast becoming clear to the authorities that they were facing a major economic disaster; the debt burden had become unmanageable, the grand dreams of a rejuvenated industry had evaporated. Poland was more vulnerable to Western pressure than at any time for a decade. A relatively open approach to the Pope would win friends, or keep them sweet for a little longer. As for the Kremlin, it seemed that they would allow the visit providing the Pope did not use the moment to launch an anti-Soviet crusade. This was not in any case the style of the Pope. Rather, he was determined to plant seeds – of ideas about freedom, human rights, governmental obligations, the imperative of living honestly in a country that was being dishonestly governed, the duty of all Catholics to resist atheistic ideology and retain the dignity of belief. About a quarter of the Polish nation was on the road, sleeping under hedgerows and in the fields in the blisteringly hot June of 1979. The sheer movement and congregation of people helped to break the compartmentalisation of the workers and other social groups. And although the Pope was not allowed to visit Gdansk, hundreds of thousands of workers made their way south to join in the pilgrimage. The effect on society was profound. Workers increasingly identified themselves with their parishes and parish priests gained a toehold in the factories. The Pope fuelled a new generation of activist priests who now shrugged off their inhibitions about carrying underground literature or allowing critical poetry and philosophy readings in their basements. And farmers too, for the first time, felt part of a greater national movement. Above all, the Pope's impact was linguistic: he taught Poland the vocabulary of change. On television with Gierek – one of the few direct broadcasts – the Party leader stumbled around in the clumsy half-patriotic, half-Communist rhetoric of the Party. The Pope spoke classical Polish, generous, finely rounded and absolutely firm. It was evident to all, barring perhaps the anxious Soviet monitors across the frontier, that Gierek had been fatally weakened.

Walesa did not manage to see the Pope. He had just begun work at a new factory and could not take time off. He had used the three months' legally permitted break between jobs to travel around the factories of the coast, ostensibly to apply for work but in fact to make contacts for the free trade union movement. But for Walesa, as for most Poles, the Pope's tour was a galvanising moment. There was a sense of history accelerating. And the rock-hard certainty that it was better to fight on for a just cause than to withdraw into a private life full of children and Sunday fishing. The Pope's baritone had boomed out that his Pontificate would be devoted to "the dignity of man, the threat to man, finally to the rights of man. Inalienable rights which can so easily be trampled upon and destroyed – by man."

The Pope's message that Poles had to become historically aware – and thus recognise the essentially temporary nature of Communism – was grasped by Walesa. He had his own personal history and its most important date was December 1970. The free trade unionists, helped by the students of the Young Poland Movement, decided to lay flowers at the main gate of the Lenin shipyard to remember the murdered workers. Walesa arrived late. It was bitterly cold and Danuta had wrapped his face in a thick scarf over his donkey-jacket. The effect was furtive, like a man on the run. He spoke that way too, the words pouring out as if the police were only a step away. Gierek, he said, had not honoured any of the promises made in 1970–71. He had not even built a monument in front of the yard. There was only one solution – and the Pope had pointed the way. "I appeal to you to organise yourselves into independent groups for self-defence. We must help each other." As for the monument, everyone should come back next year to the same place bearing a stone – and the Poles would raise their own monument. It was Walesa's first political speech and it made an impact. Jerzy Borowczak was there: "We never doubted that he was a leader – it was enough to see him laying the wreath. Seven thousand people were there that day and it was already clear how good he was at talking to a crowd. He was able to heat up the moods first, then to calm them down. Afterwards he said 'Go home now,' and they went."

CHAPTER FIVE

Strajk

A nna Walentynowicz, a sturdy woman with the big hands of a peasant and the feet of a trooper, always wanted to be a worker. Orphaned by the war, she supported herself by helping with the harvest in the summer, sharpening and selling kitchen knives door-to-door in the autumn and brewing *bimber* in the winter. She became a kitchen-maid and farmhand for a wealthy peasant in the Gdansk region and remembers the routine: up at four to feed the cattle and make breakfast for the labourers, at seven on to the milking shed and the fields, at seven in the evening back for the milking, and then a few hours of threshing. At midnight she went to bed. One summer night she fled the farm and landed in a bakery. Here she was allowed to eat as much bread as she wanted but it was still grinding, badly paid work. She lived in a cellar and kept herself warm by rubbing herself with petroleum jelly and then standing in front of a borrowed heater. One night, she recalls, she prayed intensely to the Madonna of Vilnius who rewarded Anna with a small miracle: she was accepted at the Gdansk shipyards for training as a welder. That was in November 1950. In August 1980 she was sacked.

The records of the yards show that Anna Walentynowicz, welder from the Roza Luksemburg work brigade, was a model worker. There is still a photo of her from the 1950s – that month's top worker, welding-mask in one hand, and the announcement that she had over-fulfilled her norm by 270 per cent. In the year 1964 she married and the following year she contracted cancer. Bombarded with radium treatment, the illness receded but the doctor gave her only five years to live. By the time the troops fired on the shipyard workers in December 1970 her time should have been up. But she felt fine, and guilty, and annoyed too at the cheating she saw around her: the arbitrary giving and cancellation of bonuses, the long hours and sloppy safety standards. By herself, she concluded, there was little to be done. But there were little things that could improve working life. First she thought: why should the workers from her team have to go to the opposite side of the yard to eat in the canteen? She collected the luncheon vouchers from her workmates and started to organise meals at the workplace. The management banned the meals: all attempts at self-help were forbidden. In front of the assembly hall there was a barren patch and so Anna decided to plant flowers there. "All this was in my free time, you understand," recalls Walentynowicz. "I wouldn't have dared to do it during working hours." The flowers were banned.

Anna Walentynowicz first heard about the free trade union movement in 1978 and visited the Gwiazdas in their apartment. It seemed like a good idea. She brought little pamphlets into the yards and began to hand them out. It was time, she told her friends, to do something for ourselves. The management reacted immediately. She was allowed only to move from the work gate to the changing-room and then to her crane. Since her treatment she had been shifted to the cranes, lanky orange flamingos that hover over the yard. A special key was cut for her so that she could use a nearby lavatory and not cross another shopfloor. She was in quarantine. Once Polish television arrived to show the healthy work conditions in the yard. Five workers were given clean overalls and had to sit on a bench lest they dirty their clothing. A West German boring machine that had never been used because its deployment would have put three people out of work was rolled out. And Anna Walentynowicz was told not to come down from her crane. There followed a year of harassment.

Once she was locked in the changing-room all day, another time she was hustled off by plainclothes officers, yet another time she was kept at the entrance to the yards by the factory security guards. The free trade unionists had taught Walentynowicz the labour laws and she knew that it was not easy to sack her. But if the management could establish absenteeism and unauthorised departure from the workplace – article 52 of the Communist labour code – they could throw her out. The man in the personnel department was taking tranquillisers when he sacked her. "Got no choice," he told her. "If I don't do it, I'll be sacked and then somebody else will sack you." In that case, replied the crane-driver, that one should also refuse to hand out a fake dismissal, and the one after that, and the one after that. "They can't sack everybody, can they?"

Everybody in the yard knew Walentynowicz – "the crazy woman with the flowers" – and very few knew Walesa. He had been watching the shipyards from the window of a nearby apartment on and off for a few days.

54

14 August was to be the decisive day. Walentynowicz had been fired exactly seven days before and immediately told the Gwiazdas and Bogdan Borusewicz. They ran off several hundred copies of a strike appeal – "We are calling on you to defend Anna Walentynowicz" – and many had been distributed in the trams and electric trains that brought workers to the yards from the housing estates. The sirens wailed and the shipyard, by six o'clock in the morning, was on strike.

It was not a good time for Walesa. Danuta was still sore from giving birth to their fifth child, Ania, a few days earlier. But he had agreed with Borusewicz that he would climb the fence – his official pass had been withdrawn in 1976 – and see if he could give some shape to the strike. Walesa remembers that he had devised with Borusewicz a basic set of demands: the reinstatement of Walentynowicz, the sacked worker Andrzej Kolodziej and Walesa himself, permission to build a monument to the victims of December 1970, and a pay rise for every worker in the yards. More ambitious demands, for free trade unions and fundamental reform, could come later, after Walesa had judged the strength of the strike. Gwiazda did not recall the moment quite like that: "There was no commonly agreed strategy on this, no decision to send Walesa in."

The idea for a strike emerged at a party on 8 August. The free unionists were celebrating the release of Tadeusz Szczudlowski, who had been jailed for a small demonstration on 3 May. Some vodka was drunk and Walentynowicz turned up, completely shattered by her dismissal. Jerzy Borowczak and two other members at the free union had started to have problems at work – their lockers were searched every day. "It was Walesa who first said: 'I guess we will have to go on strike'," remembers Borowczak. "Then Bogdan Felski, one of my colleagues, replied – 'easier said than done'." The day after the party Bogdan Borusewicz visited the young worker to develop a plan. Borusewicz, Felski and a third worker were supposed to be the vanguard. "I agreed and added that Walesa should be allowed to participate." Felski visited Walesa in the Stogi district and they drew up a list of sympathisers within the yard. The strike was set to begin on 13 August at 6 a.m. But that plan fell through when Walesa remembered he had to collect Danuta and the baby from the maternity ward. The next deadline was at 5.30 a.m. on 14 August – but only Borowczak and another worker showed up. Felski had overslept. And Walesa said that he had been followed – a frequent event – and could not shrug off his tails. The strike went ahead without him. Borowczak led the workers out of the K-5 assembly hall, another worker led the men out of K-3 and they converged, a few hundred nervous men in the middle of the yard.

Like many other historical turning points that have been predicted for years by learned academics and dissident thinkers, the 1980 strike came as a complete surprise. Adam Michnik had decided to spend the summer in the Tatra mountains writing a new essay. All the prophets of a social explosion were packing their bags for the Mazurian lakes; few, if any, considered the seaside. Yet there were clear signals. On 1 July the government set up a new price system that transferred better cuts of meat to special "commercial" shops with higher prices. It was undoubtedly a price rise but introduced with more subtlety than in 1976. For one thing local authorities were allowed to decide the timing of the increase and many were obviously waiting until the summer holidays. But the measures were not allowed to slip by unnoticed. One by one factories throughout Poland – from the Ursus tractor works to the aircraft engine factory in Mielec in the south of Poland – stopped work and demanded pay rises. The managers, obviously authorised to head off a general strike, conceded five, eight and ten per cent increases usually with an empty clause linking the rise to higher productivity. The official euphemism for these strikes was "interruption in production" as if the strikes were glorified tea-breaks. By the time the strikes reached Lublin, close to the Soviet Union, the Lublin strikers demanded equal family allowances with those received by the police, more independent trade unions and an end to censorship. By 20 July the workers – partly cowed by threats that blocking rail lines would anger Moscow – settled for wage rises and let the political demands drop. But Lublin was important for both sides. It gave the government the false impression that strikers were raising political demands only to secure a better wage deal, that the political could be separated from the financial. And for the workers on the coast, Lublin was a great encouragement. For the first time since Szczecin in 1971, free trade unions were back on the agenda. This time, thanks to KOR, the workers were better placed. Jacek Kuron – who had not gone on holiday – was acting as a clearing house of information between the factories. A simple police measure, such as cutting off the telephones of Kuron and a dozen other activists, would probably have saved Gierek, or at least given him a few more months. But no plugs were pulled and the workers began to feel less isolated, acted like a national rather than a sectional force. The conspiracy theory is that Mieczyslaw Moczar, the old partisan general who had tried to outmanoeuvre Gomulka in 1968 was now putting his chips on worker unrest as a way of displacing Gierek. Certainly

Moczar, head of the neutered monitoring agency the NIK, the Supreme Chamber of Control, later leaked documents about the high life and cheating of the Gierek leadership to Solidarity. But Moczar's time was long past. The most plausible explanation for the myopia of the government was that it was poorly informed and over-confident in its analyses.

Gierek went on holiday to the Crimea on 27 July; he was due to meet Leonid Brezhnev the following week and that took precedence over domestic affairs. On 15 August, the day after Walesa had climbed the fence, a Politburo member rang Gierek in the Crimea and he broke off his holiday. So too did the dissidents. Nobody was in any doubt that this was now a major showdown; few realised that the outcome would determine the future of Communism.

It was no surprise to Walesa, says one of his greatest admirers – Jerzy Kolodziejski, governor of Gdansk province and one of the chief government negotiators during the strike. "Much later Walesa told me that he led the strike according to a strategy that he had worked out long before and which he amended in the course of events. He did listen to other arguments, but only to enrich or correct his strategy." Kolodziejski, reliving the negotiations, believes this version and indeed it is crucial to assessing his importance as a revolutionary. The alternative view – that Walesa was an accidental man, a crowd player who was steered by various groups of advisers – is strongly held and conditions the popular assessment of him not only as a revolutionary but also as a president. Who on earth, Poles ask, after spotting a new blunder, is advising him? Nor did all the Communist authorities share Kolodziejski's assessment of their enemy; they did not easily shrug off their long-held belief that workers exist politically only as puppets. That, of course, is why they lost and Walesa won. Walesa's main goal was always free trade unions, stresses Kolodziejski, who was removed from his post after the declaration of martial law. For Walesa it was essential to anchor the strike gains as soon as possible, to institutionalise victory. That was the lesson of June 1956 and December 1970. "Walesa's strategy that August could be summarised as follows," says Kolodziejski: "start the strike in one of several big industrial plants; next spread it to other factories. One of these plants has to become the strike headquarters, the symbol of the struggle. In no case leave the factories and go into the streets – that could lead to bloodshed as in 1970. Organise a collective strike leadership . . . which has the exclusive right to negotiate with the government. Work out quickly the demands that bind the strategic goals with the economically popular . . . effective propaganda all the time within the striking factories and beyond creating links between the factories and society. And in negotiating start with strategic demands." This is certainly how the August strike developed but whether it was completely Walesa's brainchild is open to doubt. Even Kolodziejski confesses: "In my view his contribution to this strategy was considerable but it's impossible nowadays to determine to what degree it was influenced by his already numerous intellectual advisers." The fact is Walesa has been re-writing, as well as writing, history. To support the myth of the revolutionary leader it was necessary throughout the 1980s, and even into the 1990s, to diminish the role of others and ascribe a grand vision to sometimes haphazard and often uncontrollable events. "Lech likes to present himself as the supreme poker player," says a sociologist who advised him in 1980, "but in fact he was more of a snooker player. It was clear what he had to do to win – knock the balls into the pockets. But he did not always shoot straight, and sometimes his arm was nudged, sometimes he knocked the balls off in the wrong order. He understood quickly, though, that he was up against a weaker player."

Walesa almost arrived too late for the revolution. By the time he climbed over the fence, the strikers had marched to shipyard gate number two and were ready to march into the city. Then they hesitated, remembering the massacre in December 1970, and during the brief uncertain pause Klemens Gniech, the shipyard director, a tough but generally respected patriarch, promised that he would talk if the workers went back to their stations. For a while this seemed to deflect the workers from the essential next step, the formation of a strike committee. It was at that moment that Walesa appeared, jumped on a digger truck near the entrance and improvised: "Remember me? I worked here for ten years . . ." Gniech was one of the few to remember Walesa and, so he claims now, with some warmth: "I remember him from 1970 and when he worked as an electrician in the W-4 department. In 1976 when I had an order from the top to fire him he considered me an equal opponent. We talked man-to-man, always playing fair." Walesa quickly overcame the doubters in the crowd. He spoke quickly not only because this was his nature but also because he had a sense of evaporating time. Later the strikers would be able to call the pace, slow down or accelerate negotiation, but first they had to take control. Walesa declared an occupation strike – the crowd applauded because it meant in the first instance that they would settle the strike within the "family" and not clash with the police – and a strike committee was formed. Gniech agreed to send a black Volga limousine to collect Anna Walentynowicz from home. And then the first round of talks began in earnest, in the BHP health and safety hall with its long school-like desks and ship models in glass cases. The hall was wired up to the shipyard radio announcement system which introduced the crowd factor into the talks. Gniech agreed because he thought it would weaken Walesa's position; he thought he knew the mood of the workers better than Walesa and that they would soon settle for money. Walesa was a step ahead: the Pope's visit had changed the psychology of the least militant workers, the middle-aged family men who had bitter memories but were vulnerable to financial blackmail. The Pope had touched the conscience of precisely these men and with the younger workers – some of whom were already second-generation city-dwellers and more politically sophisticated – they formed a doughty and effective force.

Walesa packaged the various demands of the strike committee into a compact package: reinstatement of Walesa and Walentynowicz, 2,000 zlotys a month pay rise, immunity for all strikers (a lesson from 1976), family allowances on a par with the police (a lesson from Lublin) and, most important, a monument to the dead workers of 1970.

Gniech bargained hard but the pressure of the crowd outside, especially on the issue of the monument, forced him to give ground. He eventually rang the Gdansk Party leadership and was allowed to concede the monument, shape and size to be agreed, to be put outside the gate where some of the workers had died. That Thursday night the workers bedded down. There had already been messages from the Gdynia yards and other workers on the coast were preparing to join in on the Friday; the strikers were quite justifiably confident. The next morning however the management did not cave in. Gniech was still convinced that wage increases, higher for senior workers, lower for new arrivals, would carry the day. But Walesa and the negotiators stood firm: across the board for everybody. This was the first version of "solidarity". It stated clearly that workers would no longer allow themselves to be set against each other by management techniques. Walentynowicz remembers: "The management's offer to reinstate us – that is me and Leszek – was accompanied by certain preconditions. I was supposed to retire on 1 January 1981. And so on the Friday of 15 August the talks were rather pointless. On Saturday morning we agreed that we wouldn't give in under any circumstances. And at last Director Gniech accepted the demands. Leszek promised that he would work decently – though not in writing as Mr Gniech had wanted. Mr Gniech still wanted me to retire, though. We talked around this and soon it was obvious that they were trying to dilute everything again. So we became tough: 'Are you willing to reinstate us or not?' The personnel manager brought the new contracts in half an hour.

The director increased everybody's wages by 1,500 zlotys, which was half the average salary at that time. All the demands of the strike committee had either been fulfilled or were to be reviewed soon."

In the yard the mood had swung for and against the strike during the three days of negotiation. Many workers were becoming aware that their representatives – Walesa and Walentynowicz included – had very little to lose while they themselves were exposed. Most accounts of the early strike days tell of the women outside the gates sending in food and urging the workers on. But by Friday there were wives urging their husbands to return home; they needed money to feed the kids and were unsettled. Walesa was becoming well known throughout the yard but outside in Gdansk and in Poland he was unknown.

The newspapers had not mentioned the strike at all, let alone Walesa. Saturday newspapers reported a crisis in Israel, an earthquake in Chile and the visit of the Prime Minister to a metalworks. The telephone connection with the other yards and factories had been cut off. Sensible defence measures – parking heavy vehicles close to the main gate to block an attack by tanks – and humanitarian moves such as allowing mothers to go home further disturbed the workers. It looked as if the authorities were preparing for a re-run of 1970. The divers attached to the yards were told to patrol the waterfront to scout out signs of a naval assault. And the strike, as it edged into Saturday, was far from the carnival event later depicted on Western television.

For one thing it was very uncomfortable. There were some styrofoam mattresses but many had to sleep across chairs and benches in the main halls or the hospital. Outside at night it was cold and the pickets would wrap themselves in newspaper and squeeze close to each other. Walesa advised them to make fires of the piles of leaflets issued by the administration. Alcohol was banned but some had found its way into the yard and at night at least nobody complained if somebody took a swig or two out of a vacuum flask. Janusz Glowacki, the playwright and novelist, captures the hesitant mood through his Pooterish hero in *Moc Truchleje*. "Do you really think you can win against the police, the army, the Party and Edward Gierek?" a woman asks the hero. " 'I don't want to win at all,' I replied honestly. 'I'm being forced to want to win. I know that if the worst comes to the worst, I'll be hurt, but I really don't have a choice.' " Peer pressure keeps the hero in place; not, in the first instance, Walesa who is closeted in the negotiations. Many of the strikers do not see Walesa at all until the third day of the strike. The yards are a huge, sprawling wasteland and though everybody was supposed to meet twice a day it is a long haul from the outer perimeter to the main administration complex. Rumours swirl – the tram drivers have been offered 2,000 zlotys a month, have settled and abandoned their strike – and sap the resolve of the strikers; most of all they fear being left alone. But still there are constant reminders, little plucking incidents, that the workers of 1980 are different from those ten years ago. Glowacki's welder-hero goes on a reconnaissance trip with two other workmates on the first Friday of the strike. The streets of Gdansk are completely empty; despite the news blackout the whole Coast knows what is happening and is staying out of sight. A military police patrol stops their car. The police take down all their personal details. The welder is frightened: will they be arrested, beaten up? The officer asks about the flag tied to the front of the car. "What's that?"

"The Polish flag," says the welder's workmate laconically. "Red and white. The prescribed colours."

"Take it off. It's obstructing your vision."

The two men begin to argue but the third worker, a woman, reaches underneath her blouse and hauls out a medallion with the Pope's image. "Let us through," she says and stares into the police officer's eyes. They are allowed to continue. The incident is based on fact and stands in for hundreds of similar small confrontations. The dynamics of a worker–government showdown had been subtly changing. At the beginning of the strike the foremen had run around the departments telling the workers they were being manipulated by foreign agitators, that they were merely a pawn in an imperialist plot, that the grievances could be settled Pole-to-Pole. That was the language of the early 1970s and even then its credibility was wearing thin. By 1980 there were no ideological arguments left; only the implicit threat of force was sapping the will of the strikers.

After the management conceded the main demand on Saturday morning, the strike committee decided that they had won and the protest could end. Gniech promptly announced on the tannoy that the strike was over and that workers should leave the yards by six o'clock in the evening. Walesa raised his fist and yelled, "We've won – the strike is over." Several hundred workers immediately rolled up their spare overalls and headed for the gates, not exactly overjoyed but relieved. Walesa however sensed there was something wrong. He had lost touch with the crowd. Some were shouting "Traitor!", "Sell-out!" The question of what happened next is a matter of some dispute. Father Henryk Jankowski, the parish priest of St Bgydas church, which also covers the terrain of the shipyard, had asked permission to celebrate mass in the yard. Jankowski, a burly bulldog-featured man, sought permission from his bishop, Lech Kaczmarek, who panicked. "He was actually rather unpleasant – he said the strikers were drunks and good-for-nothings, that they were too lazy to work. I had to listen to this invective. Finally he gave me permission. But two hours later he rang to tell me that the strike was over and so Mass would not be needed. Something began to boil inside me and I went to see for myself." In the yards he found only a few hundred workers remaining, and a confused-looking Walesa. It was their first meeting. Walesa gave the priest the address of his wife and asked him to take care of Danuta and the children should anything happen to him. "I asked him what was the real point of the strike." He replied that it was about free unions, freeing political prisoners, access to television and other things. " 'Then we should continue the strike,' I told him. 'But, Father, how do you imagine it?' And I said: 'Simple, we'll close the gates, I'll say Mass and on Monday people will join us again.' " At that moment, says Jankowski, they were joined by the tram drivers' leader Henryka Krzywonos, a big rough-tongued woman. She said that the tram drivers also wanted to carry on striking. Walesa then made the decision that was to make him a revolutionary: "OK, if you want to support our strike, let's make it a Solidarity strike." That was the first time that the word solidarity entered the game.

That is perhaps a rather self-serving version. Father Jankowski's many virtues do not include modesty. Gwiazda simply says: "Walesa killed the strike and then realised that he had made a blunder." Walesa himself admits that he had settled too quickly with the management, and that some workers were spitting with fury. The basic complaint, of course, was that almost the whole Coast had come out on strike together with the shipyards. But the shipyards were now leaving them in the lurch; it was the biggest concern, by far the most influential. The authorities would be able to pick off the others one by one. That is why the Communist Party allowed Gniech so much leeway to end the dispute. Walesa had been duped. But apart from Gwiazda and a few other hardened Walesa critics, few hold this against him. For one thing he was profoundly tired, hoarse, barely able to stand. And it was difficult to gauge the mood of the yards. There were in fact two moods: the nucleus of those who were already in "solidarity" with all other Polish workers, a revolutionary nucleus, who would press for complete surrender; and a larger group of men like Glowacki's welder who were striking partly for money, partly out of peer pressure and who had no sense of the strategic aims. Walesa heard the second but not the first group and if he really had a master plan, as Kolodziejski claims, then he seemed ready to abandon it.

Then for whatever reason – perhaps the one offered by Father Jankowski – Walesa changed his mind. It is perhaps this ability to shift ground quickly and correct mistakes, rather than the magical intuition cited by his hagiographers and admirers, that distinguishes him both as a revolutionary and as an institutional politician.

"All right," said Walesa after being battered with complaints from all the neighbouring shipyards and factories. "If the majority decide, then we will carry on striking." He addressed a crowded conference hall: "Who wants to carry on?"

"We do!" A collective bellow.

"Who does not want to strike?"

Silence.

"So we will strike. I will be the last one to leave the yard."

The decision caused havoc. Several thousand workers had already left for home, others were approaching the gates. Ewa Ossowska of the Young Poland Movement had already been trying to stem the flow long before Walesa made his decision. Alina Pienkowska, a factory nurse and active member of the free trade union movement, was shrilly beseeching the workers to return. Now Walesa mounted an electric repair cart – a cross between a golf cart and the Popemobile – and drove around the yard shouting through a megaphone, "The strike continues." Some delegates from other yards and factories had left before Walesa had changed the strike decision and were trying to work out new solutions. Other factory delegates were arriving and grabbing passing workers and demanding, "What's going on?" Throughout the afternoon the debate continued over the public address system. "I am a member of the strike committee," came one voice, "you know me because I've been working here for twenty years . . . Do you know what the militia and the security authorities will do to Leszek? They can do anything they want because we've broken the agreement. We're supposed to leave by six o'clock. Do you want blood to flow? Do you want another December? We didn't commit ourselves to a solidarity strike. We've got to go. At six o'clock the militia and the security forces will come. Do you know what happens then? Don't you remember?"

These appeals were offset by gruff messages of support. "I'm from the strike committee in the refinery. We've been on strike since the morning. We'll stick with you but you've got to do the same by us. Thank you." When six o'clock arrived Walesa was hoisted onto the gate and said that the strike had to be fought to the end. Then in his off-key baritone he led the workers in singing the national anthem. By eight o'clock that evening the director of the yard had been refused entry, the vehicle blockade was in position in front of the main gate, heavy police patrols could be seen parading through the city with flashing lights – but there was no offensive.

Walesa nowadays blames the premature settlement on a chicken-livered strike committee; however, the real flaw, say his critics, lay in his own hesitation. He could have persuaded the committee to press for more. In any case, the turn in the strike gave the free trade union activists a chance to launch a new strike committee and put themselves in control of the protest. The so-called inter-factory strike committee was drawn from 21 striking factories. But it was really the creature of the small group that had been debating union liberties for the past two years in the Gwiazdas' apartment. There was Walesa of course, Alina Pienkowska (who was later to marry Bogdan Borusewicz), Anna Walentynowicz, the two Gwiazdas and the slender black-bearded Bogdan Lis who, like Andrzej Gwiazda, worked at ELMOR. This was the inner core of the revolution and for the most part they loathed each other. The Gwiazdas thought, and still think well over a decade later, that Walesa was profoundly anti-democratic, a worker who excluded workers from real decision-making. Lis felt bullied by Walesa, Walentynowicz was suspicious of the speed with which Walesa was willing to clinch deals with the authorities. For the time being, though, these personality differences were submerged.

The next morning, Sunday 17 August, Father Jankowski arrived to celebrate Mass. About five thousand attended and they were joined by a couple of thousand more, relatives and workers who had left on Saturday. An altar was built on a special trolley and a cross and a portrait of the Virgin Mary were set up. Father Jankowski suggested to Bishop Kaczmarek that he say the first Mass. "But," says Father Jankowski crinkling his nose, "he refused – he was an awful coward." The priest's car – "my mobile tabernacle" – was at the centre of the service. "I heard the confessions in the car and gave Holy Communion from it. The previous night I had told all the kids on the way home to tell their parents about the shipyard mass and it worked – we were besieged." His sermon was entitled "Work as a blessing, work as a curse", and put together the various biblical texts supporting the strike. And, since it was the 60th anniversary of the Miracle on the Vistula, when marauding Bolshevik troops were repelled by the apparent intervention of the Virgin Mary, Father Jankowski declared a "miracle of the Baltic". The priest's chief concern was to dissuade the

64

workers from running onto the streets of Gdansk – Jankowski had just taken over the parish when the workers were gunned down in 1970 and one of his first duties had been to administer the last rites to bleeding marchers.

The Mass set the tone not only for the strike but for the emerging Solidarity union; Christian imagery and priestly discipline became part of the union culture, confounding the many West European socialists who had already begun to trumpet the triumph of genuine workers against bureaucratic, fossilised Communism. After the embarrassment of the Afghanistan invasion and Brezhnev's brutality against dissidents, it seemed as if a new dynamic force had burst on the scene, cleansing the creed. And then, suddenly they were all on their knees! Very odd, these Poles.

From that Sunday a daily prayer meeting was held by Father Jankowski and the prayers were usually led by Walesa himself, or Magdalena Modzelewska from the Young Poland Movement. Pictures of the Pope were strung up around the main gate. Walesa started to wear a rosary around his neck. Father Jankowski remembers an atmosphere of spiritual revival. "The strikers were bitter, hated the system, although vodka was brought to them they usually poured it away and stayed sober. Some confessed every day, others had ripped up their Party cards and were confessing for the first time in thirty years. It was a lot of work."

But the gut egalitarianism of the workers emerged strongly in the 21 demands chiselled out by the strike committee on the Sunday night after the mass. A special commission had been set up to compile the demands from the different plants but the final list was a combination of the strategic demands devised long before by the free trade union activists, material concessions to the workers, a few classically revolutionary demands – such as an end to police privileges – and some nods in the direction of individual strike committee members. Thus, because Alina Pienkowska was a nurse, there was a very thorough set of demands relating to the health service. Gwiazda thinks the demands were genuinely representative of what the workers wanted and resists any suggestion that he pushed his own vision of a fair Poland. "My only contribution to this list was that the commission considered ELMOR's demands most typical and so they became the foundation of the final list of demands."

Gierek sent a Politburo member, deputy premier Tadeusz Pyka, to Gdansk as soon as he heard that the strike was continuing. His hope was still that money could solve the problem. Pyka's brief was to deal with each individual yard and factory and buy them off – indeed sometimes he offered more than the strikers were demanding. But it was too late. There was now a strong commitment to keeping "solidarity" and though it was difficult without telephones, messengers and couriers came in and out of the shipyard like soldiers carrying dispatches to Caesar's tent.

The following week was a period of intensive education for the workers on the Baltic coast. The yards and factories became like self-governing communities. Food had to be bought, brought into the yard and distributed. Money had to be collected in and out of the yards. The strike committee set up its own security service – wearing red and white armbands – to watch the gates, regulate who came into the BHP hall and ensure that machinery was not harmed or tampered with. As farmers brought a truckload of potatoes, poultry breeders donated five thousand eggs, amid much applause a live pig was taken to the cookhouse. And the whole time there was a drumbeat of talk about free trade unions – what they should do, why they were essential. At times the yard was like a Fabian summer camp; until then the workers had only the tea-breaks for conversation, time to grunt out the weekend football scores or moan about the cost of living, no more.

The government meanwhile was in a spin. Gierek, by his own account, was feeling terrible, gulping back aspirins by the handful. Pyka was failing and there were not many tricks left. It was time to send in the suave Mieczyslaw Jagielski. Mocked for his well-tailored, man-of-the-world image, Jagielski was in fact the son of a farmer and was capable of blunt talking. But he was on an impossible mission. He was under orders to persuade the strikers to accept the old union structure – completely rejuvenated, with democratic elections and wide-ranging powers, but still the same organisation performing the same function within the system. That was offered to the protesters in Szczecin in 1971, and the authorities soon scratched back the lost ground. The previous month in Lublin, railway workers had been offered something similar: government recognition of the right of the workers to elect their own representatives to the leadership of the old Party-controlled unions. "They were mugs in Lublin," said a speaker over the PA system when the news of Jagielski's arrival spread. "We mustn't fall into the same trap." Jagielski, unlike Pyka, agreed to talk to the MKS, thereby accepting that the strike committee had some legitimacy. On the same Friday, 22 August, two intellectuals, Tadeusz Mazowiecki (the Catholic editor of the monthly *Wiez*) and history professor Bronislaw Geremek (an expert on low life in medieval Paris), drove up to Gdansk to present to the strikers a letter of support from 64 intellectuals. This, and the presence of the two KOR activists (Konrad Bielinski and Ewan Milewicz), and news that the strike was firming in Szczecin, hardened Walesa's position. It was fast becoming obvious that he was in the van of a national, and not just a worker movement. Walesa decided that intellectuals – called experts though they were nothing of the kind – should take over the sharp end of the negotiation. This was partly because he sensed that the authorities were ready to give some important ground – but only in private, and hidden in the detail of an agreement. Partly Walesa was protecting himself. He had already been denounced as a traitor once during the strike and he did not like it. If there were secret compromises to be made, it would be better for the visiting eggheads (his term) to do the dirty work. And he knew, better perhaps than Gwiazda and others on the strike committee, that the final agreement would have to be packaged in a way that would allow the Party leadership to sell the idea to Moscow.

Walesa had placed free trade unions at the top of the 21 demands and he insisted that it be resolved first before any of the material demands were considered. That was common sense; trade unions and not wage rises were now the issue. Walesa, flanked by Gwiazda and the electrician Florian Wisniewski, stressed to Jagielski that the strikers had no political ambitions. They wanted to help solve the economic crisis which had come about because there was no authentic worker representation. Jagielski made his pitch for reformed unions, not new unions. "It is planned to hold leadership elections without delay in every factory where the workforce wishes them." The "wish" of the workers was his escape clause. The Party was confident enough of its control, outside Gdansk, to believe that it could persuade factory workforces to renounce free elections or accept Party-sponsored candidates. The MKS rejected this offer and the union dilemma was referred to the experts. Mazowiecki, in the lugubrious tones that were to become well known ten years later when he became the first Solidarity premier, assured the workers that the experts would keep their place and not take over the running of the strike.

And Walesa presented the experts to a rather sceptical MKS with some high-speed salesmanship: "In connection with, um, so that we will all benefit, um – we must call into being a group of advisers. Well, we must be, when all is said and done, well enough informed and clever, true? So that's what we've done. And were we right?" In the secret working groups the government quickly dropped the public demand for free participation in the official unions. It was obviously unacceptable to the strikers. Instead they tried to limit the new unions geographically (to the Baltic coast) and politically. The experts (Mazowiecki and Tadeusz Kowalik) refused to accept the idea of limiting the free unions to the Baltic but did come up with a protective preamble that made possible the agreement of the government. The workers would recognise the "leading role of the Party in the state" and would not "undermine the established system of international alliances". The youngest of the experts, the sociologist Dr Jadwiga Staniszkis, refused to accept such a qualification, saying, with some justice, that it contradicted the whole spirit of the strike movement. Other members of the MKS felt the same way: this was not the time to subordinate their new unions to Party control. But Walesa knew that the wording was hollow, just as the Party's leading role had lost its meaning. Kowalik argued that the experts had won a new principle. The constitution stipulated that the Party has the leading role in state and society. The Gdansk agreement dropped the word society. In other words, the new social contract could shape up by allowing the Party to dominate politics and giving the workers, ordinary people, the right to run and live in society as they pleased.

For Walesa, both points of view – those of Kowalik and Staniszkis – were largely semantics, a common-room discussion. The unions, once legal and institutional, would take on a life of their own and simply ignore or discard verbal limitations. That was the nature of true, rather than steered, social movements.

Walesa was growing up quickly. Tadeusz Wozniak spotted the turning point. "I saw Walesa reading *Polityka* – he spread it out in front of him and studied it closely. That was an important transition – a striking worker, a man who shouted at rallies, was becoming a politician. He himself had noticed that change so he had to check 'what's new in *Polityka*'. It was a time when reading *Polityka* was the thing to do. Even those who didn't read it, stuck the paper in their pockets, suddenly, there was Walesa, alone in a lunch break at the shipyard canteen, reading the liberal paper of the ruling classes." His negotiating tactics also suggested a new maturity. Without doubt the star of the negotiations was Gwiazda. Wozniak remembers: "Gwiazda really stood out. He was very accurate, very precise – and like all anarchists, narrow-minded and very concrete. Walesa had only a general idea of where the negotiations were headed. His role was only to control the pace of the negotiations. He would be silent and say suddenly – 'No we shouldn't overburden Mr Premier on this point just now, so let's stand up and sing the national anthem.' " Gwiazda kept the government to the point – a vital but ultimately transitional role. Walesa quietly assessed the scope for deal-making.

A close study of Walesa's actions and often fractured statements shows that in crude terms he understood far more than his advising experts, the worried statesmen abroad or the more sophisticated colleagues on the MSK. First, he sensed the true weakness of the government position. The economy was rotten to the core and the Party had lost control of it; Gierek admitted as much halfway through the strike when he threw out his main economic ministers and brought in one of his fiercest but economically most able critics, Stefan Olszowski. The rapid spread of the strikes also demonstrated that Gierek's propaganda machine, the Big Lie that camouflaged the economic disaster, had also failed. Hence the sacking of Jerzy Lukasiewicz, the propaganda chief, and the fast-living television chairman, Maciej Szczepanski. So, Walesa reasoned, if even Gierek himself admitted that the economy was a failure and could not defend himself, what was left? The Party had either to use force, or to make concessions. The Catholic Church had come round to the same conclusion and Cardinal Stefan Wyszynski, seared by the rough treatment in the 1950s, was sure that the outcome would be violent; in his experience it was how Communists at bay reacted.

On Sunday 26 August Wyszynski broadly supported the worker demands in a long, important sermon – but he also had some criticism for the strikers and the use of the strike weapon. The authorities seized on the sermon and released a mangled, though credible, version. Father Jankowski, who actually had no idea of the real version, scurried around the yards reassuring the workers that the text had been manipulated. Two Church experts meanwhile had been sent to Gdansk to ensure that control of the strike did not lurch into the hands of KOR, whom most of the Church hierarchy still regarded as a Trotskyist cell. Walesa was never completely sure that force would not be used but as long as Jagielski continued to talk and as long as Gierek was driven by his critics in the Party to admit past errors, then it seemed unlikely. The key point was to keep the protests within the walls of the factories and yards and not to make any comment that seemed like a grab for power. Andrzej Drzycimski (then a journalist, later presidential spokesman) noted an off-the-cuff remark by Walesa that he was waiting for more ministerial heads to fall. Walesa told the reporters to forget the comment and a Walesa aide tried to snatch Drzycimski's notes. There was too the outside chance of a Soviet intervention but as the strike spread to Warsaw and other cities, as it sucked in Poles from every walk of life, so that threat too receded: the Soviet army would have to put down a nation.

Like all revolutionaries Walesa was gambling, but it was a game full of inspired calculation and absolutely no intellectual baggage. Adam Michnik admitted as much. Both he and Jacek Kuron had been arrested and prevented from coming to the yards: "Jacek, like me, was very uneasy about the situation in Gdansk . . . the wildest idea was that of independent and self-governing trade unions. Jacek knew that this was impossible in a Communist system. I also knew it was impossible and that's why I wanted to go to Gdansk and explain to them that it was senseless. Since I was well known and rather popular there, I might have convinced them. Fortunately, I was arrested. I couldn't go to Gdansk and convince them and so Solidarity was created."

Not everybody liked the Gdansk agreement when the government finally caved in. There were those who thought it would give the Communists too much leverage. But Walesa, who signed with a giant ball-point pen emblazoned with the Pope's face, knew that they had won an important battle, the first of many.

If the Gdansk agreement had been implemented overnight Poland would have hopped, skipped and jumped from an authoritarian regime to a near-democratic state. True, there was no mention in the agreement of a democratic parliament or national elections or anything that explicitly challenged the Communists' control of political institutions. But it was nonetheless a formidable charter of change which, had it been honoured, would have made the passage to a complete democracy inevitable. New trade unions set up a direct competitor not only to the corrupt and Communist-run official unions, but also to the Communist Party itself. Despite the wording of the preamble acknowledging the Party's leading role in the state, new legal unions upset the Leninist orthodoxy. And by giving the workers the right of association, the authorities had opened the way for a multitude of other free-spirited organisations not only among workers, but for writers, doctors, architects, musicians, museum employees. That would stunt Party influence in almost every niche of society. Teachers, reprimanded for telling the truth to their pupils about Soviet war crimes, could find a defence from a teachers union; the directors of hospitals, inevitably Communists, suddenly had to listen to their overworked junior colleagues; the culture ministry was hesitant about denying funds to films that a few months earlier would have been throttled at birth. The Gdansk agreement gave the unions access to economic figures, a basic threat to managers (who could previously argue that they were firing troublesome workers for economic reasons) and to ministerial planners who had been juggling and shuffling statistics for over a decade. The accord promised that the government would insert the right to strike in a new trade union law. And within three months the authorities were obliged to pass a censorship law setting out precisely what could and what could not be said publicly. The mass media were to be loosened from Party control, Sunday mass was to be broadcast each week on state radio. Private farmers were to be given equal access to fertilisers and equipment. Meat supplies were to be improved. Hard-currency shops were forbidden to sell staple foods.

It was not a "political" document – article two explicitly stated "the new trade unions will defend the social and material interests of employees and do not intend to play the role of a political party" – nor was it a commitment to capitalism ("the unions approve of the principle that the means of production are social property – a principle that is the foundation of the socialist system in Poland").

It was, however, a remarkable victory for Walesa. He was obliged to peddle the public line that there was no single victor – that the only victor was Poland. But anyone who had contact with Walesa at the time was left in no doubt. He had beaten back an attempt to unsaddle him during the strike and he had turned the passion of his opponents against them. When Joanna Duda-Gwiazda – perhaps out of no more than loyalty to her husband – denounced Walesa as a traitor and an agent, it was Mrs Gwiazda who was taken out of the yard and not Walesa. "Walesa's power in the shipyard had become practically unlimited," said Borowczak. "Nobody was able to question his position."

Walesa had learned more than the dynamics of crowd control. He had come to understand the politics of committees, how to form coalitions of support and how to abandon them when the need arose. Borowczak studied Walesa closely: "Walesa had become an expert in plucking people out of a hostile group and attracting them to himself. He chose one or two from such a group, made them his own men and that in turn made the whole hostile group quarrel among themselves and reduce the danger. Sometimes people would say: 'What's Walesa doing, picking people who used to spit at him?' But Walesa knows what he's doing – he has destroyed every coup attempt against him in this way."

The day after the signing he set up an office of the future union in Machlewskiego Street and though he was outwardly unchanged, walking in a fast waddle like someone trying to escape inconspicuously from the scene of a crime, puffing a pipe ("cheaper than cigs") and flirting with women journalists, he seemed constantly flushed and laughing. But within

71

a few days the carnival spirit had ebbed and the offices were overwhelmed not by well-wishers but by complainants, men and women who wanted to put right past injustices at the workplace. Most of them came with cases as rock-solid as that of Anna Walentynowicz. The sheer number of wronged workers made Walesa think carefully about the shape of the future unions. To cope with this bottled-up anger, not to mention solving the daily crises at the workplace, would mean either a dense network of local union cells, or a large centrally controlled union. Neither seemed quite to fit the bill. The Gdansk agreement was only just beginning to filter through to the provinces. The Communist unions and the local managers were not enthusiastic about the accord; a journalist who tried to read it to a factory crew in southern Poland found himself ejected by the security guards. As enthusiasts set up union cells in central Poland they found themselves harassed and bullied. Women workers were told they would no longer be given access to the crèches and kindergartens funded by the Communist unions; holiday rest houses owned by the official unions were declared out of bounds for members of the new unions. These complaints too were reaching Walesa. Obviously, outside the Baltic coast and Warsaw the new unions were too vulnerable to attack. Yet a centrally run union would contain all the inherent problems of the official union structure: top-heavy with bureaucrats, out of touch with workers, its leadership growing too chummy with its regular negotiating partners in government. In the Machlewskiego Street office, Walesa was forced to listen to the complaints and had no time to think through the next step. Within days the union – the name "Solidarity" already in play – had moved to a squalid seaman's hotel, the Hotel Morski, where Walesa could have his own office and be protected by secretaries. Lech Badkowski, a writer who had joined the Gdansk strike committee, recalled how disorganised Walesa was at this stage: "Walesa has no organisational sense or even any understanding of the need for an orderly and productive organisation. He is an improviser."

But it was political enough to worry the Communists. The factory was the very core of Party control and although Solidarity members were not yet strong nor angry enough to cart Communists out of the factories in wheelbarrows, the challenge had been clearly stated to both the Party cells and the Communist-run unions. Stanislaw Kania, who had taken over the Party from Gierek, was a man of the apparat – his features were curiously blurred as if by a stocking mask – and a reformer out of necessity rather than conviction. The divisions in the Party were already becoming clear. Stefan Olszowski, an economic reformer in the 1970s (and therefore an opponent of Gierek), was now emerging as a rallying force for the political conservatives. This was partly opportunism – it was a natural way to gain the support of Moscow, but it was also his genuine belief that the Party leadership was dodging difficult questions about the permissible limits of change and thus rotting the authority of the Communist centre. The economy needed an overhaul, but not by giving workers a greater say in the political process. The point was to harness worker enthusiasm, to lead the workers, not to let them slip away.

Kania, sometimes described as a "centrist" though the political middle was constantly shifting, had no real plan to offer. He was aware of the economic disaster looming for Poland – over \$20 billion in debts and a dislocated economy – and could see only one way out: to buy social peace and eventually put himself in a position where he could credibly ask for sacrifices (higher prices, rationing) from the workers. Since he plainly had none of the populist appeal of the early Gomulka or the early Gierek, his approach would have to be different. A social contract but not on the patriarchal terms offered by Gierek in 1971 – "Will you help me?" Rather Kania could offer a web of agreements that were based on the premise of the Gdansk agreement – that is, legally anchored trade unions providing they did not try to overthrow the political order. That did not mean however that the Party was condemned to a passive role. On the contrary, Kania was fresh from his job as Party controller of the security services and he now presided over the most dramatic growth in secret-police activities that Poland had witnessed since the 1950s. Since local authorities would have to deal with the new unions, they would have to be given all available political weapons. The police machinery in the provinces was given considerable powers in the factories and out of the factories. Who after all was to determine whether the new unions were sticking to their end of the agreement to keep out of politics? And who was to define political activity? Factory rooms were bugged, individual workers were quietly threatened; it was the beginning of an era of dirty tricks.

Kania (who in his memoirs naturally presents himself as a dedicated reformer) not only let the police off the leash, he started to manoeuvre around the new unions. If there was to be a social contract, it was for the Party to negotiate the best possible terms. Why for example should Gdansk act as a model for the many unions springing up throughout Poland? It could be argued that Gdansk was a local oddity. The Szczecin agreement was far more useful to the Party. It had the drawback of conceding free trade unions, but there was an important codicil: the self-governing trade unions should possess a "socialist character". And there was no mention of the word "independent". For Kania's purposes, that was a far more practical model for Poland.

Self-governing was an all-purpose term that had not inhibited the Party from taking them over in the past. And whereas Gdansk won the right for the strike committee to become the nucleus of new unions, the Szczecin accord inserted an extra element: strike committees would become worker commissions, "which will hold where necessary general, direct and secret elections for trade-union leadership". Where necessary? And could not the workers be persuaded to hold secret elections within the old union framework? There was room here for the Communists to wriggle and argue with the usually very inexperienced worker activists in the provinces. Indeed, part of Szczecin's problem was that it had allowed in only a few intellectual advisers.

Kania's position then was to give some ground and take some back. In Moscow he emphasised the ground he had reclaimed; the Kremlin, though initially shocked by August, was relatively calm. The precedent of 1971 showed that the Polish leadership knew how to neutralise and contain worker discontent after an angry outburst. To the workers at home meanwhile he seemed like a man they could deal with; the villains were General Moczar, Olszowski and other more obviously authoritarian figures. Walesa, though, had learned his lesson with Gierek. Kania was no hero, no "father of the nation". He would be careful.

There was however a more genuinely reformist wing of the Party. Many of the complaints voiced by the strikers had been heard already from grassroots Party activists in February 1980. They knew the mood in the factories and various warning signals had been passed upwards to the Gierek leadership, who had in turn shrugged them off. Party activists began to wonder if the Gdansk experience did not provide some useful lessons for regenerating socialism. Why for example should factory cells not have contacts with university workers in the same city? The answer was that Leninist democratic centralism was based on the idea that information flows vertically from the bottom of the ladder to the top (central committee, Politburo) and then down again. To forge horizontal links was an ideological heresy. Nonetheless many reformist Communists started to embrace this heresy. Many others took the Gdansk agreement at face value and enquired about joining the new unions.

And in Gdansk, Walesa found two Party men – the local Party chief Tadeusz Fiszbach and the provincial governor Kolodziejski – who were

74

willing to adapt the dogma to the new events. That was crucial. Since the new unions were committed to working within the socialist system, not to overthrowing it, the socialist system had to be changed. The change could partly be brought about by strike pressure from the workers. But the engine of change had to be within the Party itself. That this was not an entirely naive hope on the part of Walesa is shown by the unfurling of events that autumn. Despite all the chicanery, the Gdansk agreement was firmly praised in speeches by the Party leadership (mainly Kania and Kazimierz Barcikowski). On 13 September the council of state passed a decree allowing new unions to seek registration even before the passage of a new union bill, and eventually in November (admittedly after the threat of a general strike) the union was registered, under the name of Solidarity. The Catholic Church also seemed to accept a corporatist solution to Poland's problems.

Walesa travelled to Warsaw from Gdansk and for the first time met the Primate Cardinal Stefan Wyszynski. The Primate had frequently been criticised for excessive caution, not only during the August strike and later. The wariness was partly coloured by his arrest during the Stalinist years and partly by a sense of Soviet malice; anti-Communism strongly felt can sometimes be a paralysing creed. The Primate's advice was thus to ease up on Kania and to define the new unions as a controlling force rather than as a power broker. "It's not a question of wanting to change the leaders, it's they who must change. We must make sure – and I make this comparison quite deliberately – that one gang of robbers does not steal the keys of the state treasury from another similar gang. What is at stake is the rebirth of man himself."

Walesa was deeply impressed by this; it confirmed his instinctive judgment that in open conflict the defeated party should be able to retain some sense of victory. The harder he pressed the Communists, the more obvious would their August humiliation become, and the harder they would fight back. There were different ways of packaging this philosophy (as Christian charity to the defeated, for example) but it was an essentially tactical judgment. The fundamentalists, such as Andrzej Gwiazda, were to find Walesa's malleability suspicious. "Walesa has always had an exaggerated respect for authority," said one member of the original free trade union group. "The Primate's advice merely gave him an easy, Christian, escape route when the going got tough." Walesa though was very careful not to become a pawn of the Church. It was always plain for example that the Primate disliked Jacek Kuron, who had been demonised by the Communist press. Yet Walesa was not prepared to distance himself from KOR. Now,

Walesa presents this as an act of loyalty – KOR had helped to get him out of jail a few times, had been a vital information exchange during the strikes – but in 1980, he really needed Kuron. The earthy former Communist was a brilliant analyst of power and capable of adapting quickly, of reading the runes of Party meetings.

Soon enough Walesa was to learn these skills too and Kuron became less important, but in the early stages Walesa was in regular contact. The Church advisers were more cautious and, like the Primate, tended to overstate the unity and resolve of the Communists; this applied not only to the Primate's emissaries, but also to the advisers from the Catholic Intelligentsia Club (KIK) and the lay Catholic editor Tadeusz Mazowiecki. Walesa understood that the point lay not in endless argument over how much the Communists could yield. The Communists had become a reactive force; Walesa and the strikers were a novelty in this quasi-totalitarian system and so, as long as the Communists did not use armed force, it was the protesters who had the initiative, who could shock and innovate.

It was rather like ju-jitsu, says Walesa. "We couldn't win in an all-out duel. They had everything. We had almost nothing. But we could keep them off balance, make them shift their weight and twist their ankles."

That was Walesa's position before an important session, on 17 September, to determine the future shape of the union. For the union, the question was whether to be a centralised national organisation, or a decentralised weave of local unions. For Walesa, the question was how to maximise his power.

The debate in Gdansk that day, and the final compromise deal supported by Walesa, was sunk in a heavy mist of ambiguity. Many delegates from provincial strike committees had come to the conference convinced that they could lose all the gains of the past few weeks if they were submerged in a big bureaucratically centralised structure. The Gdansk agreement indicated that every strike committee – and there were several hundred throughout the country – could be the founding commission of a union. But what did Gdansk know of local conditions? The local strike leaders knew the weaknesses of the local party bosses, knew roughly the bargaining capacity of factory managers and the resources of the secret police. There was a clear democratic case for keeping local unions which would nonetheless pool some functions with unions from other regions and occasionally act in sympathy. The negotiating power of Wroclaw bus drivers, for example, was their ability not only to strike but to ensure that other Wroclaw factories laid down their tools. That would have a national impact since the economy was so heavily centralised. If a Wroclaw factory was not delivering parts then factories elsewhere would have to slow down or stop production. More: strong local unions would increase the sense of resistance, the mood of civil society.

The arguments ebbed and flowed all day. The centralisers took up what they regarded as a much more realistic position. A strong central union was needed to counter a central state. Who, after all, would sit down with the government – the Wroclaw bus drivers, the inexperienced activists from Kielce or Bialystok? The Communists would pick off one local union after another and unravel the movement. Some unions would be dragged into cooked-up corruption scandals and their leaders arrested, others would have anti-Communist materials planted in their offices, others would be bought off with important-sounding titles. Of course the Gdansk shipyards could come out on a solidarity strike with any persecuted local union but that would soon cease to be effective or rational. That was the case argued by the human rights lawyer Jan Olszewski (in 1992 he became Solidarity's third premier) who put the crucial motion: all local unions should seek to register as one national union. Walesa was in sympathy with the local unionists rather than those who wanted a mammoth unitary union. He understood though that whichever way the decision fell, he would be the leader of the new movement. If the decentralists triumphed he would be the *de facto* chief since the Gdansk shipyards would always carry the most muscle. If the centralists won out, Walesa would become the elected leader obliged to consult the rank and file and follow statutory rules. Walesa had already discovered that he acted best independently of the workforce, freely interpreting their demands and gauging on the spot exactly how much he could sell to them. Walesa was always at his worst when following a closely agreed agenda.

After Olszewski put forward his motion, the two sides started to work out a compromise. There would be unified union – Solidarity – but the regions would be almost completely autonomous. Thus the Warsaw Mazowsze region would follow its own strategy tailored to the complexities of a capital with heavy industry (a steelworks, a tractor factory) and large numbers of already very politicised students and social welfare facilities. Katowice could adapt its strategy to the coal miners and their special needs. Yet every region would liaise through a Coordination Commission. It was in a sense a federalist solution but the frontiers between local and central authority were deliberately blurred. The point was to keep the Communist authorities in a state of confusion, constantly unsure whether the union would throw its full weight – in the form of a general strike – or let the regional barons settle the matter. Walesa presented the conclusion of the meeting to the press – "We will adapt one set of statutes together. A joint statute. But the regional unions will stay."

From that moment, critics of Walesa began to accuse him of muddled thinking. How could there be a legally autonomous national union encompassing dozens, perhaps hundreds, of equally autonomous local unions? It did not make any kind of sense. But the confusion was deliberate; Walesa's ambiguity was that of Solidarity. The whole idea of the union was impossible in a socialist state, as Michnik had made so plain. It could only survive in a situation of complete unclarity. And who best to represent this tactical fuzziness than Walesa himself? This is how he summed up the 17 September session: "Everybody should know that Gdansk has become the headquarters for everybody. No, wait, that's not right! No, this is it – a central authority has emerged in Gdansk, but it's not really that, something like it, but not exactly."

Walesa never really abandoned this style even when he became president and needed to state clearly what he and Poland stood for. "I am for and simultaneously against," became his famous catchword as he played off one side against another. A generation of Polish journalists has grown up interpreting and then substantially cleaning up Walesa's fractured remarks before publication. (This has also suited Walesa. If he makes a gaffe, journalists are promptly blamed for setting down his words incorrectly.)

Having settled, or at least fudged, the question of Solidarity's future structure, Solidarity could start its campaign to register in the courts. Legal status would not only give embattled local unionists some measure of protection against arrogant managers and Party bosses. It would also allow the union to expand quickly; to gather funds, open bank accounts, employ activists – most Solidarity organisers were simply seconded from their factories in the early months – to lobby the telecommunications ministry for more phones.

Three lawyers who would later turn into bulky centre-right politicians – Olszewski, Wieslaw Chrzanowski and Andrzej Stelmachowski – were given the job of drafting the statutes of the new union. And applications to join the still non-existent union poured into the Hotel Morski, into the offices of the Warsaw region on Szpitalna Street, into all the regional centres. By October almost three million Poles had expressed their readiness to sign up; three million was also the number of Communist Party members. The Party was melting as quickly as Solidarity was growing. This put an end to the Kania pretence – that the Party and the worker protests were somehow part of the same great movement for renewal. The conservatives in the Party actually had a more accurate appraisal of Solidarity: it was a competitor. The longer Solidarity was allowed to flourish, the more life would drain from the Party. But as long as the Party could not seize control of the economy, the Party was condemned to watch passively, or at best try to prick Solidarity to see how it would react.

A month after the signing of the Gdansk accords, very little – apart from broadcast Mass – had been delivered by the government. Above all pay rises were supposed to be granted by the end of September yet when the provisional national committee of Solidarity met on 29 September it was obvious that some regional authorities had not even begun pay negotiations. The food shops which briefly had looked better at the beginning of September were emptying again. The pay rise would not exactly improve this situation – indeed it was likely to emphasise how little there was to buy – but it might allow some families to buy meat on the private market once a week, or spare parts for the car, or coffee from the hard-currency shops. Anger was building up against the authorities. If the Party had imagined that the Gdansk agreement would lance the boil of discontent, they were wrong. It merely fed the feeling of the government being on the run. A plenum that pinned the blame on Gierek and threw out some of his cronies strengthened this sentiment. As for the unions, the rank and file felt a need to test their strength, to establish the new frontiers of power. The slightly accidental figures that had been thrown up by the strikers – Zbigniew Bujak from Warsaw, Andrzej Slowik from Lodz and many others – also needed to be tested.

They were unknown to most workers and had to carve out a profile for themselves. Solidarity decided that the pay issue merited a strike: a one-hour general strike was announced for 3 October, a Friday. The government promptly announced that many public-sector workers would receive their higher wages by the end of October, but it was too late. Walesa was against this strike. His advisers warned that it might tip the balance in the Party – due to resume a central committee session – against Kania and towards the use of force. Walesa was still star-struck by his success in August. He was certain that he could lever concessions out of the authorities, that his negotiating style had dumbfounded the Communists. There was however a clear emotional need for the strike and it went ahead. Compared to protests in the years to come it was a relatively mild-mannered affair: wailing factory sirens, the hoisting of Polish flags, the donning of red and white armbands. Noon is a good time for such short symbolic strikes. Although technically only a one-hour protest, in practice nobody resumes work before the end of the morning shift at two o'clock, and the incoming afternoon shift, infected by the carnival mood, takes it easy too. And the great thing about a one-hour strike is that it is almost impossible to assess its success. But it was hailed a victory and, especially in the deeper provinces, it whetted the appetite for more. When the workers were on strike they felt the still faintly mysterious "Solidarity"; when they were working, separated in their different departments and under the thumb of sometimes unpleasant foremen, that August communion disappeared.

The lawyers, having completed the statutes of Solidarity, submitted them to the Warsaw district court for approval. The judge dispatched various other union applications and then announced the decision on Solidarity: positive. There was much cheering and the judge adjourned the session for half an hour. Then, to the consternation of Walesa, he added a condition for accepting the statutes: they should be adjusted to recognise explicitly the leading role of the Communist Party in the state. And a new clause was to be inserted stating that "the organisation of a strike must not contradict the legal regulations in force". Walesa and his advisers (Krzysztof Sliwinski from KIK, Professor Geremek, Mazowiecki) stormed out of the courtroom and drove to the Warsaw KIK offices to think about the court statement. Evidently the Party, nervous about the 3 October strike and perhaps under some pressure from Moscow, had dictated the amendments to the judge. It was an attempt to box Solidarity in right from the beginning.

Kania had misjudged the feverishness of Solidarity and the workers. To the Party the insertions probably seemed like a reasonable safety clause. The leading role of the Party had already been acknowledged in the Gdansk agreement and it was not particularly provocative to ask that strikers act within the law. But Walesa was already being regarded with deep suspicion by the Gdansk strike committee. Gwiazda, Walentynowicz and the inner circle from the free trade union movement were becoming convinced that Walesa was too conciliatory to the authorities. It was this group rather than Walesa that set the pace in the registration crisis. The government should come to the shipyards and explain itself immediately otherwise there would be a nationwide general strike, said the Gdansk team. Instead Deputy Premier Mieczyslaw Jagielski flew up and persuaded the Solidarity leaders to come to Warsaw a few days later (hoping that tempers would cool in the meantime). But the worker anger was not confined to Gwiazda and the other radicals. It seemed that the regime was about to tear up the Gdansk agreement. The Solidarity regions started to prepare for a devastating general strike.

When Walesa met the authorities again in October, he brought with him other demands – an end to harassment of unions and, most important, the call for a farmers' union. The government pushed these additional requests aside, partly because they were not prepared for a suddenly extended agenda and partly because the Party itself had to find its new direction before agreeing to anything quite as dramatically different as a farmers' union. To radicalise the countryside would fundamentally shift the terms of the political game; it would push at least some of the peasants beyond the moderating influence of the Church, it could endanger food supplies and it would mean renouncing one of the most useful tactical devices of the Communists, the ability to set town against country, the honest worker against the greedy private farmer. But on registration, it seemed, there was readiness to clinch a deal, if only to head off a general strike. Secret talks were held and by 11 November, Polish Independence Day, Walesa could celebrate the registration of his union by attending a grand gala concert in Warsaw. "Don't be afraid! The whole nation is with you," said the placards as Walesa entered the opera house.

A few days later Walesa met Kania and it seemed that the Solidarity leader was ready if not to enter a corporate partnership, then at least to ease some of the pressure on the Party. "Even when there is just cause, there are other methods apart from striking to settle our grievances," said Walesa. The aim was not only to offer Kania a breathing-space, but also to consolidate his own power. For it was becoming obvious to Walesa that his personal authority depended not so much on calling a strike as being able to stop it after the demands had been won. Wildcat strikes seriously restricted his power and played into the hands of the "free unions are anarchy" school of Communist doctrine. Equally dangerous was the explicitly political strike. Such was the Narozniak affair, the arrest of a young printer who had published a secret document. Narozniak was from Warsaw and the region's Solidarity chief, Zbigniew Bujak, was determined to show that he would not allow his footsoldiers to be harassed in this way. He gave warning of a strike in Warsaw, and threw in some extra demands apart from the release of Narozniak. But most significantly he went well beyond the Gdansk agreement – by, for example, demanding a commission of enquiry into the activities of the secret police and cuts in the police budget.

This propelled Solidarity into a land without maps. A political strike that pinpointed the secret police and the prosecutor's office as its main enemy; a strike initiated by Warsaw, by a regional warlord exploiting the local powers worked out in the September 17 meeting; and a strike in which Walesa had almost no role. It proved difficult, after a concession or two from the authorities, to persuade the steelworkers to go back to work and some of the persuasion came from Walesa, flown in from Gdansk. But if Walesa had thought that Solidarity was his union, he was now forced to reassess the situation. The sound of Soviet tanks revving on the borders, the invasion phobia that gripped the West and Poland at this time, should have concentrated the mind, pushed reformist Communists, the Solidarity leadership and the Church closer together in a coalition of common sense. That was the line urged by Western ambassadors (some of whom decided that this was a remarkably good time to leave for a holiday), by the Pope and the Primate, and echoed by Warsaw intellectuals. It even seemed to take hold when, in a deeply emotional ceremony, Walesa stood alongside Professor Henryk Jablonski, the Polish head of state, local Party chief Tadeusz Fiszbach and Church dignitaries in front of the three tall steel and concrete crosses at the shipyard gates. It was 16 December, the anniversary of the 1970 shootings, and Walesa had kept his promise – there was a monument to the fallen.

Walesa, in a worker's steel helmet, used almost the same vocabulary as Fiszbach – peace, order, unity. But the ceremony which seemed to promise so much was at most a temporary alliance, a commitment to solve the Polish crisis without force. One year later, Walesa was under arrest and coal miners were being shot down by the ZOMO riot police.

CHAPTER SIX

Living on credit

Walesa left Poland for the first time in his life on 14 January 1981. He was thirty-eight years old and on his way to see the Pope. "I travel like a son to his father," he said before boarding the LOT plane. Emotionally that was certainly the case. He had long lost the tendency to look up to politicians as father-figures; Gierek was a broken idol and Kania was no replacement. His own stepfather was waiting for him in Rome but, as Walesa was to recall, the meeting merely confirmed his deep antipathy for Stanislaw. "I hadn't seen him for years, and the old resentment still smouldered between us." Stanislaw had not returned from the United States in 1975 to attend the funeral of Lech's mother and from that moment Walesa had effectively cut relations. In Rome he talked obsessively of money and Walesa, still in the glow of the papal audience, bubbled over with anger. The Pope filled the void for Walesa; apart from the obvious moral authority of the man, his status as a good Pole, he was also an intellectual who had done time as a labourer (as a quarry worker under German occupation). That marked him out, clearly distinguished him from the historians and sociologists advising Walesa. Andrzej Drzycimski remarked on how devout Walesa had become since the strikes. "He was discovering his strength in the Church. Faith was growing in him – it was becoming something durable." Yet Walesa had a tendency to drift, to have a burst of very strict devotion and then slack off. As even Drzycimski, his most faithful chronicler, admits: "For some time after the meeting with the Pope he began each day with a quiet mass at the new church in Gdansk Prymorze, but after a while his visits became more and more rare."

The Pope for his part did not know quite what to make of Walesa. The pontiff was in a certain sense the father of Solidarity – his pilgrimage in 1979 had sown the seed. And the ideas that were to make up the core of *Laborem Exercens* – the Pope's encyclical on the dignity of work and the duty

83

to avoid exploitation of any kind – had already been shaped and tested against the Polish events. "The Holy Father liked the idea of finding one worker who incorporated all the dilemmas expressed in *Laborem Exercens*," says a Polish cleric who was working in the Vatican at the time. And of course he needed one that resolved those dilemmas through Christ." Walesa, with a Black Madonna badge in his lapel, seemed to fit the bill. The workers, said the Pope, had to be the subject of work, not its object. Solidarity, by linking men at their workplace, came close to this aim. Above all it made a nonsense of a state system whose claim to legitimacy was its mystical commitment to the proletariat. But was Walesa the appropriate embodiment of his new social teaching? The Pope probably knew of the doubts in the Warsaw episcopate and the Vatican Curia. First personal contact did little to reassure him. Anna Walentynowicz recalls: "The Pope was smiling and giving us all books as gifts. I asked him to sign one for my sick friend. But Walesa jumped out from behind Karol Modzelewski and yelled: 'You've got a nerve – I've got precedence here!' " The Pope asked them to settle the row and it was only after a bishop whispered in Walesa's ear that he apologised to Walentynowicz. The whole atmosphere of the Rome trip was poisonous. Father Jankowski from Gdansk and Father Jastak from Gdynia were competing for places in the delegation and Father Jankowski eventually bounced his colleague from the list. Walesa, indeed the whole Solidarity team, was a little rough at the edges. But in Walesa's case it was more than that: he wanted a special relationship with the Pope that would consolidate his position as leader of the movement. Too many people, not just the Gwiazdas and Walentynowicz, were talking as if Walesa had fulfilled his historic function after the registration of the union statutes.

The Curia, the Vatican establishment dominated by Italians, appears to have been at odds with the Pope over Walesa and the future direction of Solidarity. Both the Pope and the Vatican foreign-policy makers Agostino Casaroli and Archbishop Luigi Poggi were plainly in agreement that a confrontation with the Soviet Union had to be avoided. The Curia's question was how: how much restraint should be put on Solidarity to appease the Russians? A Soviet attack would put the Vatican's Ostpolitik back a decade or more. If Walesa could restrain the "extremists" then he should be supported; if he would not, then he should be dropped. Moscow had sent an emissary to Casaroli in September 1980 and the Russians had been told that the Vatican would do everything "to ward off the misfortune facing Poland". That did not provide the necessary clarity for the Kremlin who in

December 1980 sent an experienced troubleshooter, Viktor Zagladin of the Central Committee's international department, to Rome. His contact with the Curia was informal (he was officially the guest of the Italian Communist Party) but at a very high level. This time the Russians were given a more differentiated message: the Vatican would do what it could to encourage moderation in Solidarity, if the Polish Communist Party was also urged to tread carefully. A Soviet invasion would meet with the strongest possible response from the Pope.

Pope John Paul supported this diplomacy but put the matter into a different context. Ostpolitik had exhausted its possibilities for the time being; the Solidarity revolution had changed the terms of the debate. Incremental diplomacy was merely allowing stagnant regimes to prop themselves up for longer. New, harder-edged policies were needed, and the Church had to choose sides. That, he gauged, was the mood following the election of President Ronald Reagan who was already talking about throwing Communism into the trash-can of history. Since December 1980 the Pope had been receiving detailed intelligence reports on Poland from the Americans; these tended to be tougher, and more supportive of Walesa, than other reports from Church channels. The Cold War context of the crisis became plain about a year later when the would-be assassin of the Pope, Mehmet Ali Agca, claimed that there was also a plot to kill Walesa during his stay in Rome. According to Italian investigators, the Bulgarian secret police had at the very least drawn up a contingency plan for the assassination of Walesa at that time but it was never put into effect. A trade union activist, Luigi Scricciolo, was the Italian liaison officer for the security and itinerary of Walesa – yet he was later arrested on charges of collaborating with the Bulgarians.

The Pope after some thought decided to trust Walesa, and much of Church strategy from that month, January 1981, hinged on the personality of Walesa. There would be various moves, within both the Polish episcopate and the Curia, to drop the shipyard worker and seek out a smoother, more pliable partner, but the Pope never wavered in his support. Walesa was a believer and was willing as far as he could to make a Christian-national movement out of Solidarity. For that at least, the Polish bishops were grateful. There was a real fear that Solidarity would turn into a Trotskyist movement, run by KOR, directed not only at the Soviet Union but also the Church. On 13 December 1980 (exactly one year before the declaration of martial law) the director of the episcopate press bureau, Father Alojzy

Orszulik, warned against the rebels whose "noisy and irresponsible declarations are directed against our eastern neighbour".

The Church accepted the Pope's judgment that Walesa should be supported (and correctly guided), but the doubts remained: was Walesa strong enough to stop Solidarity drifting into open confrontation with Moscow? And was he morally robust enough to shrug off the temptations of power?

Rumours were beginning to swirl around Walesa. He was much in demand for interviews and undoubtedly favoured pretty women journalists. Walentynowicz was convinced that Walesa was having affairs. "We all knew that they were bringing girls for him – he had a sofa in his room. Outside, his bodyguard [Henryk] Mazul would block the door and say: 'You can't go in, Walesa's relaxing.' But I managed to get in – and he had company, his hair was completely ruffled." Walentynowicz and a handful of very devout assistants decided to move the sofa out of Walesa's office. "I scolded him: 'You sinner, how can you wear the Black Madonna in your lapel?' and he replied: 'I confess every week.'" These stories were also reaching the Gdansk bishop, Lech Kaczmarek, who was no great admirer of Walesa. Yet, on balance, the stories were probably not accurate. Those who knew him better than Walentynowicz, such as the strike organiser Jerzy Borowczak, tend to discount the rumours. He was very close to Danuta. Occasionally during interviews he would bounce some of his children – there were now six – on his knee. Father Jankowski visited Solidarity offices on a regular basis; there was not great scope, or time, for dalliance.

Walesa was however a flirt, and remains one. Ewa Berberyusz, writing in the Catholic weekly *Tygodnik Powszechny* in December 1980, concluded: "He likes women. With the kind of emotion that is disappearing among men, and which is based on total lack of complexes, complete self-confidence, a shade of old-fashioned courtliness and the rock-solid conviction that women will never harm him." The fact was that women played only supporting roles in the Solidarity revolution and when they aspired to more – as did Joanna Gwiazda or even Anna Walentynowicz – they were quickly sidelined. Women were no political threat to Walesa; if they visited him, even with serious entreaties or proposals, Walesa treated it as a welcome break from the hour-by-hour politicking. Since the contours of Solidarity were still vague, so too were his responsibilities. Petitioners were trying every trick to gain even a few minutes of audience, since the verbal backing of Walesa carried the day in most local disputes. Walesa thus created a buffer: Bozena Rybicka, a student whose long raven hair and attractive face fuelled new speculation about his fidelity, was supposed to fend off all but the most important visitors. Mazul, a burly former Home Army partisan who had worked on a floating crane, was supposed to protect Walesa from the more excitable Solidarity sympathisers and to be at hand if the secret police tried to arrest him. And Tadeusz Mazowiecki, adviser during the strikes, had become by 1981 the most trusted of Walesa's intellectual companions. In February of that year he was made editor of the new Solidarity weekly. *Tygodnik Solidarnosc.* Walesa captivated all three – Mazowiecki even switched to pipe-smoking in emulation of his hero – and strained their nerves. Rybicka admitted: "He is very unbalanced. It's not easy to get on with him. He fired me four times, and then withdrew the decision." Mazowiecki's function was to put an end to the constant battle for Walesa's ear. Mazowiecki was the man to approach with new strategies and the slow, deliberate essayist and ex-MP would sift through the advice, discard the high-risk proposals and then contact Walesa. "It was calming for Lech," says a member of his staff at that time, "amid all the hurly-burly and intrigue, Tadeusz would come in and talk very, very deliberately, like a priest, and as he talked Lech would start to organise his thoughts. Tadeusz helped Lech to put his ideas into categories, to get rid of the detail and concentrate on the big goal: a self-limiting revolution. That is what the Pope wanted, and Tadeusz was the right man to understand and translate this strange concept." Eventually the idea and its purveyor began to look absurd, like a mutation of history, and Mazowiecki – the gradualist – was shed, losing significance until the spring of 1988 when it seemed that Poland could negotiate its way out of Communist rule.

But in early 1981, the Church – the hierarchy still with some reluctance, the young grassroots priests with enthusiasm – could find common cause with KOR and most opposition groupings on the lines of a revolution that recognised its frontiers. Morally it was a real revolution, since it was a complete rejection of atheistic and Communist values. Politically, it was more a rebellion since it was not prepared to cross certain boundaries and challenge for power. Only the most ultra-nationalist of dissidents, the Confederation for an Independent Poland, rejected this formula. Solidarity was capable and frequently willing to topple a government – that was the workers' *liberum veto*, the unspoken right exercised in 1970 and 1980 – but it was not ready to fill the empty chairs. Yet how, in practice, was a revolution to limit itself? There was only one way: constantly to threaten confrontation with the authorities, and then, having displayed muscle, to pull back. That suggested an organisational power which Solidarity did not really possess. And it required the quality of leadership.

Walesa's task was to protect Solidarity's independence, to compete with and neutralise the official pro-Communist trade unions, to keep pressure on the government to acknowledge Solidarity as an equal bargaining partner. At the same time Solidarity had to be reminded that it could not hope to overthrow a system that had the backing of the Soviet Union and the tanks of the Red Army. More, it was in nobody's interest to crow over victory. If Moscow was left with the impression that the Polish government was surrendering under pressure, then the rulers would be swiftly replaced by hardliners. Thus, advised by Mazowiecki, Walesa arrived at a form of improvised power-sharing; not quite the neo-corporatism with which some Western sociologists claim was emerging at the time, not even a social contract, but a type of co-existence nonetheless. In Piotrkow Trybunalski workers in some 130 factories and offices staged a sit-in strike for higher meat rations. After threats and poker play a deal was struck: not only would the government improve rations, it would also allow Solidarity activists to watch over the meat distribution process. The more serious crisis over a five-day week was also resolved in a way that shared power. The government stonewalled on the demand which was part of the Gdansk accord and repeatedly insisted that the economic crisis was too deep to allow free Saturdays. Solidarity, in short, was being irresponsible. Solidarity insisted that the government provide official documents proving that the economic crisis was as profound as claimed. The government balked. Solidarity showed its strength by urging its workers to stay at home on one Saturday. Finally the government handed over its economic forecasts to Solidarity and the union experts offered a compromise – to work one Saturday every month. But Solidarity also agreed that the workers who had boycotted two Saturdays of work in January, at union behest and at some considerable risk, should make up for lost time by working overtime.

Here then was the making of a compact. Solidarity would enforce internal discipline (the offer to compensate for the two boycotted Saturdays cost Walesa some popularity) while the government would make a series of small, quiet surrenders and tacitly admit that Solidarity should be drawn into economic decision-making. For outsiders (a category that included almost all of the political establishment) this made Walesa a baffling figure. Was he a firebrand intent on mobilising his proletarian troops at any excuse? Or was he a responsible partner who could order his troops back to barracks? The answer, of course, was that he was both, balancing the entirely essential element of worker militancy with his mastery of the conciliatory fudge.

To cope with this new form of government, the Polish authorities had to reshuffle their cards. The first step was clearly to separate the Party from the state. This seemed to be a liberalising gesture in the spirit of the Gdansk agreement. In fact it was the only sensible way to cope with the self-limiting revolution. The Party would continue to fight its ideological corner and send the correct signals to Moscow: no concessions on the "leading role" of Communism, no challenge to Warsaw Pact membership, no insults aimed at the Kremlin or socialist principles. The government meanwhile was to be a more flexible machine, absorbing some of the shock of the rebellion, negotiating in the national interests. Kania realised that a new man also had to be put into place to cope with Walesa. On 9 February, the Central Committee agreed that General Wojciech Jaruzelski, the defence minister, would be prime minister. This was regarded at the time as a master-stroke. The general had a typically tangled Polish past. His father had been sent to work camps in Siberia and his son had suffered snow-blindness (hence the tinted glasses) and Jaruzelski had refused to deploy soldiers against workers in 1970. To these credentials were added the patriotic image of the Man in Uniform, above social conflict, a man who was perhaps capable of being firm with Moscow. That at any rate was the popular perception. Even Walesa responded favourably: "The opinion was that the general had shown good will and that we should therefore cooperate with him."

Jaruzelski's first step was to call for a ninety-day ban on strikes but he promised that the time would be used to push through an anti-crisis programme. To Walesa that did not seem an unreasonable position. He came in any case anxious to slow down the pace of wildcat strikes since they sapped his negotiating power. Within a week of Jaruzelski's inauguration local bushfires in Lodz and Jelenia Gora had been quenched. The general appointed Mieczyslaw Rakowski, editor of the weekly *Polityka*, as deputy premier. Since Rakowski had a reputation as an economic and social reformer, this too was regarded as a promising sign. The public perception of both Rakowski and Jaruzelski however was not entirely justified. Jaruzelski had come of political age as a young defence minister in 1968. He had been shocked by the anti-Semitic nationalist-Communist games played by Mieczyslaw Moczar. It was then that he had forged contacts with Rakowski, a former military counter-intelligence officer, who was one of the few editors to speak out in favour of the many Jewish intellectuals who were being thrown out of jobs or forced into emigration. Yet Jaruzelski had also been decisively influenced by his part in the Warsaw Pact invasion of Czechoslovakia in August 1968. That had shown him the limits of socialist reform and the human cost of crossing those limits. As the main Kremlin players involved in the Prague invasion were still in power, it seemed that the rules were still the same. At the heart of his reformism there was thus the real, deep fear of Moscow and of invasion. This eventually made a captive of the Polish hardliners who argued that social order should precede even the most cautious social reform. If Kania, Jaruzelski or Rakowski had argued with Moscow with anywhere near the same intensity they deployed against Solidarity, then much more could have been achieved. But Rakowski turned out to be a poor negotiator with Solidarity and was almost supine in his contacts with Moscow, while Jaruzelski was paralysed by risk. Gradually those who had cheered Jaruzelski in February began to remember the general's real biography: he was a political, not a battlefield officer; a conventional thinker rather than an innovator.

The patched-up compromises of this honeymoon period had left out a crucial element: the registration of Rural Solidarity. This was one of the main political goals of the Church hierarchy since the farmers, who had not been collectivised as in other East European countries, were the social grouping closest to the Church. An alliance between Church and countryside would certainly offset the "Trotskyist" tendencies of industrial Solidarity and its ex-Communist advisers. More, it would increase the Church's ability to broker a political solution since anyone with control over the food supply had real power; both the government and the Solidarity radicals would have to listen to the Primate. Yet Moscow in particular feared such an alignment and pressure on Kania was strongest on two issues: separating the factory workers from KOR; and separating farm workers from the Church. In the blurred Soviet view of things, Rural Solidarity would mean a return to the pre-war order, a decisive move towards capitalism and the politicisation of an anti-Communist and anti-Soviet Church. Kania and Jaruzelski knew better and were edging tentatively towards recognition. But the hardline opposition within the Party – Stefan Olszowski, Tadeusz Grabski, Andrzej Zabinski – and within the security services grasped that Moscow was on their side on this issue and they could force Jaruzelski's hand. If they stampeded Jaruzelski into declaring a state of emergency, into using force, then that would scuttle the despised "dialogue politics" of the reformers, the Jaruzelski team would have to go and be replaced by . . . well, by Olszowski, Grabski *et al*.

That was almost certainly the strategy behind the brutal quashing of a sit-in at Bydgoszcz city council. Solidarity activists led by Jan Rulewski, a radical on the Solidarity National Commission, had been squatting in the pro-regime Peasants Party headquarters demanding the recognition of Rural

Solidarity. After three days, on 19 March, Rulewski and his fellow protesters were invited to the city council to work out how at least a local farmers' union could be legalised. After a few hours it was plain that the Solidarity activists had slipped into a trap. A police officer arrived and told the protesters that they had to leave the council hall, otherwise force would be used. The protesters linked arms, formed a circle to protect a few women dissidents, and the police started to grab individual members of the chain and thrust them downstairs where they ran a gauntlet of truncheons and kicks. Rulewski was singled out for a particular tough beating.

Walesa cancelled a planned trip to France and sped to Bydgoszcz. He had been tipped off that the hardliners had planned to provoke a showdown there – "it was obvious that the authorities intended to pick a quarrel with us and incite us to do something rash" – and he had warned Rulewski. Rulewski had always distrusted Walesa's instincts and had gone ahead anyway.

Solidarity frothed with rage. It was the first time that naked force had been used to break up a protest and clearly it was a turning-point for both the movement and Walesa. There was now a choice: either Solidarity could launch a strike wave (Jaruzelski's 90-day strike ban was no longer valid) and the popular anger could be channelled into gaining recognition for Rural Solidarity and other concessions; or Solidarity could contain its anger, and negotiate its way to something more fundamental, a permanent institutional set-up that would anchor Solidarity in Polish political life.

Walesa took a middle path – and in so doing lost the game. The National Commission wanted an immediate general strike. For them it was a matter not just of venting anger but of establishing the principle of Solidarity: Rulewski was an elected leader of the union. If no, or little, action was taken then each member of Solidarity could expect brutal treatment. Mazowiecki, the eternal *Realpolitiker*, said that a general strike would topple Jaruzelski and would thus serve only the hardliners. Geremek, rightly nervous about the organisational discipline of Solidarity, warned that such a strike – egged on by police provocateurs – would end in blood.

The Solidarity line was that the Jaruzelski government had asked for trust and goodwill and through police brutality had forfeited the confidence of the workers. In other words, no movement. The warning strike went ahead as planned. It was a crisp, well-planned action that ended exactly when the factory sirens sounded at noon. Compliance was almost total. Even Party members, under strict instructions to set an example and put in their shift, either openly sided with Solidarity or took the day off sick. By the

91

end of that day Rakowski was talking in slightly softer terms. He handed over a government report that went some way towards apologising for the beatings. That was on Friday 27 March. On the following Tuesday the general strike was planned. In the interim both Walesa and Rakowski were subjected to huge pressure. Moscow, reporting on the breakdown of order in Poland, tried to panic a Communist Central Committee session on Sunday into endorsing a tougher course. The move failed. The Central Committee delegates started to show some pluck. They had learned to live with the Gdansk agreement and many of the grassroots Party activists had joined Solidarity, or were close to it. The mood was so hostile to the hardliners that there was even talk of making Tadeusz Fiszbach, Solidarity's best friend in the Communist ranks, Party chief. That did not work out and Soviet sponsorship (in the form of dummy motions from stooge delegates) ensured that Olszowski clung to his seat. The state-of-emergency option was put on ice. More precisely, it disappeared from view. Although Party politicians stopped thundering about a crackdown, the Soviet Union, through its embassy and military channels, started from that week to work closely with the secret police and Polish army counter-intelligence on a detailed plan for martial law.

In the midst of the crisis, Cardinal Wyszynski had seen General Jaruzelski. On the Saturday before the general strike he also saw Walesa and the Solidarity leadership. The Pope, said the Primate, was very anxious and required Solidarity to behave with due caution. Gwiazda remembers a phrase from that audience: "If the minority is in the right it has no duty to take notice of the majority opinion." In other words, the Church would support any attempts by Walesa to act independently of the radicals in the Solidarity leadership.

Walesa had already decided that this would have to be his course. He had cut the leadership out of decisions before but never on such a major issue. The mood of the regional chieftains, the local Solidarity cells and the intellectuals like Jacek Kuron, was that the time had come for a showdown. But he was convinced that Solidarity would lose such a duel. In fact there were so many ways to lose that even Walesa, who liked to think through every feasible Communist option, had lost track. It was time, he decided, to back off. While the Solidarity leaders were scrambling around the country getting ready for the strike, or waiting by telex machines for the next stage of strike alert, Walesa struck a deal with Rakowski. Since both men agreed that the Bydgoszcz beatings were an attempt to dethrone Jaruzelski and since both men agreed that it was necessary to keep a reform-orientated

Party leader in power, there were plainly the makings of an agreement. Rakowski promised that Rural Solidarity could begin to act as if it were a completely legal body pending its official registration. Those responsible for the assault on Rulewski and his colleagues would be punished. In return, the general strike would be cancelled. Geremek and the lawyer Jan Olszewski were set to work drafting the details of the accord. According to Gwiazda, waiting impotently in the shabby Hotel Solec on the banks of the Vistula, the government delegation eventually emerged brimming with good humour and presented one copy of the Warsaw agreement. Gwiazda, as bewildered as the rest of the Solidarity team, eventually signed in his capacity as deputy Solidarity chairman. Geremek urged him to read out the agreement instead of Walesa since Lech was too nervous and would gabble the words. Or perhaps it was a ploy to deflect the disappointment of the workers from Walesa? In any case Gwiazda, who was thoroughly committed to a general strike, was humiliated and resigned as deputy chairman shortly afterwards.

Eventually the Commission accepted Walesa's proposal of a short warning strike, to be followed four days later by an all-out general strike if the authorities did not punish the police thugs from Bydgoszcz, recognise Rural Solidarity, guarantee the security of all union members and scrap all criminal proceedings against dissidents. That satisfied the radicals, at least to the extent that it provided time to prepare for the general strike. Although the union was now a large organisation – almost ten million members and a full-time staff of 40,000 – it had not mobilised on a nationwide scale since August. Food had to be stockpiled, factories put on alert, telex lines secured and clear instructions printed and distributed. Regional treasurers withdrew Solidarity funds from the banks in case accounts were frozen. The union, indeed the whole country, was in a frenzy.

Everything hinged on Walesa's skill as a negotiator. He did not want a general strike. Not only were Mazowiecki and Geremek telling him that it was folly but also the Primate (through his emissary Romuald Kukolowicz) and the clamour of world opinion. The White House was warning that "the Soviet Union may intend to undertake repressive action in Poland". Warsaw Pact manoeuvres were under way in Poland, East Germany and the western republics of the Soviet Union. The Pope appealed for compromise. Even during the August strikes, Walesa had not come under such pressure. Then invasion talk was little more than rumour scoffed at by the strikers. But only a few weeks before the Bydgoszcz flare-up Walesa had met Jaruzelski for the first time and had started to grasp the military dimension of the crisis. That may explain why he lost control of the negotiating initiative; he was simply overwhelmed.

An initial session with Rakowski produced nothing. The journalist's tendency to drift into histrionics when pushed hard was obvious from the moment that Walesa sat down at the table: How dare Solidarity become political! How could it breach the Gdansk agreement! The world, both West and East, was rightly alarmed by the irresponsibility of Solidarity!

Calling off the strike for such low returns was a devastating blow not only to the pride of Solidarity but also to its future development. As Zbigniew Bujak remarked later: "General strikes are like swords – once you take them out of the scabbard and fail to use them, they are no more use than useless hunks of iron. Walesa by making this agreement in effect demobilised the union and received nothing in exchange . . . it deprived us of our basic weapon and thus became the source of our subsequent defeat. The authorities counted on this when they prepared the 13 December martial law operation."

The Church hierarchy was naturally well pleased and in the Catholic understanding of the crisis, Cardinal Wyszynski had saved the day. As far as the Church was concerned Walesa had now proved himself to be the unquestioned leader of the union. The earlier doubts about his moral or political calibre had been pushed to one side and, in the internal Solidarity disputes, the Church threw its influence behind Walesa. The Kania–Jaruzel-ski–Rakowski team was also relieved. They had bought time – though not, as it subsequently emerged, for serious dialogue and reform. The real reform-ists in the Party, the so-called "horizontalists" who wanted to discard the Leninist tenet of democratic centralism and create a grassroots structure, were knocked out of the game by the Warsaw agreement. If there was no longer a general strike threat, then a Party alternative to Solidarity was no longer required. Jaruzelski had committed himself to a special Party congress in July. His idea was to trim the edges – the radical Communist reformers on one side, and the more extreme hardliners on the other – and end up with a more malleable Party that would mouth the correct words for Moscow while stealing some of Solidarity's proposals for economic change. Jaruzelski had drawn the correct conclusion from the handling of the Bydgoszcz crisis: Solidarity had been fatally weakened. It had lost not only its chief weapon, but also its unity of purpose.

Gwiazda, now an embittered man living in a cramped Gdansk apartment and turning out cyclostyled Samizdat-style pamphlets, was probably right. Walesa's supporters pooh-poohed his insistence that the core issue of Solidarity was whether the union should be run as a one-man dictatorship or as a less efficient but nonetheless open democracy. "Walesa tried to take over the organisation according to the slogan 'I play to win.' In other words, leave him alone while he plays on our behalf." That philosophy, which still guides Walesa as President, has undermined the consistency of his politics, and presents him as an erratic leader. "Any dictator deprived of the police and the army is condemned to maintaining his popularity and good relations with the authorities," says Gwiazda. "That meant making more and more concessions to the government, until the factory workers began to say, 'Enough!' Then in order to restore his popularity he had to change his course and become the leader of the rebels. This leads to a catastrophic, chaotic policy, one that has to be changed according to the whim and influence of different factions."

But Walesa's contradictions were also partly those of the big amorphous movement that Solidarity had become. If Solidarity's credo was based on the premise that it would not seize power from the Communists, then there was no choice ultimately but to back down. Walesa, and indeed Poland, could have ridden out a general strike in March 1981; or he could have captured lasting, important concessions from the government in return for cancelling the strike. That, with hindsight, seems a reasonable assertion. But eventually Solidarity would have to cave in and fit itself into the straitjacket of a Communist power – or become a truly revolutionary body and overthrow the system. Walesa was not equipped for either cause, he was neither an institutional politician nor a revolutionary; he was, and is, a man for transitions, an illusionist. He himself says now that in 1981 he was "living on credit", hoping that nobody would call the necessary bluff that kept Solidarity together.

Bydgoszcz showed Walesa just how fragile was his position, how thin his bluff. He admitted freely that he might have blundered: "Tomorrow we might achieve more, but today we should not go to the very edge. I know too that what is good today may be bad tomorrow. The historians will perhaps say: he was out of his mind, the authorities were bluffing, really they were weak . . . they (Solidarity) could have won but missed their chance. In ten or fifty years I can be judged like that . . . All I know is that the risk was too great."

After the March crisis, the tension in Poland eased somewhat. Life was difficult; food rations were low and frequently even the ration cards, presented after hours of queuing, could not be honoured. The black market blossomed. Even dedicated Solidarity activists took time off from the revolution to travel to Berlin, where no visas were needed, and work on a building site or as a waitress. A month's earnings in the West could tide a family over the summer, make a down-payment on an apartment, or buy a car. But most Poles suspended major decisions – to get married, have a baby, leave university – because the March clash had shown how unfinished was the Solidarity revolution, how uncertain the future. The sense of carnival passed from Solidarity to the Party. In factories and offices there were elections to the congress and they were being conducted with more than a dash of freedom. Nobody could remember such lively debates, such open criticism of the leadership or factions, in Party meetings. Each delegate was given a specific agenda, usually completely unrealistic, and dispatched to the congress like a favourite son to battle.

Both Solidarity and the Party were thus absorbed by their own affairs rather than with the running of the country or managing the crisis. Solidarity agreed again to restrain strikes but even the fireman rhetoric of Walesa and Kuron began to sound a little tired. Walesa began to feel, for the first time since August, that he was slipping out of control.

He had been remarkably self-confident for the seven months preceding Bydgoszcz. Even criticism, the constant sniping in the leadership, appeared to have given him energy. It was rather like the typology devised by Archilochus and developed so effectively by Isaiah Berlin: there are hedgehogs and foxes. "The fox knows many things, but the hedgehog knows one big thing." Walesa was a fox who needed hedgehogs. There was Mazowiecki with his commitment to evolutionary change, a negotiated exit. And there was Gwiazda, committed to open, participatory democracy at any cost. Walesa could not be pinned to any coherent philosophy apart from a rather general belief in a self-limiting revolution. But Bydgoszcz swept away even this vague concept. Walesa had "limited" the revolution by pulling Poland back from a general strike. One hedgehog, Mazowiecki, told him that a general strike should never have been threatened. Another hedgehog, Gwiazda, told him that scrapping the strike without consulting the Solidarity leadership was a betrayal of the revolution. To "limit" the revolution, it seemed, was to lose it. Walesa in May 1981 was a confused man. "He was convinced then that Solidarity was going to be snuffed out," says a member of his entourage at that time. "He did not talk much and he brooded a lot. Maybe Solidarity would tear itself to pieces, maybe the Russians would come, maybe both. Well, OK, that was always the risk. But in a way Walesa already had his mind fixed on the post-Solidarity era.

What would remain afterwards, after jail or blood? Wasn't there anything noble that could be saved from the wreckage?" Walesa was in Japan when he heard that somebody had tried to kill the Pope and he immediately made the connection with the future of Solidarity. "I was overcome by a feeling of intense loneliness; the whole world seemed to have been turned upside down; with our lodestar gone, some of us were wandering in a wilderness of Poland and Solidarity: they were inextricably bound together; this was just the beginning." The Pope, of course, recovered. But Walesa became a lacklustre leader for the last few months of Solidarity's legal life.

Solidarity was inching towards power. The Party congress marked the end of the fiesta for the Communists. Having turned the agenda upside down and shaken the Politburocrats, the delegates excluded energetic reformers from the new line-up but gave a cautious go-ahead to the Kania–Jaruzelski team. It was a bewildering congress. Rakowski, knocking hardline Communists and Solidarity "extremists" just about equally, won loud applause – yet failed to be elected to the Politburo. There were many well-received speeches attacking dogmatism, yet Stefan Olszowski was returned to the Politburo and he did not lack allies in the Central Committee. The reason for this patchy message was that the delegates, though infected with the new freedoms, voted not according to their consciences but out of anxiety. A letter from the Soviet leadership, addressed to the Polish Central Committee in June, had become public knowledge and it seemed to show that Moscow had not abandoned thought of an invasion. "One position after another is being surrendered," thundered the Soviet Party, ". . . there is not much more than a month left before the congress, yet increasingly forces hostile to socialism are setting the tone of the election campaign." The Polish Party could not accept this degree of intimidation and so rallied to Kania. But neither could it shrug off the fear of invasion. And so known friends of Moscow were allowed to cling on. The result was a paralysis of the state administration; for the summer and autumn of 1981 the government of Jaruzelski (who in October also took over the post of Party chief alongside the prime minister's office and the defence ministry) and Rakowski did precious little governing.

Solidarity moved steadily into the vacuum. In many cities women and children banging empty pans had been marching through the streets and demanding action against food shortages. Solidarity, which had pledged to avoid strikes, nonetheless supported these so-called hunger marches. There was little else they could do. Rakowski, meeting Walesa in early August, started to yell about this new pressure on government and said the union had "to cooperate, or to follow the road to nowhere". Walesa bawled back that Solidarity's only fault was not to press the government harder. But when the shouting finished, there was a sober dialogue. Solidarity admitted it had no real control over the marchers and was losing its grip on the factories. If the government gave Solidarity an institutional role in the running of the economy, above all in food distribution, then it would be able to argue more convincingly with the workers and persuade them that the government was not artificially creating the food shortage. Many Poles were convinced that food was being stockpiled in police warehouses to heat up the political crisis and ease the way for martial law. Yet Rakowski refused to accept the proposal at face value and interpreted it as a bid for all-out power: control food production in a hungry country and you have political power. The talks broke down.

Solidarity was moving on other fronts. In the factories workers were electing councils that could choose managers and share power, albeit in a very restricted way. The Party rightly regarded this as a direct threat to the influence of Communist cells in heavy industry. And soon enough, from slightly different perspectives, Karol Modzelewski and Jacek Kuron began to argue that economic reform and industrial democracy were not enough. Why, asked Modzelewski, were workers organising at factory level? Answer: the Party and government were paralysed, incapable of taking economic initiatives. Then why the paralysis? "Because Rakowski tells Solidarity: first you tie our hands, then you accuse us of not doing anything. Well, Rakowski was right except that his hands were tied not because of some devilish conspiracy, but because of the democratic rights that had been won by Solidarity." Here was the nub according to Modzelewski: "The state is capable of governing only in conditions where those rights are lacking." The logical conclusion was that Solidarity had to shift quickly beyond economic reform. Perhaps, in Kuron's concept to form clubs – not parties yet, but almost – that would group self-governments. They would become the nucleus of a social-democratic political force. Or a second house of parliament could be set up, to which democratically elected local councillors would be returned. In theory the central powers of the Communists would not be touched. Much talk then, for even the simplest of Solidarity leaders, was groping for a way to keep the strength of the union after the setback in March. To stay in the game it had to keep on moving and prodding, and if it could not move (because of the obstruction of government, or because of vagueness about direction), then ambitious talk would have to suffice.

In his memoirs Walesa barely mentions the first Solidarity congress of

September 1981. Other Solidarity leaders, writing or speaking at a distance of a decade or more, also tend to contract the period between Bydgoszcz in March and martial law in December. It is as if the grand sweeping phrases of those months were cancelled out by the force, as if the period from March was a mere waiting-room. Did Walesa still believe that some kind of partnership, some neo-corporatist solution, could be worked out, or was he just trying to lengthen the rope that would eventually hang the movement? "Walesa was constantly on the move at the time," recalls a woman on his staff, "and he told us once, 'This is the time for tactics, not strategy.' " He was uneasy about the congress, for he disliked putting himself up for election. He did not however have to think deeply about his congress tactics since his rivals (Marian Jurczyk, the Szczecin strike leader, his persistent opponent from Gdansk, Gwiazda, and Rulewski from Bydgoszcz) would all press for varying degrees of confrontation with the authorities. Walesa could either out-trump them with radicalism – a move that would be unacceptable to the Church, that would ditch any hope of a deal with Jaruzelski, and that would in any case go against the grain – or he could argue restraint and warn of the restless eastern neighbour. That would be unpopular but it was preferable to making an elaborate apology for his conduct in Bydgoszcz. Rulewski had told Walesa that he could negotiate with the authorities over onions, but not blood. That was still the feeling of a substantial minority, perhaps a majority of delegates: Walesa, faced with the first naked display of force, had backed down. By September the delegates had forgotten the national sense of relief when the strike was cancelled, and remembered only the sense of betrayal. Walesa then was in for a rough ride.

For Walesa the key question was not his re-election – which he thought certain – but what powers he would retain as chairman. The first and most important battle of the congresses then was with critics like Gwiazda whose major theme was Walesa's lack of accountability and his tendency to strike unauthorised deals with the government. Walesa still enjoyed the support of the Church though the death of Cardinal Wyszynski in July had dulled its impact. Archbishop Jozef Glemp, a stumpy canon lawyer, lacked the solid anti-Communist credentials of his predecessor as Primate. He was a man of small, controlled gestures, more corporate than canon lawyer. Even so he had been close to Wyszynski and was pledged to continue the same line. The government too wanted Walesa to win the congress. This was partly because the leadership was publicly committed to dialogue and thus needed a talking-partner. None of the other contenders had the remotest intention of talking. But the chief reason for the government's backing of

Walesa (never publicly stated, of course, since that would immediately have torpedoed his chances) was a cynical calculation. A Gwiazda or a Rulewski victory would have hastened the declaration of martial law. The Jaruzelski team wanted to make some last attempts at persuading Solidarity to play by institutional rules. Martial law, as it was conceived by the Jaruzelski inner circle, was to be a mere interruption. It was to crush the radicals and leave "honest workers" under a neutered worker-leader and at the same time it was designed to break the back of the Party conservatives in the state apparat. Then after a month or two of enforced calm, with the Kremlin tranquillised, "dialogue" could be resumed. Walesa was a necessary part of this equation. Even the censor's office had been under instruction from October 1980 to block any critical comment on Walesa's personal life.

Walesa lost the struggle for a powerful central Solidarity leadership. Geremek's idea was that Solidarity would be split into a supreme council that would hammer out all the doctrinal points while the Congress would directly elect a praesidium that would have wide executive powers. The supreme council would be a kind of parliament, the praesidium a government. Or, put another way, a central committee and a Politburo. The obvious charm of this idea for Walesa was that all the feverish talk would not interfere with the real decision-making. It was a vehicle for the "dictatorship" of Walesa and his closest advisers. More, it would allow Moscow to discount the talking-shop (just as it wrote off its own Supreme Soviet) and measure Solidarity by its practical deeds rather than by its rhetoric. But it was not to be. Too much power would be snatched way from the regional chieftains and there was too much distrust of Walesa's intentions. More democratic, said the delegates, and therefore infinitely preferable, was a larger national commission representing all regional forces, discussing and shaping all decisions. A small praesidium concerned only with the daily running of the union would be elected by the national commission. Walesa knew that he could dodge around these restrictions but the National Commission nonetheless took away much of his ability to manoeuvre with the government, and almost all scope for spontaneous initiative. It also gave little space to Walesa's experts.

That is why Walesa entered the leadership elections in a dispirited way. He was constantly losing his temper and was convinced that the congress was sinking Solidarity under the weight of its slogans. As a result the two stages of the congress were punctuated throughout with rowdy stage effects. "The body of decisions and motions adopted had, in my view anyway, only a theoretical value, for only one thing was important now: to see if we could

100

create in Poland a tripartite system involving government, Church and Solidarity." If that really was his main focus – and not hindsight – he presented it poorly. Most of the time on the podium he was fidgeting, yawning, breaking pencils; at lunchtime, instead of power-broking with his colleagues, he was driven to his apartment in the Zaspa housing estate, "out of the madhouse" as he put it. Not, in short, the image of a man burning with a vision of a new ruling triad. His election speech was a rambling unprepared affair, calling for respect for the authorities. Instead of a Party–Church–Solidarity triad, he stressed, the three essential pillars of democracy were the workers' councils, Solidarity and the Party–state administration. "The replacement or dislocation of any one of these elements would weaken democracy."

That was directed at his other (perhaps principal) audience – Jaruzelski. It was a plea for partnership. The other candidates made a bigger splash at the congress. Jurczyk wanted free parliamentary elections, Gwiazda wanted worker co-determination in factories, Rulewski – to the gasping horror of the West – wanted out of the Warsaw Pact. A decade later the wishes of Jurczyk and Rulewski had been granted, but at the time the speeches seemed both brave and foolhardy, shock-politics. The voting showed that there was little support for extreme politics; Rulewski was applauded for his grasp of theatre, not for his common sense. Jurczyk picked up 24 per cent of the votes, Gwiazda and Rulewski shared 15 per cent between them. But Walesa did not exactly sweep the board – his surprisingly low 55 per cent reflected the dissatisfaction with his poor speech, his muddled vision of partnership (with whom, for what, to what end, for how long?) and his performance after Bydgoszcz. For better or for worse, they were saddled with Walesa. But *next* time, the delegates were saying, next time he will not get it so easy. Next time turned out to be nine years hence, and even then the delegates ended up voting, against their better nature, for Lech Walesa, the shipyard revolutionary.

CHAPTER SEVEN

Corporal Walesa

"When we say confrontation, we don't mean it in the way you think, we mean arguments, strong arguments," Walesa was speaking in a cigarette-and-coffee break at the Solidarity National Commission meeting in Gdansk on 12 December 1981. The reporters wanted to know if the fighting words spoken at a leadership session in Radom the previous week, taped by the secret police, edited and published in a Communist propaganda stunt – added up to a declaration of war. "We don't have tanks, and don't want to have them. If those in power stopped distorting our words and looked at the real message they would see it is about non-violence." Walesa returned to the session, somewhat reluctantly. Since the Solidarity congress he had skipped a few leadership meetings and at those he did attend he could barely disguise his irritation. The shift of power to the National Commission, to the regional chieftains, and away from his praesidium had blunted his political talents. His instinct told him it was time to drive a fast bargain with the government on the co-management of the economy, but the mood of the National Commission was now set against any kind of neo-corporatist solution. In particular Zbigniew Bujak, the Warsaw chieftain, was opposed to deals with the authorities: Solidarity had to prepare for a government assault and at the same time display its muscle. A demonstration was planned in Warsaw for 7 December and the marchers would be protected by worker-guards. At this final Gdansk session Walesa sat passively, absorbed in thought. Pieces of paper were passed to him on the podium. The first: odd troop movements had been spotted along the Baltic coast, water cannon and riot squad units were on the move. Aides checked with the police and were told that an elaborate anti-crime operation was under way, codenamed Operation Walls. The last message of the day was put in front of Walesa: telex and phone lines had been cut. Walesa, sensing the end, called a halt to the session.

That night the National Commission, and over 4,000 other activists throughout Poland, were picked up. A few were drunk, most bleary with sleep. (Kuron was giving a late-night interview to two women journalists in his hotel room.) They were loaded into blue police trucks and ferried through the long night to camps, well away from major cities, many in the far east of the country. Walesa, however, was given special treatment. He had been driven home, through the snow, and had settled into bed when the doorbell rang. The first caller was the wife of Mieczyslaw Wachowski, his driver (and ten years later his chief adjutant at the presidential palace). Wachowski had been arrested. Then members of Alexander Hall's Young Poland Movement arrived to relay news of other detentions. And then came the police equipped with crowbars. They stood outside the apartment in Pilotow Street awaiting orders. But Walesa was not about to be arrested and for a while there was a pretence that he had not even been interned; he was still, it seemed, a *partner*. Party chief Tadeusz Fiszbach and Gdansk governor Jerzy Kolodziejski – both in their ways admirers of the Solidarity leader – turned up at the apartment to persuade him to travel to Warsaw where General Jaruzelski was awaiting him. "Tell him: not while there are people under arrest," said Walesa. Then after consultations with Warsaw (Fiszbach had one of the few functioning phone links in Gdansk) the Party men told Walesa there was no choice. The police would take him by force if necessary. The authorities had in fact been trapped by their own propaganda. If only, they had been wailing for months, Walesa would separate himself from the extremists and the malevolent experts, then the worker movement could return to its sober path and all would be well. The authorities would be able to do a deal with Walesa, "Pole-to-Pole". Now the National Commission and the undesirables had been put away – let the dialogue begin! But of course the mere implementation of martial law had squashed this possibility: a political manoeuvre had become a military operation on a national scale. There were schedules to keep, lists of people to be detained, troops to be deployed, communications to be secured: this was not politics by other means, but anti-politics.

In fact the Jaruzelski leadership had abandoned the dialogue "option" some months earlier. Colonel Ryszard Kuklinski, a member of the Polish defence planning staff, had defected to the United States in November and set out the timetable. First contingency plans for martial law were drawn up after August 1980, activated and refined in October 1981, awaiting the final signal from General Jaruzelski. Food inspection teams sent to the countryside by the army in the autumn – thought at the time to be a sign that the military was ready to help the government more actively in running the country – were a part of the pre-martial law reconnaissance. And the storming by Interior Ministry troops of the Warsaw Firemen's Academy, occupied by striking students, was also a signal. That was on 28 November. How far apart were the perceptions of Solidarity and the government at the time can be illustrated by quotations from Rakowski and Walesa. Rakowski, in his 1982 interview with Oriana Fallaci, remembers the militia operation as follows: "The operation happened at ten in the morning, and before ten Ciosek went to Walesa, who was staying at a hotel, to inform him and show him that we were playing openly. Walesa answered: 'Well then, Mr Ciosek, this is the end. Then we will have to take over power. Don't worry for yourself though. You are a good man. I'll find you a job.' " Walesa's version, given in the first volume of his memoirs, is rather different. Ciosek visited Walesa at the Hotel Solec. "He is a talkative man but on this occasion I had the impression that he had some hidden motive for prolonging our conversation. And so it turned out. When he was called to the telephone for a moment, Ciosek left a piece of paper on his chair with a simple handwritten note: Keep Walesa in his hotel at all costs!" In other words Walesa was not to be given a chance to end the student strike; the authorities had decided to use force and Walesa was not supposed to get in the way.

The government had proposed a Front of National Understanding in which Solidarity would be one of seven social organisations. The other participants were aligned one way or another with the government and it was plain that the point was to outnumber the union while at the same time saddling it with responsibility for the crisis. The general had little more than that to offer when he, Walesa and Archbishop Glemp met to work out a mode of cooperation. The Church–Solidarity axis was Walesa's only real hope. He had come to the talks cold, without priming by his advisers and with a minimal amount of consultation with the National Commission. It is what the Germans call a *Flucht nach Vorne*, a retreat disguised as an advance, and a wholly typical Walesa strategy. Sometimes the technique works; more often it has sown suspicion in his own ranks. Some workers even nowadays remember Walesa not as the hero of the August 1980 strikes but as the young worker in December 1970 who broke off from the crowd, ran into the police headquarters and started to speak to the demonstrators from the window of the police commander who would later shoot at them. That was poor judgment, an emotional rather than a political judgment. So was his meeting with Glemp and Jaruzelski at a time when neither had anything new to offer. Glemp was preparing for a visit to the Pope on the following day; the general had already made up his mind on martial law. The meeting with Walesa was convenient. It showed that the general was "willing" to have another go at dialogue and contributed to the image of a patriotic reformer. But in terms of brute power all the tripartite summit seemed to prove was that Solidarity was on the ropes: one knockout blow should suffice. Why then did Walesa bother? "I am sure that Walesa felt it was the endgame," said journalist Stefan Kisielewski, a wise outsider who understood Walesa and the Church better than most. "Something, perhaps somebody, had told Walesa and, since politics was dead, he began to act emotionally – to seek protection for Solidarity, for its idea, if not for its organisation. He thought the Church could provide it. But he was wrong about the Primate. Later he would come to understand Glemp, but he didn't then. You see, the Church had already been persuaded that the general was the 'lesser evil', that martial law was preferable to Soviet tanks. That is what Glemp told the Pope the following day in the Vatican."

Walesa later described the session as a dead end. It was also the beginning of a long period of loneliness when Walesa could find no natural allies. Gwiazda claims that Walesa had been tipped off about martial law well in advance, that he was the lonely keeper of the secret. There is, however, not much evidence for that. It seems unlikely that he would have appealed to the West for urgent food aid for the winter had he known of the date for the imposition of martial law. But the former Church adviser, historian Andrzej Micewski says, with some credibility, that the Church leadership was told three weeks in advance about the decision to impose military rule. The Church may in turn have told Walesa. In any case Walesa was philo-sophical enough on the night of 12–13 December. He had been arrested over a dozen times in his life and knew the rules; even Danuta knew exactly what had to be packed in his grip. Walesa was not frightened of prison. It was a time to catch up on sleep and to think a bit, a sabbatical from politics.

For the rest of Poland it was as though a thick blanket had suddenly been thrown over the head of a sleeping child. First there was the panic, the blackness, the uncertainty whether you were awake or asleep, then difficulties with breathing, loss of direction, anger. Danuta recovered more quickly than most Poles. The television and radio broadcasts from early Sunday morning showing the general, in front of a heraldic Polish eagle, woodenly reading his prepared speech about the great abyss – Soviet invasion? – facing Poland, about the drift into anarchy, about the need to defend the structure of the state and the constitution. And there were all the new rules to be absorbed: no phones, no unauthorised movements, a dawn-to-dusk curfew; all public gatherings apart from Church services were banned, key enterprises were "militarised", most independent organisations were suspended, personal post was to be censored, shortwave radios banned, the sale of petrol restricted. Every detail had been worked out (even water-skiing in the bay of Gdansk was explicitly forbidden) and the posters had been printed in the Soviet Union.

Partly because it was a weekend, partly because the lightning arrests had destroyed most of the first-echelon leadership, workers reacted only fitfully. Some, as in the Wujek colliery, staged a sit-in. But most were baffled. At six o'clock on Sunday evening Danuta and Father Jankowski were able to speak to Walesa in Warsaw. The priest urged the shipyard workers to be patient, Walesa would be speaking to government representatives; there should be no strike. Danuta added her voice: "Lech asks you not to make any rash decisions." To the radical workers it seemed as if Walesa had struck out on his own again and was set to do a deal while the rest of the leadership languished in jail. There were fierce arguments but eventually they abandoned their attempts to organise a strike. Most, after all, were as tired as Walesa.

The government was going through the motions of a dialogue with Walesa. He had been taken to the former villa of Jerzy Lukasiewicz, propaganda chief under Edward Gierek. The former Party leader and a few of his cronies had also been picked up in the weekend raids and, much to their irritation, were interned on the Hel peninsula not far from a Solidarity internment camp. Jaruzelski wanted to prevent a Party conspiracy. The Gierek team still had links with Moscow and could have tried to outflank the generals. Walesa's villa in Chylice, in the leafy outskirts of the capital, was deemed secure – a muddy approach road could be blocked off with only a platoon of soldiers and a nearby field could provide a useful helicopter pad. The jovial, flabby figure of Stanislaw Ciosek was to be Walesa's interlocutor, the government side of the great dialogue. Ciosek had been a youth activist in the Party but he was not a conformist. In many ways he was more mentally agile than his mentor Rakowski. He had been given the difficult job of Labour Minister and though some Solidarity leaders were irritated by his slightly owlish manner he had established a reasonable rapport with Walesa. Ciosek looked shaken and, accompanied by two generals and a brigadier, he was not his usual expansive self. There were many apologies for the inconvenience to *Mr Chairman* – a good sign, thought Walesa – and he was shown to his bedroom and marble bathroom from whence the razor had thoughtfully been removed. Walesa fell into a deep sleep and was wakened only by a thunderous knocking at the door. Walesa had a visitor, said the staff officer at the door, was he willing to receive him? Walesa, who understood the name to be Makowski, told him to go away and plunged back into his interrupted sleep. Later Walesa was to find out that the visitor was Rakowski, who to this day does not believe the explanation of a simple misunderstanding. Rakowski, the committed "reformer", the Western-style dialogue-politician, did not try to talk to Walesa again; his pride had been hurt.

The basis for any sensible negotiation had been pulverised by martial law. Walesa may have been in a gilded cage but he was a prisoner nonetheless. There was no question of behaving like an equal partner. Martial law as an attempt by the Jaruzelski team to regain control over the pace of change. But by resorting to force, to *total* force, he had destroyed the Poles' last illusions about reform Communism. Reform Communists had to win by persuasion, otherwise they represented nothing. Perhaps Jaruzelski's greatest historical act was to demonstrate this to the rest of Eastern Europe. By the revolutions of 1989 none of the flawed and failing Communist regimes considered the use of martial law to cling on to power. When they failed to persuade, they surrendered.

For the time being the Jaruzelski team had to play charades. Since the truth – that martial law was put into place solely to reduce Russian anxieties – could not be admitted, the politicians had to carry on talking to Walesa for a while. Ciosek saw Walesa on the Monday after martial law was declared and tentatively suggested that Walesa appear on television to urge national unity, calm, determination to reform through the Party. Both men knew it was a hopeless request.

The following day two key churchmen drove out to Walesa. Father Alojzy Orszulik was technically press spokesman of the episcopate – that is, the voice of the bishops – but he was also one of Archbishop Glemp's inner circle. It was Orszulik who had attacked Kuron and KOR in December 1980. Orszulik, along with Bishop Bronislaw Dabrowski – a gaunt, church politician who served as Secretary to the Episcopate – and the younger, more urbane Bishop Jerzy Dabrowski, made up a strong policy-making nucleus in the Primate's palace. For sixteen months their main thrust had been that Solidarity should not be allowed to drift to the extreme Left, steered by "Trotskyists" like Kuron. Solidarity, in claiming to be a national reform movement, had to speak with a Christian union voice since society was rooted in Catholicism; it also had to accept Christian restraints. Glemp's first sermon after martial law, and his Christmas message, was that blood should not be spilled, Poles should not resist and that there were even worse things awaiting Poland should Jaruzelski lose the game. The brief of Orszulik and Bronislaw Dabrowski on that snowbound Tuesday was to ease Walesa out of his anger and move him towards a negotiated solution with the general before martial law froze; for a few days, perhaps weeks, Walesa's bargaining power was quite strong providing that he accepted the advice of the Church. Walesa was suspicious of Orszulik at this first session. For one thing, the government and the Church – Orszulik's church, Glemp's church – seemed to have lined up with each other, if only because neither wanted violence on the streets. Accompanying the two clerics was an Interior Ministry official described only as Colonel Matuszko. A few years later Walesa would realise that "Matuszko" was in fact Colonel Adam Pietruszka, deputy head of the secret police church department, who helped to arrange the murder of Solidarity priest Father Jerzy Popieluszko. Even on this occasion Pietruszka/Matuszko had a quiet menace about him. For Walesa, Orszulik's pragmatism seemed at best premature; certainly talk of a deal was misplaced when, as Walesa heard via the BBC and Radio Free Europe, there was resistance in the factories and ill-treatment in the internment camps. He had been allowed a shortwave radio and was constantly switching from channel to channel in search of news. Most shocking was a report that miners had been shot down by riot police at the Wujek colliery. That, and Danuta's first visit the same week, hardened him. Danuta told her husband about the friends in jail – though his driver Wachowski had been freed – and the rumours of beatings and the clothes collections for the interned. It was, in short, no time to rush into the embrace of Jaruzelski's Military Council of National Salvation. "They will come to me on their knees!" Walesa yelled at Orszulik after a dose of "common sense". Orszulik was shocked. Polish workers do not shout at priests, they show due humility.

The outburst soon got back to the authorities, who were taping all conversations in the villa. Rakowski and the Interior Minister General Czeslaw Kiszczak, studying the transcripts of the first few days, made a number of decisions. Walesa should be transferred to a more secure place, but still within reach of Warsaw – the villa in Otwock where Wladyslaw Gomulka had had to sit out his house arrest. Second, Ciosek should take over the main responsibility of government contact with Walesa. Kiszczak would keep track of Church proposals and ensure that they did not drift too far away from government thinking. Since Walesa was obviously not going to plunge into a cooperative deal, the emphasis had to change. Perhaps

Walesa could become the head of the official union movement? Perhaps he would care to leave the country for a while? Perhaps, but probably not. Egged on by Rakowski the government preferred to put off the Walesa question. Rakowski, though he now writes with some admiration about Walesa, was sure that the electrician would eventually break down. Without access to advisers, Walesa would run around in circles like a decapitated hen and eventually collapse. That was the intellectuals' fallacy; how could a simple worker handle complicated political decisions? And how could a man constantly at the centre of a crowd survive alone?

The answer was that Walesa managed rather well. In part because of his faith, in part because of regular visits from Danuta, but chiefly because Walesa was always a solitary person. "He walks alone like a cat," says Walesa's sister Izabella. Rakowski never grasped this, nor did he ever make a serious attempt to understand Walesa. And that is why Rakowski ended his career in the humiliating position of General Secretary of the Communist Party on the day that it dissolved itself. Ciosek, doodling and sketching diagrams, spent hours with Walesa. His thrust was that Solidarity, currently suspended, could be revived and even operate within its statutes if the leadership was in the hands of Walesa and his praesidium, and not the National Commission. Walesa could not even contemplate the idea while the National Commission members were in jail (though some, it was gradually becoming clear, had escaped and were fugitives) and anyway wondered whether Ciosek was speaking with the full authority of his masters.

By Christmas 1981 it was obvious to the Jaruzelski team that they were in for a long and bumpy ride. There had been a naive calculation that the West would quickly come to terms with martial law and even be secretly relieved that the Russians were not going to march into the heart of Europe. This indeed represented the thinking of some West German politicians who were sure that a Soviet invasion would fracture relations with East Germany for years to come. But the enduring reaction was outrage. Solidarity had been at times uncomfortable but the manner of its crushing reinforced the anti-Communist crusaders in the White House, Downing Street and the Vatican. Economic sanctions were on the agenda: the jailed Solidarity opposition were treated uniformly as martyrs. The Pope sent a firm letter to General Jaruzelski, appealing to his conscience: "Every effort must be made so that our compatriots will not be forced to spend this Christmas under the shadow of repression and death."

Early on Christmas Eve, a secret-police officer asked Father Jankowski to accompany Danuta to Otwock. "We were driven in a secret-police car and the driver kept on reporting into the radio: 'The objects are on their way.'" He collected the chalices, wine and vestments from the Primate's palace and that night celebrated Mass. The next day Bishop Zbigniew Kraszewski, a tough flush-faced cleric, and Father Orszulik brought a letter from the Pope – "I am heart and soul with you and your family and with all those who suffer" – as well as the Pontiff's reprimand to Jaruzelski. That cheered Walesa.

Father Jankowski was allowed to visit Walesa every ten days. "I was always driven in a secret-police car. The luggage was searched, toothpaste tubes cut to check if I wasn't smuggling messages, chocolate bars were broken open." Walesa understood that there was another form of dialogue with the authorities. By speaking openly in a bugged room you pass on messages to the eavesdroppers and hence to the government. "In January," remembers Father Jankowski, "I took Lech's kids along and they found bugs in the bedroom. Kids always have to scramble around everywhere, so they found a piece of green sponge covering a microphone hidden in the air-conditioning vent." Real communication was more difficult. "I wrote messages on paper while we were talking," recalls the priest, "and Lech either ate them or flushed them down the toilet. But we were watched all the time – there was a camera in the lamp on the ceiling." There was also the nagging fear that the authorities might simply kill Walesa. "We were worried whether they might be using some sort of radiation device on Lech. He often said that he heard noises above him, as if some trolley were being moved on the floor above him. That's why he never slept on his bed. Whenever he heard the noises and the scrapings he would take his pillow and blanket and move to the corner of the room, changing several times a night. He was very cautious."

The Church was coming up with new formulae for freeing Solidarity and Walesa. As a starting point, the Church had proposed to the government, Walesa could be allowed to meet Solidarity advisers and some members of the National Commission on neutral ground. Walesa insisted that Geremek and Mazowiecki be among the advisers at such a meeting, but the Church stressed that their participation would antagonise the government. There had to be second-rank, less controversial, men. That was Orszulik's caution again. Walesa eventually accepted all the Church's ideas and pre-conditions for a meeting – but it never happened.

There were two reasons for this. The first was that the Church was divided in itself about its mission and was constantly changing and shifting its ground. The second was that the Jaruzelski team felt that it was running out of time. It wanted to exploit the enforced calm of martial law and impose food price rises (which were announced with relatively little resistance in February) and push through, by decree, economic emergency measures. If negotiations were started with Solidarity at this stage, the government would have to slow down. Moreover, the Russians would be furious. The concept, by mid-January, was the so-called zero option: banning rather than merely suspending all social organisations created over the past 16 months and starting afresh. New trade unions, new newspapers, a new look. That did not leave much space for Walesa, the leader of an old trade union, and none at all for the National Commission.

But equally important were the splits in the Church. Cardinal Wyszynski had made the role of Primate into a kind of superman position; his influence was felt at parish-priest level, by the bishops and by all lay Catholics. The combination of a Polish Pope and a strong Primate had given the Church unprecedented muscle since 1979. Archbishop Glemp, though well schooled in the politics of the Primacy, wanted to shift the emphasis of the job. The Primate, he believed, should represent the sum of the Church; he should be the Chairman of the Board, with a casting vote, but nothing more. Unfortunately the change of focus occurred at a critical political time, the second half of 1981. The result was that the Primate seemed to the ordinary Poles and to the priesthood to be a weak figure, sapping the central power of the Primacy in the middle of a crisis. Aware of the criticism, Glemp turned to his small inner circle and let the bishops go their own way. Some bishops, such as Bishop Lech Kaczmarek in Gdansk, were conciliators, ready to bow to pressure from the Communists by, for example, stifling outspoken young priests in their diocese. Others, such as Bishop Ignacy Tokarczuk of Przemsyl, were anti-Communist prizefighters. Wyszynski had managed to keep them under one roof; Glemp could not. There were thus differences between the Primate, the provincial bishops, the Vatican and grassroots priests; between priests of the younger (post-Vatican Council generation) and the older generations; between Cracow and Warsaw. All of this was flushed into the open by martial law. To what degree should the Church lobby for and help political prisoners? Was this political interference? What were the limits of denunciation from the pulpit? The internal rows eroded the credibility of the Church's various mediating attempts. The Primate, it seemed, had put his chips on Jaruzelski rather than Walesa. When on 24 January Walesa was handed his official internment order – ending his period of

111

grace – it was obvious that both government and the Primate had quietly dropped Walesa from their calculations.

As the snow began to melt in the fields and woods around Otwock, Walesa grew restless. He was receiving fewer visitors. Father Orszulik came only rarely and the whispered meetings with Father Jankowski did not amount to high-level encounters. Ciosek kept up his visits but the conversations quickly ran dry. The radio stations were carrying almost daily reports of how Solidarity was being dismantled. Ciosek had nothing left to offer. When the weather improved, Walesa went fishing in the grounds of the Otwock palace and brooded. There was no possibility of escape. He began to understand that he was a fully fledged prisoner when Danuta gave birth to their child Maria Wiktoria. He applied to attend the christening in March. "Only if the occasion is completely private, no friends, no photographers," replied Ciosek. Walesa talked it over with Danuta: it was to be an open ceremony, in the Polish Catholic tradition, or nothing. Walesa stayed in his palace-jail and shed his first tears for many, many months.

Since too many journalists now knew that Walesa was in Otwock, Jaruzelski decided to shift him to the south-east of Poland. There was no sense any more in having him close to Warsaw. He was out of the game. Walesa's new prison was to be Edward Gierek's old hunting-lodge in Arlamowo. (There were many stories about the place. Marshal Tito was invited to stay there in the 1970s and in his acceptance note told Gierek that he was looking forward to hunting the famed bison of Poland. Sadly, no bison existed in the Bieszczady forests and so a hapless creature had to be brought from a different part of the country – another version of the story says from Warsaw zoo – and for two months it was trained to commute from one part of the wood to the other. Tito duly arrived and had no difficulty shooting down the virtually tame creature; a diplomatic triumph.) Conditions in the lodge were good, barely changed from the Gierek days. The refrigerator was stacked with luxury food, snacks and champagne. A cook served Walesa and his gaolers – Walesa frequently insisted on swapping plates with the guards lest the meal was poisoned – and he had a television in his large double room. The guards were envious. "Some people claimed that Walesa had been fed drugs because he had become so puffy and overweight," says one secret-police officer who served in Arlamowo. "Nonsense! He simply loved to eat. He did not mind having drinks either but there was scarcely anything to drink. Sometimes half seriously, half joking, he scolded us for serving only Georgian cognacs because he normally drank only French.

112

When we showed the final food and drink bill for Walesa to Kiszczak he was shocked and refused to pay from Interior Ministry funds. He told us to take it to the Cabinet office of General Jaruzelski because they had more money to throw away." Walesa put on 16 kilos in his year of internment. He describes it bitterly as being like a king in exile.

Father Orszulik brought piles of books, many on Catholic social teaching. In an early interview with Oriana Fallaci Walesa claimed that he had never read a book and the bodyguards were curious as to whether he really tackled the big tomes sent by the Church. "Whenever Orszulik came on a visit with a new set of books and asked about the previous lot, Walesa would always answer, 'Thank you, they were all very interesting.' So, using the old methods, I put a hair inside one of the books: a month later it was still there untouched." Thus a secret agent quoted in Kiszczak's book. Walesa does in fact read books, or guts them. "I take in the first few pages, flick to the end to see if I guessed right and then go to the middle to see how it happened." This works better with Agatha Christie than with Catholic social teaching. As in Otwock, Walesa had a shortwave radio in his room but when the eavesdroppers picked up the fact that he was listening to the BBC Polish service and Radio Free Europe, they switched it for a less powerful set. Walesa took it apart and somehow managed to make his longwave receiver pick up news from London. The policeman changed it while he was out of his room, and Walesa would change it back again. Short of confiscating his screwdriver or nail-file there was little that the police could do. He was entitled to a radio to listen to General Jaruzelski's version of the news. The concern about Walesa's listening habits stemmed from the emergence of the Solidarity background. The so-called TKK, the temporary coordinating committee of different regional underground centres (mainly Warsaw–Gdansk–Poznan–Cracow), had been set up in April. Bujak was the Warsaw leader and in Warsaw at least his prestige was to challenge that of Walesa; for the 18–25 generation and for many others he was to become a romantic hero, combining something of Janosik (the Polish Robin Hood) and the partisans of the Warsaw Uprising. He had been hiding in monasteries and by April was moving from apartment to apartment in a series of disguises. The secret police took the underground seriously, monitored it carefully, tried, often successfully, to penetrate it. There was a risk that the fugitive leaders would be able to harness the anger of the young generation and would then lose control, leading to teenage terrorist groups and an almost permanent instability. There was the risk too that Western intelligence money would now quickly enter Poland since there was a clearly defined authority, the TKK, ready to distribute and account for it. And there was the risk that the underground would make links with those leaders in prison and be directed by the "extremists".

One almost certainly incorrect assumption of the secret police was that underground cells received coded messages through the BBC and RFE. That then was why the Arlamowo officers were bothered by Walesa's listening habits. But Walesa was picking up information anyway. Danuta brought him cassette recordings of the Gdansk demonstrations on May Day, the traditional Communist holiday, and 3 May, the anniversary of the 1791 Constitution.

Gdansk was being punished for August 1980. The round-up of local activists had been the most comprehensive in the country. And from the government side, the conciliatory Fiszbach and Kolodziejski had disappeared from the political scene. "Fiszbachism" was now regarded as a cardinal sin in the Communist Party and protesters would shout in the streets "Give us back Lech and Fiszbach." Some fifty thousand Solidarity supporters had demonstrated on May Day, easily outnumbering the official Communist parade, which was a funereal affair. The marchers started from the gates of the shipyard – gathering in front of the monument to December 1970 – then made for the police headquarters, the Party headquarters (apparatchiks were inside at the time drinking vodka to celebrate the workers' holiday; when they heard the roaring crowd outside they dropped their drinks and ran astonished to the barred windows) and on to the Soviet consulate. "Come with us!" they yelled to the Russians. No one did. Eventually they moved on to Pilotow Street where the Walesas had their apartment. There was a clear stretch of ground in front of the house and the demonstrators managed to squeeze underneath the Solidarity chief's living-room window. Neighbours from the high-rise blocks of the Zaspa estate flocked out to join the crowd. "We shall win!" "Where is the general!" "Let's march to Moscow!" Light-hearted rather than angry slogans. Danuta came out to talk to the demonstrators and it quickly became clear that Walesa's wife had developed firm politics of her own and that she had been infected by the radicalism as well as the traditional common sense of Gdansk. During her husband's internment she had become if not a spokesman for the movement, then certainly one of many standard-bearers. In an interview with Gdansk radio which was never broadcast she expressed herself very plainly, more clearly in some respects than her husband. "It's not true that somebody wanted to seize power before 13 December. Who would want to rule in Poland? It's not easy. First we should strike an agreement and then get on with the

114

work to be done — be absolutely certain what we have agreed and for what we are working . . . when I watch the news on television I get the impression that I am in a different world, that things are normal. But in the streets, in the queues, we know that things are different. We should go back to the root of things and see why it all happened, why men don't trust each other, why relations between people are so tense now."

On May Day the police did not react to the demonstrations. How could they beat workers on the workers' holiday! Two days later, on 3 May, the protests turned nasty. The ZOMO riot units hit hard at the demonstrators beating and kicking detainees in the back of police vans. Several police cars were set on fire, two Gdansk police stations were attacked and, among the many injured, a police superintendent lost his eye from a stone fired by slingshot. A strike was called for 13 May and for two days Gdansk, Gdynia and Sopot — the so-called Baltic tri-city — were under siege. Five-man ZOMO patrols blocked access to the railway station, Party headquarters, the shipyard, the Old Town. Police patrols arrested people on commuter trains, on platforms, in schools. The ZOMO, it seemed, wanted revenge for 3 May when they had been attacked with ball-bearings, cobblestones and sometimes ensnared by lassoes. Suspected Solidarity sympathisers had their phones, even their office phones, disconnected. The most effective anti-strike measures came not from the ZOMO but in the threats of dismissal from managers and factory foremen. It was not a good time to be thrown out of work. The workers therefore adapted their tactics to the level of force deployed by the authorities. ZOMO troopers in full battle gear stood at every bus and tram stop on 13 May to ensure that the drivers did not join a strike. So the drivers merely sounded their horns, drove extremely slowly and flashed their headlights; the point was made. In the shipyards, where there was an obvious split between the more fearful family breadwinners and younger more daring workers, they managed to agree on short cigarette strikes. At ten o'clock in the morning almost the whole of the shipyard — non-smokers included — stopped work for fifteen minutes and ostentatiously puffed on a cigarette. There were similar protests in Warsaw, in the steel complex of Nowa Huta and other industrial townships. Underground resistance cells were organising these actions — above all printing leaflets that alerted and involved the less politicised workers — but the most effective protests, such as the May Day counter-marches, were largely spontaneous. In Gdansk Bogdan Borusewicz of the free trade union movement and one of Walesa's closest allies at the time (Walesa has attended his wedding with Alina Pienkowska) and Alexander Hall of the Young Poland Movement were still free, switching apartments every night and putting together an underground structure for the tri-city. Yet for Walesa as he heard the reports from Gdansk, the most important fact was not the new underground cells but the more general point that the Poles were losing their fear. The great danger of the first few months after the army crackdown was that resistance would be taken over by people whom Walesa regarded as wild – especially Zbigniew Bujak – while the rest of the Poles would merely simmer, withdrawing entirely from politics. Then the radical underground leaders would turn to ever more extreme measures, fulfilling the prophecy of the military regime and in a perverse way legitimising martial law. But the events of May 1982 showed that the influence of the underground was not unduly large or ill-considered, that workers were ready to resist in what they regarded as a sensible way. Moreover, Danuta's smuggled tapes of the crowd shouting "Free Lech" had reassured him that he was still in the political game.

By the summer of 1982 the Jaruzelski team was in deep trouble. They had not succeeded in using the "breathing space" of martial law to push through anything approaching a reform socialist programme. The economy was plunging, partly because of Western sanctions but also because of sheer economic mismanagement. A year earlier the government had blamed economic shortages on Solidarity and strikes. Now there was no Solidarity and no strikes, and still the economy languished. The regime tried but failed to win over the intelligentsia. The Party hardliners had time to re-group and were sniping from the fringes. Martial law was simply stasis. Since the government could not claim to be interested in "dialogue" (all talking partners were in jail) it had the choice of somehow re-Sovietising Poland or dismantling martial law step by step. The hardliners naturally favoured the Soviet option but it would never have worked without huge, permanent prison camps and the full machinery of a police state. That left the idea of dropping martial law piece by piece in the hope that Poland could be remoulded into a version of Janos Kadar's Hungary. Some of the Jaruzelski team even started to try out the Kadarist slogan – those who are not against us are for us. This did not square with the purges of universities, schools and newspaper offices ("verification" tribunals weeded out of the office any politically suspect employee), nor with the massed battalions of ZOMO deployed on 31 August, the anniversary of the signing of the Gdansk agreements; their truncheons, acrid tear gas and water cannon put a different spin on "those who are not against us are for us". The Jaruzelski apologists argued: if the Solidarity underground stops stirring up the country, if the

116

West stops funding the underground, then we can relax a bit and start a process of careful reform. But Walesa and the rest of Solidarity knew that the struggle in the Party and government was not about reform, but about power and how best to cling on to it.

That was why Walesa quickly ended the conversation when Ciosek presented him with a memorandum outlining the government's future policy on unions. Solidarity was to be banned, not just suspended, and a new union movement would be created from scratch. Meanwhile a new organisation, the Patriotic Movement for National Renewal (PRON), was to take over the responsibility of social dialogue. It would be a forum for government critics and Walesa could be its head. If he accepted, he could be free the next day. Walesa scoffed: "I didn't ask to be brought here but I'm not going to beg for permission to leave." PRON was transparently a Communist front organisation, a means of siphoning off criticism and then forgetting it. Nobody of any stature, from Solidarity or the intelligentsia, joined PRON. "It was a fig-leaf," said the satirist Jan Pietrzak, "with nothing to cover." That was the last attempt to draw Walesa into a political institution and the government tried to forget about the prisoner in the hunting lodge. Instead he became a secret-police problem. They seemed to feel that they had the go-ahead to be as unpleasant as they wished. The months of resentment that Walesa was lording it in the woods spilled over. Walesa's brother Stanislaw arrived to celebrate Lech's birthday on 29 September. He recorded part of their conversation to be passed on to the rest of the family. But when he left the lodge the secret police took the recording and later spliced it together with another tape to produce a highly compromising conversation about money. This police stunt was shown on Polish television a year later. The gritty images of a hidden camera showed an overweight Walesa swearing, cursing the Church and adding up how many millions he had in foreign accounts. Kiszczak, apparently ashamed of this piece of black propaganda, later blamed the incident on Colonel Pietruszka. Since Pietruszka was incommunicado in prison, serving time for the murder of Father Popieluszko, that was a relatively safe way to escape blame. Shortly afterwards Danuta came to visit and on leaving was taken to a police station to be strip-searched along with two of her children. Danuta flew at the police commander, a certain Captain Bobinski, and the short dialogue indicated how little of the pent-up hatred had dissolved in the ten months since martial law. Magda, her young daughter, was being undressed and started to cry. "I took her in my arms and told Bobinski that I hoped the same thing would happen to his daughter one day. 'My daughter is six years old and they were going to kill her,' he replied."

When the formal banning of Solidarity was announced the Lenin shipyards went on strike. A sprinkling of workers elsewhere in Poland followed suit but the strike failed to ignite. Jerzy Borowczak, one of the initiators of the original August 1980 strike, remembers being disappointed by the underground's limited power to transform a regional protest into a national one. "I was in touch with Bogdan Lis and Borusewicz but we met very seldom – perhaps because I had been staying at the Walesa household, I was followed and could lead the police to Borusewicz's hiding-place. Still, I kept assuring both Bogdan Lis and Borusewicz that I could and would make the strike happen. Lis promised to appear in the shipyard if the strike started to work. They were in touch with other underground Solidarity cells in Gdansk and they had promised to support us on the day. But during the first day nobody joined us. On the second day Borusewicz promised that if we could hold out others definitely would join us. But this turned out to be wishful thinking. So the underground made very little impact." The strike was broken when Jaruzelski "militarised" the yard, that is, made the workers subject to army discipline (five years' jail for disobeying orders).

Despite the evidence that the underground was not very successful at mobilising workers, Walesa became nervous about calls for massive national demonstrations on 11 November. They would, he thought, trigger a show-down with the authorities, perhaps bloodshed. So far relatively few Poles had been killed under the martial law regime – less than fifty according to some independent calculations, and even that included a few people who had died of a heart attack rather than directly administered violence. If however 11 November were to turn out like December 1970 then the small gains by Solidarity over the past year would be lost. Jaruzelski could be toppled to be replaced by Olszowski or some hard-boiled character. A few cracks were opening up in the Jaruzelski regime and they should be skilfully exploited. A massacre by the riot police would spark off insurgency that had no chance of success.

Those were Walesa's calculations when he sat down to write a short letter to Jaruzelski. He decided to sign it with his military rank, corporal, since this would acknowledge his subordinate position – prisoner to gaoler, but soldier to soldier – and dodge the protocol problems of addressing the general as chairman of a now-illegal trade union.

Arlamowo, 8 November 1982

General Wojciech Jaruzelski,
Warsaw

It seems to me that the moment has come to take a good look at the problems and to reach some kind of understanding. Enough time has passed for it to be widely known where we stand and what our options are. I propose that we meet for a serious discussion of these matters that concern us all, and I'm sure that, with goodwill on both sides, we can come to an agreement.

Corporal Lech Walesa

Walesa's aim was to take charge of the movement again and to halt the erosion of Solidarity's authority by a weak underground leadership. The Jaruzelski team, which had forgotten about Walesa for the past month, was excited by the proposal. They had abandoned the idea of winning Walesa over to their cause but he would serve a useful purpose if he only split Solidarity. The underground might even be dissolved if Walesa re-emerged. More important, perhaps, freeing Walesa would give the West the impression that Warsaw was serious about dropping martial law and encourage it to lend money again. As for the Russians, Warsaw had just been given a windfall in the form of the death of Leonid Brezhnev. ("Release Walesa?" Brezhnev is supposed to have told Jaruzelski: "Over my dead body!") Moscow was absorbed with the Kremlin succession and let Jaruzelski go his own way for a while at least. Kiszczak remembers a Politburo session devoted to Walesa's future. "Different variants were considered – for example, to change his status from internment to arrest and then put him on trial with other Solidarity leaders, or force him to emigrate. But then somebody – I can't remember if it was Jaruzelski or I – said we should talk to Walesa since he had just sent his letter signed 'Corporal Walesa'. So, using the pretext of the letter, I was chosen to talk to him."

Kiszczak flew to Arlamowo with a television crew. "The first part of the conversation took place in Walesa's room. Then we moved to the dinner table. I must admit the conversation was horribly difficult. Walesa is very difficult to talk to, at least on such matters." Kiszczak's aim was to produce a joint communiqué that would commit Walesa to staying out of politics, and accept the fact that he would be arrested immediately if he strayed from the brief. Walesa was deliberately vague and for a while Kiszczak thought that he had secured the signature of the Solidarity chief. Then

119

Walesa burst out: "Wait a minute, I haven't said a thing, I'm not signing anything. No promises." Kiszczak returned to Warsaw empty-handed and the Politburo convened again. "I told the Politburo that in my view Walesa should be freed immediately with no pre-conditions, that it was a delusion to believe that Walesa would ever change his mind and that arresting him would just swell the number of his supporters and make him a martyr." A hardline minority argued against – raising the question of how Walesa should be treated once he was free – but Jaruzelski, Kiszczak and Kazimierz Barcikowski won the debate. The Jaruzelski team could now press ahead with their pencilled-in schedule – to lift or suspend martial law on 13 December, to free many of the low-level or medium-ranking prisoners but keep the "extremists" behind bars.

On 11 November, Gdansk was again battened down by the riot police and a hundred or more local activists were picked up and jailed for 48 hours. But it was obvious that the bruising experience of the unsuccessful strike in October had weakened public backing for the underground strike call. And then on the evening of 11 November, during a solemn service to mark the 64th anniversary of Poland's independence, a priest broke the news: Walesa had been freed! The crowds that then gathered in Pilotow Street had however to wait for three cold days before Walesa returned. After leaving Arlamowo he had been subjected to long briefings from government lawyers explaining the many things he was not allowed to do or say, every legal tripwire was identified. That was the political fee to be paid to the Politburo hardliners who continued to see the release of Walesa as a sign of weakness, of cowering to Western pressure.

Walesa returned to Zaspa like a monarch to his homeland. The crowds sang patriotic songs, "Long Live Lech", and, had he been a bit lighter, they would certainly have hoisted him aloft. Not a word, not an image was shown on Polish television. Walesa, head of a ten-million-strong banned movement, was now officially a "private person".

CHAPTER EIGHT

General Hamlet

Walesa was free. Free? He did not talk like a free man. A first press conference in his crowded living-room revealed an extraordinarily cautious man, thinking, it seemed, more ponderously. "My position as I see it today is that of a man who finds himself obliged to walk a tightrope over a prison yard. I intend to make my way to the other side." Hence: no straight answers, not even his traditional answers-as-metaphors. He stressed his adherence to the Gdansk accords – and thus to free trade unions – and to non-violent policies. The journalists came away disappointed, feeling faintly cheated. Much political capital had been invested in the release of Walesa, but he had nothing to offer. Instead a rather fat, shifty man, with none of the grace of August 1980, declared that he had no solutions. The following Sunday, he disappointed again. He was expected at St Brigyda's and the nave was crammed with wellwishers, even figures from the local underground who slipped in through a side entrance. Walesa did not turn up. Nor did he lay flowers at the monument in front of the shipyard gates on 16 December. Instead he made a short speech a few days before and allowed the video to be distributed through churches. He pleaded for the restoration of free unions and for worker management. "Each of us must know how to be master in his own house, and also at the factory and in the university, in a newspaper office, a cooperative, neighbourhood, or a city." In other words Poles were urged to keep alive some form of *de facto* pluralism, to block attempts at a government *Gleichschaltung*; a plea for the civil society and for patience. It was actually a very sensible speech but the manner of its delivery, far away from the monument and not even on the anniversary of the 1970 shootings, was lacking in revolutionary élan. The younger Poles, who had almost a year of living dangerously behind them, began to suspect that Walesa had clinched a deal with the government in return for his freedom, or at the very least that he was afraid of being arrested. Kiszczak's men had indeed piled on the legal threats and Walesa, though not afraid of prison, was keen to stay out. Solidarity was *his* movement, not Bujak's, not that of the National Commission.

Walesa's internment had been different from that of the other Solidarity leaders. They had been engaged for eleven months in an almost constant debate about the future of the movement and about the limits of socialist rule. Mazowiecki remembers strolling through his prison yard and being approached by a radical. "Well, Mr Tadeusz, look where all your expert wariness has landed us!" Mazowiecki replied, "And look where all your firebrand speeches have got us. In exactly the same place!" Internment brought the Solidarity movement together, healed some of the fractures that had crippled the union since March 1981. For the first time in the revolution, intellectuals and workers actually had time to talk to each other and form personal rather than political relationships. In many ways it helped to create the new governing class. And there was even a dialogue between the prisoners and the underground outside. Jacek Kuron and two fugitive Warsaw leaders had been exchanging letters. Kuron had told Bujak he should prepare to overthrow the government. Since the choice was between a disorganised popular uprising – that would certainly provoke Soviet intervention – and an organised overthrow led by the underground, Bujak should start to get his troops ready for a putsch. Bujak, on the outside, knew that Kuron was living in a dream world. There was no mass support for the underground. There was conditional, careful backing for the few thousand underground activists and a much more general emotional commitment to the ideals of Solidarity. That was not raw material for a political assault even on a debilitated government. Bujak replied accordingly and slowly those inside and those outside prison began to think on similar lines and form a coherent philosophy. But this educational process had not included Walesa. He had been cut off from the movement, missed out on its internal debates and was coming round to the conclusion that *he* was Solidarity, its elected leader, its figurehead but also its practical head, its chief executive, its general. It was his duty for the sake of the movement to stay out of jail.

The other pressure on Walesa came from the episcopate, and especially from the office of the Primate. Despite Glemp's unwillingness to confront Jaruzelski, the Church had behaved well in the first year of martial law. Churches had become the main focus for Western aid to Poles and for help and information about the interned Solidarity activists. Actors who were refusing to perform in state theatres or on television staged pieces in the basements of churches. There was some very plain speaking about Jaruzelski and the Communists in many parish churches – such as Father Jerzy Popieluszko's St Stanislaw Kostka – some theological academies were very close to the Solidarity underground (sheltering fugitives or printing leaflets) and the Catholic youth movement Oasis was providing real competition to the Communist youth organisations. This was the classic role of the Polish Church during occupation and partitions. Poles who could only be described as believers in the broadest possible sense started to go to church because that was where they could best express their shared sense of Polishness, and thus distance themselves from the un-Polish behaviour of the ZOMO, the army, the secret police and all the quasi-totalitarian trappings of martial law.

Glemp stayed aloof from these Church activists for, as in November 1981, he continued to believe that General Jaruzelski was a lesser evil than Soviet intervention. But his chief concern was that the boat should not be rocked before the Pope's visit. The second papal pilgrimage to Poland had become the focus of Glemp's strategy: it would be a pressure point on the government since the Pope would obviously not come if large numbers of Solidarity activists were in jail and there were soldiers on the streets. A papal trip would fortify the Church, but also Glemp's position as Primate. Glemp's authority, inherited from his mentor Wyszynski, was beginning to melt away. Poles used the term *glempic* as a synonym for sanctimonious waffle. The government was eager for the Pope to come and thus end the diplomatic boycott of the country and demonstrate that Poland was now fully "normalised".

But it was not oblivious to the tactical gains in the run-up to the pilgrimage. The Pope could come, it said firmly, only if the country was peaceful. That meant in practical terms that the Church should try to stifle underground activity, or at least ensure that priests distanced themselves from Solidarity. Glemp obliged, disciplining wayward priests and suddenly the Communist authorities had found an unexpected bonus from the Pope's trip – the Church was split. At a time when the secret-police dirty tricks unit were putting explosive charges in Father Popieluszko's apartment or setting fire to the cars of troublesome priests or harassing their friends or bugging their apartments, Glemp was calling them to order and telling them to depoliticise their sermons. That set some bishops in opposition to the Primate, and other bishops against their priests. Glemp agreed to attend a meeting with some three hundred clerics from Warsaw. The atmosphere was tense. "I do not see any chances for the political victory of Solidarity," said the Primate. "Moreover after the military victory of the authorities one should expect an attack on the Church. It is therefore the duty of priests to prepare for this assault by concentrating on religious work, strengthening the faith and completing the various matters important for the Church. Priests should stay clear of politics . . ."

One young priest exploded: "Is that any reason to do a deal with Jaruzelski over the Pope's visit at the expense of Solidarity?" The debate raged on. Young priests accused the Primate of playing an essentially supportive role to Jaruzelski, albeit for good motives. The Primate replied that the Church was abandoning its spiritual for a political mission, and that if it continued it would lose. "Some priests are behaving like journalists," he said angrily. There is no stronger insult in the priestly vocabulary.

Yet the insubordinate priest had been right. There had indeed been a kind of deal. Glemp and Jaruzelski had finalised the papal trip the day before Walesa was freed; Brezhnev's death merely made the decisions easier. But Jaruzelski was hesitant about the next step. Instead of abolishing martial law at the end of 1982, he merely suspended it. If the Poles – if Walesa – misbehaved, the military courts would be back and the Pope's trip would be off. And if there was any spark of rebellion during the Pope's pilgrimage, then the final lifting of martial law, scheduled for 22 July, could be called off. Jaruzelski has argued that this was a necessary concession to the Soviet Union and to the hardliners who looked to Moscow for support. A more likely explanation is the hesitant nature of the general, his inability to make a swift decision. "Jaruzelski was both General Hamlet and General Procrastinator," says Mikolaj Kozakiewicz, who was later to become Speaker of parliament during the first Solidarity government. "General Hamlet had to solve the conflict between his duty as head of the governing party – which ordered him to keep power at all costs – and his duty as a man and as a Pole to undertake radical reforms. General Procrastinator was unwilling to make decisions unless he could assure himself that they were absolutely necessary. That was the case not only with martial law but also with many important reforms which were not introduced at the right moment after martial law was imposed. In this sense he wasted martial law."

Walesa as a politician was equal to both these men, the general and the archbishop. But he had to steer an intelligent course. To be held responsible for the cancellation of the Pope's visit would destroy his authority at a time when he was trying to re-establish his control of the movement. The suspension of martial law freed many hundreds of activists – workers, intellectuals, advisers, organisers – but the authorities also converted intern-

124

ment orders into arrest warrants for five members of KOR (Michnik, Kuron, Jan Litynski, Jan Jozef Lipski and Henryk Wujec) and seven members of the leadership including Andrzej Gwiazda and Jan Rulewski. Those were the "extremists". Several hundred who had been arrested during the first year of martial law for underground resistance were also kept in prison. Even so, Walesa found, by the spring of 1983, that he now had access to almost all of his former advisers. The Church, wanting to keep Walesa under its wing, ensured that he met with the most moderate counsellors. "Part of the Polish Church hierarchy was saying that for the sake of the Pope's visit, a visit important for the whole nation, Walesa should stay in the shadows," says Andrzej Drzczymski. "But Bishop Bronislaw Dabrowski, secretary to the episcopate, decided that Walesa should hold regular meetings with Church advisers. Every month he was visited first by Andrzej Wielowieyski and Wieslaw Chrzanowski, and later by Jan Olszewski, Tadeusz Mazowiecki and Ryszard Bugaj." The new bishop of Gdansk, Tadeusz Goclowski, a much more politically attuned cleric than his predecessor, always attended these talks. Their joint aim was to develop a platform for dialogue in case some sudden shift of government position opened the chance for talks and power-sharing. It seemed, in the spring of 1983, to be a hopeless task. Yet the 1979 papal visit had led to stunning results. Perhaps the same would happen after the June trip. In any case Walesa had to anchor his leadership of Solidarity and he could do this only by developing a programme. The underground had channelled their activities on the release of all political prisoners. It seemed that this might well happen. And then what?

Walesa's next task was to meet the underground leaders. This required some political skill. His political position had now crystallised: he was committed to expressing openly the values contained in the Gdansk agreement of 1980 and thus demonstrating and voicing what the Poles expected of their government. But everything hinged on behaving openly and legally. He was, as the government spokesman Jerzy Urban kept saying, "a private citizen" but private Poles were still entitled to public views. The decision to link up with the underground was thus full of political risk. It would make it easier for the government to go beyond the "privatisation" of Walesa and criminalise him. Yet the meeting was essential if Walesa was to show that Solidarity, overground and underground, was one coherent whole – and that he was at its head.

The invitation came from the underground, the TKK, swaddled in the usual conspiracy. Walesa was to drive out of Gdansk on the Warsaw road as far as Karczemki. A courier would be waiting. So first Walesa launched a double bluff, talking loudly in his apartment about how he was looking forward to going to Warsaw to meet his friends. The eavesdroppers swallowed the bait and alerted the SB in the capital to expect a visit soon. Then Wachowski arrived with the Peugeot and with some fast backtracking, worthy of an Apache, they managed to shake off their tail, assuming correctly that the agents would tell the Warsaw SB to pick Walesa up as the car entered the capital. In fact Wachowski took side roads out of Gdansk and stopped well short of Warsaw. Behind a tree on the fringes of the village of Karczemki, their underground contact emerged. Walesa transferred to a small Fiat, put on glasses and a woollen hat and was taken to the underground destination. Wachowski drove back to Gdansk without his passenger. Walesa enjoyed the game and for a while he enjoyed the company. He was particularly close to Borusewicz, a chubby stoic who had done more than anybody to make Walesa the star of August 1980. Walesa easily dominated the session since Zbigniew Bujak was missing – he had narrowly escaped arrest in Warsaw and had gone to ground. The underground chieftains presented their organisational structure, their hideouts, their finances to Walesa, but soon enough their wires crossed. Walesa assumed that the underground was about to subordinate itself to him since after all he was the elected head of Solidarity. Instead they presented their case for continuing on the basis of regional commands, merely consulting with Walesa before a big protest date. Walesa was somewhat sceptical about the resources of the underground and about their ability to mobilise workers: the October strikes in the shipyard had shown that the underground was unable to respond quickly, that it was largely out of touch with workers. And Walesa was passionately in favour of a papal visit whereas at least some of the underground chieftains believed it would merely legitimise the Jaruzelski regime. "Then you simply don't understand the Holy Father!" said Walesa and pushed aside the arguments. After three days they agreed only to carry on as before. Walesa above ground, the legal, public face of a banned organisation, while the underground would prod the workers and ensure that they did not give up their fighting spirit. And both would nudge the government, highlight the limits of its power and the urgent need to reform along the lines suggested by Solidarity. There was little else that could be done; it would serve no purpose for Walesa to go underground and become a resistance hero.

Walesa issued a terse communiqué stating that he had met the TKK. He was quickly summoned for interrogation. The protocol of the interrogation shows how theatrical these occasions had become.

QUESTION: Are you involved in the illegal activities of the underground structures?
WALESA: I refuse to testify.
QUESTION: What do you know about these activities?
WALESA: I refuse to testify.

Other questions follow: What made you leave Gdansk? Did anyone accompany you? Was this trip planned? Whose car was it? Did the people from the second car talk to you before you set off? How did you meet foreign journalists earlier today? Did you comment on your underground contacts to the Western press? Do you have contacts with the TKK?

Walesa stonewalled all questions. But at the end of the protocol he added: "As a free man I have the right to go anywhere I want, meet anybody I choose including criminal groups providing that they do not result in a crime committed by myself . . . I never tried, and never will, to seize power; I would never resort to force in the pursuit of power, nor would I betray my homeland. I have never undermined the system of People's Poland, nor its alliances. I will never raise my hand against a public functionary. My area is union, not political activities. Laws can be improved or changed, not violated. Apart from this I declare my commitment to an agreement which is possible with good will on both sides." The protocol then remarks that the witness said he was tired and left the room.

That is not, it is fair to say, a typical addendum to a police protocol. Walesa, advised by Jan Olszewski, had set out to deny any of the possible political charges that could be laid against him – denouncing the Warsaw Pact say, or consorting with criminal organisations, or treason. But he did so as if speaking from a Nobel Prizewinner's podium rather than in a seedy office of the Olsztyn region police command. In later years Walesa, as president of Poland, would make terrible diplomatic gaffes chortling over the size of the beds in Buckingham Palace – "I couldn't find Danuta" – or telling German parliamentary deputies to stop asking questions since it was a basic human right to go to the lavatory. Yet in quite unexpected places – police stations – he could summon up a remarkable dignity that made a nonsense of police state bureaucracy.

The encounter with the underground forced Walesa back onto the Politburo agenda. What to do about the man? Prevent him from leaving Gdansk? Kiszczak believed that the answer was to give Walesa back his job at the shipyards. The idea was bitterly opposed. "Those people believed that once Walesa was in the shipyard again he would be staging riots and strikes every second week." Kiszczak however was in charge of internal security and at that stage he had real clout in the Politburo. "Refusing to give him a job would have meant trouble while giving it to him would give us some peace. I simply knew that at first Walesa would be the focus of attention in the shipyard but that in time interest would dwindle and he would just become an ordinary citizen. Well, I was wrong."

The local tax office turned one more screw on Walesa – playing the tape of his conversation with his brother Stanislaw recorded secretly in Arlamowo and subsequently doctored. There was enough evidence there, said his interrogator, to put Walesa away at any time for tax avoidance. With that last salvo, Walesa was free to take up his job again.

Walesa was put to work repairing electric trolleys. There were 200 in the yard and they were always breaking down; for the Solidarity chief it was a poignant task. He had been standing on just such a trolley when he drummed up the August strike. Now he was an "ordinary citizen" again, ensuring that trolleys could be driven and not used as a revolutionary platform. His then foreman Stanislaw Bulwin remembers: "They gave him the place near the window at our workshop so they could keep an eye on him. Opposite the repair shop there is a large redbrick complex, the design and construction office. Walesa was constantly watched from one of the windows. Whenever something went wrong, the manager was instantly there. But that didn't stop people from parading past the window and shouting greetings at him. "A few workers doubted that this was really Walesa. But when he changed after the shift and put on a white T-shirt emblazoned with "Solidarity" or "Man of Iron" – after Andrzej Wajda's film on the 1980 strikes – there were no more sceptics. Then the glaziers arrived, broke in the glass and installed opaque windows.

Walesa was regarded as an innovative, highly professional electrician, changing the steering system in all the carts. "I couldn't use all of his skills," laments foreman Bulwin, "because the management refused to let him do repairs outside his own workshop."

Walesa deliberately kept his distance from the underground Solidarity cell in the shipyard. Since he was so thoroughly tailed and eavesdropped, any contact would have spelled an end to the conspirators. There was no doubt though that Walesa's publicised meeting with the TKK and his other brushes with the authorities had restored his standing with young Solidarity sympathisers. That became plain on May Day. The Solidarity underground had bowed to Walesa's request to keep the lid on until the Pope's June pilgrimage could no longer be cancelled. Instead of demonstrations it requested a boycott of the Communist parade on May Day and some symbolic celebrations on 3 May, Constitution Day. The protests the previous year had rattled the authorities and they were taking no chances; ZOMO troopers by the thousand were positioned in the city centres of likely troublespots like Gdansk, Warsaw and Nowa Huta. They could be seen reading comics or playing cards in every quiet niche of Gdansk. And in Warsaw, plainclothes men detailed from the anti-Church department of the secret police were briefed to break into and smash up the political prisoners' aid centre at St Martin's church. It was a time then for "provocation", that manoeuvre specific to secret-police forces everywhere – deliberate provocations designed to embarrass or wrongfoot a political enemy. Walesa did not believe that the Pope's trip could be called off at such short notice but he knew that the Jaruzelski regime was entering a particularly vulnerable period; Kremlin-backed hardliners could have used a violent May Day clash to topple the general. As in 1981, this would not have been in Solidarity's interests. And so Walesa stayed at home.

The Walesa family had been radicalised by martial law. Danuta in particular remembers the humiliation of her body search the previous October and the thuggish behaviour of various agents. Two of the Walesa sons, Slawek and Przemek, had become pugnacious, tough demonstrators spoiling for a fight whenever Solidarity took to the streets. On May Day 1983 they all flung themselves into action. Crowds gathered on the Zaspa housing estate thronging the big dirty patch of ground outside the Walesa home. The ZOMO moved in from early morning with their brontosaurus-like water-cannon trucks and the phalanxes of troopers beating their shields with truncheons. Zaspa sprouts high-rise blocks and is working-class to the core. When the troopers walked by they reacted in the classic style of worker resistance: they whistled and booed, banged pans and threw from their windows flowerpots, buckets of water, any old metal scrap. It was a simple act of defiance and virtually undetectable, to crawl from one's living-room onto the small balcony, to peer down through the railings and when the ZOMO came into view shove a few bricks over the edge. From the eighth or ninth floor this could be very painful and the police were forced to shelter their heads with their shields like Roman legionnaires besieging a fort. That in turn made it easier for the likes of Slawek and Przemek to use slingshot at the suddenly exposed policemen.

Although Solidarity continued to mourn its martyrs from the martial law years, less than one hundred Poles were killed over the whole period. Fewer police were killed but hundreds were badly injured and a common sight in the 1990s was a desk-commander with an eyepatch.

During that demonstration Danuta rushed from one window to another urging the demonstrators on. Walesa was ready to make a speech from the balcony but the excitement of battle, the crack of percussion grenades and clouds of tear gas counted more than fine, tired words about the "search for accord". Walesa understood the impatience of his sons. There was still a huge popular anger that was normally bottled up in the daily routine of factory-work-queuing-rearing-babies-television but which from time to time was bound to break out. It was not teenaged hot-heads who were emptying rubbish bins on the ZOMO in Zaspa – it was housewives as driven and as furious as Danuta, as much victims of the police state as the professors in prison. Such fury did not augur well for a new "agreement" between society and state. The fear had gone. Now the anger had to be intelligently channelled and not squandered in demonstrations. That was the essence of Walesa's tactical disagreement with the underground. Bujak depended on popular anger, on keeping it close to boiling-point to show that he still had a part to play in any future deal with the authorities; such demonstrations were as close as Poland came to revolutionary passion. When the authorities deployed battalions of armoured riot police several times a year it showed plainly the absurdity of official claims that Poland was "normalised". Walesa, however, saw no future in demonstrations. Ultimately the police always won such showdowns. They had the prisons. Soon enough either the Russians would become fed up and put one of their placemen instead of Jaruzelski, or the West would become bored and conclude that Poles should be seen but not heard. "Letting off steam is all right," said Walesa, "but don't forget steam can make engines run. We need it. Too much energy is being wasted and we are not moving forward." On this, at least, Walesa and Archbishop Jozef Glemp could agree. Poland was becoming weaker by the day. Young Poles were emigrating, seeking asylum in droves – including Rakowski's two sons – and many of those who stayed behind were living an almost robotic existence. The future was on hold. The Pope could change that. Walesa promised the Primate that he would not stir matters up during the papal visit. Gdansk and the rest of the Baltic coast had in any case been excluded from the papal route. Walesa had submitted a written request for a papal audience but the Church hierarchy tried to persuade him that this was not a wise move for it would immediately politicise an essentially spiritual mission. Instead the Church would ensure that the most important issues for Solidarity were given due prominence in the cycle of homilies –

free trade unions, the need for honest media, the release of prisoners. The Jaruzelski regime was, naturally, firmly opposed to an audience. Walesa was a private person. A meeting would disrupt the social calm and would infuriate the Russians. Walesa might be assassinated. The Pope might be assassinated. Every conceivable excuse was slapped on the table. The Pope however was determined – against the advice of some in the Holy See – to meet the shipyard workers who had given flesh to *Laborem Exercens*. Finally the authorities caved in providing that the audience was not only private but in a secret remote location. The day before the Pope arrived in Poland on 16 June, a police major rang Walesa and told him not to leave Gdansk during the eight-day pilgrimage. At some stage he would be collected and flown to meet the Pope; he was to tell no one. In the meantime Walesa could watch the Pope on television.

The Pope did not disappoint. Soon after kissing the tarmac he made clear that he was not going to be hemmed in by political niceties. The Polish head of state, Professor Henryk Jablonski, made the welcome speech and reminded the Pope that he was the figurehead of a Marxist state. The Pope was welcome, he said, blinking through heavy spectacles, but "we will not abandon the road of socialist reforms, nor shall we cease striving to make our socialist state organism strong and efficient". The Pope deftly shrugged off this dross and declared that the Church's duty was to side with victims. "The kiss placed on the soil of Poland has a special meaning for me, it is like the kiss placed on the hands of a mother . . . a mother who has suffered much and who suffers anew." Sensing he could not fulfill all the nation's high expectations, the Pope spoke directly to the victims: "I myself am not able to visit all the sick, the imprisoned, the suffering, but I ask them to be close to me in spirit." In the Walesa household there was a cheer when he spoke the word "imprisoned": the Pope was not going to be silent about political prisoner.

That week a ragamuffin army was on the march. The Pope travelled to Wroclaw, to Poznan, to Czestechowa, to Cracow and at every stop his audience was rarely less than half a million. They trekked especially from the north, from Gdansk and Szczecin, and they slept under the hedgerows, in cinemas, in abandoned buses. By the third day, though, it was evident that the Pope was not proposing any political escape routes for the young pilgrims. From the battlements of Czestechowa's Jasna Gora monastery, the Pope's baritone echoed over the heads of the crowds, duplicated by faulty loudspeakers. "We do not want – we do not want – a Poland – a Poland – that costs us nothing – that costs us nothing." Every homily was laced with the politically salient: the dignity of work, the rights of workers to organise themselves, human rights, the need for truth, and solidarity with a lower-case "s". Every time the word solidarity was phrased by the Pope pilgrims would hoist up banners: "Ursus Solidarity greets the Pope", "Warsaw Poly-technic Solidarity is with You". A vigilant secret agent could have rounded up most of the Solidarity underground structures simply by pinpointing the banners. He would, however, have been lynched.

On that June Saturday in Czestechowa the Pope's most pressing problem was how to hold a dialogue with a million people shoehorned into the meadow underneath the monastery. When he rose from his throne on the ramparts of the monastery, the crowd shouted in deafening unison: "Long live the Pope", making it impossible for him to speak. After a while he said with mock humility: "I would like to ask if a man who comes to Poland from Rome has the right to speak." *"Bardzo prosimy"* – please go ahead – sang the pilgrims, adding, "Come closer." The Pope walked to the very edge of the ramparts, much to the bewilderment of his bodyguards. "Any other requests?"

"Stay here for ever!" came the reply.

The Pope did not stay, but he left behind some important messages. The first was this: Solidarity might have been battened down, but the fundamental values of the movement were still intact. These qualities of "interpersonal" solidarity had to be developed, treasured and preserved. Sooner or later the appropriate organisation for expressing these values would emerge. For the time being, Solidarity had to learn to function in the lower case. Stronger workers had to look after weaker workers. And there was a message to the bishops, perhaps especially to the Primate. In the absence of Solidarity and other independent organisations, it was the Church's duty to speak loudly and powerfully for the jailed and the persecuted. That was supposed politically to reposition the Church. It was no longer enough for the Church hierarchy to be equidistant from the government and from Solidarity.

All this was made clear to Walesa, Danuta and some of their children in the private audience which came at the very end of the pilgrimage. The police had whisked the Walesa family to a church house near Cracow and then taken them by helicopter to the Tatra mountains close to the Czechoslovak frontier. There, in a wooden mountain lodge familiar to the Pope since his hill-climbing days as a young Cracow prelate, the Walesa family were given their "private" audience. Three circles of security guards blocked access to the lodge. A famous underground cartoon of the time showed secret agents disguised as sheep and goats and clutching beam microphones as they tried to catch a word from the two and a half hours of conversation. The secret was quickly leaked and news of it overshadowed General Jaruzelski's nervous final session with the Pope. Walesa has never confided the details of this audience but it seems that for the most part the Pope listened as both the Solidarity chief and his wife set out the detailed problems of everyday life and Solidarity's ambitions. The Pope again stressed the need to look beyond Solidarity as an organisation to Solidarity as a body of values. Walesa said he was ready to resign as leader of the union if that was the only way of getting Poland out of the crisis. But for the time being he believed he could still serve a useful purpose.

A very slanted version of the conversation was peddled around the papal entourage and became a weapon in the hands of the Church faction that wanted to discard Walesa and Solidarity, move to a fast agreement with the Communists (a kind of concordat was being discussed) and shift the Pope's focus away from Polish domestic politics to other pressing issues. Virgilio Levi, the usually astute editor of the Vatican organ *Osservatore Romano*, published a commentary that seemed to write off Walesa, praising his historical role and stressing the need for truly great figures to step aside when times changed. Was that what the Pope told Walesa? Did the Pope sack Walesa? It seems not. Levi, not Walesa, lost his job and the article was put down to Vatican infighting. The Pope's chief object had been to ensure that Walesa kept Solidarity on a non-violent and Christian track. As long as Walesa accomplished this, he would enjoy papal support. Walesa remembers the Pope saying, "If the world appreciates you, it is exactly because you have renounced force and use the Church's social teachings as your guide."

The costs of building Poland, referred to by the Pope in Czestechowa, soon became apparent to Walesa. His public-private audience with the Pope established Walesa as a public-private person. The government spokesman Jerzy Urban, a malevolent satirical journalist with toby-jug features, had been referring to Walesa as a private citizen with no significance. Poles knew better. If Walesa was without significance why did Urban refer to him almost every week at the government news conference? This rather obvious paradox led Poles to suppose that Walesa was either not completely out of the political game or that he represented something vaguely menacing to the authorities. Now the Pope had given Walesa almost equal time to that given General Jaruzelski and it was no use pretending that Walesa did not exist. A decision had to be taken: should Walesa be treated as a future partner? That went against the whole philosophy of martial law, the "zero option" that had smashed all unions and tried to build up new pro-socialist structures. Should Walesa be ignored? That would be difficult now. Energised by the Pope, Walesa would obviously be more prone to take risks. No, the only sensible choice was to treat Walesa as an enemy. That decision was made in July at a meeting attended by Rakowski, Kiszczak, Jaruzelski and Barcikowski. The Polish government kept its promise to the Pope to lift martial law in July after the Pope was safely back in the Vatican. But the political heavyweights stayed behind bars and a new crop of laws gave the authorities martial law-style powers.

All meetings had to be registered in advance. Employees had to give six months' notice before leaving their jobs and their managers could in any case refuse permission to leave. "Recidivists" – that is those who had been arrested on political charges, freed and then picked up again for attending an unauthorised meeting – were liable to serve two consecutive jail terms. Possession of unregistered printing equipment was a prison offence. Membership of an illegal union, or carrying its insignia, could lead to jail or hefty fines. Military courts would no longer deal with such offences – though they were still to consider the treason charges against the Solidarity leadership – but magistrates' courts had been given new powers. The generals, said Poles, had sent their uniforms to the dry-cleaners, but they had not left the army.

The moves against Walesa fell into these new post-martial-law categories. Walesa was to be discredited in the eyes of the workers, cut off from the masses. And every effort had to be made to drive a wedge between the Church and Walesa. Before the Pope's trip the authorities could exploit the cracks in the Church hierarchy, play off the pro-Walesa bishops against the Primate, the Primate against his staff. The papal audience, however, despite the efforts of Virgilio Levi, had sent an unambiguous message on Walesa: he was not to be dropped or excluded, he was to be held in reserve. As long as he remained an essentially Christian leader, Andrzej Drzycimski wisely points out that the January 1981 audience with the Pope was designed to consolidate Solidarity as a movement, the June 1983 meeting was supposed to consolidate Walesa as a man. It was precisely here that the authorities saw their chance. Destroy Walesa as a moral entity, show him to be corrupt and weak, and even papal support would be withdrawn and the world would quickly forget about the electrician.

Rakowski took the first step, inviting himself to the Lenin shipyards before the third anniversary of the Gdansk accord. The meeting with the workforce was held in the Health and Safety hall, scene of the 1980

134

negotiations, and the place was spilling over with workers. Walesa was brought in through a side door and positioned next to a local Party activist away from the main crowd of Solidarity supporters. The television cameras were in the hall, the strong lights adding to the heat of the crowded room. The point of the session was to show Walesa on the television screens again, as a humble-humiliated-worker. And Rakowski wanted to show the hardliners and Moscow that the authorities had overcome the final psychological hurdle. The deputy prime minister could enter the lion's den, talk man-to-man to the workers and at the end of it all claim that it was the government not Solidarity that had won in August 1980. The idea, first put forward by Jerzy Urban, was ridiculous. For one thing there was no disguising the fact that the Jaruzelski team was frightened of the workers. The workers gave the Workers' State its slender legitimacy; if they withdrew or withheld their support then only naked force could keep the government in place. Martial law had been lifted, it was time to build a new basis for consensus. But first the workers had to be reminded that Solidarity was dead and that its leader was politically finished.

Rakowski thought he could handle the crowd, although they started to whistle and boo as soon as he mounted the podium. They were together in a historic place, Rakowski told the men and women from the shipyard, and it was just that – historic. It had no relevance for the present day. Now it was important to look coolly at the sixteen months of Solidarity and to see it in perspective. It had been a time of betrayals and anarchy. Strikes had dragged down the economy. The workers had let themselves be used.

This was familiar material for the workers. But what they most resented was Rakowski's manner, his *"if only you had listened to us"*. Everybody in the hall was sweating. Rakowski took off his jacket and loosened his tie without asking permission. A small group of Solidarity hecklers suddenly found support in other parts of the hall. "Keep your tie on – we'll need it to hang you with!" yelled one worker, and then another. Rakowski the great proponent of social dialogue and darling of Western social democrats, struck a boxer's pose and rolled up his sleeves.

He launched directly into Walesa, accusing him of setting the workers against the government. Walesa too was hot and nervous. Sitting down he read out a statement saying that sooner or later the government would have to come to an agreement with the workers. And, he said, it was precisely Rakowski and his associates who had exploited the strikes of 1980 by pushing Gierek aside and snatching power. Walesa's statement was delivered in a stumbling way and its wording was defensive. By the time that the

135

television censors had cut out important fragments, Walesa came over as a defeated man. But no amount of studio-surgery could disguise the arrogance of Rakowski, his sheer contempt for his audience. A major propaganda rally against Walesa and Solidarity had thus been fumbled. Rakowski had lost many of his political friends, "liberals", and done little to appease the hardliners. Walesa had come across as more of a victim than a revolutionary hero, but had not noticeably suffered. Chiefly it whetted the curiosity of Poles, who had not seen him on television screens for twenty months.

Enraged by the Gdansk showdown, Rakowski decided to hit harder at Walesa. The video collage compiled at the end of 1982, drawing partly on the bugged conversation between Walesa and his brother Stanislaw in Arlamowo was now authorised for public showing. The programme, entitled "Money", was supposed to present Walesa as a venal man with no respect for the Church, a vulgar oaf. It had already been presented to Vatican and Church officials to demonstrate the moral collapse of Walesa and his unsuitability to be considered a workers' leader. The Church had been rightly suspicious. The film, which must have come from the secret-police camera hidden in his room in Arlamowo, displayed a fat Walesa and his brother tucking in to food and drink and swearing like fishermen. The conversation was supposed to have been taken from a recording that Stanislaw himself made in September 1982. In fact, as Kiszczak later admitted, Colonel Adam Pietruszka had put together the tape using some of Walesa's public utterances and an actor imitating the voice of the Solidarity chief. The programme, in other words, was a fake, a piece or black propaganda. During the meeting in the shipyards with Rakowski, said the narrator of the programme, Walesa declared: "Stop talking about my millions, I am a Pole and I don't have accounts in the West." In fact Walesa had received dozens of awards that amounted to large sums of money even by Western standards. The transcript of the programme develops this theme:

LECH WALESA: You know all in all it is over one million dollars. After all it is not a fucking zloty, or one hundred – somebody has to draw it all and put it somewhere. It can't be brought into this country though.

STANISLAW WALESA: No, no, no!

LECH: So I thought about it and they came here and this priest had an idea that they would open an account in that bank, the papal one. They give fifteen per cent there. That means in ten years it will

be worth double. And there is over a million dollars! Somebody has to arrange it all, open accounts in the Vatican. I can't touch it though or I'd get smashed in the mug. So you could . . .
STANISLAW: OK, so the same as with your private account?
LECH: And you can take some out but not me, because I'm a social activist . . .
STANISLAW: But from your private, you can . . .
LECH: No I can't because then I'd get my head cut off.

There follows more money talk, more swearing and then the conversation drifts towards the Nobel Prize.

LECH: Maybe in this country we have five million, six million. But hey, listen, I'd like to get this Nobel, even though, damn it, the Church is backing out. I'd get it if it weren't for the Church. But the Church is starting to interfere.
STANISLAW: Yeah, because they've put up the Pope again.

The programme tried to play on an existing general impression that Walesa had indeed profited from international prizes. Some money had been earmarked for Solidarity or for good causes, but other cash had slipped away, apparently into foreign accounts. Moreover, wellwishers were giving the Walesa family valuable gifts – a Volkswagen van to transport his large family, money for a small Fiat. There was some resentment and some curiosity, but it had been restrained for some time, since to start asking questions about the cash was to play by the Communist rules. Walesa, in short, was vulnerable to this kind of smear campaign.

But within a few weeks all the careful propaganda preparations of the government were derailed by the announcement that Walesa had won the Nobel Peace Prize for 1983. This so completely propelled Walesa into the public domain that even such a skilled propagandist as Urban needed time to recover. It was, he said, a Western stunt, money for a man who was still under investigation for breaking tax and currency regulations, a deliberate attempt to interfere in domestic Polish politics. Walesa had been up for the prize in 1981, and had stood a reasonable chance in 1982, but by 1983, dislodged from his perch, he was regarded as at best a long shot for the Nobel award. The reference to the Nobel Prize in the "Money" programme did betray some anxiety on the part of the Jaruzelski team, but the Polish embassy in Oslo had advised that Walesa would almost certainly be passed over.

Walesa had been tipped off by Krzysztof Wyszkowski, his old colleague from the free trade union movement of the 1970s, but refused to take it very seriously. In the morning he escaped to the Kaszuby region to go mushroom-picking and await official confirmation of the award. Although he had a big staff – a bodyguard, a driver, a secretary, a housekeeper – the clamour of the phone was destroying his train of thought. He needed to work out precisely how to spend the 200,000 dollars or so that came with the Prize. In more ordinary circumstances he could have considered the matter for several weeks, but the smear campaign about his foreign earnings meant that he had to make a quick announcement. He settled on the Church's plan to help private farmers. The Church had developed a scheme to mechanise and modernise the Polish countryside. The West would give tractors, fertilisers and machinery to the Church Foundation which would then sell the donations at low prices to farmers. The resulting zlotys would be used to build roads, install electricity, water and irrigation in hopelessly backward regions. It was a sensible scheme, bitterly opposed by Communist hardliners, who saw it as a new conspiracy between the West, the Church and the private farmers. For Walesa, donating the Nobel money to the Foundation was a clever move. It demonstrated Walesa's fidelity to the Church and thus wiped out some of the propaganda of recent months, it was not as politically provocative as giving it to Solidarity, and it was mildly embarrassing to the government, which would have liked to drop the whole idea of the Foundation. And as he told the crowds outside the house: "We all have to eat – agriculture is still what counts most today."

Walesa decided not to attend the prize-giving ceremony. There was a risk that the government would not let him back into Poland; it was not a very large risk but it was plainly more sensible to have Danuta receive the prize in his stead. Listening to the acceptance speech read out with great precision by his wife, the former florist's assistant, he claims that he "fell in love with her all over again". Walesa's speechwriters had served him well. The speech quoted Henryk Sienkiewicz, who won the Nobel Prize for Literature in 1905. It was a time when Poland had been partitioned out of existence. Poland "was pronounced dead, but there is proof that she lives: she has been called incapable of thought or work, and here is the proof that she is capable of action: she has been declared conquered, and here is proof that she is victorious". Walesa's speech added: "Today few are pronouncing Poland dead. But these words take on new meaning." For Walesa, listening intently to his own words in Father Jankowski's study, the Nobel Prize was a sign that he had come back from the political dead.

CHAPTER NINE

Cats with sick bladders

This was the era not of *Realpolitik* but of *Traumpolitik*, dream-politics. The Nobel Prize had given Walesa an international dimension. He was a player now, not a pawn or even a tricky knight in centre field. Western diplomats could seek him out; a Nobel laureate, unlike the leader of an illegal trade union, was a legitimate partner and reason enough to visit Gdansk. To make the point the US chargé d'affaires John Davis and his wife had joined Walesa as he listened to the radio broadcast of the Nobel ceremony. The political complexion of East and West had changed considerably since August 1980 and Walesa was beginning to realise that it had changed in his favour. The Reagan administration had put Poland at the spearhead of an essentially ideological campaign against Communism. The Pope, while not abandoning the careful Vatican policy towards the East, had sharpened his public criticism of Communist regimes. The Thatcher government in Britain, riding high after the victory in the Falklands war, was beginning to focus on Eastern Europe. Chancellor Helmut Kohl, though critical of Western sanctions, was more determined than his Social Democratic predecessor Helmut Schmidt to avoid conflict with the White House. The Russians too were reacting to the new ideological climate. One clever old man, Yuri Andropov, had been replaced by another, less clever old man, Konstantin Chernenko, but the policy line was the same: friction between Germans and Americans was to be exploited. And in Eastern Europe, clear demarcation lines were to be drawn between the socialist and the anti-socialist.

Walesa was having to fend off pleas from younger activists to be more radical. "They asked – has anyone ever heard of a successful fight against Communism using peaceful methods? Gandhi lived in a different era, they argued, and he dealt with the British, with gentlemen; he would not have achieved anything here because the Communists think nothing of principles

139

or public opinion." There were many such arguments, usually in the parish house of Father Jankowski, in a parlour crammed with heavy black Gdansk furniture. Walesa talked about pluralism. "But many chose to wait for the order to start the final battle rather than listen to my sermons about organising themselves. Waiting for battles was simpler – they didn't have to do anything, just stay angry. Moscow-style socialism had shaped a passive person who did not like the views imposed on him but at the same time was not capable of making the effort to change the situation."

Walesa had changed, his political rhythm was different from other Solidarity figures. He barely participated in the political issues of the day, though he always produced a statement deploring the latest arrests or harassment. His friends said the year in Arlamowo had broken something in the man. Separated from the rest of the Solidarity leadership, from the embryo political class, he had drifted into a kind of Messianic direction, convincing himself that he and he alone was Solidarity. When he returned and found that to be untrue he was engulfed in a haze of contradictions, neither for, nor against the underground, neither for, nor against pressing for a deal with the government; an indeterminate man who stood for nothing. That was the view certainly in the Warsaw intelligentsia. Others, like Gwiazda, were sure that Walesa had sold out to the authorities. Many were convinced that the Nobel Prize had confirmed his tendency towards monomania. A young visitor to the Walesa household in 1985 remembers: "It was my first time close to him and I was disappointed. He was playing around with the children. Danuta had gone out to the shops and the nanny was somewhere else so he was running around changing nappies. It was as if he were John Lennon, completely withdrawn, just inside himself and his family, cut off from the world."

Something far more fundamental had happened however: Walesa had lost his faith in reform socialism. He still talked sometimes of persuading the government of adopting Solidarity ideas, but that was merely interview-fodder. By 1984, Orwell's year, Walesa had come round to the idea that there was life after Communism. Even the appointment and rise of Mikhail Gorbachev in 1985 did not cause him to doubt that Communism was doomed. From the beginning Walesa regarded Gorbachev as a transitional, though useful, figure. When the leaders of other post-Communist states rushed to Moscow to establish contact with Gorbachev in 1989–91, Walesa stayed away.

To believe in life after Communism in the mid 1980s was dream-politics. President Reagan was talking about Communism being dropped in the trash-can of history, but this – in both East and West – was widely regarded as the vague musings of a Cold War rhetorician. The Pope too was talking as if Communism had entered its final, terminal phase. That, however, was his duty as pontiff and his mission as a good Pole. It did not make the overthrow of Communism a graspable goal. Yet both the Pope and Reagan had been taking practical steps to dismantle Communist rule, acting as if *Traumpolitik* were indeed *Realpolitik*. And, thanks partly to the Nobel Prize, Walesa had a role to play in the new ideological politics. The Pope and Reagan had agreed, during their first Vatican meeting on 7 June 1982, to share intelligence resources on Poland. Three weeks before the audience the President had authorised covert operations in support of Solidarity in a secret national security decision directive, NSDD 32. The aims of the directive were quite clear: to destabilise the Jaruzelski government, to loosen the Soviet hold on Poland and the rest of Eastern Europe, to fund and supply underground resistance. The directive was supposed to fit in with the US-led public policies such as economic sanctions, diplomatic isolation of Warsaw and boosted radio broadcasts into Poland by Radio Free Europe. Reagan's advisers had told him that the martial law regime was not about to crumble overnight and so the administration was gearing itself up for a long haul. After the June audience, the Vatican and the United States decided to pool reports from Poland and to some degree to act in harness. Carl Bernstein argues that this amounted to a full-blown secret pact, a joint Church–CIA operation to overthrow Communism. Poles from both sides of the barricades tend to dismiss the idea. General Wladyslaw Pozoga, head of Polish counter-intelligence during the martial law years, was convinced that the arrangement benefited the Americans more than the Pope.

"During the first weeks of martial law, thanks to Glemp's radio communication with the Pope, the Holy See was much better informed on Poland than Washington. Later contacts between Archbishop Pio Laghi [the apostolic delegate to Washington] and national security adviser William Clark and [CIA chief] William Casey became the basis of intelligence assistance for Poland, and the CIA took over the lead roles." Pozoga claims to have had a Polish agent in the senior ranks of the CIA during the 1980s and most of the covert funding for Solidarity thus became known to the Warsaw authorities. Aid for Solidarity was being channelled through the AFL-CIO trade unionists and the National Endowment for Democracy into the accounts of the Solidarity-in-exile bureau in Brussels run by Jerzy Milewski. Milewski, a laser physicist who had been in the West when martial law was declared, liaised with underground treasurers in Gdansk and worked out the requirements of the resistance. Chiefly, there was a demand for printing machines for leaflets, pamphlets and books. These were hidden in charity shipments and sent mainly through Sweden to Gdansk. They were picked up and distributed by the Gdansk region to the other underground centres. According to both General Czeslaw Kiszczak and General Pozoga (who disliked each other intensely and who certainly did not coordinate their accounts) the Polish secret police knew about these shipments and about the recipients. "We infiltrated the underground with great precision," recalls Kiszczak. "About ninety per cent of funds arriving from the West came through our hands. The same was true about Solidarity reports sent abroad." The reasons were clear: the Polish police had a series of agents in the Brussels bureau of Solidarity, and two agents in Sweden. "Because of our agent, codename Rodon, we kept track of the huge flow of printing materials being smuggled in – enough to equip several major publishing houses – and we could intercept messages sent by among others, Lech Walesa and Jan Krzyzstof Bielecki [later to be Solidarity's second prime minister]. We broke the codes and thanks to the spy in Milewski's bureau all computer-coded intelligence sent on floppy disks was read by the secret police."

Both the Vatican and the CIA knew of the police penetration of the underground networks, though they were probably not aware how completely the authorities were in control. Pozoga says agents set up new underground groups attracting local oppositionists and kept tabs on any new flicker of resistance. To protect some US funding from scrutiny the Institute of Religious Workers (IOR) – the Vatican Bank – cooperated with Roberto Calvi's ill-fated Banco Ambrosiano in setting up shell companies in Panama and Nassau. Calvi told his lawyers that he had channelled fifty million dollars to Solidarity in this way. "If the whole thing comes out it'll be enough to start the Third World War." The only source for this is Calvi, who died in mysterious circumstances in June 1982 – that is, at the time when the Vatican and the Reagan administration were reaching agreement on cooperation in Poland. The circumstantial evidence suggests that Calvi was on the right track; certainly it would help to explain why the Pope protected IOR chief Archbishop Paul Casimir Marcinkus for so many years. But the figure of fifty million dollars was pure fiction. Almost everybody involved in Solidarity financing, from the one-time underground treasurer Janusz Palubicki to Pozoga's spies, tends to agree that not much more than one million dollars a year of covert funding was being transferred to Solidarity. Even that was a huge sum for Poland and the subject of lasting, bitter fights between Gdansk and Warsaw. Underground chief Zbigniew

142

Bujak was convinced that money intended for his cells was being siphoned off in Gdansk.

The deep penetration of the underground resistance persuaded Walesa to stay overground. The authorities were playing an elaborate game with the resistance. Why? Pozoga says he penetrated several Western spy rings via the underground. But the political calculation was more complex. By 1984 scores of underground publications were in circulation, the basic reading material for all intelligent Poles. The mere existence of these printing presses strengthened the hand of Communist reformers, who argued that to stay competitive the government censor had to relax his grip on official magazines and books. Only television, the medium most closely monitored by Moscow, stayed under tight control. Knowing about, but not arresting, underground cells was also a type of power. It helped vent the steam of popular protest and it also created a kind of dialogue partner. General Kiszczak was hunting for underground chieftain Bujak but not, it now appears, too intensely. "The existence of Bujak in the underground was convenient for us because he was a competitor to Walesa – an old method. It's true that I wanted to talk to Bujak as early as 1982. We believed that he was a serious, responsible and intelligent young activist and thought it would be to our mutual benefit if we managed to strike some political deal with him, allowing him to come above ground and legitimise his activities."

To Walesa the police games with the underground smacked of dirty politics. If the government wanted a dialogue they could talk to him. They knew his address. Instead the Jaruzelski team preferred to use Talleyrand-style police-politics and middlemen – the philosopher Adam Schaff briefly opened a link of communication between Warsaw and Washington in secret sessions with US chargé d'affaires John Davis – whose authority soon collapsed. The point presumably was to hoodwink hardliners and Moscow, but in the end Jaruzelski was merely fooling himself.

The murder of Father Jerzy Popieluszko was a turning-point for Walesa. It showed that the Jaruzelski regime would always be bogged down by dogma. There were some determined optimists – Tadeusz Mazowiecki among them – who reasoned that the international furore over the killing of the priest (by three secret-police officers) would allow Jaruzelski to flush out the remaining hardliners and bring him to the negotiating table. A manipulated show trial of the three murderers and their immediate subordinate in February 1985 quickly disposed of that hope. Walesa found that he was no longer alone in his post-Communist thinking; slowly but surely it was those who still talked about the reformability of the system who seemed to be out on a limb. Walesa put himself in the shoes of Poland's governors and realised that they had very constricted options: from the murder of Popieluszko onwards, the balance of political advantage swung towards Solidarity rather than the regime. Jaruzelski needed Solidarity. "The other side," remembers Walesa, "was asking itself what next? How to survive? Those were the signals reaching us. That was a good sign. It was no longer a question of when or if the government would reform, it was becoming a question of survival for them." It was Kuron's point again: to count not on the liberalism or reformability of the Communists, but only on the pragmatism of the people in power. Yet though logic pointed Jaruzelski towards some form of power-sharing with Solidarity, he was shackled by ideology ("the leading role of the Party" was still regarded as an article of faith) and by Moscow. In December 1984 he received a letter from Konstantin Chernenko, the old, ill man who had replaced old, ill Yuri Andropov as Kremlin leader, urging the Poles not to go easy on the opposition or the Church. This was two months after the death of Father Popieluszko, three months before the accession of Mikhail Gorbachev.

The amnesty of July 1984 revealed the limitations of the Jaruzelski regime. It was tailored specifically to meet Western demands. Sanctions – a refusal to reschedule Polish debt (around $30 billion in 1984) and a rejection of further credit – would only be lifted if martial law was ended, political prisoners freed and a dialogue begun with independent institutions. Jaruzelski needed both new money in the economy, and, perhaps even more, diplomatic rehabilitation. The amnesty proclaimed on 22 July 1984 – the 40th anniversary of Communist rule – freed 56,650 political prisoners and, to nobody's delight, 35,000 common criminals. There had been an amnesty in July 1983 that left only 50 political prisoners, but soon enough the prisons had filled up again. The 1984 amnesty freed almost all the key activists including the Solidarity 11 who had resisted various attempts to persuade them to emigrate. It did not apply to Bogdan Lis, the number-two man in the Solidarity underground, who had been charged with high treason, nor to the investigations against the two most radical priests, Father Jankowski and Father Popieluszko. There was no martial law, and very few political prisoners – that was the reluctant gesture to the West. The amnesty text clearly showed though that martial-law legislation was to be replaced by straightforward police-state treatment. Thus if any person amnestied committed a similar offence again he would be immediately returned to jail with a more severe sentence. Underground Solidarity leaders wanting to benefit from the amnesty would have to surrender their networks, funds and equipment. Those who carried on in clandestine Solidarity, promised Jaruzelski, would be "hunted down without pity". That, presumably, was to please Moscow, which was extremely uneasy about the amnesty. Perhaps too that was the point of the brutal murder of Father Popieluszko who had become a target of secret-police interest not only because of his sermons against the evils of Communism, but also because he stored cash for the Solidarity underground cells in northern Warsaw. The murder was thus an act of violence against Solidarity, a jolt for those who had been lulled into thinking that conditions for a power-sharing deal had improved since the lifting of martial law. Walesa, delivering the funeral address for the priest at St Stanislaw Kostka church, told the crowds: "Solidarity lives on because you have given your life for us." The biblical cadence was deliberate. The struggle with the Jaruzelski regime had shifted ground. It had become less political and more ideological, the goodness of the Solidarity ethic (rather than the turmoil of the Solidarity organisation) was set against the badness of Communism. There was not much space in this Manichean scheme for the reform socialism of Gorbachev; the system had to be broken and this, as Walesa told the mourners at the Kostka church, was essentially a Christian task.

Father Jozef Tischner, a theologian who had written an extended essay on the ethos of Solidarity, set out how martial law had flushed out the innate crisis of Communist rule. "Quite simply, the labour structure of Communism had doomed the system to a gradual death. The Solidarity movement had an instinctive awareness of this structural flaw and that explained to some degree Solidarity's growing appetite for power in the country. One can hardly be surprised – as one doctor put it to me – that the people wanting to cure the ill suddenly discovered that the hospital was sick, and when wanting to cure the hospital they discovered that the whole system was sick." Some Communists continued to believe that violence "in the name of progress" could in some way extract the system from its crisis; violence, the use of force, was part of the revolutionary ideology, a positive element. But, argues Father Tischner, martial law "revealed the simple truth that violence cannot cure the labour disease".

Martial law was Communism's last card. When it failed, so did Communism. "Suddenly I got the distinct impression that the Party had stopped believing what it was saying . . . and the lack of belief which engulfed Poland at the time, and specifically Polish Communists, soon spread to other countries in the Communist bloc." The Polish Party under Jaruzelski had gambled for high stakes and had ended up scrapping the last scraps of

145

ideological or economic control. When the threat of Soviet intervention disappeared, shortly after the accession of Gorbachev, there was almost nothing holding the system together. He was not exactly an emperor without clothes, but the threads of his uniform were unravelling fast. By 1985–86 the only dynamic force in Polish society was the secret police.

The Jaruzelski team decided that food prices would be raised again. On 13 February Lech Walesa called a session of the Solidarity leadership – Bogdan Lis (who had the treason charges against him dropped after international pressure), Adam Michnik, Wladyslaw Frasyniuk, who had been leading the underground resistance in Wroclaw, Janusz Palubicki from Poznan, Jacek Merkel and Mariusz Wilk. Bujak was still in the underground but he had close contacts with at least three of the participants in the meeting. The point was to prepare a uniform national strategy, not only towards the price rises, but also towards the Church. The trial of Popieluszko's killers, with its deliberate shielding of senior secret-police officers and even Politburo members, had left a sour taste. The betting was that the authorities would now launch an offensive against Solidarity to prevent it regrouping and to show that the Popieluszko trial had not been an act of weakness. How should Solidarity cooperate with the Church and individual priests? How to keep up pressure for economic reform that went beyond mere price rises. A general strike was one possibility; the popular anger at the Popieluszko murder, coupled with fury about price increases, would be sufficient to mobilise the factory workforce. Or perhaps not. In any case the discussion did not reach a natural conclusion since police agents, who had been in a neighbouring apartment eavesdropping on the meeting, burst in and arrested everyone. This broke new ground. Even immediately after martial law, even in Stalinist years, Poles could talk about what they wanted in the privacy of their homes. Tape-recorded conversations could later serve as evidence in a political trial but to arrest people in the middle of a discussion plainly demonstrated that the police were now improvising the law. It was, said the prosecutor, a conspiratorial meeting to plan the illegal act of a national strike. Michnik, Lis and Frasyniuk, as beneficiaries of the amnesty clause on "recidivists", were sent for trial. Walesa and the others were called as material witnesses. "Lech Walesa," Urban told Western reporters a few days after the raid, "has turned out to be a comical figure, pathetically trapped in a tragic situation. The state authorities feel they would make themselves ridiculous if they arrested him. He merely dances to other people's tunes."

But it was the trial of the three men that seemed to be drawn from a farce by Slawomir Mrozek. Observers and journalists were banned. Thuggish judges told the defence lawyers to shut up and sit down, the defendants were prevented from speaking and Michnik was at one point thrown out of his own trial. Walesa had drummed up a letter of support from 28 Nobel laureates but the verdict had been worked out long in advance: Michnik three years in jail, Frasyniuk three years six months, Lis two years six months. Even the jail terms were part of the police game to sow suspicion about Lis.

Walesa became more outspoken. His mission was the same: to represent something that could be called the spirit of Solidarity while waiting for the internal collapse of police-Communism, *Panzerkommunismus*. But he was willing to test the limits of his status as a Nobel laureate. The authorities had not arrested him in February. Would they jail him if he called publicly for a boycott of parliamentary elections? The elections, in October 1985, were supposed to breathe new life into democratic socialism ("fried snow-balls" according to philosopher Leszek Kolakowski). Solidarity had called for a boycott and Walesa had done everything short of it.

On the day of the voting he told Western reporters that he was staying at home and that indeed it was a splendid day for everybody else to stay at home too. Solidarity volunteers hid in front of polling booths and counted voters. Democracy, as a Tom Stoppard character says, is in the counting, not the voting. The government announced a 78.8 per cent turnout – far below the 99 per cent turnouts recorded in the Communists' days but hailed nonetheless as a triumph. Walesa declared the results of Solidarity's secret monitoring: between 35 and 50 per cent of the nation had boycotted the election, a triumph! Few people bothered to ask who had actually been elected to parliament; decisions were taken, or dodged, in Politburo and not in elected chambers. The police decided to close in on Walesa, to clip his wings. He was to face trial for slandering the vote-counters. He was taken for interrogation on 6 November 1985 but refused to say anything. More precisely, the protocol from the interrogation declares: "The shameful course of the trial of Lis, Frasyniuk and Michnik and the stepping up of official repression has convinced me that the only way to behave in court or a prosecutor's office is to refuse to testify. I declare only that I will continue to act as I have so far, despite the penal proceedings." During a break in the questioning, Walesa went home. A police captain was sent to collect him. One of Walesa's staff recorded the exchanges, which give a glimpse not only of Danuta Walesa's pluck but the generalised distaste for police authority.

CAPTAIN MAREK ROGOWSKI (*rings the door bell in Pilotow Street*): Where's Walesa?

DANUTA (*seven months pregnant*): So walk around the place, feel at home! Mr Walesa! Militia here to see you! Hey, you! (*to a young policeman*) careful, where do you think you're going? My husband will be here in a second.

CAPTAIN M R: Let me in. I haven't come to see you.

DANUTA: Oh, just you wait. What do you think you're doing? You're behaving like a thug. What do you mean, you have orders? To break into somebody's place and start recording things? What do you want with this sick man anyway? (*Walesa was on sick leave.*)

CAPTAIN M R: Keep your hands off, Mrs Walesa. Stop pushing me!

LECH WALESA *arrives*: I'm on sick leave and I'm not supposed to go out. You can't take a sick man by force.

CAPTAIN M R: Yes we will.

DANUTA: So four bulls have come to take my husband away! You're a thug! Hey, don't be so nervous! Oh, look at that one, he looks almost normal, just like Pietruszka [one of the murderers of Popieluszko]. Take your gun out and shoot, what do you have to lose? Swines, cannibals! Yes, keep on recording! I'll smash this ashtray on your heads, you blockheads.

CAPTAIN M R: I warn you that offending a policeman on duty –

DANUTA: I don't care! I'm a citizen like you. But can I come to your place and record you?

WALESA: Calm down, darling. There may be trouble.

DANUTA: You cops are running around like cats with sick bladders.

WALESA (*to the police*): This is simply an assault on my home.

DANUTA: Those shits! Kill a man on the street and call it an accident! You can't frighten me though.

CAPTAIN M R: I will ask our doctor to examine Mr Walesa.

WALESA: I've already got a doctor's certificate saying I can only leave the house for injections or tests. I don't want to be examined by your lady.

DANUTA: You animals!

Eventually WALESA *submits to a medical examination.* DANUTA *has the last word*: I wouldn't strip if I were you! Such handsome men but such swine! You're not worthy of being called human!

CHAPTER TEN

Constructive chaos

The authorities were determined to build a stockade around Walesa. All earlier propaganda ploys had failed. The attempt to smear Walesa as a corrupt money-grabber had struck no chords with the workers. Jerzy Urban's weekly ridicule of the "private" politician was merely making the government look absurd. A visit to Walesa in Gdansk, along with homage at the grave of Solidarity priest Father Popieluszko, was becoming part of the ritual of diplomats and Western politicians. A certain taboo had been shattered by the British Minister of State at the Foreign Office, Malcolm Rifkind, who ostentatiously laid a wreath at the tomb in Saint Stanislaw Kostka's church. This was a clear statement: the West was opting for the people rather than the authorities. Even the arch-conciliator, West German Foreign Minister Hans Dietrich Genscher, was tugged along and started to lay flowers from Bonn – and grudgingly to accept Walesa as a serious player. The Jaruzelski team hated this shift but recognised it as a necessary step towards receiving economic concessions. The alarm signals from the economy were flashing red and the piecemeal offerings after various amnesties did little to help a system creaking with debt. If the West wanted to play with Walesa, well, let the game go ahead. But Walesa would be tied down, like Gulliver, with a thousand threads; his mobility was to be restricted, his political energy diffused.

A few outraged vote-counters had been drummed up to explain about Walesa's attitude to the elections. Walesa, they said, had insulted them by suggesting that the turnout figures had been cooked. That was libellous and Walesa should be brought to book. With the help of a clever human rights lawyer, Anna Skowronska (later to be a Solidarity member of parliament, and later still, as the Solidarity revolution entered its Thermidor phase, to be accused of collaborating with the secret police), Walesa dodged the charges and the case was settled without a jail sentence. Walesa, though, took the case seriously. Could it be the first move in a more elaborate hardline plan to criminalise him? That is how it seemed at first to Walesa. The authorities ploughed considerable resources into an essentially trivial affair.

The trial documents show that the prosecutor had authorised the tapping of Walesa's phone three weeks before the elections and had ruled that Suspect L. Walesa would not be informed of the investigation until 31 December 1985, that is two and a half months after the "offence". In other words, it was a straightforward entrapment operation whose various "disclosures" would be released according to a political rather than a legal timetable. Walesa's telephone had of course been tapped for years. The prosecutor's intervention was to authorise the official transcription and publication of the conversations. Until that moment Walesa's conversations, monitored live, were only transcribed if they had operational relevance – if, for example, they were in code, or related to a meeting with the underground. Daily conversations with Western news agencies were not usually entered into Walesa's thick police dossier. It was cheaper to use agents planted in journalists' offices, run off a photocopy of agency reports, or clip items referring to Walesa from Western newspapers. The costs of the limited three-week monitoring of the Walesa household were huge. The Gdansk police records show that monitoring and transcription of 170 hours of Walesa conversation – 21 times eight-hour working days – could have financed a complete month's work by the welding unit of the Lenin shipyard. And that did not include the night-shift nor the translators, nor the informers and clerks of the prosecutor's office. "Plus," Walesa says in amazement, "several cars, kilos of tape and equipment, the police van in front of my house – all this just to privatise an ordinary worker!"

The point was not only to unnerve Walesa and feed his sense of persecution. If that gave him a slightly crazed air when he talked to Western diplomats, so much the better – government money well spent. But the aim was to tie him to Gdansk where he could be called to testify as a witness at any time and prevent him travelling to Warsaw. From the secret-police point of view Warsaw was a dangerous destination for Walesa. The regional structure of the underground had kept alive rivalries and friction within Solidarity. But the anger at Popieluszko's murder was a unifying force, a reminder of the beast that lurked behind the bland, rather ineffectual, Jaruzelski team. Popieluszko's death had also galvanised Walesa. At the funeral Walesa had addressed his biggest-ever crowd and it had become clear from that moment that Walesa should take control of the underground as well as the overground union, that the natural direction now was towards a more open political challenge.

At the funeral, which rippled with banners from illegal Solidarity cells throughout Poland, Walesa's surface message was that Popieluszko, the peasant boy who sided with workers, was the very essence of Solidarity, rather than its martyr. A Christian Solidarity, as represented by Popieluszko, could overcome its fear and self-doubt, and eventually crack open a faltering regime based on an atheistic and implausible ideology. That is what Walesa's words promised. But there was a nuanced message too, understood by the crowd of hundreds of thousands. It was this: "Walesa is still Solidarity; I understand Popieluszko because both he and I were products of socialist Poland who withdrew our allegiance and chose instead to learn from Mary, Christ and the Polish Pope; and so, disgruntled, cheated Poles – follow me! I can see the way forward." Some of the listeners resented this subtext, feeling that Walesa should have addressed himself to the martyrdom of Popieluszko and Poland rather than pumping so much of his own personality into a graveyard speech. Yet Walesa's historic sense, if not his funeral protocol, was correct. The tide was turning, indeed had turned. The way forward was by means of a patriotic Church which had, through the Popieluszko affair, set very definite limits to the power of the state. "The worst you can do is kill me," Popieluszko had told his murderers and that was now the watchword of Solidarity. There was now the civil courage to resist an invitation from the police to inform on workmates and school colleagues; the courage to organise openly. The Fear, the cohesive power of all authoritarian societies, had not disappeared completely, but it was melting fast. That in turn gave Walesa a new leadership role. For five years he had been the leader of a mass movement whose mass was in doubt and which was not allowed to move. Those restrictive terms had been changed by a priest whom Walesa barely knew.

The Church hierarchy in Warsaw was not much pleased with this development. Glemp had disliked Popieluszko and the whole notion of a politicised clergy. Openly political priests threatened the unity of the Church, diluted the spiritual mission and weakened his bargaining power with the Communists. Glemp's closest advisers, above all Bishop Jerzy Dabrowski, had been determined to send Popieluszko to Rome both for his safety and to relieve themselves of a serious disciplinary problem. Glemp had tried to fudge his differences with Popieluszko and other similar priests by saying that the clergy should be patriotic rather than political. But the term "patriotic" had already been taken over and mutated by the regime and the

151

distinction merely highlighed the failure of Glemp's post-martial-law strategy. To most Poles, it was becoming a patriotic duty to oppose any Communist regime. What could be more political than that? Yet the Primate held on to the idea that Jaruzelski was the lesser evil, better by far than Soviet intervention. Popieluszko's killing, the accession of Mikhail Gorbachev, the stagnant, rudderless policies of the Jaruzelski team made a nonsense out of the "lesser evil" theory. Glemp did not however abandon the line. The Pope was due for a third pilgrimage to Poland in 1987. He could put heart into the Poles but also turn them away from fruitless conspiracy. Yet Jaruzelski was insisting on political stability before approving the visit; the pilgrimage should avoid any hint of confrontation between Christianity and Communism for that would give hardliners in Warsaw and their allies in Moscow an excuse to topple him. It was Glemp's failure that he accepted such reasoning and interpreted it so narrowly. As far as the Glemp inner circle was concerned it meant that the Pope should not have a public meeting with Walesa, that Gdansk should be avoided, as in 1983, and that Solidarity should show real restraint.

"The Primate saw me less and less," remembers Walesa, "and I heard that he did not like the traditional workers' pilgrimages to Jasna Gora which were changing into political demonstrations in favour of Solidarity." The pilgrimages which criss-crossed Poland every summer culminated on August at the Jasna Gora monastery in Czestechowa. Walesa was always there – and so were hundreds of thousands of workers with red and white Solidarity banners. "Jasna Gora made people feel safe and courageous – so of course the pilgrims carried thousands of banners condemning Communism. Cardinal Glemp felt responsible for the Pope's visit and argued that stability – even the semblance of it – was more convenient for him than our ineffective activities." Some Church advisers and opposition activists actually shared this opinion. In fact there were opinions that Walesa had already played his role and was finished.

The Pope however had not written off Solidarity or its leader. He had been very struck by his visit to India in 1986. The nephew of Mahatma Gandhi had told him, "We thank you for Poland, your country." Before his trip to India, he had steeped himself in the works of Gandhi as a normal part of his pre-pilgrimage homework. Now he began to think about how Solidarity could be transformed into a Gandhian struggle for independence. This was part of his *Traumpolitik*. He saw most clearly that Communism could not last and that its survival was perhaps only a matter of years. But he understood too that Communists would not, in the nature of things, be inclined to surrender power peacefully. The priority was not therefore the one set by Glemp – to work out ways of reasonable co-existence with the authorities in the hope of winning territory inch by inch and slowly expanding individual freedom. Rather the question was how to maintain pressure on the Communists without triggering the kind of violent behaviour that was used against Popieluszko. The method was to change Solidarity from a closely focused union movement to a broader civic resistance that drew in not only workers but also doctors and students and farmers. These groups all had their Solidarity chapters but they were being run by small knots of organisers and were not making much impact on society. If Solidarity was prepared to lose its capital letter and become simply solidarity, interpersonal *solidarnosc*, then it could never be banned. The broader the movement, the more likely it would be to stick to peaceful resistance. That was the lesson of Gandhi. The Pope, who in 1982 had been prepared to use that arch-instrument of the Cold War, the CIA, was by 1987 looking beyond the epic confrontation of East and West. The Solidarity underground was precisely a child of that era, financed by the West to destabilise the East. Left to its own devices, the underground would soon become a cockpit for personal vanities and arguments about money with, on its fringes, perhaps, a potentially violent grouping. The Pope was concerned that Solidarity, which in 1980 had some nobility, would soon degenerate into a small set of conspirators on one side and a mass of largely passive supporters on the other.

These thoughts were best articulated in Gdynia in June 1987. The Pope had insisted on the Baltic coast being included in the pilgrimage and on a meeting with Walesa. The Pope urged Walesa to read Gandhi and for the first time they talked in detail about the future of Solidarity. But the Pope's thinking about the movement was too complex for the rather reverential conversation and only the most careful listeners picked out the points in his Gdynia homily, "To the maritime People". Chiefly they cheered when the word solidarity, with a small "s", was peppered into the text. As a crowd event it was merely an extension of the 1983 pilgrimage, but it was much more than that.

The sea, said the Pope, does not just separate, it also unites. The sea "speaks of the need for solidarity between human beings and between nations". It was therefore significant that Solidarity was born on the Baltic coast. The August 1980 strikes "gave the term 'solidarity' a new meaning that confirms its eternal significance", said the Pope and predictably harvested long minutes of applause. The excitement drowned the intricacy of the argument that followed. "Does not the future of people on our planet, on every continent and throughout the seas, speak in favour of the very need to comprehend this meaning? Can the world – this great and ever-growing family – persevere and develop itself in the midst of multiple contrasts between East and West? . . . can the future, a better future, be born of multiple differences and of contrasts on the way to struggles among themselves – from the struggles of one system against another? of one person against another? In the name of the future of mankind and of humanity, the word *solidarnosc* must be pronounced. Today it fades away like the waves that extend across the world. In view of this we realise that we cannot live according to the principle of 'all against all' but only according to the other principle 'everybody with everybody' and 'all for all'."

The regime liked this better than the crowd. Was not the Pope pronouncing an obituary on Solidarity and calling on Poles to cooperate in forging the future of Poland? In a way he was: Solidarity in its old institutional form no longer made sense, the Pope was saying, the goal now was to extract the spiritual kernel of the movement, the sense of social cohesion against tyranny or dictatorship, and move forward. Walesa, partly through an intuitive grasp of the Pope's words, and partly with some interpretative help from his advisers, found a way of converting the Pope's words into action. It was to come in the difficult spring of 1988 and took everyone, apart from the Pope, by surprise.

There is a theory that the Pope's trips abroad lay a time fuse. Whenever he visits authoritarian or closed societies, the sheer volume of people gathered from different regions, and hearing firm words about truth and deceit in social life, changes the political equation; South Africa, Chile and Poland support the idea. The 1979 pilgrimage was plainly connected with August 1980. The 1987 pilgrimage also sowed the seeds of trouble for the authorities. His homilies, as in Gdynia, were intended precisely to fend off naked public confrontation with Jaruzelski, and the Solidarity leadership had taken note; they were preparing for a long battle of ideas, the intellectual rather than the physical defeat of Communism. The Pope had shown them that this was the only sensible battlefield. As long as the Communists had the secret police and the tanks, there could be no victory on the streets. Perhaps there were some power-political calculations behind the message – certainly Cardinal Agostino Silvestrini and other Vatican *Ostpolitikers* had persuaded the Pope that Gorbachev should be given a chance and that upheaval in Poland would strengthen his opponents. But whatever the calculations

154

in Rome, the Pope's homilies seemed eminently reasonable to the Solidarity leaders. Since the 1986 amnesty, Zbigniew Bujak had been making clear that the political fight should come to the surface. The Solidarity policy document – a thick dossier proposing alternatives to Communism in areas as diverse as health reform and housing construction – was a useful starting-point. Walesa formed what was in effect a shadow government, a team of dissidents that could provide expert and public criticism.

And yet all this was not really enough. It was an extension of common-room politics, at its weakest, a kind of café-talk; at best, the worthy deliberation of a high-powered think-tank. Ideas were thrown – by Church advisers, academics, the emerging right-wing thinkers, social democrats – into a great casserole and baked. By and large the workers were excluded from the debate. The evangelising zeal of the Flying Universities, when dissident historians carried their ideas to young alert workers, had ebbed away. Even Walesa did not notice the shift at first. But there was a new generation entering the factories. An 18-year-old signing up in the Nowa Huta steelworks in early 1988 was a mere ten years old when Walesa had launched the August strikes. These 18-year-olds had an instrumental rather than an emotional connection with Solidarity. They had digested the ideals second-hand but they judged Solidarity harshly. For this generation it appeared that Solidarity had failed. It had its chance but could not win – even though the government was virtually swooning with weakness. The authorities had embarked on a strange stunt in the autumn of 1987 – a referendum asking Poles whether they were prepared to accept radical economic change. It was an absurd time-wasting manoeuvre – since Jaruzelski lacked the political will to carry through even the mildest of reforms – designed to give Jaruzelski a popular mandate that would allow him to bypass sluggish apparatchiks. It was a simple matter for Solidarity to call for a boycott of the vote and Jaruzelski failed even to muster the required fifty per cent.

The beards and the pipe-chewers of the original 1980 revolution did not seize the initiative. If anything, the more anaemic the government, the closer drew the moderate advisers. To young Polish workers it was beginning to look a little too chummy in Warsaw. As for the older workers, they were still traumatised by martial law, the shock of tanks and internment camps. In the shipyards and the foundries this contempt was becoming obvious, a source of real friction. Walesa, still isolated within the yard and taking long sick leaves to run his chairman's office, missed this significant shift. As he freely admits, he shared the view of most of the 1980 generation that these youngsters were punks, frisky but with no sense of commitment to the workplace. The newcomers were not like that, but they did not much like the way the workplace was organised; the internal hierarchy had barely changed since the 1970s. Apprentices were bullied and underpaid, the best jobs went to senior workers, foremen continued to press hard to fulfil production norms, safety rules had to be ignored to finish work on time, the management was inaccessible. What had changed? The older Solidarity generation who had lived through two politically sensitive papal pilgrimages had heard and cheered the Pope's tough words about honesty at work, but they had not stopped pilfering or faking work sheets: that was their due. The old joke – "They pretend to pay us, we pretend to work" – was as relevant as ever; work was guerrilla warfare by other means. The young workers, however, felt the direct shock of the Pope's message: do not settle for personal compromises, speak out against injustice, protect each other. Food prices were raised steeply in February 1988, the steepest increase since 1982. There were scattered protests but mainly in the smaller factories. The large combines were bought off with "compensation" payments, one-off payments that were supposed to soften the blow. By the end of March, however, this money had been spent and did little to appease the poorer-paid. Again it was the young generation that was smarting. Most of the senior workmen had working wives and lived in flats with controlled rents. Bachelors who had moved to the cities from the countryside had to rent pricey rooms, often sent part of their pay packet home and lived close to the poverty level. Gone were the days when workers were the pampered darlings of the system. And, as their pockets were pinched, so the young began to remember the Pope's texts. Was it right that smaller factories had received no pay-offs? Was it just that food prices could be raised at the whim of an unelected leader? Was it acceptable that workers were being quietly fired for complaining? Where was Solidarity when solidarity was called for?

The first strike was announced in April by the bus drivers of Bydgoszcz. It was swiftly settled; the drivers were promised pay rises after only a day of strikes. There was speculation that the strike may have been a "provocation", an event steered by secret-police provocateurs. That certainly is the opinion of Wojciech Lamentowicz who was closely watching the protest – "many things point to a deliberately manipulated protest" – and Walesa too had his suspicions. Why should the Communists stir up such protests? First, General Jaruzelski had been given a hefty analysis of social moods in Poland, warning of an imminent explosion. The reasoning was that Solidarity

156

had lost control of its followers and would be driven into ever more desperate actions unless the government accelerated the pace of political reform, prompting a strike or two before Solidarity had time to organise a more comprehensive nationwide protest, buying off workers in strategic factories (and not just with wage rises – many malcontents were being offered promotion): that made a kind of sense for the regime. Strikes had also become part of the political game. Hardline Communists welcomed them as a sign that the jelly-ish Jaruzelski regime had lost the support of the working class. They favoured the use of force to end such strikes, since that would discredit Jaruzelski once and for all. Even the "reformers" in the Jaruzelski team were not completely averse to isolated strikes. Managing strikes was one of their few lines of communication with workers; it gave them the opportunity to explain their position and set out the limits of change.

Bydgoszcz may have been responding to somebody's puppet strings, but Stalowa Wola and Nowa Huta were not. Encouraged by the quick settlement with the bus drivers, the workers of Poland's industrial heartland laid down their tools. Nowa Huta was particularly delicate. Built on the fringes of Cracow with Soviet help it turned out steel for the nation. Political rather than economic considerations had determined its site. A new town, filled with young migrants from the countryside, was supposed to counterbalance the middle-class, Catholic, potentially anti-Communist metropolis of Cracow. For decades there was no church in Nowa Huta. The steelworkers were supposed to be New Socialist Men, clean-cut poster-men from the radiant Future. Naturally it had not worked out that way. The first generations did not forget their rural Catholic traditions, priests evangelised from door to door, and the later generations, instead of embracing socialism, merely drifted. Alcoholism and juvenile delinquency were the norm on the prematurely ageing high-rise housing estates; punks fought motor-cycle gangs on Saturday night; swastikas and "Screw Communism" were daubed on the walls. The Nowa Huta strike was led by a 38-year-old with impeccable Solidarity credentials, but it was the young post-Solidarity men who followed his call. They wanted not only more money but also the reinstatement of fired workers. It was not, despite the blaring propaganda on state television, a particularly political strike. In fact the strikers did their best to stick to the law. They did not seize the local radio station or take over the factory printing works, nor did they clash with the local factory guards, nor did they appeal to other Cracow and Nowa Huta enterprises to join in. The strike began on 26 April. By 29 April, the management was making

157

serious threats. Unless the workers gave up the strike by ten o'clock that night, the management could no longer guarantee the security or safety of the workers. What did that mean? Within hours ZOMO riot troopers with their dinosaur-like water cannon and tear-gas launchers were ringing the large factory. On May Day, the workers' holiday, they briefly returned to barracks. On the same day, Walesa attended mass at St Brigyda's shipyard church. After the service he told a crowd that the government was condemned to reform the economy and the policy. If it failed it would perish. Then he shouted: "I demand that you show your solidarity with Nowa Huta!" Walesa later claimed that he had not intended the shipyard to stage a strike. He was thinking more along the lines of a petition or a go-slow.

It is difficult to believe Walesa on this point. Jerzy Borowczak had visited Walesa two days earlier and told him that the younger workers in the shipyards were brewing for a strike both to support Nowa Huta and to advance their own claims. Moreover, go-betweens were constantly travelling between Gdansk and Nowa Huta – nobody trusted the telephones – and Walesa knew that the only hope of the southern steelworkers was for big factories to come out in support. Walesa, though, was not ready for a general strike. He says that he had such a move planned for the summer and that a spring strike was bound to fail. What he really meant was that a spontaneous strike, arranged without his knowledge, would undermine his authority. At the same time he was unable to resist the pressure of the crowd. "He missed applause," says an intimate from those days. "He needed to be popular and especially in 1988 he was at his most vulnerable – no real position, not recognised by the government, out of touch even with the shipyard. He wanted to hear cheers again and 'Long Live Lech' – that's why he made his delphic statement. I was there and it was obviously a strike call."

Borowczak, like many of the skilled strike organisers from 1980, had been fired from the yards and was working in a cooperative that repaired factory chimneys. It was dangerous labour but it allowed him and his colleagues to enter virtually every factory premises on the Baltic, apart from the Lenin shipyards. For the yards, he had a fake pass. He was a good listener, an expert at judging mood and the potential for unrest. It was obvious to him that the yards had reached boiling-point but when the time came for Walesa to take a decisive lead, he hesitated. Walesa was afraid of leading a losing strike.

"I told Walesa on 29 April that the shipyard would go on strike on 2 May, the Monday. He promised me then that he would join us immediately

– and I told the workers that he would. He said: 'Even if there's only one of you on strike I will join him and stand by his side at once.' His words were quite inspiring for the workers but we ended up having a little argument about it." Borowczak owes much to Walesa and is reluctant to spell out his grudge, but he was plainly shocked by Walesa's lukewarm commitment to the cause at a critical moment. "I came to the shipyard in the morning. Jan Starecki [a 29-year-old welder] was originally made strike leader – but people kept asking when Walesa would come and take over. Eventually I found him at Father Jankowski's place and told him how the strike was going. He started to mumble: 'Come on, how many of you are actually on strike? Only a handful – I have to think about the whole country.' " Borowczak had a blazing row and accused Walesa of breaking his promise. When Walesa arrived he started to tell the workers: "I haven't announced this strike! This is not my strike!" The strike committee asked him to stay in the shipyard, to sleep with them on the cork mattresses. Walesa refused, saying that he had to stay outside the yard to coordinate the national protest. Yet only Nowa Huta was out, and Walesa made no attempt to win support in other industrial centres. Danuta seems to have played an important part in making her husband stand side-by-side with the workers. She was being flooded with phone calls from the wives of strikers saying "Our husbands are in the shipyards, and where's yours? The cops will smash their skulls unless your husband is with them." Eventually Walesa agreed to join the occupation strike and see the protest through.

The dynamics of the strike reveal a great deal about Walesa: his expertise in running a strike, his sense of the popular mood, but also his ability to shift blame and manipulate even his friends and allies. By the second day of the Gdansk strike, the strike committee had worked out its aims: a pay rise of between fifteen and twenty thousand zlotys, the restoration of Solidarity, the release of all political prisoners, reinstatement of those fired for their politics and immunity for the strikers. Walesa still distanced himself from the strike but addressed the workers in a typical circular speech that seemed to contain a note of apology for Solidarity's apparent passivity, and a warning that the strikers should not imagine they were in the vanguard of a new revolution: "Solidarity has committed a few mistakes but its failure stems from the bad atmosphere, the terrible political climate in Poland . . . but you have to remember if we do not have peaceful perestroika and reform then we will end up with a bloody revolution . . . still, constructive chaos is better than the calm of a graveyard . . . now it is for you to learn quickly, create many Walesas, fight and negotiate – because I'm just tired, dog tired." Adam Michnik told Walesa that he should leave the yard after the speech and guide the strikes throughout the country. Walesa left, but within minutes saw a column of ZOMO troopers approaching the shipyard gates and hurried back. It was a false alarm and Walesa went home to Danuta, partly to avoid contact with Andrzej Gwiazda, who had arrived in the yard to instruct the young workers on how the 1980 strike was set up. Throughout the day, advised by the old hands – though not by Walesa – the strike was taking shape. Some members of the Anarchist movement and the Freedom and Peace pacifists had arrived with printing machines. "They had never had an emotional tie with Solidarity and in fact considered most of the leaders senile," said Wojciech Gielzynski, the talented journalist who had participated in both the 1980 and the 1988 strikes. "Yet they came immediately. This time around young students had a much better relationship with young workers." At night the workers clustered in the administrative hub of the yard got hold of a guitar and tried to sing the subversive songs from 1980. Few could remember the words.

By the third day of the strike intellectual advisers were thick on the ground. There were two emissaries from the Church – Tadeusz Mazowiecki and Andrzej Wielowieyski. There was Alexander Hall from the Young Poland Movement, a pale 30-year-old historian with a reedy voice and an unconvincing manner. There was Andrzej Celinski, tall with chiselled features. Both men were close to Walesa. All four joined Walesa in a formal meeting with Alojzy Szablewski, the chairman of the strike committee. Walesa had some useful tips – he told Szablewski to grab the yard's public address system since that was the key to mobilising the workers, keeping them involved in negotiations and warning them of attack. But beyond such practical advice, Walesa was rather aloof, as if the strike had in some way offended him.

Talks between Mazowiecki and the director of the yard, Czeslaw Tolwinski, were getting nowhere. The police cordons around the yard were dense. Indeed one of the cardinal differences between the early days of the August 1980 strike and May 1988 was that the earlier strikers were free to move out of the yard. In 1988 contact with the outside was maintained through gangs of fourteen-year-olds known as kangaroos who knew every bit of loose netting. They spent joyful days mimicking Rudyard Kipling's hero Kim, smuggling supplies from Father Jankowski's church through the porous shipyard wall to the strikers. Workers however were at liberty to leave the yard and the hope of the authorities was that the strike would haemorrhage. The government had learned some psychological warfare techniques over

160

the years and, from the fourth day of the strike, started to batter the morale of the workers. Tolwinksi, obviously with the full backing of Jaruzelski, announced the suspension of the shipyard. That meant nobody would be paid and it was obviously the first move towards closing down the yard altogether. When the decision was transmitted to the strikers there was utter confusion; it was almost certainly not a bluff and it showed the full power of the authorities. Everyone knew the yard was not making money, perhaps never would. If the government shut the yard the strike was pointless. At this moment of bewilderment Walesa showed his strength. He grabbed the microphone and ordered the strikers to march around the yard – any kind of activity was better than brooding – and shortly afterwards promised that strikers would be paid out of Solidarity funds for the duration of the protest. Although Walesa was critical of the strike, he saved it with his quick thinking. Soon however reports came through from Nowa Huta. The ZOMO had broken through the gates and, not sparing the baton, had shattered the strike. Rumours swept Gdansk; there was talk of dead bodies in the steelworks, of drug-crazed riot troopers allowed to run wild, of strike leaders being deported to the Soviet Union. The shipyard managers seized the moment: anyone who chose to leave the strike now, of his own free will, would be regarded as being on paid leave. Those who stayed could face the Nowa Huta treatment. The strikers began to trickle out. Originally there had been 3,000. Between 200 and 300 were leaving every day. Wielowieyski, depressed by the poor bargaining prospects, returned to Warsaw. Most of the August 1980 generation went home. Gielzynski describes the political mood: "At the outset young workers amounted to two-thirds of the strikers but as the strike wore on they made up ninety per cent. They had the least to lose and they were most angry – with the foremen, the frauds, the informers, the arrogance. That's why they insisted on their own trade union. Best if it could be Solidarity."

General Kiszczak, later to present himself as the man who peacefully surrendered Communism, ordered the use of psychological terror. On the night of 6 May, a battalion of ZOMO appeared at the shipyard gate closest to the Gdansk railway station. In the canteen where the strike leadership was bedded down on scratchy Styrofoam mattresses, everybody was asleep apart from Mazowiecki who was chain-smoking and worrying about the next day of negotiations. Suddenly Walesa's big radio, permanently tuned to the police frequency, began to crackle into life. Commands were being barked and gruff shouts of: "We are going in – let's finish the buggers off." Mazowiecki woke his colleagues and a few hundred of the strikers ran to the gate. Instead of charging, the ZOMO turned their backs and withdrew. Then they came back beating their shields with their batons like a Zulu battle ritual. They stared at each other through the railings: the drowsy, terrified strikers, and the crazed troopers in their reinforced helmets. The tension was taking its toll. The next morning a worker, scarcely out of his teens, threw himself at a window-pane in the canteen, broke it with a chair and attempted to slash his wrists. Walesa reacted intelligently, assuming a patriarchal role: "Each of us has thousands of problems – and each of you can come to me and tell me about them. If some of you have to see your wives, then go. And they can come here if they want to." The next night, again at about 2.30, police trucks disgorged a large number of ZOMO. Again they seemed to be gearing up for attack and the guards on the gate had resigned themselves to a beating and arrest. The ZOMO phalanx moved closer, stamping their boots but otherwise silent. Suddenly their commander made a sign and the troopers started to chant: "*Dobra Noc!* We wish you sweet dreams!"

One night before the end of the strike, General Kiszczak launched his most perverse operation. In the middle of the night five strike guards heard the sounds of a distant street battle – human screams, the rumbling of tanks. In the distance across the bay of Gdansk the lights of two helicopters glowed like silkworms. The strikers panicked, convinced that a massacre was taking place near Gate Number Two. In the morning it turned out that nothing had happened. The helicopter had been equipped with powerful loudspeakers and a recording of battle. The intended audience was not so much the shipyard as the city where the battle noises could clearly be heard in the centre. The point was to disorientate the whole of Gdansk, to convince ordinary people that the strike had been brutally crushed, or that it could be.

Walesa's strength was his ability to shrug off physical threat. He had retained his peasant common sense on these matters. Of course the ZOMO could come in and murder everybody, or murder a few, or injure a few. But none of this was very likely. A striker asked him what he would do personally if the ZOMO came in. "I would ask them what language they spoke," he said, "ask them whether they were really Poles." That was not bravado. Walesa was thinking on Gandhian lines. A fan had given Walesa a present during the strike – a fine-looking Japanese rooster. Some of the strikers wanted to cook it for lunch. Walesa grabbed the rooster by the neck and said "No, don't kill him. You've struck lucky, little one, lucky that you've landed in Walesa's hands." Walesa, like most of the strikers, slept off the

162

night's excitement during the morning. After waking up he would be brisk, firing off decisions, keeping the workers active. His mood would swing dramatically. This was partly because of his stomach ulcers, the painful legacy of years of stress, missed meals and unhealthy prison diet. The stomach cramps became more acute during the strikes, and Walesa was rarely seen without a glass of mint or camomile tea. Sometimes, though, his temper would change for the most whimsical of reasons. Some workers tried to enlist Walesa in a poker school. He refused – poker was for political talks, serious business – but agreed to draw cards from a deck, the winner taking the whole kitty. He drew the ace of hearts, won the game and was in excellent humour the whole day. Then, as now in the presidential palace, when Walesa was in a good mood everybody around him lit up. Yet Walesa was worried. He knew that the strike would fail; Kiszczak's psycho-terror made it clear enough that the government was not preparing to surrender anything as central as the recognition of the Solidarity union. The phone calls from Kiszczak – mainly addressed to the lawyer Wladyslaw Sila-Nowicki who despite his sound human rights record was playing an odd role in the yard, acting as go-between and explicator of government policy – showed willingness to talk about money and even about releasing political prisoners. But Solidarity, the prime goal for the strike, would never be restored under the pressure of a strike. The young workers over-estimated their power. Walesa though knew there was an essential difference between Nowa Huta and the Lenin shipyards. Blocking steel deliveries from Nowa Huta could quickly cripple the manufacturing economy and so it had to be settled quickly – with force, as it turned out. The shipyards had very few contracts, most of them with the Soviet Union which would surely rather wait a month or two for their container ships than see the return of Solidarity. The government could thus sweat out the strike, squeezing the workers, making life uncomfortable and waiting for the defections. Walesa could have tried harder to make the strike succeed by drumming up support from other regions. He did not because at a certain level he wanted the strike to fail. Solidarity had to come back as part of a much broader pluralistic package, as part of a huge institutional change that would see the Communists voluntarily restricting their role in political life. That would not come about as the result of a single strike. On the other hand Walesa could not allow the strike to end as a fiasco, as a personal humiliation.

Walesa and Andrzej Celinski came up with the idea of an "autonomous" end to the strike. That meant refusing to accept a partial deal with the government and choosing instead a moment at which the strike could be abandoned on their own initiative. That was a more dignified ending than picking up crumbs from the negotiating table or waiting for the ZOMO to attack. Politically, it would, in Celinski's expression, be a ceasefire rather than a surrender. But how to sell this plan to the workers? It would be difficult even to convince Mazowiecki who had invested much time and prestige in his negotiations with the shipyard director. His aim was to gain more than money and non-harassment guarantees for the workers. He wanted a joint committee, composed of strikers and the government, to oversee the implementation of the deal. That would have given the strike committee *de facto* recognition, a small step towards recognition of Solidarity. Walesa did not believe that the Jaruzelski team would ever allow such an arrangement, but he had been allowing Mazowiecki to carry on talking to buy time in case other Polish factories joined in.

Celinski, his unusually large Adam's apple moving nervously up and down, read out a letter from the strike committee which recognised that the restoration of Solidarity was outside the scope of the shipyard management, that it was a decision for the government, and should therefore be dealt with at that level. Celinski says he had expected angry questions, a full-blown argument with the workers which would have given him the chance to explain to them the relative balance of forces. Instead there was a long silence and suddenly the crowd chanted "No freedom without Solidarity" (*Nie ma wolnosci bez Solidarnosci*) in a low, sad tone, like a dirge. Celinski was baffled by the response. Walesa was not. "Exactly!" he bellowed at the workers. "Don't you see, that's what it's all about. We're not giving in. This is just a very tough game of poker." The crowd changed their chant: "We will win! We will win!" Walesa then hooked the workers. "Yes, we will win – because we are stronger than them." It was a rhetorical flourish that completely inverted the situation – he was after all preparing the workers to give up because they had no chance of victory – and yet tapped a bigger truth; perhaps Solidarity really *was* stronger? In any case Celinski was used by Walesa, and discarded.

Although Celinski and Walesa had jointly worked out the approach, it was Celinski who emerged looking like a beached fish and Walesa like the revolutionary uniquely in touch with the workers. Mazowiecki too felt crumpled when Walesa told him of his plans. "So what am I supposed to say now?" said Mazowiecki, somewhat wounded but also genuinely concerned about what he could legitimately offer or accept during negotiations. Gielzynski recalls the scene: "Walesa hated clear statements and would rather speak delphically, giving him a chance to change his mind as soon

164

as he noticed some more profitable option on the horizon. Thus, ignoring the conciliatory concepts worked out the previous night, he suddenly began to insist – like the crowd – that there was no freedom without Solidarity and assumed a very radical stand." Mazowiecki was furious and walked around the yard with some other advisers to cool off. Mazowiecki later told a friend, "Sometimes dealing with Lech is like dealing with a difficult child." Later Mazowiecki, disappointed by the hardening attitude of the government negotiators, came round to the Walesa position. Since legalising Solidarity could only be authorised at the top, there had to be talks with the top; the strike had made that plain and thus served its historical purpose. Even so, neither Celinski nor Mazowiecki emerged from the strike unbruised. Walesa may have chiselled out the right strategy but the price was a strained relationship with those closest to him politically. That has been a theme of Walesa's political biography both as a revolutionary and as an institutional politician. To stay friends with Walesa is to accept continued and abject humiliation. Typically, Szablewski was persuaded to read the final statements to the workers. Since it contained an admission of defeat, Walesa would not read it. "We have not managed to win," said the declaration. "We are not leaving the shipyard in triumph but with out heads held high, convinced that our protest was necessary . . . we are not giving up our struggle for Solidarity." The faces of the workers were wet with tears. They still did not want to go, not like this, empty-handed. Walesa chipped in, got them moving, gave them a time to march out of the shipyard; the skills of a good schoolteacher, field commander or strike organiser: never give them time for reflection or boredom, give them schedules, things to do and places to be.

At eight o'clock on the evening of 10 May 1988, a thousand or so workers formed a broad column and gathered behind the main gate. They sang patriotic songs and then fell silent. The gate opened. The march was led by a man carrying a simple wooden crucifix, then by Polish and Solidarity banners. Walesa was in the vanguard, arms linked with Mazowiecki. Walesa still looked chubby despite the bad food during the strike, Mazowiecki, drawn and weathered, like a Goya portrait. The ZOMO stepped aside and let the marchers through. The bells of St Brigyda's church, their destination, pealed out a welcome, and an enthusiastic crowd thronged the pavements shouting "Solidarity!" But the workers stayed silent. Gielzynski explains: "It was only a ceasefire, after all, and one does not celebrate ceasefires."

The May strikes shook up Polish politics, indeed decisively changed the equation. The mere fact of the strikes in the country's two major industrial centres showed how little had been achieved in seven years. The use of gas and batons against the Nowa Huta strikers and the psycho-terror against Gdansk was, in Adam Michnik's view, "a nail in Jaruzelski's coffin – he lost his last chance of rebuilding his credibility". Many myths were shattered. Solidarity, despite many funeral notices in the West, was not dead. It had taken over the Gdansk strike, refined its political demands and ensured that the legalisation of the union was the chief item on the political agenda. Another myth – that the workers were now only interested in their bellies and their pockets – had also crumbled. Above all, the conventional wisdom that Poland was doomed to a kind of permanent stasis had to be revised. But Solidarity too was forced to shrug off its complacency; it had after all failed to put together a general strike. The lazy premise of the past two years had been that one big industrial conflict would be enough to trigger a social explosion in Poland. But the May strikers had waited in vain for support.

Walesa now had to honour his promise to organise a serious protest that would bring the government to its knees. Despite much talk from Walesa and other chieftains that the May strikes were premature by some six months, there were no comprehensive plans for a summer or autumn stoppage. That had to be changed. The initial step was to state again, with some precision, what Solidarity now represented. Walesa had been surprised by how little the younger shipyard workers knew of Solidarity. Few had bothered to read the underground news bulletins and picked up their information second- or third-hand from Radio Free Europe and BBC Polish services. Walesa called in his advisers and after two weeks of brainstorming they managed to produce a document that was remarkable in showing how far the union had departed from its quasi-socialist (some would say true socialist) roots. "It is no secret any more that market mechanisms are the most efficient economic principles," said the report, hinting at the influence of an emerging group of market liberals in the group around Walesa. Gdansk in particular was becoming a hive of Thatcherite economists, active not only at the polytechnic and university but also as consultants to local private businesses.

For a time it had seemed as if Solidarity would repackage itself as a reform socialist grouping *à la* Gorbachev. Walesa kept referring to the Polish perestroika whose guiding principles had been laid down by Solidarity. This, however, was little more than a tactical game. The Jaruzelski team and Solidarity were competing to show that they had the backing of Gorbachev.

A similar game was under way in Czechoslovakia where Charter 77, some of whose signatories had known Gorbachev as a student, were scoring a few points off the Communist leadership of Milos Jakes. In Poland the Jaruzelski team, though obviously in sympathy with Gorbachev, had made very little use of the Kremlin changes since 1985. The breakthrough, said the regime's apologists, would come when Gorbachev visited Warsaw in early summer of 1988. The main Solidarity experts were divided over Gorbachev. Most agreed that the decisive moment had to come from above with a little pushing from below. Gorbachev seemed capable of such a shove – he had after all ended the Afghanistan war at a stroke – but there was a growing feeling that Gorbachev-style solutions would not carry Poland much further. There was more political imagination in Moscow than in Warsaw, so it seemed, but it was still not enough. Gorbachev came and duly announced that Warsaw could solve its problems in its own way, albeit in a broadly socialist framework. Yet shortly afterwards, on 26 July, Jerzy Urban told reporters that Solidarity was "a thing of the past, a relic". That appeared to put an end to the hope that a Jaruzelski-led administration, no longer nervous about Moscow, would come up with a solution that embraced Solidarity. It was plain to Walesa that the power-sharing deal with the Communists – tentatively brought into play in April by deputy premier Zdzislaw Sadowski – would have to be forced through. There was even a school of thought that the Jaruzelski leadership was waiting for pressure, for another round of strikes. The government analysis of the May strikes had been weighted against Solidarity. To generals Kiszczak and Pozoga, who were most closely in touch with the factory moods, Solidarity had yet to prove that it was still a political partner. Walesa had shown that he could end a strike with dignity, but there had been no general strike. How well organised was Solidarity, how angry were the workers? Despite the extensive network of police informers, the authorities had no real answer to these questions. The public line was therefore that Solidarity was dead. The private line was that perhaps, *perhaps*, a deal could be struck but first the relative strength of government and opposition had to be worked out.

When the Silesian miners stopped work that August, Walesa was sure that the moment for a showdown had arrived. They were striking for money (the traditional privileges of pitworkers were being eroded quickly by the general economic decline) but they also insisted on the restoration of Solidarity. By 17 August the coal strike had spread to 16 pits and the shipyard in Szczecin had joined in. The Gdansk yards said they would come out on 22 August unless the government started negotiating on legalising Soli-

167

darity. The government did not oblige, so Gdansk joined the strike wave. This time the strike committees had established lines of communication between striking plants and the atmosphere was quite different from that in May. The young workers were now strike veterans, not so easily intimidated, and were quick to set up printing machinery. There was time too to enlist sympathisers, like singer Piotr Szczepanik who lent his audio equipment to the Gdansk workers. (Szczepanik was later rewarded by being made President Walesa's personal emissary to the world of culture: any film director or actor who wanted a favour from the Walesa court had to go through Szczepanik.) The Kaczynski twins arrived again and Professor Andrzej Stelmachowski, who had been the Church's man in Nowa Huta, became the episcopate's link to the shipyards. Mazowiecki, stung by his experiences during the May protest, was not part of the team.

The strike dragged on, negotiations leading nowhere. But the festive spirit endured. By the fifth day of the strike Kiszczak appeared on television and suggested a meeting with various "social and workers' milieux". To Walesa the offer sounded promising, not part of the usual strike-breaking deceit. "This meeting," Kiszczak said, "could assume the form of a Round Table. I have no pre-conditions about the subjects to be discussed at the table or who may sit at it." That last pledge – no conditions about who could take part – was crucial; it suggested that Walesa could attend with his full complement of experts, and that the legalisation of Solidarity was not far away. The strike committee was jubilant – "Better a Round Table than a square cell" was Jacek Merkel's comment – but the workers were not convinced.

"They have woken up," Walesa told the strikers, "but they are not going to give up their territory too easily. So we will have to quarrel to work out the kind of answers that will let us heal Poland together." As Walesa recalls it, the strikers were brimming over with anger and frustration. "I was so struck by it that I couldn't utter a word. I didn't expect that degree of radicalism, the sort that can fuel a civil war." The fact is, the workers were right to be suspicious. Kiszczak was not offering much, and to give up the strike on the basis of a promise of future talks needed a great deal of faith. And it demanded popular trust in Walesa. Kiszczak, after a three-hour session with Walesa, umpired by the Church, was not prepared to budge from his formula: Solidarity would be restored only if the Round Table talks produced a national accord, all strikes had to end within 18 hours, and there would be a two-week pause while both sides drew up their lists of negotiators and advisers.

Walesa accepted the terms and thus embarked on the biggest risk of his political career. If the Round Table turned out to be a sham he would be fatally weakened as Solidarity leader. Not only the shipyard workers but also the miners had made clear that they did not believe in the Round Table. Walesa was shrewd enough to prevent himself being made into a puppet, but he was dangerously vulnerable to the whim of the government. The Communist press was rabidly attacking Solidarity, some of those who had taken part in the recent strikes were being harassed, and on 13 October the ineffectual premier Zbigniew Messner was replaced by Mieczyslaw Rakowski, a personal enemy of Walesa. Within a fortnight Rakowski, still regarded in the West as a sensitive semi-democrat, declared that the Gdansk shipyards were going to be shut down for economic reasons. It was regarded by many as an act of personal spite, revenge for his hostile reception in 1983. Whatever the reason, Rakowski did nothing to build up the necessary trust before the Round Table.

Under pressure from the rank and file, Walesa began to argue during his regular preparatory meetings with Kiszczak and Stanislaw Ciosek that a timetable had to be worked out for the restoration of Solidarity. The government insisted that this was out of the question. That was a prize which might, or might not, be granted as the result of the Round Table talks; it could not be treated as an independent issue. There was considerable body-language involved. Without putting it into words, Kiszczak and Ciosek were indicating that they had real problems with their hardliners. The outlawing of Solidarity was an item of faith for many Party members and the present Central Committee was vehemently opposed. Walesa in turn was hinting that he needed a gesture to ease the impatience of the factory crews. In mid-November, the same theatre was enacted. Walesa warned that the Round Table could not go ahead without some movement on Solidarity. Kiszczak said: Very well — and ordered the dismantling of the large table which had already been set up in the Jablonna Palace. It then spent ten weeks in a furniture factory warehouse while tempers cooled.

There were indeed hardliners active in the Central Committee and in the nooks and crannies of the Party machine. They no longer had Kremlin backing, but there were those in Moscow who nonetheless supported their cause. The Round Table was an unorthodox solution that could only entail a loss of power and authority. It would dilute central power and sideline the official pro-Communist trade unions. It could be, the hardliners correctly surmised, the beginning of the end. The chief obstacle to the Round Table, however, was the contempt felt by Rakowski's men for Lech Walesa.

Rakowski had his own bitter memories of Walesa (the time that Walesa had refused to see him soon after being interned, the shipyard visit in 1983) and he was keen to do business only with other members of the Solidarity élite, preferably professors or journalists, who could construct grammatically correct statements, who were capable of drafting legally consistent and binding agreements. The view was shared by other members of the Jaruzelski team who, since Rakowski's elevation to the premiership, were becoming more assertive. Urban in particular regarded Walesa as little more than a wily peasant. Wieslaw Gornicki, Jaruzelski's chief speechwriter, saw Walesa as a kind of Holy Fool, capable of truth-telling but not to be trusted with responsibility. Above all they believed the propaganda that they had peddled for most of the decade: that only his vanity kept him in the game, that he was weak and vulnerable. Only Kiszczak did not fully support this view. Apart from his many personal contacts with Walesa and Walesa advisers, he had his agents in the Walesa entourage. They gave him the image of a far more complex man, a potential winner rather than a certain loser.

The assessment of Walesa changed decisively after a television duel between Walesa and the head of the OPZZ Communist-backed unions, Alfred Miodowicz. As a sign of the new Round Table mood – even if the table itself had been unscrewed – Walesa was to be allowed to confront Miodowicz during prime time. Miodowicz was an affable pipe-smoking man, keen on woolly cardigans and walking his dog. He was a member of the Politburo, but he was supposed to be Communism's comfortable lived-in face. He knew how to talk to workers and had a simple straightforward manner that came across well on television. It was thus assumed that Walesa would be dealt if not a knock-out blow, then at least a good crack to the chin; Walesa, ran the conventional wisdom in and out of government, was a disaster on television. He sweated, became red in the face, lost control of his sentences and his argument. If Walesa were outpointed by Miodowicz then the government could play off the official unions against Solidarity. At the Round Table the Communists would be able to claim that Solidarity did not speak for the whole union movement. And if Walesa messed up in a spectacular way then he might end up alienating intellectuals and workers. This after all would, for most Poles, be the first glimpse of the man since 1981.

The gamble did not pay off. Walesa beat Miodowicz with some ease and re-established himself as one of Poland's leading political figures. Even Rakowski had to admit that Walesa had brilliantly used state television to sell the Solidarity cause, and himself. Walesa had prepared himself thoroughly, taking camera advice from film director Andrzej Wajda, learning television debating techniques from the sacked presenter Andrzej Bober, and packaging his thoughts together with skilled political performers like Jacek Kuron, Adam Michnik and Janusz Onyszkiewicz.

Miodowicz stuck to the line that pluralism was over-rated, that Poland needed unity to pull itself out of the crisis:

MIODOWICZ: Can union pluralism solve all our problems? We won't get much help from the West if we are jumping at each other's throats, like in Lebanon. Even if we get it, it won't last long. We have to count on our own strength . . . the first step should be having one trade union in each factory, and exactly which one should be decided by a free vote.

WALESA: Solidarity is ready to make compromises but after the elementary questions have been looked at again. The union monopoly, the political monopoly, the economic monopoly – they have to be destroyed at last! No, Mr Miodowicz, we will never be able to deal with the fundamental issues without first introducing a pluralistic system . . .

MIODOWICZ: Our society needs peace rather than slogans like: "No freedom without Solidarity" . . .

WALESA: Mr Miodowicz, I don't have time to deceive the public that something is going on when in fact nothing is going on. The talks with the Agriculture Fund have been going on for five years – with no results. I will fight for Solidarity because Poland needs it. Lack of pluralism equals Stalinism.

MIODOWICZ: Is union pluralism the only answer to Polish problems? We must see some opportunities in the Party, which is changing so much . . .

And so on. By why was Miodowicz, the smooth television performer, looking so uneasy throughout the debate? Perhaps it was because of a bit of gamesmanship by Walesa. Moments before walking into the studio, Walesa hissed into Miodowicz's ear: "I'm going to destroy you!"

CHAPTER ELEVEN

Furnishing democracy

Polish streets presented strange spectacles at the end of the 1980s. Those battered men wheeling two-metre-high piles of newspapers on old pram-carriages – where were they going? To *maklatura* collection points. In return for several kilos of waste paper they received free lavatory paper, ten rolls strung into a necklace. After forty years of socialist rule, lavatory paper was still in short supply. So were most medicines, cotton wool, sanitary pads, most cuts of meat, mineral water in summer, shampoo, washing-powder, milk. Prices were on an ascending escalator but there was still no balance between supply and demand. Some private markets were allowed to charge any price and did so, aiming for a few wealthy clients or the wives of foreign diplomats. One writer took his children to such a market, much as he would take them to a zoo or a museum, to point to the exotica; look, children, there is a banana! It comes from South America. A newspaper told the sad story of a couple who had met and fallen in love in a meat queue in the early 1980s; there was plenty of time for romance, by the late 1980s they were divorced and could be seen in separate food queues, seeking new mates. By 1988 moonlighting had become as prevalent as in Hungary and bribes were essential. A spot police check in Poznan revealed that about a third of prostitutes working the streets on a Friday night were registered nurses unable to make ends meet on a state salary that was barely above the poverty level. Nuclear physicists doubled up as plumbers or spent their summer holidays as night porters in Amsterdam hotels. Yet there was not much chance of a shipyard worker or a foundryman or a miner picking up such after-hours work. They were left behind, increasingly bitter not only about the government but also about other social groupings which seemed to have such easy access to dollars and to privilege. So-called Pewex shops sold goods imported from the West only for hard currency. The fact was that the Polish economy was in a state of ruin – recession was too mild a term

172

– comparable to Germany after the war. Germany, that is, without the promise of Marshall Aid, without established markets, without managers, without capital.

It was this sense of utter collapse that drove the government into accepting that power had to be shared. The economy, in the government view, needed Western credits and a long period of industrial calm. Both elements required the cooperation of Solidarity. The economy of course required far more – a fundamental overhaul – but the authorities did not have the political will to ditch the command economy. The short-term goals, though, could be achieved by doing a deal with the opposition. Could such an arrangement be struck without legalising Solidarity?

Both the Party and the Jaruzelski team seemed to think so for much of 1988. That was the logic behind Rakowski's appointment. Rakowski was unpopular in the Party because of his cleverness, yet was deemed suitable for the present mission for precisely the same reason. If anyone could talk the West out of its obsession with Solidarity and Lech Walesa, then that man would surely be Rakowski. He spoke foreign languages (and not just Russian!), he was open about his personal problems (his children had stayed abroad after martial law, his ex-wife was sympathetic to Solidarity, his current wife did not much like what was going on), his suit fitted and did not slop over his shoes or stretch over his stomach. In short he was a tricky sort of person who could be relied on to bamboozle the Germans and to box Solidarity into a corner. Bronislaw Geremek spotted this quickly: "Rakowski's accession to power was a substitute for legalising Solidarity. He had assured the Party leadership that he would gain Western aid even without restoring Solidarity, relying on his old contacts with European politicians." The pre-Round Table negotiations – through the mediation of Sila Nowicki in May and August and the first brushes with General Kiszczak – all talked *around* Solidarity.

The Miodowicz debate put an end to these illusions. Jaruzelski's advisers grudgingly accepted that they had to grasp the nettle. The new line ran like this: co-opt Solidarity, give them economic portfolios and ensure that they shared responsibility for the crisis. Worker anger would be turned against Solidarity, not Communism, the West would be dazzled by the "liberalism" of Jaruzelski and Rakowski and pay up. Since the economy was forecast to get dramatically worse within a year, it was a gamble worth taking. Walesa and the Solidarity leadership had no illusions about the government plan. As Geremek saw it, "Their bet was that such a manoeuvre will cost them only a little and yet bring substantial profits." In his earlier (confidential, but leaked) letter to the Central Committee, Rakowski had clearly explained the doctrine: "The opposition should be dragged into the orbit of power and thus stripped of its excellent position whereby it amasses political capital by simply doing nothing." Anything bad was automatically blamed on the government and those who criticised it gained strength. "What they meant to do," says Geremek, "was corrupt Solidarity, divide us, compromise us. And they were pretty rational in this plan. The plan had only one irrational element – the assumption that the Communist Party would survive it."

The hardline Marxists understood the situation much better than Rakowski. To share power was to surrender it, and after the first surrender there would have to be many more. It was one thing to recognise the existence of a non- or anti-Communist opposition, quite another to announce that it was no longer regarded as an enemy. Jaruzelski thus faced a difficult task in selling the idea of a legal Solidarity to the Party; the Party had lived through 16 months of direct competition in 1980–81 and had come close to breaking up. The plenary session of the Central Committee which began on 20 December, and which staggered into a second session in January, was therefore critical to the chances of a Round Table power-sharing arrangement. There had been something of a Party taboo on open criticism of Jaruzelski but the delegates at the plenum swept this aside; this was their last stand, their last attempt to keep intact the old black-and-white categories, the Demon Solidarity, the epitome of clericalist, CIA-backed anti-Communist reaction, pitted against the Party that had rebuilt Poland and which enjoyed the support of the working masses. Jaruzelski and Rakowski were trying to blur the categories and should be stopped.

At the outset of the plenum, held as usual in the large white Party headquarters on the corner of New World Street and Jerusalem Avenue, that seemed to be the majority view. The leadership was given a rough ride. The leadership replied by saying that it was perhaps the Central Committee and not the Politburo or government that was out of touch. Rakowski recalls: "I decided to ask the members of the Central Committee, and indeed all Party members, several crucial questions. How many of your fellow workers are for restoration of Solidarity? What should be your next steps in the new circumstances? Should we include that Walesa's standpoint has opened the way for dialogue? . . . Walesa suggests a compromise and wants to discuss its shape. Should I, as premier, pretend I am deaf? . . . How can we prevent the opposition from seeming to be the personification of everything that is promising and beautiful while we represent nothing but austerity and tough decisions? Should we share responsibilities with them?" The plenum adjourned, ostensibly to consult the grass roots on these important questions (why had they not been posed before?), but in fact to allow Jaruzelski supporters (known as Jaruzeleks) and the hardliners to regroup. It was a busy Christmas for Polish Communism.

When the plenum resumed on 16 January 1989 the hardliners took the offensive. Miodowicz stressed that only a national conference of Party members would have the authority to share power. But such a conference would not be able to meet before May. The timing would destroy the Round Table. The point of the Round Table, as far as the government was concerned, was to secure a deal allowing for Solidarity participating in, or at least supporting, parliamentary elections in June. Stretching the political calendar further would sabotage the talks and that naturally was the intention of Miodowicz, whose unions were surviving only because of the absence of Solidarity.

After listening to the debates Jaruzelski took his biggest risk since declaring martial law. He called in Kiszczak and the Defence Minister Florian Siwicki, the two politicians closest to him, and told them he would offer his resignation to the Party. Kiszczak and Siwicki said they would join him. Later, when Rakowski was told, he too promised to resign. If the Central Committee failed to vote for Jaruzelski – and the Round Table – Poland would thus be left without a Party chief, without a head of state (the job was also filled by Jaruzelski), without a prime minister, without an interior minister and without a defence minister. Jaruzelski gave the Party a choice – vote for the Round Table (and the legislation of Solidarity) or plunge the country into constitutional crisis. When it came to the confidence vote, only four members of the Central Committee voted against. The vote on political and trade-union pluralism was less clear cut. There were 143 votes in favour, 32 against and 14 abstentions – that is, about one-third of the Central Committee were against opening up to Solidarity. Rakowski believes, probably correctly, that if Jaruzelski had not blustered the Central Committee into a vote of confidence beforehand, the voting would have gone against the restoration of Solidarity. Walesa began to respect Jaruzelski as a political actor from that moment. Earlier he had felt some sympathy for Jaruzelski as a man – Walesa sided with those who regarded the general as a supreme patriot – but was not overly impressed by his political skills. "The ten-hour discussions on restoring Solidarity were stormy enough for General Jaruzelski to demand a vote of confidence for himself and the result was highly positive for him," writes Walesa in the second volume of his memoirs. "No matter what one's views are, it is obvious that on 18 January, at three o'clock in the morning, the Party came to a historic decision."

Within a week Walesa was meeting with General Kiszczak to work out the three main working groups at the Round Table. There was to be a group on economic and social policy led by Professor Witold Trzeciakowski for Solidarity, a group dedicated to restoring Solidarity led by Mazowiecki, and a third group on political reform whose chief negotiator, on the Solidarity side, would be Bronislaw Geremek. These were the so-called little tables that would handle the kind of detail that could not be discussed in full sessions. The little tables were in turn split into other groups dealing with the reform of the judicial system, the mass media, local government, education, science, youth, housing, mining, farming, health and many other subjects. It was becoming a huge undertaking and Walesa found himself at the centre of an intellectual hive, a queen bee served by sociologist drones, scores of doctors and professors with contributions to the future blueprint. Walesa had spent the months of bargaining calming down expectations, warning Poles – and intellectuals seemed to need greater reassurance than workers – that the Round Table would not lead to the immediate overthrow of the Communists. Even Rakowski had been impressed by the moderate tones that Walesa had struck on a visit to Paris at the end of 1988. To some it seemed as if Walesa was becoming more like Jaruzelski and Jaruzelski more like Walesa. But these were merely surface impressions. Walesa was taking his usual vague tack, wary of committing himself before the bargaining began in earnest.

On a bitterly cold January evening in 1989 students packed into the Rudy Kot (Red Cat) club in Gdansk to listen to Lech Walesa. The mood bordered on the carnival. There was a reasonable hope that if Solidarity was allowed back, then so too would NZS, the independent students' organisation that had been providing so many underground writers and printers. But the students wanted to know more. How far was Solidarity from sharing power? Or how close? And where were the limits of compromise? Walesa was good, quick on his feet, convincing. "The Germans, in particular, are asking me why we refuse to fill the posts of deputy premier and four cabinet positions. They are saying, take it, Mr Rakowski is giving these posts to you. But we won't because it is just an invitation. The system has always worked on the basis of invitation. Even in the times of Mr Sadowski [deputy premier in the preceding government] they told us: please, opposition, join us, help us arrange credits or debt forgiveness. And eventually you will help us to build prisons. If you're still naughty, we will lock you up in them."

The students roared with laughter, slapping their knees. "That was a joke of course. Of course." More giggling. Walesa had developed the high-speed delivery of a stand-up comic. "But in any case: we say no. The point is that we may have one instead of four ministers, providing we get the post in accordance with the law. We're going to take things when we deserve them, not when we are invited. Today they want to give some room away to us because they are getting thinner. We will sit there but what if they regain weight? Then they will push us off again! So everything has to be divided structurally. Of course with the leading role [of the Communist Party] in mind, but slowly we will build different structures."

How slowly? Rakowski's diary records a meeting with a Mr M and a Mr G, presumably Mazowiecki and Geremek. They are asked about timing and G replies that he can see Solidarity being fully restored in five years. Rakowski's memoirs are not wholly trustworthy and the initialled Solidarity advisers are a particularly arch gesture. But there was a consensus among Solidarity experts that the restoration of Solidarity had to be viewed over the long term. The priority was to gain a watertight government committee and then to change the political environment to allow Solidarity to function properly. Solidarity underground leaders like Wladyslaw Frasyniuk knew that this was nonsense; government promises were designed to be broken. Walesa agreed with him. There had to be an early determined push to legalise Solidarity. If everything else failed at the Round Table, he would still emerge as a victor.

The plenary talks which began on 6 February were held in the white-washed Radziwill Palace on Krakowskie Przedmiescie Street, the place where the Warsaw Pact was born. The table had been rescued from the factory warehouse. It was some eight metres broad because, as the Warsaw wits had it, the world spitting record was only seven metres. Kiszczak in his opening speech stressed that Solidarity could become legal again only if the opposition helped to work out a programme of economic reconstruction and participated in "non-confrontational" elections to parliament. Walesa followed the secret-police general and said Poland was still "feeling Stalin's breath on their backs". If Solidarity was to participate in an arrangement that would drag Poland out of this systemic crisis then it must be given more responsibility. Indeed there should be "a direct relationship between the degree of participation and the degree of political responsibility". This broadly defined the position of the two sides after months of exploratory talks. The government wanted Solidarity to acknowledge the socialist system and strike a historic compromise with it. A constructive opposition could be allowed in a limited dose in the lower house while a newly created upper house, a senate, with limited powers would accommodate even a majority of dissidents. Solidarity would curb strikes, help work out an economic policy with market elements (including unemployment and bankruptcy) and share some government responsibility. Solidarity wanted to broaden the agreement and ensure reforms in every corner of society, thus making a nonsense of the constitutional provision for the leading role of the Communist Party. Apart from Walesa the opposition keynote speakers were a farmer activist, Josef Slisz, and the veteran Catholic editor Jerzy Turowicz. In that way Solidarity showed that it was shadowing the government in every sphere – workers, peasants, intellectuals. Walesa was determined to demonstrate that Solidarity was not entering these talks as a junior partner but rather as a legitimate spokesman for most of Polish society. That, and not its capacity to call strikes, was its bargaining power.

The important horse-trading, however, was not contracted in the Radziwill Palace but at a government villa in the small village of Magdalenka outside Warsaw. The house was a recreation centre for secret-police officers, set in woods and always ringed by Interior Ministry guards. In the lead-up to the Round Table, Walesa and his team had been dealing with Kiszczak in a comfortable four-bedroomed house in Zawrat Street, barely fifty metres away from Jaruzelski's home. But as the need for more experts grew the two teams moved to Magdalenka, which had a large conference room and its own telephone exchange. Magdalenka became a contemptuous label among Walesa's critics for secret deals struck with the Communists both before the Round Table and during it. But as Walesa points out, all serious negotiations had to have a private dimension. The Round Table plenary sessions were something of a political circus with regular briefings and photo-opportunities and leaks from both sides. Magdalenka was where the serious dealing was done and Walesa, who rarely attended the official sessions of the Round Table, was in his element there. Somewhat nervous when making formal prepared speeches, Walesa preferred the hard-edged poker play in which the crucial thing was not to speak grammatically correct Polish but to guess the hand of the opponent. The two Magdalenka teams – bussed out to the village like rival football squads heading to a match – met five times during the Round Table and essentially settled the future of Poland there. Information from these sessions is sparse but Krzysztof Dubinski, Kiszczak's personal secretary, took notes. After a month of formal Round

Table talks the two sides were not making much progress so the Magdalenka troubleshooters were called into action. Kiszczak, anxious to hold parliamentary elections as soon as possible, urged Solidarity to speed up its work on a draft electoral law. The government version expanded presidential powers (on the assumption that Jaruzelski would become president and act as a guarantor of Poland's socialist status), the senate was to be appointed not elected, and opposition candidates were to be placed on the so-called national lists which allowed individual candidates to enter parliament more or less automatically. According to Dubinski, Walesa chipped in: "I do agree that a president is a necessity and I accept the need for guarantees. But it has to be a more democratic president. A presidency as you suggest it would probably end up as a presidency for life and you could probably only get rid of him by execution. So what you seem to be saying is: here you are, boys, you're getting more than you wanted but your bill is also four times higher. We can't accept that. We don't want to end up in a corner worse than Stalinism." Geremek added that a non-elected senate was out of the question. Moreover the president should be elected by the whole nation and have less power to dissolve the parliament.

Dubinski's notes laconically sum up how far the two sides were from an agreement despite a month of talking. "They listed the problems on which there was still disagreement: the legal status of the independent student organisation NZS, reforming the courts, amending the law on assembly, creating Solidarity newspapers, access to television and radio (Solidarity insisted on setting up additional TV and radio channels). Ireneusz Sekula then said that in order not to worsen the atmosphere he had postponed price rises until June. Solidarity men still insisted that they be given 40 per cent of the seats in the Sejm but the government is prepared to give only 35 per cent."

The meeting then took a curious turn. Walesa and Geremek again stressed that they were not interested in a second house of parliament that was not elected. It would suggest that Solidarity was being co-opted and would disguise the real strength of the opposition. Suddenly Alexander Kwasniewski, the youngest and most imaginative member of the Communist Politburo, came up with the idea of an entirely freely elected upper house (still with limited power) and a 35 per cent bloc for the opposition in the lower but more important house. The president would not be chosen by a national vote – Jaruzelski would not have stood a chance – but by both houses of parliament. Some quick calculations on an envelope convinced Kwasniewski that even if Solidarity won every seat in the Senate, the arithmetic was still in the Communists' favour and Jaruzelski could be elected. Walesa declared this proposal to be "interesting" and the meeting broke up. That, then, was how power subtly shifted hands. There are many unresolved mysteries which simply add to the general aura of conspiracy that surrounds Magdalenka. Kiszczak and Jaruzelski had wanted to compartmentalise the opposition, giving them a talking-shop – perhaps making Walesa senate speaker – while using the lower house to pass the really important decisions. Who then authorised Kwasniewski to present the new idea? Rakowski, perhaps, since he was Kwasniewski's political patron. Did that mean there was infighting between Rakowski and Kiszczak? Certainly there was not much affection binding them, if only because they were competing for the ear of Jaruzelski. Such speculation attended the whole Round Table process. Nobody pretended that it was democratic.

The Round Table established a common language between these two polarised groups, the ex-political prisoners and their warders. This was a matter of some amazement in the West and in neighbouring Eastern Europe but in Poland it was not quite so astonishing. Reform socialists on the Jaruzelski team had more than ideas in common with liberal members of the Solidarity élite. A photograph from the 1970s shows a crowd of intellectuals, mainly journalists, posing outside Rakowski's dacha on the Mazurian lakes. Sprawled on the grass there were the men who would be the intellectual core of the Jaruzelski–Rakowski team (including Jerzy Urban and Wieslaw Gornicki) and some of the most gifted critics of martial law (Dariusz Fikus, Ernest Skalski and many others). Most were associated with the weekly *Polityka* and, at the time, almost all admired Rakowski for opposing Communist-steered anti-Semitism in 1968 and numbskulled economic planning. That group was the nucleus of a new political class but it split, first over the meaning of the 1980 Solidarity strikes, and soon afterwards over martial law. Yet Warsaw is not so much a city as a set of interconnecting villages governed by ritual. These old colleagues, newly minted political enemies, kept in touch. Long ago they had inter-married and shared girlfriends so it was natural that gossip from the boudoirs of ministers would reach Solidarity, and that Solidarity intimacies would reach members of the regime like Urban. This cosiness made it possible for the government to consider a Round Table. They knew that there were "sensible" people on the other side because a few years back they had got drunk together, discussed the world's problems after midnight, been on joint holidays. But this Warsaw ménage was not enough to run Poland or to carve it up. For one thing it excluded the bright workers who had won their spurs in the underground resistance. Bujak, well read and articulate, found some room for him in the Round Table salon, but the Wroclaw bus driver Wladyslaw Frasyniuk felt like a man from Outer Space when he sat down with the likes of General Kiszczak. He refused to shake hands. "Frasyniuk was at first very aggressive," recalls Dubinski, "and said that he just didn't understand why he was supposed to sit at the same table with the same people who had put him in prison and persecuted his family." Even Walesa had been something of an unknown quantity until the Miodowicz debate. Jaruzelski had called in Walesa's former platoon commander from his army days to try to understand his character. To Jaruzelski, Walesa was an almost completely baffling combination of respect and rebellion, of courtliness and brash vulgarity; Walesa made Jaruzelski angry. The fact was that Jaruzelski, from his sheltered army background and family roots in the minor nobility, was never part of the Warsaw circle. Nor was Walesa. They knew vicariously about the various ties connecting Warsaw intellectuals, but they were not in the gang and Jaruzelski at least had to grope to find ways of communicating. Kiszczak, though not in the Warsaw group, knew the opposition best, having had hundreds of individual meetings with dissidents since the declaration of martial law. But even for him the Round Table was a revelation. These men were not only intelligent – you could do business with them! "I wish I had got to know people like Geremek, Mazowiecki, Kuron, Modzelewski, Michnik, Frasyniuk, Bujak and Jaroslaw Kaczynski before," he lamented later. "We didn't know our opponents too well. Someone somewhere had once defined them, and we simply added to this definition later."

By and large the Party regarded the opposition as a monolith and did not really distinguish between Michnik, on the liberal-left of Solidarity, and the determined anti-Soviet nationalism of Leszek Moczulski. As far as the average Communist was concerned it was all much of a muchness, a demonic goulash kept on the boil by the Western intelligence services and stirred up a bit by the Pope. But some names did stand out. Geremek was feared, perhaps because he had been in the Party and was therefore bilingual. And Kuron and Michnik were fixed parts of the Rogues' Gallery. There was therefore strong resistance to the participation of these men at the Round Table. Walesa stood firm.

Geremek, whose personal loyalty to Walesa was being seriously tested by Walesa's temper and whims, was reassured by this gesture. "The authorities had believed for years that the Evil Spirits of Solidarity and the puppet-masters of Walesa were the intellectuals and advisers, especially Mazowiecki

181

and myself. Suddenly they saw that Walesa himself was absolutely determined to include Michnik and Kuron in the delegation and that he ruled out any negotiations without their participation. I suggested compromise then but he rejected it. He grasped that the Round Table talks should not begin in an atmosphere of concessions and weakness." Kiszczak eventually took the personal responsibility of allowing Michnik and Kuron to take part. By most accounts it took some time to persuade Jaruzelski, who shared the Party prejudice against the two dissidents.

After the sides had lined up, the political lexicology could begin. Dubinski captures the mood well: "The essential element was translating the language of our side into the language of the other, how we understood different concepts and named different things." Stanislaw Ciosek said the Communists and the dissidents had to work out which values they shared. How for example did Solidarity understand the term socialism? Geremek replied: "You mean what kind of socialism do we accept? Well, as far as state ownership of the means of production is concerned we won't be able to make an agreement. But if we look at the Pope's encyclical *Laborem Exercens*, his writing about man's relationship to labour, well there we can find a starting-point." Papal socialism? Not exactly, but they could start talking about removing ideology from everyday life, from the running of the state and the economy.

It was a time of mutual fascination. "The authorities eventually saw that the guys facing them were not enemies or foreign agents but rather normal people who were thinking in terms of the national interest," says Dubinski. "As for the other side, it had to overcome similar fears. They expected stupid thugs, eating raw meat with their fingers and dreaming of locking them up in basement cells." The educational process of the regime was helped by a massive eavesdropping operation. General Pozoga writes that Kiszczak knew almost everything about the intentions of the opposition "because their phones had been efficiently tapped". Even the Church advisers were being bugged.

The Round Table also introduced, or re-introduced, Solidarity figures to ordinary Poles. Every evening a Solidarity leader – Geremek with his pipe, Kuron in jeans, Janusz Onyszkiewicz carefully positioning a microphone – would appear on state television and give their version of the day's talks. After several years of Urban's sarcasm and half-facts, the candour and straightforward language of the Solidarity spokesmen was both shocking and refreshing.

The talks made Solidarity *salonfaehig*. Not only the Poles were surprised by this government somersault. Every regime in Eastern Europe was running scared. Above all the East Germans, treated to thorough daily coverage of the Round Table by West German television, started to ask themselves some fundamental questions. For East Germany to abandon socialism – and there was little doubt that this would be the ultimate effect of the Round Table – meant not reviving the state but scrapping it completely. Without a Communist regime East Germany had no *raison d'état*; it might as well become West Germany. Soon enough, hundreds of thousands of East Germans had come round to this opinion. The huge East German exodus through Hungary and Poland that summer was directly triggered by the Polish experience. The average East German had sneered at his Polish neighbour yet it was obvious that Poles were carving out more individual freedom than East Germans could ever hope for. It was no longer a matter of waiting for Honecker to go or even giving him a bit of a shove. The state was *by definition* unreformable. That was why Walesa claimed with some justice that he played his part in dragging down the Berlin Wall. His contribution was duly credited by Chancellor Helmut Kohl.

Walesa's role in the Round Table has been played down in Poland partly because he did not take part in most plenary sessions, partly because much of the brainwork was obviously carried out by Mazowiecki and Geremek and the army of over one hundred experts and analysts. Yet Walesa's was the decisive voice. Geremek, who had the chance to watch him closely, was impressed.

It was Walesa who decided to meet Kiszczak on 31 August 1988. "All Walesa's advisers could do was argue for or against the idea, and we were not unanimous about it," remembers Geremek. "The situation in Poland certainly demanded a show of goodwill but that could be done in a number of ways. So the decision was left up to Walesa because it was he who was taking the risk." During the Magdalenka talks Walesa was tough not only about the legalisation of Solidarity and the participation of Michnik and Kuron, but also about rescinding the decision to shut down the Gdansk shipyards. He eventually won that fight too. When Kiszczak made opening speeches at Magdalenka, it was Walesa who usually replied – without a script and without time to consult his advisers. He was, in short, anything but a marionette. "The key decisions were always made with Walesa's participation," stresses Geremek. Moreover, Walesa was also travelling the country urging patience on factory workers. The talks were being held to a constant drumbeat of wage protests and warning strikes. Sometimes these helped the Solidarity negotiators since they added a sense of urgency to government decision-making, but it was a time for closed Solidarity ranks and Walesa pulled the movement together.

The Round Table was Walesa's political coming-of-age. It was not just that he outboxed the Communists. He showed himself to be a good cabinet politician, capable of leading government. There was perhaps too much conspiracy involved in his style of leadership. Then, as now, Walesa preferred to play one adviser off against another, and would later shrug off criticism by declaring it to be "pluralism". After his first session with Kiszczak his closest advisers tried in vain to find out details of the discussions, but Walesa preferred to wrap the conversation in mystery. Although the Round Table had tried to expand the political class beyond the reform socialists on both sides, the talks excluded many of the fringe players in Polish politics: the nationalist right was under-represented, so were worker radicals and of course hardline Communists.

The sense of exclusion helped to foster the idea that Walesa had sold out, that he was by his very nature predisposed to compromise with the Communists; that he was far too intimate with Kiszczak. The Round Table outsiders had by 1992 come to form a substantial chunk of the Polish political spectrum. And they asked what seemed to be pertinent questions about Walesa's behaviour during those early talks. Why was it necessary to make foul compromises with the Communists when Communism was about to collapse? The Round Table froze Poland in a compromise when the rest of Eastern Europe was ditching the Communists. Did Walesa agree to leave the Communists alone, to protect them from show trials, to let them slip into private businesses and become comfortably rich?

Predictably, all the Round Table participants deny that any secret deals were struck: Kiszczak, Pozoga, Geremek, Mazowiecki and many others are on record as saying that the closed sessions in Magdalenka did not offer an escape clause for the Communists or in any way corrupt the policies of the future Solidarity governments. Walesa is quite straightforward about Magdalenka. First it was entirely natural that he should have private talks in parallel to public negotiations: that was the way of politics. "There were no additional contracts signed at Magdalenka. It was simply a place where both sides could negotiate the most important issues in peace without television cameras and crowds of curious onlookers . . . all experienced politicians know that such informal groups have to exist behind the scenes of formal negotiations. Certain concessions, ideas and bargains demand privacy." Second, nobody could predict that Communist rule would tumble quite so rapidly in Central and Eastern Europe. To say that the end of

Communism was inevitable, especially after the Round Table, was not the same thing as saying it would break by the end of 1989. Everybody – dissidents, Western observers, politicians in East and West – had been operating on different time-scales for the previous four decades. Solidarity had become accustomed to a set political choreography; they were prepared to seize the initiative but only within the established rules. It was Walesa's genius to think three steps ahead and while he too was surprised by the swift surrender of the Communists, he was not paralysed by it. The June elections, the voting for Central Europe's first semi-free parliament, provided an example of his particular genius.

The large group of intellectuals who had been meeting with Walesa – originally known as the Group of 60 and then as the Citizens Committee affiliated to Lech Walesa – became the Solidarity campaign team for the elections. During a session in a Warsaw church they agreed that Solidarity should make full use of its legal status (granted on 17 April) in the election campaign, that local branches of the Citizens Committee should be set up, that candidates for parliament should be drawn from all social classes and from the right and left of the Solidarity movement. The group already sensed the divisions within Solidarity. The union was an anti-totalitarian coalition and was geared to fighting a particular brand of Communist rule. As the regime weakened, and sought partnership, so Solidarity was losing its cohesion. Walesa told the meeting: "We're not a political party and yet we have to fight in an election. We have to do it as a formation that unites the whole opposition." The talk at the Round Table was of "non-confrontational" elections. What did that mean? Geremek stressed that it should not mean Solidarity pulling its punches: "We must be sure not to lose these elections because they will be a test of strength for Solidarity and civil society."

The regime, by contrast, was rather complacent about the elections. It was the Communist side of the Round Table that had pressed for early elections mainly because it wanted to wrongfoot Solidarity. The Party and its two allies, the ZSL peasants party and the small Democratic Party, had ample funds, local organisations, placement throughout every level of the state machine, and clear identities. If they acted quickly they would gain from a Round Table bonus; look, they could say, we did this, we're both decent and safe. Solidarity? A bunch of dissidents with their heads in the sky, some rabble-rousing workers – a chaotic combination despite their popularity. The main concern of the Party campaign managers was to avoid winning by too big a majority. That would look bad, like the old days; the

West and most Poles would think that the counting had again been cooked. It is difficult to say whether this was naivety, arrogance or a suicide instinct. There was always a strong body of opinion in the Party that believed in a suicide-faction, avowed liberal Communists whose every action appeared to be geared to the ultimate destruction of the Communist Party. Stanislaw Ciosek, the chubby Communist youth league organiser who was rolled out against Walesa in the early 1980s because he could speak without resorting to ideological clichés, was regarded as the head of the suicide-faction. It was significant then that the most important figure in the Party election campaign was Ciosek, and interesting that Walesa honoured Ciosek's incompetence, or death-wish, by keeping him as Poland's ambassador to Moscow well into the 1990s.

Solidarity was far from confident about the outcome of the election. Walesa told his associates that he would be happy with some 25 per cent out of the allotted 35 per cent of seats in the Sejm and some 70 per cent in the freely elected senate. It was the enthusiasm of the campaign that tipped the balance and gave Solidarity such sweeping victory. The campaign began formally on 10 May 1989 but in some senses it had been under way for over seven years. It was to be a plebiscite on Communist rule and specifically the first honest chance for Poles to say what they thought of martial law and the men who had imposed it. There were naturally disagreements over how the campaign should be fought, and Walesa won every major point. Mazowiecki, for example, wanted Solidarity to put forward several rather than only one candidate for every seat. Walesa rejected the idea. Bujak remembers: "As a result Mazowiecki refused to run for parliament. Lech was angry with him because he wanted to see Geremek as head of the Solidarity faction in the Sejm and Mazowiecki in the senate. Had Mazowiecki's concept won, our victory would not have been so spectacular." Instead Solidarity candidates were put forward by regional Citizens Committees and the national committee then verified the choice. The future MPs and senators tended to be ex-underground activists, members of the Catholic Intelligentsia Club, academics associated with the Primate's advisory council – people known and trusted within the Solidarity milieu but not necessarily to the public.

To promote their candidates, Solidarity ran an improvised, but very effective propaganda campaign. The Round Table had cleared the way for a Solidarity daily newspaper, provisionally called the Election gazette, *Gazeta Wyborcza*. A cooperative including Bujak, film-maker Andrzej Wajda and journalist Alexander Paszynski, secured a bank loan and guaranteed the paper's independence, though the slogan on its front page – "No Freedom without Solidarity" – plainly identifies its politics. At the head of the editorial collective was Adam Michnik and he gave a spark to the new paper, which was snapped up quickly at least in Warsaw where it was printed. By its third issue it had published the 26 points of the Solidarity election programme which promised that Poland would have moved to full democracy within four years and that a market economy would be in operation. Other issues of the paper profiled candidates for parliament. These articles were in turn picked up by Radio Free Europe and the BBC Polish service (no longer jammed) and broadcast throughout Poland. The Church, which had benefited from the Round Table (it was again allowed to buy and sell property, to run hospitals and schools and radio stations, nuns and priests were now eligible for state pensions), was unmistakably on the side of Solidarity. This made itself felt particularly in the countryside, where the priest still had the ability to steer the public opinion of a whole village. All this weighed heavily against the government, which was relying on the state monopoly of television and radio. Television had penetrated virtually every household in Poland and was regarded by the Communists as the most important mobilising force in society. While newspapers devised ways of wriggling past censorship, television was kept under firm central control. Walesa realised that despite all the energy being ploughed into the Solidarity propaganda campaign it was still an uneven match. He thus agreed to have his photograph taken with every Solidarity candidate and to have hundreds of thousands of wall posters run off. The aim was to give the blessing of Walesa – instantly recognisable – to even the most obscure aspiring politician. Walesa's critics immediately accused him of starting a personality cult. Afterwards he would be able to say, plausibly, that Walesa, rather than Solidarity, had won the election. That certainly was the suspicion of Zbigniew Bujak, who refused to stand for parliament rather than stand for a mug-shot with Walesa. "I didn't want to be an MP on the basis of a picture. My relations with Lech were quite specific – because I represented Warsaw he regarded me as a rival. A photo with him – a kind of knighting ceremony – did not appeal to me."

Walesa also resisted pressure to stand for parliament. There were many reasons for this decision. The first was that Walesa has never felt at ease with the idea of parliamentary democracy. His personal experience, as a child of the Polish People's Republic, was that parliaments were peopled with eunuchs. The historical experience, of squabbling nobles talking endlessly, was not encouraging either. Moreover, Walesa still did not feel comfortable with the idea of becoming an institutional politician. He toyed with the presidency but realised that it was destined for Jaruzelski. Walesa's instinct as usual was to avoid commitment until the political landscape could be clearly viewed.

It was the sense of political acceleration throughout Eastern Europe that probably sealed Solidarity's triumph at the polls. There were cracks emerging everywhere. In May Vaclav Havel was freed from jail in Czechoslovakia, and in the same month the parliament of Soviet Lithuania passed a declaration of sovereignty. The Soviet ambassador to Warsaw indicated that Moscow was giving Poland full freedom in sorting out its problems; there was a conviction in both the Solidarity and the Communist Party élites that Gorbachev was treating Poland as a kind of laboratory for socialist reform.

On election day, 4 June, every wall, every tree seemed to be plastered with portraits of Walesa and the local candidate. Some priests gave their congregation a last-minute shove. In Przemysl the doughty bishop Ignacy Tokarczuk told his parishioners: "I think you know by now who God would vote for in today's election." Millions turned out, though a significant chunk (38 per cent) stayed at home, apparently motivated by distrust of the Round Table agreement. Probably the decisive vote came not from the young but from the older generation, always the most disciplined voters. Those bitter at the treatment of the anti-Communist Home Army after the war, those who had been dispatched to Siberia, those who demanded the truth about the Katyn Forest massacres – they at last had somebody to vote for because Solidarity was committed to filling in the blank spots of Polish–Soviet history. The election was thus not only an anti-Communist plebiscite, but also an anti-Soviet one.

The victory was sweet, but slightly embarrassing. Solidarity candidates won 91 out of 100 seats in the senate and in the second round managed to capture a further eight. The lone non-Solidarity senator was a millionaire, Henryk Stoklosa, who had used his considerable fortune and local clout – his factory was a major employer – to mobilise votes. In the Sejm, Solidarity won 160 out of 161 seats available to it. The remaining seat was picked up in the second round. Solidarity had thus gained its full 35 per cent entitlement. The biggest humiliation for the government was the showing of the National List which comprised some 35 candidates who were deemed so important that they should be returned unchallenged. In the old days National Lists were a painless way of ushering into parliament members of the Politburo, and thus adding a deputy's stipend to their pay-packet. But under the Round Table deal List candidates had to win fifty per cent of the vote: 32 out of 35 failed. Solidarity supporters simply crossed out all the names on the List and put the obliterated paper into the ballot box. After some negotiation, Solidarity allowed new names to go through unopposed; it was not the time to upset the Round Table deal.

Walesa was overjoyed and kept breaking out in smirks even during official business. Jaroslaw Kaczynski remembers travelling to Gdansk the day after the results were known and finding his brother Lech breaking open a bottle of champagne with Walesa. Walesa playfully stood up from his desk and offered Senator Kaczynski his seat. "Quite right too because you are just an ordinary citizen," joshed Kaczynski. ("I didn't take the seat though – it doesn't do to take a joke too far with Walesa.") Writing in *Gazeta Wyborcza*, the poet Wiktor Woroszylski published a story: "Let us take joy in it!" The article struck a strange note for ordinary Poles because they were indeed celebrating rather as if they had just won a crucial football match, against, say, the Soviet Union. But the Solidarity leaders did not quite know what to make of the new situation. Four days after the elections there was an emergency session of the Military Council, the political command of the army. Jaruzelski, Kiszczak and a few other architects of 1981 martial law attended the session. According to leaks from the meeting various options were considered (and perhaps also ruled out): introducing a state of emergency, invalidating the election under some pretext. It was not entirely clear to these army politicians how the Russians would react, despite the numerous pledges of non-interference before the elections. The meeting was thus prompted by genuine anxiety but as far as Jaroslaw Kaczynski was concerned it was simply a way of frightening Solidarity into sticking to the terms of the Round Table. For Solidarity was indeed divided. Mazowiecki argued that Solidarity should now advance extremely cautiously and not pose an open challenge. For him the shootings in Tiananmen Square which had occurred on the same day as the elections was as much a warning signal as the Military Council session on 8 June; events in China showed that the pace of political and economic reform had somehow to be calibrated. The priority now should be to consolidate the political gains and work for economic changes. Kaczynski saw the humiliation of the Communists in more tactical terms. The Communists had lost their National List candidates; Solidarity should allow the Communists to fill the posts anyway – but only if the Communists agreed to quick, democratic local council elections. That way the impetus of revolution – or Garton Ash's "refolution" – could be maintained.

A new important debate had thus began, a debate about the pace of change. This issue was to dominate Solidarity's first four years in power and force Walesa to shift from one position to another, first presenting himself as an accelerator and then as a consolidator. As an accelerator he was denounced for destroying the Solidarity movement that he had created. As a consolidator he was denounced as a post-Communist stooge willing to tolerate old Communist structures in the army, the police, the foreign service.

The Solidarity élite was confused. What kind of victory had they achieved, what was its true value? "The iron rule of democracy is that if somebody wins elections, he has to start ruling the country," reflected Kuron. Poland was a democracy and the regulations had been constructed to ensure that the Communists would win. Yet not a single Solidarity candidate lost. All those deputies from the ZSL peasants party and the Democratic Party that backed Solidarity also won their seats. "At dawn on 5 July I immediately understood that the Communists would not be able to hold the government any longer unless they introduced a new form of martial law." The Round Table process however made martial law if not impossible then at least highly improbable. "So on that night I understood that we had to take the government and yet at the same time I quickly persuaded myself – and later, others – that we were in no position to take it, we were totally unprepared." The essential problem was a lack of people and a lack of governing experience. Only a parliamentary opposition has access to the necessary experience in working out a budget, the art of compromise and brokering between parties. Solidarity however had been a clandestine opposition, skilled at conspiracy, organising cells in factories, at printing books and leaflets, at writing stinging articles about the Communists. There were people of high calibre involved – professors, writers, shrewd workers like Bujak. "But," confesses Kuron, "we had no politicians in the sense of running the country. Taking power is more than joining the government élite. You need people to man ministries, local administration, right down to the lowest level of control, and so it was clear that we were condemned to a Communist administrative machine. I was certain that this machine would boycott us and we would end up as a government making decisions that would be worth no more than lavatory tissue." Solidarity thus had to concentrate on moving from the clandestine into the parliamentary opposition and wait its moment.

Walesa was not as certain as Kuron. He relied not so much on his instincts – events were moving at a speed that baffled even his sensitive political nose – but on his sense of natural justice. Solidarity had won the election. Yet the Communists would retain a powerful presidency, the government, the bureaucracy and dominate parliament. All Solidarity would have to show for its election performance would be a talking-shop in the Senate that could slow down unpopular or poorly formulated legislation. That did not seem right.

Walesa realised that most Poles would soon feel cheated, that their problems had not been solved and would not be solved in a framework that lacked a substantial Solidarity presence. There was thus a clear choice. Solidarity could make a run either for the presidency, or for the government. Walesa liked the idea of being offered the presidency though he would almost certainly have turned down the post; it was too early for him to make statesmanlike speeches and put on frock coats. The post, however, was never offered. The Communists insisted that the election of Jaruzelski was part of the Round Table deal. And even those closest to Walesa at the time could not see how the Solidarity leader could pull it off. Jaroslaw Kaczynski: "I thought then that there was no chance of Walesa becoming president yet – although it seems to me that he was already thinking on those lines. The Russians were probably not the problem but our army and our police would not have agreed. Still, who knows – perhaps I was wrong?" The acquiescence of the army and the police was essential not only because of the experience of martial law, but also because the newly defined powers of the presidency included supervision of defence and security policy. In 1989 Solidarity had barely penetrated the great Communist institutions of the Defence Ministry and Interior Ministries. KGB and GRU officers were very active, prowling around the ministries like nervous landlords worried that the tenants' children were scrawling on the wallpaper.

If Walesa was not to challenge for the presidency, then why should Solidarity not make a bid for the government? Kuron's objections had weight but for every one of his points there was a counter-argument. Who would reform the Communist-dominated bureaucracy if not a Solidarity-led government? The Citizens Committee, which despite fierce arguments (Walesa having been both for and against) had refused to disband after the elections, could become an important talent-spotter and allow budding young politicians to come to the fore in local and national government. The main thing was to find the right man for prime minister and to change the political debate, to steer it towards acceptance of a Solidarity government.

Many claim to have come up with the idea of a Solidarity government. Jaroslaw Kaczynski claims that it was one of his first thoughts after the June election, and unlike Kuron, he did not immediately have second thoughts. Kaczynski can of course say this because very few were interested in his thoughts at the time; even Walesa valued him more as a skilled reconnaissance pilot than as a squadron commander. "Walesa had the nose, Kaczynski had the ears," says a close member of the Walesa team. A Solidarity government was simply in the wind. Even reform Communists, such as the Politburo member and wily sociologist Janusz Reykowski, had been mulling over the plan. It was part of the informed, private debate that was continually under way in the narrow political class of Warsaw. Michnik seized on the idea and travelled to Gdansk to persuade Walesa. The Solidarity leader had decided that the presidency was impossible partly because of lack of support from Solidarity itself. On 1 July the Solidarity faction had decided not to put forward Walesa's name for the presidency because of "the lack of democratic conditions". It was the right, logical decision and yet Walesa was smarting; it was difficult to shake off the impression that his Solidarity colleagues did not take him seriously. There was some ritual tugging of the forelock, phone calls from his former advisers, but they often came after the event. Walesa was thus in a receptive mood when Michnik arrived at his home. That feeling of injustice could be corrected in another way. "Solidarity is being left on one side," he told Michnik, but perhaps he meant Walesa. More attentively than usual, Walesa listened to Michnik and caught some of his enthusiasm. Unlike most clever people with stammers Michnik's fluency tends to improve with excitement. He had in any case carefully worked out his pitch on the way to the Baltic. Michnik was convinced that he had found a formula not only for Poland but possibly even for the rest of Central Europe. The assumption was that Solidarity would do a deal with the reformist wing of the Communists, men like Alexander Kwasniewski, the chubby puppy-like figure who had first come up with the proposal for a freely elected senate. Such a coalition would split the Communist Party. Then, instead of the Party domesticating Solidarity, Solidarity would tame the Communists. Solidarity would run the show and blame all setbacks on the Communists of the past and the few Communists in the cabinet; it would be the exact reverse of what Rakowski had planned to do to Solidarity a few months earlier. The problem of a reluctant or hostile Communist bureaucracy would also be solved in this way. Kuron the doubter had already been convinced. After a night of hard drinking and talk with Michnik he agreed that it would be irresponsible not to make a grab for government: inflation was soaring, the shops were nearly empty, both society and the economy were close to a complete breakdown. Kuron told the Solidarity faction in parliament (known as OKP) that they should make government their next aim and extract a fair price for the election of Jaruzelski to president. The OKP was not very impressed, saying with some justice that Kuron had been arguing the opposite case for the past three weeks.

Walesa agreed with Michnik on the principle of a Solidarity government, but he was unsure about the soundness of clinching a coalition with reform Communists. He did not know well the new generation of Communists – Kwasniewski, Slawomir Wiatr with the permed black hair, the prematurely grey Leszek Miller – but he knew well enough how the Party worked. Walesa had too great a respect for the conspiratorial gifts of Communists to enter quickly into a political coalition with them. But he was sufficiently keen for Michnik to read approval in his response. By 4 July Michnik had gone into print with a crisp front-page article in *Gazeta Wyborcza* which announced, as if it were already fact, "Your President, Our Prime Minister." For many ordinary Poles it was the first glimpse of the discussion, since most of it had been carried out behind closed doors. Polish newspapers had yet to discover investigative journalism. The publication of Michnik's article suddenly spotlighted some fundamental questions raised but not answered by the Round Table process. Why should Jaruzelski, burdened by his martial law years, be so swiftly rewarded with the presidency? Why should this be regarded as an automatic decision? If there was to be a Communist president why did there need to be a Communist government to "guarantee" Poland's membership of the Warsaw Pact? Was head of state – with considerable, if ill-defined, powers over the army – not sufficient? Poles, carried along by the pace of change, had broadly accepted that the Round Table had to be a negotiation between two non-elected groupings. Now, for the first time, they were beginning to suspect that they were being railroaded.

Kaczynski and others on the centre right of Solidarity picked up these rumblings and made capital of them. "In my view," says Kaczynski, "there was a faction of Solidarity which believed in the reformist wing of the Communist Party and was planning to unite with it in some way. It was always striking how they fraternised during the Round Table negotiations. Probably the Communist negotiators did it on purpose – they wanted to create a new élite and opened themselves up to the new eager partners from Solidarity." Some, like Mazowiecki, believed that it was too early to move into government. Mazowiecki, who had taken over the new organ *Tygodnik Solidarnosc* (Solidarity Weekly), wrote a reply to Michnik: hurry up *slowly*. Kaczynski however drew a different conclusion. Why did Solidarity need to ally itself with Communists to form a government? Two other parties, the

ZSL peasants party and the Democratic Party, were both in play. For decades they had been the poodles of the Communists, pliant allies in parliament. But Solidarity had helped some of their deputies into parliament in June and they could be viewed as crypto-Solidarity men. Certainly, with the Communists obviously on a downward course, the ZSL and SD had to find a new foothold in parliament and society. With some careful seduction, Walesa might be able to woo these parties into a government, thrusting the Communists firmly into opposition. Kaczynski explained the arithmetic to Walesa, who then authorised Kaczynski to make the appropriate soundings. Two attempts at coalition-broking – with the Communists, and with the fickle allies of the Communists – were thus set in motion. The negotiators from all sides thought they were acting with Walesa's blessing; he could not lose.

Since the focus had shifted away from the presidency, Jaruzelski's managers assumed that their boss would be voted through parliament without a hitch. But this new parliament was a strange brew and the election of Jaruzelski presented an equally odd spectacle. On the Solidarity side many of the key deputies had served long years in prison. It was enough to look at the broken yellowed teeth of ex-KOR members like Jan Litynski, or Kuron, or Michnik to grasp that they did not have conventional political biographies. They were rubbing shoulders with members of the regime. Some, like Kwasniewski, were more or less on the same wavelength. Others had police backgrounds. One was a prison doctor at a time when Kuron as a young prison inmate was raped by convicts. That was not easy to forget or forgive. Others smugly claimed that martial law had been justified because without it, the Round Table would have been impossible. Andrzej Gdula, a Central Committee secretary and Round Table participant, shared this view. Kuron bumped into Gdula in the corridors of the Sejm. Gdula: "A minute ago I was asked by some French journalist what made me so happy about the fact that we have just given away power. And I answered – because I know the state in which we are leaving this whole business to them. They're welcome to it!" The parliament was like a city at war, with no-go areas, barricades, but also oases of peace. It was not a place where easy voting deals could be struck.

The election of Jaruzelski was the first serious act of parliament and the mood was tense. In the end, after anxious recounting, Jaruzelski scraped into office by one vote. Several members of the Communist alliance had voted against the general – but he had been saved by a handful of Solidarity deputies who, seeing how the tide was turning, clenched their teeth and abstained to save the general and the Round Table agreement, and thus ease the passage toward a Solidarity government. The most important election help for Jaruzelski had been rendered by Walesa who a few days earlier had stated that only "a representative of the government–Party coalition" could be elected president. It also said that Walesa would cooperate with any president, whoever was elected, because the well-being of Poland made it imperative. Jaruzelski was also given flanking support by President George Bush who had spent two hours with Jaruzelski before the election, when Jaruzelski's prospects were far from certain. He had also visited Walesa in Gdansk but it was the Jaruzelski encounter that was most politically influential. Walesa got on well with Bush (and Danuta Walesa with Barbara Bush) but he squeezed little out of the US President. Walesa told Bush that Western investment was urgently needed if political reform was to survive. The killing on Tiananmen Square had graphically shown what happens when economic and political reform was not coordinated. Bush, under budget constraints at home, talked freedom, not money.

Jaruzelski pledged as president to represent all Poles, not just the Party. On 25 July he called in Walesa and proposed a Grand Coalition, citing the example of West Germany's alliance in the 1960s between the Christian Democrats and the Social Democrats. That alliance, said Jaruzelski, had benefited the Social Democrats and the Polish equivalent would benefit Solidarity. It would grow into power. Walesa asked for concrete proposals but Jaruzelski made plain that Solidarity would be the junior partner in such a government. Solidarity would be given the ministries of Industry, Health, Ecology and Housing. Since industry made no sense without other economic portfolios, and since effective management of health, housing and the ecology – the three most serious crisis areas in Polish society – would depend on the goodwill of the Treasury, which would be under Communist control, Walesa politely declined. Under the circumstances, Walesa said, the opposition would stay in opposition.

Despite Walesa's conversation with Jaruzelski, Solidarity was preparing in earnest to take over government. There had been a meeting in a convent (to avoid bugging) and Walesa had heard again the powerful arguments for a coup in parliament. Michnik and Kuron – who were putting together a team of economists including market liberals like Stefan Kurowski and Jan Winiecki to work out a programme – put the case in favour, Mazowiecki the case against. Geremek stayed silent, as did Walesa who finally ordered "Mr Geremek" (Walesa always used the formal mode with Geremek and

Mazowiecki) to form a shadow cabinet. The assumption was that Geremek would be the prime minister of whatever government emerged.

Meanwhile Jaruzelski was reordering the Party and state hierarchy and perhaps unwittingly playing into the hands of those who wanted a Solidarity cabinet. Jaruzelski handed over the Party leadership to Rakowski. Every political mission that Rakowski had taken on since 1981 had ended in failure and there was no reason to believe that his Party leadership would be any different. He was given the job because he coveted it (all the old pretenders shrewdly withdrew) and because Jaruzelski wanted him to vacate the premiership. That was how Rakowski became the first – and the last – secretary of the Polish United Workers Party, presiding over its dissolution within six months. And Jaruzelski appointed his old army colleague and trusted police chief General Kiszczak to be Premier-designate. Although there was some Solidarity sympathy for the soft-spoken counter-intelligence commander, the sentiment did not overwhelm the memories of martial law. It was one thing to strike bargains with your former gaoler, quite another to join him in bed. Solidarity sharply protested at the choice of Kiszczak, but secretly rejoiced. As it was unthinkable to form a coalition government under the general's leadership, the whole idea of an alliance between the Solidarity left and the reformist Communists was now doomed. The picture might have been slightly different had Jaruzelski charged Kwasniewski with forming a cabinet. As it was, all the left-leaning Solidarity politicians approached by Kiszczak – the health system reformer Zofia Kuratowska, the economist Ryszard Bugaj, Kuron – rapidly turned him down. "I didn't even have to think about it," said one ex-dissident phoned by Kiszczak.

The Russians too seemed to be helping matters along. A Warsaw Pact session which a few years back would have shot warning signals towards Warsaw and started tank engines on the border, came to the conclusion that each member of the alliance could go their own way – the Sinatra Doctrine. A Kremlin functionary, Vadim Zagladin, went on record as saying that Moscow would accept whatever government eventually emerged from Poland; the impression given was that *any* government was better than none. The economic collapse of Poland was far more dangerous than the collapse of the Communist monopoly on power.

As Kiszczak struggled to find a cabinet – even Communists did not want to serve – Walesa put his cards on the table. "Once again I wish to protest against General Kiszczak forming the new government. The only solution in the present situation is appointing a government based on an alliance of Solidarity, the ZSL and the SD, and that will be my target." There had been soundings between Solidarity (mainly Jaroslaw Kaczynski) and the two Communist satellite parties, but so far nothing very concrete had been stated. Walesa's declaration sent the two parties into a spin. The atmosphere at the ZSL headquarters was like the morning before a débutantes ball; all humming and buzzing and fretting.

Two days after Walesa's statement, the ZSL had renounced its coalition with the Communists. The smaller Social Democratic Party was heading in the same direction. Plainly they could be lured into a Solidarity government with the promise of high posts – Solidarity was prepared to offer deputy premierships to both parties – a sensible economic programme and a mutually acceptable prime minister. It was that last point which caused the problems. The head of the ZSL, a big lumbering man called Roman Malinowski, considered himself to be a friend of Jaruzelski and shared the Communist élite's distrust of Walesa. But Malinowski himself was quickly losing influence within his party. Kaczynski, as the politician authorised by Walesa to talk to the other parties, thus had to adjust to a very fluid situation. The priority was to establish who Walesa wanted as prime minister. A little earlier in the game both Kaczynski and Adam Michnik had been convinced that Walesa should head the government. Kaczynski had driven up to where Walesa was spending the first part of his holidays, in the house of Danuta's mother in Sokolow Podlaski. Kaczynski arrived late (Walesa was in his pyjamas) and the two talked through the night. Kaczynski put the orthodox view: Kiszczak was failing, now was the time to move in, cobbling together a new coalition that would bring Solidarity to power, would Walesa take on the premiership? Walesa did not give a direct answer but commented that nobody had contacted him from Warsaw on the issue, not even Geremek who as head of the Solidarity parliamentary faction should have done so. Kaczynski was intrigued by this information. It suggested, he thought, a plot to move Walesa out of politics altogether. "On my way back to Warsaw I was thinking that either Kiszczak was stronger than he seemed to be – or that somebody was playing a different game and did not need Walesa for it at all." After Walesa's declaration that there could be no Communist–Solidarity alignment, Kaczynski and his twin brother Lech visited Walesa again to straighten out who should be the prime minister of the first Solidarity government. They found Walesa fishing in Wesiory. On the river bank the twins and Walesa's secretary Krzysztof Pusz talked through the choices with Walesa. The candidate had to be a symbol of the Solidarity movement and yet not paralysed by history. Preferably of the younger generation, suggested Walesa at first. But the only person of the young generation that the Kaczynskis could think of was Alexander Hall. Walesa waved away the suggestion. Walesa's original preference had been for Geremek – that is, he had charged Geremek with forming a shadow cabinet – but the Kaczynskis persuaded Walesa that Geremek was still emotionally wedded to the concept of an alliance with reform Communists. Kuron was not acceptable to the ZSL and SD; they had swallowed the decades of propaganda that had portrayed Kuron as mad, bad and dangerous. Jaroslaw Kaczynski put forward his friend Jan Olszewski, the burly human rights lawyer who had fought many good causes including defending the reputation of Father Jerzy Popieluszko at the trial of his killers. Walesa, however, distrusted Olszewski. He knew the lawyer was stubborn and strong-willed and that did not fit well into his plan for the future. Olszewski had publicly criticised the decision to enter Round Table talks and refused to stand for the Sejm. He had been closer to the Church than to Solidarity and was not a master of theatrical politics. He did not for example spend the strike days of 1988 inside the shipyards or the steelworks. Mazowiecki had made the gesture and was as close to the Church as Olszewski, perhaps closer. The more that the group brooded on Mazowiecki, the more appropriate he seemed either as Prime Minister or, if Walesa decided to take the premiership, a deputy. He was a conciliator, he had an international standing and he understood Walesa.

Walesa was thus talking himself out of the presidency and the premiership. Why? He was still head of the Solidarity union but strictly union affairs had no great fascination for him. It may be that Walesa had predicted the events that would follow: the break-up of Solidarity as a uniform political movement, the emergence of a party system, the political difficulties that a Solidarity government would face as soon as economic reform began to bite, the possible fall of Gorbachev in Moscow. All this was easy enough to foresee and it made a certain amount of sense to stay out of the fray. Walesa kept talking of himself as the "last card", the "matador" who goes into the arena to finish off an angry wounded bull. The most likely explanation of his self-exclusive behaviour during that hectic summer was that he envisaged an Italian-style *partitocrazia*. Governments would rise and fall and true power would be at party headquarters (in Gdansk, of course). In Italy it is party leaders who do the horsetrading and steer government; any prime minister who loses touch with his party chairman soon finds himself slaloming downhill. The informal role suited Walesa better than the premiership with its many technical detailed decisions and daily frustrations. The presidency, he was now convinced, was unattainable for the time being and was in any case moulded around the personality of Jaruzelski rather than Walesa. That left the role of puppet-master, and to pull those kind of strings he needed a more pliant figure than Olszewski. Mazowiecki seemed just right.

Jaroslaw Kaczynski at last managed to prime the ZSL and SD for a fully-fledged coalition with Solidarity. It had taken some skill and Kaczynski, who could never quite shed an air of self-importance, had made a few enemies on the way. Why was he bargaining secretly with the party machines of the ZSL and SD, and not with those parties' deputies in parliament? Why was Geremek not entrusted with the negotiations? Kaczynski flourished a letter from Walesa that gave him the personal authority to find a coalition. Kaczynski explains the anger of the Solidarity establishment in two ways. First, Kaczynski was a minor figure, a walk-on character in the revolution. "It was an absolute precedent, that is what shook them," wrote Kaczynski. "For the last eight years various Solidarity people dealt with various problems but when it came to really important matters it was only Mazowiecki, Geremek and sometimes Stelmachowski who took care of them . . . it was a total change of front on the part of Walesa, an experiment." The second reason for Solidarity's irritation with Walesa and Kaczynski was that Kaczynski had thwarted a future Solidarity–Communist government. This explanation is presented by Kaczynski himself and is rather suspect especially because it endows him with near-heroic status: the man who single-handedly prevented a creeping Communist counter-revolution. Certainly Kuron and Geremek deny that there was any conspiracy to side with the Communists. The most important factor behind the rows and suspicions of those days was that the Solidarity deputies were beginning to savour the importance of parliament and wanted to protect their independence, their separateness from Walesa. The Solidarity leader was behaving as if he still controlled events. To the new deputies it seemed that Geremek had become more important. Where was Solidarity power concentrated? In parliament. Who led the caucus? Geremek.

None of this washed with Walesa. He had after all helped each deputy win his constituency by posing with them on posters. They were elected on a Solidarity ticket and Walesa was Solidarity. Mazowiecki returned from a trip to Belgium and was sitting in his untidy cramped office in *Tygodnik Solidarnosc* when Kaczynski announced himself. Kaczynski's brief was to find out whether Mazowiecki, having been pinpointed by Walesa and his associates, was actually prepared to take on the Prime Minister's job. Mazowiecki had had rather strained relations with Walesa since the 1988 strikes and he had openly opposed the idea of Solidarity taking over government. The visit was thus essential. But Kaczynski's manner jarred with Mazowiecki. The plump lawyer was offering different posts to Mazowiecki – a senator's position that had become vacant, deputy premier if Walesa were to become Prime Minister – to find out his general attitude towards power. Mazowiecki, tired and with a hacking smoker's cough, was not interested in this conversational foreplay, nor did he find Kaczynski an attractive emissary. "If Walesa has something to say to me, let him say it," he said after a while. "I don't see any point in passing on my thoughts through you." Kaczynski stressed that he was just trying to help and told him that Walesa could be found at the Europeijski hotel, a faded once-grand place that had become a Graham-Greeneish haunt of money-changers and prostitutes. Kaczynski was interested in more than the fleeting authority of the King's messenger. He was angling for a cabinet position and was thus keen to give the impression that the premiership was his brainchild. "Walesa was always aware of Kaczynski's ambitions but did not feel they got in the way," comments a former Walesa aide. "Everyone in Warsaw was saying that the Kaczynski brothers were manipulating Walesa. But of course it was the other way round."

The same day, Walesa and Kaczynski met Roman Malinowski and Jerzy Jozwiak at the ZSL headquarters. After a while they mentioned Mazowiecki's name as premier and the other two party leaders nodded agreement. Then Malinowski lumbered over to the telephone in the corner of the conference room and rang Jaruzelski. The President agreed in principle. Walesa was skating on thin ice. He had put together a government coalition on the basis of a prime minister who had not yet officially been approached, who had barely begun thinking about the half-offer. Worse, the whole deal had been worked out over the heads of the Solidarity parliamentarians. It was Walesa's characteristic fast shuffle, but this was the first time that he had used it in democratic circumstances; every one of Walesa's moves in those August days showed a contempt for the almost democratic parliament.

Walesa left it to Kaczynski to present the new alliance to the Solidarity deputies. The MPs were predictably furious. They had only been in parliament a month and already they felt like impotent backbenchers. Moreover the Solidarity–ZSL–SD line-up could only be set out in the sketchiest manner – Mazowiecki's name could not be mentioned – and this, added to Kaczynski's nervousness and unconvincing public speaking, gave the impression that the whole manoeuvre was a Walesa improvisation. Walesa was not yet at war with parliament, but he had made plain that it had only a subordinate role in the future Poland.

The next day Walesa, Malinowski and Jozwiak paid a call on Jaruzelski to secure his blessing for the new alliance and the *de facto* displacement of the Communist Party. Jaruzelski insisted that the army and Interior Ministry should be occupied by Communists and it became plain that the future government would have to live with General Kiszczak as Interior Minister and General Florian Siwicki at the Defence Ministry. Both officers were intimates of Jaruzelski and the president could thus claim to Moscow that the security of Poland within the Warsaw Pact was guaranteed. Jaruzelski also liked the choice of Mazowiecki as premier since he knew how to work within a broadly socialist system, had the trust of the Church, and was the last word in caution. Walesa portrays this meeting in a rather different light than some of the other participants. According to his version, he offered Jaruzelski a choice of three Solidarity premiers: Geremek, Mazowiecki and Kuron. In fact, Mazowiecki had already been approved the day before by Jaruzelski and there was never a chance that either the president or the prospective coalition parties would accept Kuron. It seems highly likely that Walesa lied about this encounter, and the reason is revealing.

Walesa knew that he would have to face the Solidarity deputies that same night. Kaczynski, humiliated the previous day, was determined that Walesa address the caucus if only to reinforce Kaczynski's authority. Walesa had virtually to be dragged to the meeting. Although the popular view of Walesa is that he is a man who does not shirk confrontation, he was simply scared of explaining himself to a justifiably angry gathering of his colleagues. Some, like Andrzej Celinski, could claim to have been among Walesa's closest associates. And somehow Walesa had to explain why he had overlooked Geremek in choosing the prime minister. Many of the deputies had been arguing that Geremek was a far wiser choice than Mazowiecki, quicker at making decisions. Zbigniew Bujak was fairly typical of the liberal-left of Solidarity in his judgment of Mazowiecki. Like many of his colleagues he liked and respected Mazowiecki but regarded him as too slow and too scrupulous, a man who would place personal loyalty over the smooth running of the state. "The decision was wrong and had Lech consulted me, I would have opposed it. I think only two people were qualified for the job: Lech himself and Geremek." Even some people who subsequently served in the Mazowiecki government shared this view. Still, Mazowiecki had become a necessary part of the equation. Certainly Primate Glemp was very pleased; he had been dreading the prospect of a Prime Minister Walesa.

Walesa steeled himself for the session with the deputies. He could not give Mazowiecki's name before, but after Jaruzelski's go-ahead he had to show his full hand to the Solidarity caucus. It was Jaruzelski who had chosen Mazowiecki out of the offered trio, because the general wanted someone who had the unquestioned support of the Church. This was undeniably true. By most accounts Primate Glemp had heaved a great sigh of relief when he found out that he would not have to cope with a Premier Walesa or a Premier Kuron or even a Professor Geremek. Mazowiecki, in his early days a member of the PAX pro-Communist church grouping, understood the ways of the Church, its internal politics and its limitations. But Walesa had not of course offered the trio to Jaruzelski. Walesa wanted to shift some of the responsibility for the choice to Jaruzelski in case it all went wrong. And he could see Geremek's face, flushed with anger at being passed over.

People who lie to save the feeling of others are not usually judged too harshly. But Walesa had set an uncomfortable precedent in his relations with parliament. This time his side-deals looked set to pay off, at least in terms of winning a Solidarity government. The price was the friendship of Geremek and the trust of many Solidarity associates. There would be more to pay later.

Walesa may have ridden roughshod over the feelings of his fellow-revolutionaries, but he had correctly judged Mazowiecki. Despite his show of reluctance, Mazowiecki would take the job. Before being driven to parliament, Walesa had dinner with Mazowiecki in the restaurant of the Europeijski hotel. Over pork chops, Mazowiecki had stressed that he did not want to be boxed in by anybody; he wanted to be prime minister in the British rather than French manner. It was a time, he said, for Poland to have good cabinet government and a strong executive. Walesa agreed – and disagreed. The Prime Minister obviously had to snatch as much power as he could from a Communist presidency. The Communists would certainly try to exploit their grip of the Defence and Interior ministries and expand their influence in other departments. Perhaps local Communists would try to block Solidarity decisions. No, Mr Editor (*Pan Redaktor*) should not let himself be pushed around. As for the Solidarity side, the Prime Minister should not become a plaything of the parliamentary caucus. The premier should lead parliament, otherwise it might end up like earlier Sejms, a chaotic distraction. Mr Editor was quite right. But Mazowiecki was not worried about being manipulated by the Communists – he had their measure – even less so by Geremek and parliament. He was nervous about Walesa and Walesa's men. The last thing he wanted to do was stuff his cabinet with the likes of Jaroslaw Kaczynski or even his more sympathetic brother. His condition for taking on the job would be that Walesa kept his hands off. Mazowiecki was too discreet to spell this out and so Walesa made no commitment. It was simply understood that there would be close cooperation between the two men, between Warsaw and Gdansk, between the Solidarity executive and the Solidarity symbol.

Kaczynski arrived to take Walesa to parliament and though the meal had dragged on, Mazowiecki had still not formally accepted the offer. But in the car Walesa said: "I can bet my head that Mazowiecki will agree." He had understood that Mazowiecki was not governed by vanity or ambition – the easiest qualities to manipulate – but by a priestly sense of duty and a web of personal and social commitments. More than any other leading opposition politician, he applied a moral litmus test before every decision.

The mission was accepted, the Sejm gave the go-ahead and the 62-year-old journalist tackled his first difficult task – finding a balanced and effective cabinet. The Communists, though excluded from the coalition, were prepared to be supportive of the Solidarity premier. In return they wanted more than the Interior and Defence ministries. They pushed for the Foreign Ministry, the head of the cabinet office, transport, communications and control of television. Mazowiecki showed his mettle and the Communists ended up only with Transport. The Foreign Ministry went to Professor Krzysztof Skubiszewski, a specialist in international law, who was acceptable to the Communists because he had been a member of Jaruzelski's broad consultative council. Geremek, a natural choice for the ministry, was not offered the post. Walesa's destructive influence was probably at work. Not only were relations between Geremek and Walesa strained, but Mazowiecki and Geremek were also now set on different paths. The trio who had made the Solidarity revolution, so complementary in many respects, had been pulled apart. Meanwhile Kuron was given the Labour Ministry – an inspired move – and a young economics lecturer, Dr Leszek Balcerowicz, was given the Finance Ministry, which soon took the major part in the running of the economy. Kuron had been working intensively on an economic programme for this government. Apart from professors Kurowski and Winiecki, Harvard professor Jeffrey Sachs (who favoured a shock-therapy treatment for Poland) had become involved in solving the very complex riddle of how simultaneously to cure hyperinflation – 1,000 per cent inflation was forecast for the end of the year – and to change from a highly centralised planning system to a market economy. Balcerowicz, a Solidarity sympathiser, was regarded as energetic and firm enough to launch such a plan. His fluent English would be an asset in negotiating with the International Monetary Fund and the Western creditor organisations.

All in all, it was an impressive team that included at least four former political prisoners. They were a modest-living bunch. Skubiszewski had been living in a one-room bachelor apartment with a windowless kitchen. Balcerowicz was taking buses and trams because someone had stolen a wheel from the family Polski Fiat. He carried his IMF papers in a US army surplus kitbag. Kuron's neighbours rang him early one September morning to warn him that a secret-police car was waiting for him in the drive. This had become normal procedure on Mickiewicz Street and was supposed to give Kuron time to pack his clothes and toothbrush before the police carried him off to prison again. This time it turned out to be his ministerial chauffeur. Half-naked, his face smothered in shaving foam, he leaned out of the bathroom window and bellowed at the driver: "Come back in an hour, nobody goes to work so early." Mazowiecki had also been living a dissident lifestyle. A widower, he had been sharing a cramped apartment with his two grown sons and spending more on cigarettes than on food. Their first moral decision came quickly. Should they return the smart navy-blue Lancias ordered by the Communists, should they take on the trappings of power? Most of the ministers favoured giving the Lancias back to Giovanni Agnelli or, more rationally, selling them off on the free market and giving the budget deficit a small boost. Healthier by far to bicycle to work. But Fiat was insistent: the Lancias had been sold at a substantial discount on condition that the cars were used by the government, a promotional concession. If the government was going to sell them off they should pay the full amount to Fiat. The Treasury could not find the necessary dollars and so the Solidarity ministers found themselves chauffeured to work in air-conditioned limousines with electric windows. Poles waited for the Solidarity cabinet to follow the example of Orwell's pigs and scrawl on the farmyard blackboard "Four legs bad, two legs good."

Warsaw enjoyed this comic-opera spectacle, beggars turning to princes; it had a certain charm even for the steelworkers, who were forced on payday to rush to the city centre and change their full salary into dollars since zlotys were losing value by the day. Gdansk, however, was not amused. Walesa complained that Mazowiecki's cabinet was too one-sided, too left-liberal. Above all he was angry that he had not been consulted in the fortnight of cabinet formation. True, Alexander Hall had been taken into the cabinet – as minister in charge of coordinating with non-Solidarity groupings – but Mazowiecki was probably planning to do this anyway. Jaroslaw Kaczynski, Walesa's eyes and ears in Warsaw, had been frozen out of the new establishment. "Mazowiecki's behaviour at that time was very clear," said Kaczynski, "the point was to deprive Walesa of all support. Nobody was suggested whom Walesa fully trusted, none of his closest milieu was given a permanent job." On 12 September 1989, Mazowiecki presented his government programme and his cabinet and became the first non-Communist prime minister in the Communist bloc. During his speech delivered in his usual ecclesiastical cadence, he stumbled and announced that he felt faint. Parliament was shocked. No cardiological equipment could be found on the premises and so a search ambulance (a vehicle specific to Eastern Europe, designed to speed around the main hospitals and find missing equipment or medicine) was dispatched. While the deputies sweated and speculated – could the first Solidarity premier have suffered a stroke within minutes of assuming office? – Mazowiecki disappeared through a side exit and emerged in Warsaw's royal Lazienki Park, a fine place that crosses the spaciousness of Hyde Park with the elegance of St James's. His jacket strung over his shoulders like a pre-war Polish officer he went virtually unrecognised until a crocodile line of schoolchildren passed by. "Look, children," said the teacher, *"Nasz Premier* – Our Premier." Nobody had said that of a post-war Polish prime minister before. Heartened, Mazowiecki returned, passed his ECG examination, resumed the speech and took office.

But the stage had been set for the Thermidor of the Solidarity revolution. In Warsaw, there was a morally rigorous, physically frail premier whose mission did not see much of a role for old revolutionary heroes. In Gdansk, there was a robust union leader without a real job, spoiling for a fight.

CHAPTER TWELVE

Ping-pong

The politics of Poland was defined by two factors in the autumn of 1989. First, neighbouring Communist regimes started to crash like airliners with defective engines and leaking tanks. Second, Lech Walesa had a headache.

Walesa was always offhand with interviewers and often tried to dramatise his indifference to journalists. Oriana Fallaci had been forced to question the solidarity leader in his bathtub, and his press spokesmen became skilled at soothing the wounds of visiting diplomats who were given similar treatment. This was easily forgiven. Rudeness, after all, is part of the revolutionary temperament, an impatience with protocol and form. Even so, our meeting in the autumn of that year was particularly brusque. We had talked several times before but Walesa was not interested even in exchanging a greeting. He was in a bad mood that would last almost uninterrupted for six months. "Just ask me what you want," he snapped as I entered his Gdansk Solidarity office with its G-Plan furniture and statuette of Pilsudski. His aide, Piotr Nowina-Konopka (later to be denounced as a "louse" by Walesa) looked up with the clenched anxiety of a political public-relations man while the Boss flicked through a newspaper. It was *Trybuna Ludu*, the Communist Party organ, and somebody in the Solidarity secretariat had underlined with a yellow marker pen all the crucial bits. Walesa did not give the impression of a happy man. The Springtime of Nations, the collapse of dictators in the East, the jubilant politics of the piazza in Prague, even in dour East Germany, all this merely deepened Walesa's depression. He had become particularly unpleasant to his courtiers, barked at his elder sons. On Saturday afternoons he would stride into the garden of his new villa in the Gdansk suburb of Oliwa and dig furiously with a spade.

The reason was simple enough. The telephone should have been ringing, and it was not. It was Walesa who had put together the first non-Communist government in Eastern Europe and the first dissident-turned-premier, Tadeusz Mazowiecki, was his creation. Yet Walesa, or "Gdansk" in the Polish political shorthand, was barely being considered by Warsaw. The Sejm was behaving like a free parliament and was beginning to accrue real power. And Mazowiecki was building up his own power base, separate from parliament and miles away from the Solidarity union. Kuron, as minister of labour, was setting up a network of soup kitchens and appeared on television every Tuesday night, his voice as usual branded by scotch and smoke, to present the social policies of the Mazowiecki government. A cool buck-toothed blonde, Malgorzata Niezabitowska, was government spokeswoman with a brief to give only neutral information and avoid the barbed polemics of her Communist predecessor Jerzy Urban. Their task, the task of most of the cabinet, was to prepare Poland for the harshness of market reform. Should that not have been Walesa's job? What exactly *was* Walesa's job? Walesa too had a regular spot on television – news conferences, every Thursday, from Gdansk. But over the months it was becoming clear that Walesa had little to say at those conferences. "Walesa had asked for and was readily given access by Andrzej Drawicz [Solidarity-appointed chairman of television]," says a television producer. "But it was obvious that Walesa had cornered himself. He wanted to criticise the government and yet he sensed that it was folly to do so. His phrasing became more and more Byzantine– nuances and jumbled metaphors that tried to disguise the fact that he had little new to offer." The very existence of the conferences showed that Walesa was dissatisfied, but Mazowiecki's team regarded this chunk of vanity-television as a cheap price to pay for institutionalising Walesa. He was a profoundly uncomfortable political presence. Chairman of Solidarity certainly, but elected rather narrowly by a very different union in 1981. Yet his pronouncements, prefaced by comments like "Polish society is unhappy/restless/dissatisfied . . ." were bowled from Gdansk at a more or less democratically elected government. Did Walesa have the right to speak for "society"? "I put them where they are and they would do well to remember it," barked Walesa during our talk that autumn. "Study the opinion polls – I'm top of every list."

But even his unchallenged popularity was beginning to fade. Mazowiecki was enjoying a long honeymoon. People liked his fatigue. Even his habit of sighing deeply into the microphone as if about to gasp his last breath, even that was attractive. Later, it would become boring and the premier's strenuous efforts to be fair would be held up as weakness. But for a while, as a contrast to the mannered slickness of Rakowski the premier pleased the

Poles. He did not please Walesa, however. Walesa had not reckoned with the personal popularity of Mazowiecki. The government would soon become swallowed up in the economic crisis and would have to betray the workers; that was built into the market-reform programme. That was why Walesa had been reluctant to take on the premiership. He preferred a Messianic role, to be the man, the only man, who could pull Solidarity out of the mud. Yet the workers proved more intelligent, more elastic than Walesa had expected. The months of hyperinflation were proving to be a swift lesson in market economics. A few years back workers were prepared to storm Party headquarters to protest against price rises. Now prices were going up by the hour, savings were being wiped out, many on a fixed income or with no access to dollars were being driven into poverty. The queues outside Western embassies were measured not in metres but in weeks; emigration seemed for many the only way out of the crisis. The Solidarity anti-inflation plan seemed credible, and so workers accepted the demands made of them. There was no choice; striking for higher wages made no sense at all if the value of the wages was eaten away by pay-day, and if there was little to buy in the shops. When Boris Yeltsin embarked on a similar anti-inflationary course in 1991 he had a similar experience – instead of mass worker protests, there was a great deal of understanding. But in Russia, as in Poland, the workers had merely put their government on probation. How long would it last? Walesa, who had braced himself to "save" the Solidarity government, suddenly found himself sitting on the reserve bench asking the same question.

Walesa's exile in Gdansk was not made any easier by the sense that other Central European states were rapidly overtaking Poland. The Poles has manoeuvred their way out of Communism, bargaining like carpet dealers. But the Czechoslovaks were making a rock festival out of their revolution, moving faster and with more brio. Most irksome for Walesa and his advisers was the fact that the Czechoslovaks appeared to have more control over their destiny. By the end of November the Czechs had jettisoned Milos Jakes and the Politburo. By the end of December, after a few rallies, Vaclav Havel was installed as president. There was a big fiesta under way on the other side of the Tatra mountains. As 1989 spluttered to a close, Poland still had a Communist president (he had swapped his uniform for civilian suits but the dark glasses and the stiff gait remained) and Walesa was virtually unemployed. Mazowiecki took Walesa's calls but rarely rang on his own initiative. The premier's view was that Walesa as king-maker had not lost his capacity to be king-breaker. There was thus a need to find a useful mission for Walesa but in the rush of events and the enormous workload – Mazowiecki's team was working 16-hour days – in the roar and the rattle, the "problem" of Walesa seemed to be of secondary importance. And the political class of Warsaw was growing cocky. The cocktail-party line in the capital ran as follows: the working class has had its day. This is an essentially bourgeois, liberal revolution: parliamentary democracy, property ownership, the establishment of sound middle-class values and an end to the artificially high rank ordering of the working class; that was now the order of the day. According to this argument, Solidarity had to wake up and realise that it was never really a union but an anti-totalitarian coalition that had accomplished its primary task. So too had its respected leader, Lech Walesa, who would always retain (the inevitable appendix) his mythic importance. He was the man who had thrown Communism on the rubbish tip. We wish him a happy retirement and we will never forget him. There was another, even more dismissive version: poor Walesa, he was losing his grip, becoming greedy, out of his depth, in psychological tilt, looking dreadful.

That was the tone of the intelligence reaching Walesa in Gdansk. It enraged him. Our talk during those days was larded with paranoia, with a sense of conspiracy and grievance. "Do you think I couldn't have had it all – the big cars and the girls?" His critics were "ticks on the hide of a rhinoceros". His head was bent seemingly staring at the sports page of *Trybuna Ludu*, and the words came out in an unstoppable gush. A young clean-cut man interrupted the conversation and Walesa shifted an attaché-case onto the desk, unlocked it and started to hand out wads of dollar notes. The Chairman had been to the bank before our meeting. At the end of the conversation, Walesa moved to the corner of the office and opened the case again, absentmindedly fingering the bank notes. "Well, that wasn't too bad, I always give good value, don't I." Then for the first time he grinned and started a low chant: "I'm so conceited, so conceited, so-o-o-o, so conceited."

The chattering classes had misjudged not only Walesa but also the political dynamics of Poland. The workers had not yet been displaced. Unlike the other anti-Communist revolutions – notably in Czechoslovakia – workers were the crucial element in overthrowing the Communists and while market reform cast them as victims any government would have to secure their acquiescence. As under Communist rule, the workers retained their collective power to defy leaders and derail unpopular policies; those were the terms of the modern *liberum veto*. Walesa understood the blocking power of the workers, especially in heavy industry, he had misjudged only the present mood. But few in the Mazowiecki administration had such insight. They believed that the relatively calm industrial climate signalled fundamental, not conditional, approval of the austere monetarism of Leszek Balcerowicz.

Walesa hated to mark time and such static periods always took their personal toll, bringing out his bitter, petty side. His personality had been fundamentally changed by the year of house arrest in 1982. In 1980–81 he had been the genius of the fast ricochet; ping-pong was his game. After the year of internment in Arlamowo he had become a more deliberate man. Isolation from the rest of the Solidarity élite had given him a sense of separate destiny, differentiated him from the union movement. Women who knew him then, and now, are particularly perceptive about his personal change; Lech became less charming, they say, and the light capriciousness that could thrill and motivate had given way to a duller, denser complexity. Walesa, speaking after the Round Table agreement was signed, publicly recognised that he had grown up as a politician and perhaps lost something as a man. "Many people complain that I have changed, that I used to be more emotional and that my smile was more sincere. Well, at a certain moment I had to descend from the trees and stop making faces. I have simply begun to calculate, to be flexible and smart. That's probably why those who liked to see the Good Old Boy Lesio are now yelling, 'Who is he really? A worker or a politician?' "

At the end of 1989 and the beginning of 1990 Walesa was trapped in another period of waiting. He was committed to action. At the age of 46 there was not the slightest question of retirement, though as usual he set riddles for visiting journalists ("perhaps I'll set up a business and become rich"). Like a parachutist he had to secure the best combination of posture and timing, while keeping his nerve and looking for a place to land. He could only act from a position of loyalty to Mazowiecki. To betray the Solidarity government after a few months, when it was still riding high, would have been absurd. Yet he had to begin a process of differentiation. The shades of difference that were already apparent in Solidarity had to be developed into alternatives. Ultimately Walesa was beginning to realise that Solidarity had to be destroyed in order to pave the way for a multi-party system. He had to take into account three elements. First, only he, the creature of Solidarity, could wield the hammer. Second, to break up Solidarity he had to establish definitely that he was still in control of the movement. And, crucially, he had to show that destroying the Solidarity movement was the wish of the majority of Poles. What happened later was still uncertain. "There'll be maybe twenty or thirty parties, but only a few will survive."

Walesa began to search for the appropriate blunt instruments and quickly came up with Zdzislaw Najder who, helped along by the Kaczynski twins, rivalled Walesa for destructive talent. Najder was a scholar, a literary critic who had written extensively on Joseph Conrad. He had also been a signatory of the Polish Independence Agreement in 1977, along with Jan Olszewski and others. This gave him solid dissident credentials, though more to the right of KOR. Najder had been out of the dissident mainstream in the 1980s chiefly because he took up the position of head of Polish section in the US-funded Radio Free Europe. The Munich-based station has always been a veritable cockpit of personal rivalries and Najder did not settle well in that most politically charged of broadcasting jobs. He stayed long enough for General Jaruzelski's military courts to sentence him to death for treason and espionage. The sentence passed *in absentia* kept Najder out of Poland until some months after the Mazowiecki government had been established. This profile suited Walesa well. Najder was not tainted by the Round Table, had roots in the Warsaw cultural élite but was manifestly not part of it, he was an international figure and, as far as Jaruzelski was concerned, an unforgiving one. He would make a good hammer.

Najder's return to Poland was one of the landmarks on the 1989–90 road away from Communism. In December parliament had changed the official nomenclature of the country to The Republic of Poland, dropping the Communist tag "People's". Factories, steelworks and shipyards were no longer named after Lenin or the glorious revolution. Mayors were obliged to draw up lists of politically suspect street names. Out went the old Marxist heroes, even quite brave ones, and in came saints and holy men. Warsaw gained a Pope John Paul Avenue and an entrepreneur, exploiting the open economic climate, promptly set up a sex shop in the street. The Royal Crown, knocked off Polish insignia by the Communists, was replaced and sewn or nailed to heads of eagles in every office of the land. The guaranteed "leading role" of the Communist Party was dropped from the constitution. Somehow none of these gestures quite met the mood of the Poles. In Prague the carnival-revolution was continuing, the Germans were storming towards unity (Chancellor Helmut Kohl had interrupted his sensitive reconciliation mission to Poland and dashed back to witness the pulling down of the Berlin Wall) and even Romania seemed to be having a tyrannicidal revolution. In Poland, the pioneer of the eastern revolutions, inflation was going through the roof and unemployment exchanges were being opened. Attempts to

211

revive the old insignia of pre-war Poland appeared more an admission of impotence than a symbol of triumph over dictatorship. Najder's appeal to Walesa was that he showed the next step forward in this rapidly changing world: the Round Table agreement had to be scrapped. Power-sharing with the Communists had shown itself to be an outdated and over-cautious policy. More, by leaving the Round Table accord untouched, the Solidarity revolution was being fatally compromised, robbed of vision and direction. Najder made a radio address on Radio Free Europe on 27 December – responding specifically to the new situation created by Romania's Christmas uprising – and had expanded it into an article for the government daily *Rzeczpospolita*. It was phrased in rounded, cultured terms but seemed to Walesa to go to the heart of the matter. There was, said Najder, an uneasy contrast between the great enthusiasm of the residents of Prague, Brno, Dresden and Leipzig and the muted sentiment in Warsaw or Lodz. "I believe that the Poles will survive because after all what else can they do? Lech Walesa is right when he says that a revolt against the government would be an act of disastrous folly. But there are other, no less important, more difficult questions: how will they survive this operation? In what moral shape will Polish society pass through this most critical stage of the crisis?" There was much resentment, he said. Czechoslovaks and Hungarians had stated clear demands for the withdrawal of Soviet army units yet the Poles in garrison towns were having to put up with the Russian presence with not even a distant prospect of their withdrawal.There was envy about the new rich, a collapse in social solidarity. "I'm afraid that the premier's right and cautious words about 'the prospect of better times' will not suffice. Steps towards democracy were at best faltering, amounting to an uneasy compromise with what was until recently the ruling party and, which is much worse, squabbling between groups and milieux that were recently in opposition." The army, militia and judiciary should be completely over-hauled. The Communists were still in control of the two vast ministries, Interior and Defence, and "they are changing very slowly, incomparably more slowly than in East Germany or Czechoslovakia". In short, Najder argued, to share power with a discredited partner was to deny the Poles the new world that they craved.

Walesa liked this text. It gave him the ammunition he needed. Instead of irritable backseat driving from Gdansk, he had been shown a way in which he could criticise Mazowiecki from the high moral ground. Significantly all the points mentioned by Najder became part of Walesa's presidential election programme nine months later. Najder's article mentioned Solidarity only once, the movement was treated as a thing of the past. The point now was to build a "state of our common good".

Walesa invited Najder to head the Civic Committees, or rather the Civic Committee attached to Lech Walesa. Winning a competition with the British embassy, Najder's committee managed to secure the lease on a small, elegant palace on Aleja Ujazdowski. Walesa told him: "You will be Walesa's man in Warsaw." Najder's specific brief was to mobilise the nation for early local council elections and later for parliamentary elections. "We will be a clearing-house for information, a telephone exchange connecting the masses with the leaders as well as a bridge between Walesa and the authorities in Warsaw. There should be less room for springing surprises." Perhaps Najder really believed this. In fact the Civic Committees were about to be remodelled into an offensive weapon, a revolutionary tool. Lenin had defined the aims of the October revolution as "electrification plus Soviets". Walesa's formula for the next stage of the Solidarity revolution, the 1990 phase, was "privatisation and Civic Committees".

Civic Committees were odd hybrids. The members included intellectuals, local teachers and doctors, men and women who had carried out minor but plucky tasks for the underground, anti-pollution experts, and, though they were clearly in a minority, some workers. They were the spontaneous off-spring of the revolution. Paris in 1870, under siege by the Prussians, had (in Frank Jellinek's phrase) "spontaneously reorganised itself into a miniature federal body" which then became the hub of the Commune government. The Russian strikes in 1905 and the 1917 revolution threw up Soviets, councils which incorporated many political leanings. Rebellious Berlin in 1918 created *Räte*, the Hungarian uprising of 1956 drew on councils. The original structure of Solidarity was the factory and regional cell, a useful network in 1980–81 in that it provided a connection between otherwise isolated white- and blue-collar workers. This as well as the new (rather than fake Communist-steered) coalition between workers, farmers and intellectuals supplied the true meaning of "Solidarity". But more refined instruments were needed. The intellectuals had been summoned to Gdansk by Lech Walesa before the papal visit in 1987; their follow-up session that November created the first pool of Committee-men. Then they took on the function of organising the Solidarity campaign for the June 1989 elections and expanded their functions to include fund-raising and head-hunting. By the winter of 1989–90 they had begun to resemble other revolutionary organisations: they were pre-party in that they brandished the Solidarity banner in anticipation of the setting up of more formal parties. For the

213

most part such groupings have been regarded as temporary or transitional devices – Lenin's Soviets soon gave way to the Bolshevik party with its elaborate rules and choreography – and, as Hannah Arendt notes, they invariably strive to cling to power after their obvious function has ended. "Such councils obviously were spaces of freedom," writes Arendt of the Soviets and similar arrangements. As such they invariably refused to regard themselves as temporary organs of revolution and, on the contrary, made all attempts at establishing themselves as permanent organs of government (Arendt, p. 264). Walesa's fear was that the Civic Committees, having little else to do, were transforming themselves into a supportive arm of the Mazowiecki government and were thus fossilising the revolution. Civic Committees should have been providing new blood; instead they resembled a recycling unit supplying Committee-men to central and local government, and then applauding. For Najder, for the Kaczynski twins, and eventually for Walesa, the Committees showed not only that Mazowiecki was trying to build his own political base separate from Gdansk but also that there was a plan to create a monolithic Solidarity party. For Walesa that was tantamount to benign totalitarianism. The Communist Party structure was to be replaced by a Solidarity party structure, more democratic of course and more transparent but still vulnerable to the old temptations of unchallenged power. Najder's job was thus to take the Committees and turn them around: to shatter Solidarity, not to preserve it.

Najder thought that he had been chosen by Walesa because "I stay outside all mythical or real côteries – I am not a deputy or a senator or the editor in chief of a paper or a member of the government". This was a sound assessment. Walesa preferred to drum up what he called reservists who would owe their very career to him, who would be personally loyal because there was really no other choice. Najder, though, had his own circle of political friends, including Jan Olszewski, essentially national conservatives. And he had a difficult, prickly personality.

Adam Michnik flew to Gdansk as soon as he heard that Najder was to be made head of the Civic Committees. Michnik set out all the personal arguments against Najder: his rows and enmities at Radio Free Europe and at other times in his life. In short, said Michnik, Najder was a man of great integrity but he was not able to operate within a team; he divided rather than united. But Walesa was far ahead on this: he wanted Najder precisely for his fractious qualities. Najder, the excluded politician *par excellence*, was to work for the many (politicians and ordinary people) who had been excluded from the political process. His brief would broaden the Civic

Committees – Najder eventually admitted 22 new members representing groups previously unrepresented in the Committees – and thus throw open the gates. Najder would either dilute the influence of Civic Committees by making them so general, or at the very least he would fracture the special relationship between the Mazowiecki government and the Committees. Michnik had warned Walesa that Najder was a splitter – but a splitter was exactly what Walesa wanted.

Najder and the Kaczynski twins enjoyed an uneasy relationship. As Najder told friends, he would never had imagined six months earlier sharing a dinner table with Jarek Kaczynski. Najder liked politics and power but he was also a formidable intellectual with deep literary knowledge. By contrast Jaroslaw Kaczynski has no conversation and probably no waking thought beyond the political chessboard. The twins and Najder were bound only by their respective parts in the Walesa strategy. Najder was to break up Solidarity and ensure that it would not regroup in a huge combine linking the Mazowiecki team with Geremek parliamentary deputies and the supportive Civic Committees. The Kaczynskis were to take this process one step further and translate Solidarity factions into proper political parties. Despite Najder's sometimes visible contempt for the twins, the Kaczynskis were the politicians of the future. Slowly the age of dissident-politicians, moral giants who would not bow to totalitarianism, was coming to a close. The dissidents with roots in KOR had grown up with the idea that the opposition had to preserve unity above all else. That was the only sure method of building a civil society and outwitting a system that relied on police methods. These dissidents-turned-politicians then took this principle with them when they became ministers and editors, but by that time the principle had become mere sentiment, the stuff of movement not party politics.

The contrast between the different kinds of politicians became plain when the Polish Communist Party dissolved itself in January 1990. The Kaczynskis seized on the moment. Since the old Communist Party no longer existed, their signature on the Round Table accord was no longer valid. Ergo, power-sharing could be pronounced dead and the next stage of the revolution could proceed. Walesa had met Rakowski in December 1989 and exchanged some public joshing. Walesa had called Rakowski Mr Mietek – strangely familiar considering their past personal enmity – and Rakowski acknowledged Walesa's status as Solidarity leader by calling him Mr Chairman. Even so, the meeting did not make much sense, since Rakowski came away with the impression that Solidarity had in some way blessed his Party leadership. After some sharp criticism, Walesa met a genuine Party reformer,

Tadeusz Fiszbach, who was planning to launch a breakaway social democratic party. Fiszbach later supported Walesa's presidential campaign but that was not the aim of the talk. Walesa had been trying to engineer a split – two- or three-way – of the Communist Party with the ultimate aim of creating a young, untainted leftist party that could act as a potential coalition partner in a centre-left alliance. Walesa thought that Polish politics would eventually stand on two "legs" – a centre-left and a centre-right. The Kaczynskis were well on their way to making a centre-right. But the centre-left could not form an alliance with an unreconstructed Communist Party. The Party had thus to be split into acceptable and unacceptable sections. Walesa's attempts to push along this process merely ended up muddying the waters. The Kaczynskis thought Walesa's moves ill-judged but could not sway Walesa on the matter. Jaroslaw Kaczynski argued that two legs were all very well, but what if the left leg was longer than the right? There was a real risk, he said, that the left wing in Solidarity would grow fast. World Bank projections for unemployment in Poland during 1990 were for well over one million. From zero unemployment to one million in one year in a society with no recent experience of joblessness – that was a recipe for discontent. Since it was a Solidarity government that was passing the tough market reforms, who would speak for the workers? A left-leaning Solidarity grouping, penetrated by defectors from the Communist Party, was Kaczynski's answer. "The Solidarity leftists' close ties to post-Communist leftists on the political and social scene are pretty obvious," Jaroslaw Kaczynski told a reporter (*Zycie Warszawy*, 7–8 April). "If a very prominent Solidarity leftist keeps saying in his paper that reformists from both sides must form an alliance, and if he shows himself repeatedly on television with a leading figure of the other side, that makes me wonder why." The reference was to Adam Michnik, editor-in-chief of *Gazeta Wyborcza* and a deputy in parliament.

Michnik was indeed on the left of Solidarity but he was not in the business of striking deals with the Communists. The difference between Michnik and Kaczynski was not so much the gap between left and right, but rather in their dissident backgrounds. Since 1968 Michnik, who was then a student leader, had been a target of the secret police and he had been in and out of prison for two decades. He had the revolutionary's talent for converting a prison cell into a place of study; jail helped him clear his mind and think in terms of moral absolutes. If Michnik chose to forgive Communists (he had appeared on a good-natured television debate with Kwasniewski and later helped to promote Jaruzelski's memoirs) it was not because he had suddenly turned into a Quisling or been overtaken by left-wing sentimentality. It was because only the wrongly imprisoned can forgive the gaoler, a personal not a political act. Michnik thought beyond the fixed political positions and often came up with judgments that were both startling and obvious. He had written a definitive essay that questioned why the Catholic Church should be viewed as the natural enemy of the Polish left. Surely, he argued, the Church had shown how well it could defend democratic values and it was therefore an ally of the thinking, democratic left though not, of course, of the totalitarian, Bolshevised left. It was Michnik too who had promoted so effectively the idea of splitting the premiership and the presidency between Solidarity and the Communists; another somersault which could only have been performed by someone with strong dissident credentials.

Kaczynski did not have that kind of authority, and he craved it. He came into the dissident movement through the side door. His mother had been a friend of the socialist dissident Jan Jozef Lipski and through this connection he had started to help KOR with legal advice. He was not greatly respected or even trusted. When Lipski was jailed or hospitalised with a heart complaint, Kaczynski found there was not a great demand for his services. He made contact with the Gdansk underground, but he was never imprisoned or interned; he was quite simply not dangerous enough.

The contrast between the two types was physically striking. Michnik, who had been an angelic-looking schoolboy, his face framed with curls, had become a craggy figure with bad teeth and a vulnerable stomach. That was the legacy of prison. While Michnik was in jail, Kaczynski was living with his mother. He resembled the cats he kept in his bachelor apartment: sleek and well padded. Kaczynski, like Najder, was not enmeshed in various old-boy networks formed in internment camp or underground groupings. That allowed him to emerge first as a Walesa loyalist, then as a party-politician and tactician. But he still had to compete against the dissident generation with their moral certainties. Kaczynski therefore made it an item of faith: never forge an alliance with the Communists, no forgiveness.

Kaczynski targeted Michnik. The balance had to be restored in the propaganda war within Solidarity. *Gazeta Wyborcza*, which carried the Solidarity logo, was becoming an organ of support for the Mazowiecki government and was helping to pump up the premier's popularity, especially in Warsaw. Mazowiecki had been editor of the Solidarity weekly, *Tygodnik Solidarnosc*; the editorship was now vacant. The paper, which had become somewhat boring under Mazowiecki's editorship, was more directly linked than Michnik's paper to the Solidarity union. The editorship was technically in the fiefdom of the chairman – or perhaps the National Commission – of the Solidarity union. In other words, Walesa could install his placemen. Kaczynski asked for and, despite Mazowiecki's objections, was given the job. From that moment the break-up of Solidarity was inevitable. At *Tygodnik* a group of journalists – Krzysztof Czabanski, Wojciech Gielzynski, Jacek Maziarski, Piotr Wierzbiecki – plunged into combat with the Mazowiecki government, the Round Table agreement, with Communists who had profited from the latest economic changes and, of course, with Adam Michnik.

Walesa let the conflict develop. He did not share the anti-Communist phobia of the Kaczynskis but recognised its value as a popular mobiliser. For Walesa the threat from the Left did not exist as such; the only peril came from a unified Left. Divided, scratching and stabbing each other, the ex-Communists, the neo-Communists, the social democrats and left-leaning unionists could all be a useful part of the equation. Nor did Walesa share the Kaczynski twins' antipathy towards Michnik. There was even some mutual respect. Michnik defended Walesa against charges of anti-Semitism. Walesa became godfather to Michnik's son. Opinion polls showed that Mazowiecki was overtaking Walesa but they rarely awarded Michnik more than one per cent. Walesa could afford to be generous to the ex-KOR man. He was not a captive of the prejudices of the Kaczynskis or any other ambitious advisers. Walesa was thinking a few steps ahead for his plan was, with the aid of the Kaczynskis, to become President of all the Poles.

At the latest since the end of November 1989, Walesa's thoughts had been on the presidential track. Not out of pique with Vaclav Havel (though there was an element of that too) but because there were few other options available. There was one role to be seriously considered: the leader of a fortified Solidarity union which would not only keep alive the revolutionary flame, but also be a useful base for challenging the government.

Walesa had lost any enthusiasm for union matters. He had taken over the chairmanship of the Solidarity cell in the Gdansk shipyards in the autumn of 1989 but it was plainly a temporary move; it was power and not the detailed bargaining for workers' rights that now held him in thrall. There he had a proprietorial air as he showed Barbara Piasecka-Johnson around the yards trying to persuade the soap heiress to buy up the place. His prickly, breezy manner at first charmed and then offended Johnson; his estimate of the value of the yards was so inflated that it became clear that Walesa was not serious about a deal; he was waiting, if not for a better offer, then at least for better times. Edmund Szczesniak, one of the closest observers of Walesa, remembers how the shipyard union election was rigged. "He simply manipulated the results of the deputy-chairman elections. Although Alojzy Szablewski won he insisted that somebody more dynamic take the job, Zbigniew Lis. The workers insisted on Szablewski because they knew him well from the 1988 strikes, he was trusted. But Walesa wanted a younger man, more pliant and more loyal." Szczesniak was present when Walesa bullied Szablewski into withdrawing. "It was then that I saw the coldness in Walesa: he was wiping Szablewski off the slate and there was a cold warning in his voice. If the man tried to contest Walesa's will it would end badly for him. Szablewski, his voice trembling, tried to continue the conversation but to no avail."

To grapple with the intricacies of wage negotiation at a time when trade unions were in decline held no charm for the ex-electrician. As Margaret Thatcher fought to de-claw the trade-union movement in the 1980s, Walesa's sympathies were noticeably with the British premier rather than with his fellow workers. He was more certain that he wanted to be president than to be Solidarity chief, but both ambitions were cloaked. In one interview Walesa ruled out running for the leadership of the union "unless Jan Rulewski stands". There have been many such caveats in Walesa's career. On the presidency too he qualified heavily: he would not be a candidate unless the country could not survive without him. He was to be the last resort, the white knight, the trump. Yet the preference for the presidency was becoming obvious. When, on 12 December 1989, he demanded special powers for the government, he gave an ultimatum to the Warsaw political establishment. Look, he was saying, I am being supportive, I understand the problems, take me seriously − or else.

Walesa's idea was that the government be given the power to rule by decree on pressing economic issues; parliament was already logjammed with legislation needed to transform the planned economy, to change the justice system, housing policy: all the nuts and bolts of the Communist system had to be changed one by one and while this was being done the vehicle was immobile. Mazowiecki was thus giving the impression of slowing down the revolution but Walesa was convinced that it needed more pace before the honeymoon came to an end. Yet the way Walesa launched the plan showed that he still had no grasp of institutional politics. Walesa strode into his Gdansk office, as usual at 9.45 − he hated to be late and would prowl outside his house impatiently waiting for the chauffeur to appear − opened his briefcase and handed a slip of paper to Jaroslaw Kurski, his young press spokesman. "Type that out and circulate it, will you," he said. The statement read, in part: "I hereby propose that the government be given special powers to reorganise the economy, amend the property laws, demonopolise the state and cooperative sectors, reform the tax, accounting and banking systems." This right to rule by decree would, as Walesa saw it, be granted only for a short, defined period. In the meantime parliament could get on with other important legislation.

When Kurski had deciphered the scrawl, he realised that he could not just issue a press release. Did Walesa really understand the present powers of the prime minister? Somebody had to talk to a constitutional lawyer. Kurski managed to find one and then released the statement. Somehow Walesa had forgotten to mention the idea to the government beforehand. The first that Mazowiecki heard of it was on the television news. Kurski's assessment is sound: "The idea was controversial, totally different than the premier's philosophy but definitely worth some quiet discussions. Walesa, knowing Mazowiecki's commitment to the rule of law, should have guessed that the premier would reject this surprise gift."

Najder and the Kaczynski twins were helpful in explaining how the presidency could be tailored to Walesa's needs. The post of president, with an eye on Jaruzelski, had been created in rather different times. The Kaczynskis in particular argued that there were real merits in a French-style presidency if the constitution could be appropriately changed. The French model would offer Walesa the scope he needed. He could "co-habit" with a premier of different political persuasion, he could manoeuvre governments, dictate the policy agenda, establish real control over foreign and defence policy. Walesa needed a job description that made space for his personal whims, that allowed him to exercise his famous intuition. A member of the Chairman's staff prepared a synopsis of a biography of Charles de Gaulle and Walesa liked it, drawing large circles around the already underlined key points. That kind of presidency made sense to Walesa; it had smoothed de Gaulle's passage from war leader to head of state, and Walesa could make a similar transition from street-fighting revolutionary. Various dates were considered for the launch of his presidential bid. One school of thought favoured early January; another, the end of January after the likely fracture of the Communist Party. But Walesa put off the date again and again. First, he could not simultaneously run for the presidency and for the chairmanship of the union. He had decided that his fundamental platform for the presidency was to show that the workers were being abandoned not so much by market reforms as by the arrogant way in which those policies were being implemented. Why the arrogance? Because intellectuals, Warsaw eggheads, were running the government. Did Walesa present an alternative – after all, he had many times publicly asserted his agreement with government policies? Yes, because he was still the tribune of the workers, and to demonstrate this he would stand again for the leadership of the union. That was the campaign approach worked out essentially by the Kaczynski brothers, though others – such as Jacek Merkel, the former underground organiser – were consulted. This tactic locked Walesa into a tight timetable and necessitated a great deal of pretence. To ensure his election as Solidarity chairman he would have to hedge about his presidential ambitions. The delegates would not be keen, in their first congress since 1981, to vote in a new leader only to find him stepping down a few months later.

The other factor delaying a presidential bid was the rapidly shifting sands of international politics. The Soviet Union was bursting at the seams. German unification seemed inevitable. Sandwiched between these two unstable countries, Poland was confused, and the muddle showed in its foreign policy. Janusz Reiter, Solidarity's main expert on Germany (and later ambassador to Bonn), argued with some force that Poland should not follow Hungary and Czechoslovakia in demanding the withdrawal of Soviet troops. They should be allowed to stay in Poland at least until the future of Germany was clarified. They were a bargaining chip that gave Poland a stronger case for participating in the Four plus Two talks on Germany. Walesa took the point but it struck him as needlessly contrived. The Soviet ambassador Vladimir Brovikov – a hardliner who was fulfilling the mission with clenched teeth – came to Gdansk to invite Walesa to Moscow. Before Brovikov had settled into his chair, Walesa declared that it was time for a man-to-man talk rather than diplomatic niceties. There were many painful problems that had to be aired and so it would be a good thing if their talk could be recorded and publicised.

"When will you withdraw from Poland?" barked Walesa to the dumb-founded diplomat. "It has to happen before the end of the year [1990]! And what about letting Poles return to former Polish territories? What about compensation for Poles who were deported to the east?" Suddenly, Warsaw was making quite different, much more radical demands of Moscow. The previous month Walesa had flown with Michnik to Moscow to attend the funeral of Andrei Sakharov and though he was there for only a short time he had quickly absorbed the mood, at least of the strongly reformist part of the political class. Demanding the withdrawal of Soviet troops was no longer tantamount to stinging the nose of an irritable bear. Mazowiecki and the Polish foreign-policy makers were stuck in an over-cautious, if not servile, policy towards Moscow. Mazowiecki had taken his cabinet to Moscow but they had barely left an impression on Gorbachev's Kremlin. It was by most accounts a charming trip, but it had accomplished little. Mazowiecki had decided one evening that his cabinet would go for a night on the town instead of attending an official function. They talked their way into a table at the Praha restaurant on the Arbat – the doorman refused to believe he was dealing with the Polish government ("Anyone can say that, can't they?") – and they drank toasts with black-marketeers at a nearby table and whirled around the dance floor. But while this underlined the changes of 1989, it was the continuities that mattered more: Poland needed Soviet oil shipments, needed a friendly neighbour. "We didn't find Mr Walesa's comments very helpful at the time," recalled a suave department director, glossing over the turmoil that Walesa's intervention caused. "Our main aim that winter was to ensure Polish participation in the Four plus Two talks on Germany and secure guarantees on the western frontiers. The motto was 'Nothing about us, without us.' Putting up unrealistic demands for a more or less instant withdrawal of Soviet troops might have affected Moscow's support for our participation." It was, in short, a matter of priorities. The Mazowiecki government was sure that it had got its priorities right. Walesa was following his nose. Later he would claim that the government simply missed his pass from across the field, that he was giving the government useful flanking support by shaking up Moscow and showing how radical the ordinary Poles felt about the Russian presence. But it was nothing of the kind. It was a piece of electioneering. A "Soviet Troops Out" call was to be his most effective rallying call for young Poles during the presidential campaign later in the year, and the diplomatic successes of the Mazowiecki cabinet were forgotten. The fact is that Walesa had always understood the Russians rather well and Polish–Soviet relations were the one area of foreign policy in which his intuition could be deployed. Addressing a crowded auditorium in Gdynia Shipping College (23 February 1990) he was asked by a fresh-faced cadet if he supported the Warsaw government's bid to take part in the Four plus Two talks on Germany. "Yes, I do," said Walesa. "But I still insist that Soviet troops get out of Poland – the world is running in a different direction and it will soon be an anachronism to keep foreign armies anywhere."

Walesa, then, was less dazed than the political establishment by the speed of German unification and its implications for Polish–Soviet relations. He sensed that the only concession that had to be given to Moscow was loud reassurance that Poland was not going to export its revolution eastwards. The first Soviet visitor, indeed the only important one, to Solidarity-controlled Poland had been the KGB chief Vladimir Kryuchkov, who had made this point with quiet menace. If Poland started to spread the revolution to the Ukraine or the Baltic republics then Moscow's benign passivity could change rather rapidly. Mazowiecki's aides report that the premier was extremely nervous after his session with the KGB man and tried to walk off his tension in a nearby park. On this at least, Walesa was aligned with Mazowiecki. He told a Soviet newspaper (*Ekha Planety*, 27 December): "Your country is obviously a great superpower and cannot afford to take very sharp turns – that could be too dangerous."

By spring 1990 the international configuration was more or less clear. Gorbachev had been elected Soviet president and seemed unassailable. The future of Germany was put onto the safe tram-tracks of an election calendar. It was therefore easier to imagine the problems that should be tackled by a democratically elected president of Poland. In Gdansk the planning began in earnest. In Warsaw, though, there was no sense of an imminent presidential contest. Walesa was at worst an irritant, at best a man who could keep the workers in check. The first-quarter economic results were quite encouraging – hyperinflation was being successfully throttled by the Balcerowicz–Sachs plan and the IMF was well pleased – but the government knew it was in for a long haul. It was to be said, half a year later, that the Mazowiecki cabinet ignored the workers. That was not completely accurate. The government was terrified of the workers. Since the ministers were too honest to make empty promises, they preferred to remain silent. Walesa on the other hand was licensed to talk, to explain. Nobody bothered to work out a strategy with Walesa, to make him part of a tandem. It was merely assumed that Walesa would play along. Walesa obliged, but as soon as he sensed that he was being taken for granted, something in him snapped.

It was a strike of railway workers that was to be the first real challenge to the strict financial policies of the government. Yet the government dithered. It was torn between doing nothing – waiting for the strike to fizzle out – and a belligerent we-will-give-no-ground Thatcherite position. Whatever the reason, the striking workers in the railway station of Slupsk found that nobody was talking to them. Their only visitors were Miodowicz of the pro-Communist OPZZ and Walesa's old rival from Szczecin, Marian Jurczyk. Both men merely succeeded in radicalising the strike. By the end of May 1990 the strike had spread to many key rail yards and junctions. Walesa decided to end the strike. Lech Kaczynski had gathered the exact details of their pay and pension demands and Walesa was well informed. His position, he told the workers, was that their strike was entirely justified but that it was not the right time for such protests since they seemed to be aimed at market reform as such. This did not much impress the strikers. As Walesa was speaking a group of workers interrupted and said that if Walesa ended the strike one of the men, already on hunger strike, would commit suicide. Others yelled that they would carry on with the strike whether Walesa liked it or not. Walesa left and issued a furious communiqué blaming "extremists" for keeping the strike alive. His gamble was that within the day the more moderate strikers would call him back and he could then pull the rabbit out of the hat. It did not happen. Walesa's magic with angry crowds had been tarnished by his association, however uneasy, with the government. He could not simultaneously be with "them" – the authorities – and with the workers. It did not function that way in Poland; you had to choose your side. At last, the strike committee regained control of its strike, persuaded the hunger strikers to end their action, and urged Walesa to visit them again. Swiftly, and with some of his old confidence, Walesa drew up a draft agreement, which he would personally guarantee, and the strike was suspended. The Polish media were exultant because for a dangerous week or so it had seemed as if the workers would launch a counter-revolution.

In his role as Great Explainer, Walesa next talked to angry farmers, an almost cartoon-like image of flush-faced men with pitchforks, baying for justice. He damped down the crowd, said he sympathised with their problems and urged them to be patient. But they demanded for the first time a clear statement of where he stood: was he against them or for them, was he the ventriloquised voice of the government or the voice of all those who felt frustrated? "There is no argument between the prime minister and Lech Walesa," he said, in an obvious lie. (One easy way of spotting a Walesa lie or deflection is when he talks of himself in the third person, as in: Walesa would never let you down!) "I may get furious at times, I may blame some ministers. But if I were to propose a candidate for the prime minister of Poland again, I would propose Tadeusz Mazowiecki. There is no doubt on this point." (*Rzeczpospolita*, 3 April). There was much more of this talk at the time and the mistake of the Mazowiecki information managers was to believe it, or accept it at face value. More important, and closer to the truth, were articles by members of the Gdansk court such as Krzysztof Czabanski. Typically a piece written as early as February 1990 for *Tygodnik Solidarnosc* was concerned with the technicalities of getting Walesa into power; the "if" had already been replaced by the "how". In phrasing strongly reminiscent of Jaroslaw Kaczynski, Czabanski shrugged off the fact that Poland already had a president. "It is often argued that by keeping a rein on the nomenklatura, Jaruzelski guarantees the evolutionary character of the Polish transformations. That is important. But perhaps we have already reached the wall, the limits of his usefulness? Perhaps Jaruzelski by now slows down changes instead of guaranteeing them?" Then came the Soviet card: "Poland should gain independence and sovereignty before the Soviets close their ranks and return to an aggressive imperial policy." Finally Czabanski admitted that there might be a few hitches in exchanging Walesa for Jaruzelski, "unless of course the chairman of Solidarity, having strengthened his union first, would turn to society. First free elections – then a free president – and all of it within this year?" That was a precise statement of Walesa's timetable.

The lead-up to the Solidarity congress was a difficult time for Walesa. The Solidarity leadership had lurched into middle age. Some of the original 1981 élite had emigrated, some had peeled off to lead the Solidarity 80 breakaway group, others had given up union politics, a few (surprisingly few) had been unmasked as secret agents. They knew and understood Walesa; after a bit of grumbling they would return him to office. There was much less certainty however about the future of Solidarity as a trade union. Nobody seemed to be asking why eight million Poles had left the union over the preceding decade, nor who exactly made up the remaining two million. Walesa's mind was elsewhere.

A fortnight before the Solidarity congress, Gdansk shipyard workers met to consider a strike. It was a cold April day, the last sting of winter. There had been a steady throb of protest from the yards since the Solidarity government took over. The Rakowski team had wanted to privatise the yard but in a way that penalised the average worker and opened the way for profitable joint ventures, some of them remarkably close to the Communist administration. After Solidarity had come to power, Walesa had flirted with Barbara Johnson. When those negotiations broke down, the yards were understandably nervous. A Sejm deputy, Czeslaw Nowak, said that the shipyard would be registered as a company, that ships built for the Soviet Union would continue to be subsidised and that workers would receive bonus payments. Many such promises had been made to the yards and broken; the workers were unimpressed.

Then Walesa appeared on the platform, sporting a padded shipyard jacket. There was a buzz around the crowd and a few chirpy shouts: "Tell them, it's not enough, Lech!" Them? Walesa pulled his jacket closer around his stomach and puffed out his cheeks. "I am in the same situation as you, I'm with you – especially those who are jeering. This rally shows that democracy is democracy but that we must eat all the same. The prime minister was appointed thanks to this shipyard and now he must help it." There was applause at the last statement and somebody yelled: "So you tell him, Lech!" Walesa, for the purposes of this meeting, was borrowing from the wisdom of 1980. Since there was no democratic accountability – the president was a Communist, parliament weighted with Communists too – it was the government that had to speak directly to the workers. The welders and fitters in the shipyard on that April day were happy with the thought, but it was largely bluff on Walesa's part. For Walesa, like everybody else in the political class, was preparing to dump the workers. The final words of his speech were the important ones: "My role with you is ending. Now your future is in your own lap."

The last waltz with Solidarity was not a particularly jubilant occasion. Through Jaroslaw Kaczynski Walesa had leaked his determination to seek the presidency and officially confirmed it to the PAP news agency on 10 April. "We have many wise and valuable people in various government posts, but it is necessary to speed up the pace of reforms and demolish the old structures," he told PAP. But Walesa was deliberately vague about *when* he would press his candidacy. The implication that Walesa would force Jaruzelski to leave early was obvious but this still gave him considerable time for manoeuvre. Walesa thus began the Solidarity congress with two agendas. The first was his semi-secret presidential timetable worked out with the Kaczynski twins; the second was the open "I am at your disposal" line to be offered to the Solidarity delegates. At the climax of the congress after his landslide victory he assured the delegates, "I have agreed to give you two years", the official tenure of chairman. One curiosity about Walesa that became plain at the congress is that while Walesa repeatedly tells his worker audience half-truths, they intuitively grasp the full truth and continue to admire, or at least vote for him. During the congress debates Walesa was again and again asked about his plans for the presidency. His standard reply: "Imagine this – a union leader becomes president, head of state – wouldn't that be marvellous?" He was more open to journalists than to the union delegates. How, he was asked, would he ever be able to combine the two jobs of union chief and president of Poland? "I'll live in Gdansk and go to Warsaw on the morning express train every day. I'm used to getting up early. I had to when I worked at the shipyard." (Naturally when he became president, he did nothing of the kind; he lived in Warsaw and flew to Gdansk by air-force jet at the weekends where secret-service bodyguards firmly barred workers from approaching his villa.)

Walesa opened the congress with three sharp raps of a golden hammer. Probably it was a mistake to hold it in the Oliwa sports hall where in 1981 Solidarity so noisily challenged Brezhnev and the whole structure of Communist power. This time the delegates wore suits rather than T-shirts with anti-Communist slogans, their average age was 42 and the atmosphere was slightly stuffy, like a marketing conference in Wolverhampton. Walesa was in poor form. He was supposed to present a speech on Solidarity's activities over the previous nine years. The hall and the galleries were full, the lobby bars (poorly stocked and overpriced) emptied. "You liked the way I jumped over the shipyard wall and so you elected me to drive this vehicle whose name is Solidarity," he began. The rest was barely comprehensible to the delegates. There was no report. Instead there followed a rambling attack on "eggheads and pretentious intellectuals". Later, Walesa's spokesman Jaroslaw Kurski would try to piece together the speech for journalists rather as President Reagan's men would mop up after a particularly inept statement. "You should consider his speech from three aspects – first, Lech Walesa's grudge against Warsaw intellectuals who have been reacting coolly to his presidential aspirations. It was also outrage at the undemocratic behaviour of the delegates and his indignation at the resolution passed by them." The resolution in question was a call by the delegates (prompted mischievously by Jan Rulewski) to invite all members of the praesidium of the first congress. That would include Andrzej Gwiazda who was openly contemptuous of Walesa. "I will not sit at one table with these gentlemen," spat out Walesa, "for all their offences, for splitting the union, for ruining its foundations, they don't deserve it. If they come – I go." To onlookers, high up in the spectator stands of Oliwa, it seemed a rather base way of starting a historic congress. After a night's sleep, Walesa relented and the Solidarity dissidents – Gwiazda, Jurczyk, Seweryn Jaworski – were formally invited; to no one's surprise they did not turn up. Yet the skirmish was important. Somehow Solidarity had to digest its past before it could move on. The presence of Walesa made such digestion very difficult. His personality continued to dominate the union, much as a domineering mother cripples her children. Once it was plain that Walesa wanted to stand again, no serious rival – Wladyslaw Frasyniuk, say, from Wroclaw – came forward. A virtually unanimous vote approved the work of the past nine years – thus sweeping aside many festering issues – and the most vociferous critic of the Solidarity leadership, Andrzej Slowik from Lodz, was bizarrely sponsored by Walesa as a contender for the chairmanship. There were some high-carat speeches – by Alexander Malachowski and ex-Warsaw underground chief

Zbigniew Bujak – appealing essentially for Solidarity to set the tone for a tolerant Poland. But the early days were peppered by slightly crazed appeals for revenge and reckoning. A delegate from Piotrkow proposed that all Poland's Communists be deported to the USSR where "they will live in a Communist fashion, in the red fashion they like so much – after first being stripped of any possessions". The power struggle barely touched on the key issues of the union future: the fundamentals had to be frozen until Walesa's presidential ambitions were satisfied. The heads of the regional delegations agreed to support Walesa for the chairmanship of Solidarity – but only on condition that Walesa was cut off from his entourage. The only way to achieve this would be to elect a strong national commission which would act as the union's parliament, independent of, and immune from, Walesa's influence.

There was thus a procedural battle common to union politics in the West as different groups tried to maximise or minimise Walesa's influence. The Solidarity regions confederated with Gdansk preferred to elect a large National Commission, ostensibly because it would be more democratic but in fact because a larger body would leave power in the hands of a strong praesidium – and thus Walesa and his allies would be in charge. Some six hours of exhausting and often baffling voting appeared to swing the congress behind the Gdansk version. Ridiculous, said the Warsaw delegates: Solidarity would have a National Commission more bloated than in the days when the union could boast ten million members. Shortly before midnight the mood changed again, away from Gdansk and Walesa, towards those who favoured a powerful, relatively tight-knit national commission. It was the first sign that Solidarity, as a union, had entered its post-Walesa phase. The union, in its voting, had shown that it still honoured Walesa but not his entourage. Walesa had stressed before, during and after the congress that Solidarity headquarters should stay in Gdansk. But when Walesa stepped down later in 1990, Solidarity chose not a candidate from Gdansk but a shrewd Silesian academic, Marian Krzaklewski, as chairman. Walesa accepted these setbacks with equanimity. He had long ago stopped being a real worker; soon he would no longer be a leader of workers but of the nation.

CHAPTER THIRTEEN

Discarding friends

How was it that the Solidarity revolution, that great rolling social movement responsible for the fall of Communism, could degenerate into a slugging match between two old friends? By the spring of 1990 that was the nature of Polish politics. Walesa was hitting with his right fist and explaining: "I did not mean to do that, Mr Tadeusz!" Mazowiecki was parrying, blocking and lamenting: "I shouldn't be defending myself!" Revolutions can crystallise around personalities – Danton versus Robespierre, Stalin against Trotsky – but rarely is the struggle so fraught with guilt and personal emotion. The break-up of Solidarity was a messy divorce staged in front of 38 million bemused spectators. Poles, ordinary Poles who had only a passing interest in the dissident politics of the 1970s and the 1980s, now had the chance to study the contrasting personalities and state their preference.

After half a year in office, Mazowiecki was run down. Power may inject adrenalin in politicians but Mazowiecki, already frail and wracked with a smoker's cough, was not feeling the benefits. He slept for only a few hours, took pills to counter the endless cups of coffee. Every small decision was a small agony. He read everything on his desk, was determined never to lie, always to play straight. His chief merit as a strike adviser had always been his ability to stop and reflect in the middle of a crisis. In trouble, he took a walk in the woods near a convent on the fringes of Warsaw, trying to sift out the trivial and concentrate on key issues. Given a choice, Mazowiecki would rather read a book than make a speech.

Walesa, the fast, almost torrential, speaker, had little time for books in 1990; books took away hours that he needed to fuel himself up for the fight. You can win elections, lead revolutions, even lead nations without having to read books. It may even be better that way. Walesa had lost the physical agility of a decade earlier. During the strikes he had been a lithe

229

figure, his machine-gun speech somehow matching his physique and abrupt movements. But he had never been a great sports player – as a schoolboy he had always insisted on being goalkeeper so that he did not have to run so hard – and his body had gone slack. By 1990 he was having bursts of high energy, followed by long depressive interludes. Doctors warned him to watch his sugar level. And as the phoney war with Mazowiecki wore on, his stomach ulcers flared. The Solidarity chairman, the President-in-waiting was rarely seen without a cup of mint tea to still his stomach. The physical contrast was obvious, even to the politically indifferent. Mazowiecki was ponderous, fair-minded, able to motivate those close to him but not the masses; Walesa was cold, rough-edged, hungry.

Jaroslaw Kurski watched the contest from his vantage-point as Walesa's press spokesman, a young subaltern on the front line. He describes it as the year of the scorpion. "Walesa needs an enemy. Once he defeats him, he has to find a new one in order to live. So, since the moment that the Communist Party dissolved itself, Mazowiecki became enemy number one. He needed a rhetoric of threat, anxiety and fear to justify his hyperactivity, and his political existence. First Walesa began to talk about the danger of civil war, the dwindling patience of the Poles, the smell of gunpowder in the streets."

It is difficult to stop Walesa when he has launched himself on a campaign of this kind. "He antagonised almost all of his advisers," recalled Kurski, who resigned shortly before being sacked. "Within a couple of months he constructed a whole army of opponents for himself – thus creating a job that would keep him busy for years. Just think of all those battles and wars that would have to be fought! Exactly what he needed – the prospect of a clash." The tension with Mazowiecki had been there from the beginning, from the moment that the new premier did not consult Walesa on the formation of a cabinet. Walesa had wanted portfolios for "Gdansk", for one or both of the Kaczynski twins, for Jacek Merkel. Mazowiecki in turn had been angered by what he regarded as a cheap trick over the timing of local council elections. Aware that there needed to be some speeding up of political reform, Mazowiecki made a rare visit to Gdansk and told Walesa that he was thinking of announcing early local council elections. He was going to make the announcement at the next session of parliament. But Walesa was quicker. Two days after his talk with the prime minister, Walesa made a formal appeal for early elections making it look as if Mazowiecki was trailing behind the chief. Walesa expressed amazement that his actions could be interpreted in a subversive way. Mazowiecki, though, had learned a lesson: Walesa was now playing for the other side (whatever that meant) and should not be made privy to government plans. The new mood was obvious in a telexed letter to Mazowiecki.

> Dear Mr Prime Minister,
> I'm sorry to have to inform you that a television report from my meeting with the Gdansk citizens on 14 January 1990 was withdrawn because of a personal decision by Jan Dworak (earlier dismissed from *Tygodnik Solidarnosc*). The vast majority of the people present at the above-mentioned meeting supported the policies of the government. The withdrawal of the TV programme makes me conclude that the government does not need support any longer. I will take this into consideration.
>
> Regards, Lech Walesa.

Dworak was a good friend of Mazowiecki – and was set to be Mazowiecki's successor as editor of the Solidarity weekly until Walesa handed the paper to Jaroslaw Kaczynski. Walesa was thus declaring that the Friend of my Former Friend is my Enemy and that Mazowiecki was unfairly using his control of state television against the Solidarity chairman. Whether Walesa really believed this is another matter. Certainly he was building up a head of steam. In a strange, almost mystical way, his resentment was being fused with the resentment of Poles everywhere. His sense of personal slight was most apparent in his relations with Vaclav Havel. A matter of months after the Velvet revolution, the craggy playwright-philosopher had been installed in the Castle, Prague's presidential palace, while Walesa was stewing in his own juice. Havel's first trip abroad had been to Germany, not to Poland. Walesa did not like that. Now Havel was visiting Poland but spending the time in Warsaw, claiming that he had no time for a pilgrimage to Gdansk. For Walesa this was proof that the Mazowiecki team were kidnapping the revolution. Havel and the Charter 77 dissidents who formed the bulk of the new Czechoslovak government had been close for years to the people around Mazowiecki. There used to be secret meetings along the Polish–Czechoslovak border in the Tatra mountains between Kuron, Michnik, Jan Litynski and Havel, Jiri Dienstbier, Father Vaclav Maly and others. It was a subtle meshing of the dissident élites. Walesa was out of this. It was difficult enough for him to take time off from the shipyards and he was never invited into the club. Walesa's assessment of Havel was not unreasonable. The carnival, he predicted, would soon be over in Prague and then the Czechs and the Slovaks would have to grapple with the kind of problems facing Poland. "Now they applaud Havel but soon they will begin to boo him because our car [the economy] has already stopped while theirs is still driving in reverse." But chiefly his view of Havel was coloured with envy: Havel could float effortlessly into the presidency because he was an "intellectual", while Walesa was told to wait his moment. Jaroslaw Kaczynski was certain that a feeling of rivalry with the Czechoslovak leader propelled Walesa towards the presidency. "Ever since Havel became president, I was sure that Walesa was seriously considering taking a similar step . . . I had been suggesting the presidency to Walesa for a long time but he just answered along the lines of "Yes, but . . . and then again, no." The first time that we talked directly about the presidency was around the new year of 1990, after Havel had become president."

The Mazowiecki team pleaded with Walesa to come to the Polish capital to meet Havel. Walesa replied that he had an important meeting in the Gdansk shipyard. This was not true. After a while, the Warsaw politicians gave up. Some weeks later members of the Polish–Czech dissident group, including Michnik and Litynski, travelled to Gdansk and persuaded Walesa that the two giants of the anti-Communist revolutions had to meet, had to be seen to be friends. Out of strategic necessity, the advanced reformers of Central Europe – Poland, Czechoslovakia and Hungary – would have to cooperate more intensely. There was no question of immediate entry into the European Community, still less to NATO, and Soviet army behaviour in Lithuania had shown that cooperating with Gorbachev was also out of the question. That left the Czechs and the Hungarians. Walesa should do his bit. Reluctantly, Walesa agreed to his own rendezvous on the Tatras. The summit meeting was on the Karkonosze Pass. It was supposed to be a symbolic encounter but it failed even in that modest aim. Havel tried his best but Walesa was reticent, like a political débutante. The Czech leader arrived in a woolly mountain sweater and had apparently had a few beers before Walesa arrived. The Tatra dissident summits were always occasions for heavy drinking and late-night talks and Havel expected some of the same informality this time round. Instead Walesa came wearing a tight suit. A planned closed-door meeting was cancelled apparently for lack of time. After a bit of hand-shaking they had a semi-public lunch at a wooden chalet on the Czechoslovak side of the frontier. By the main course of beef and chips Havel was addressing Walesa as Lech, but Walesa struck to the formal mode of address. Then they walked over to the Polish side of the frontier for coffee and, at the urging of photographers, they shook hands again. That was it. The revolution was not going to be shared. There were differences on almost every major policy issue – from privatisation to Lithuanian independence – but they were most visible on Germany. When President Richard von Weizsaecker had visited Prague he was greeted more enthusiastically than any foreign visitor since Empress Maria Theresa; Havel had apologised for the brutal expulsion of Sudeten Germans, and he declared that "All of Europe should be grateful to the Germans that they destroyed the Berlin Wall, thus beginning to undo the split of the old continent." When Weizsaecker visited Walesa in Gdansk he received a rather different lecture. Kurski and German diplomats recall how unimpressed Weizsaecker had been with the Solidarity chief.

Walesa talked at length about the need to secure the western border of Poland and of the threat of mass migration from East to West. But his manner was combative and barely gave the German President time to reply. "I was a little flustered," admits Walesa, "by trying to get von Weizsaecker to speak. I soon discovered that what impressed American or Soviet officials left this inscrutable, coldly intelligent German untouched ... How could an ordinary electrician with just three years [sic] of education and all the cunning of a farmer from Mazowsze challenge an intellectual with an intimidatingly aristocratic 'von' in his name? I tried to say exactly what I meant and welcome him in Polish. Was this tactless?' Perhaps not. But von Weizsaecker may well have been remembering an interview given by Walesa to a Dutch newspaper in which he warned that if a unified Germany started to become aggressive "it would be blown off the map of Europe". Poland's room for manoeuvre was and is more limited than that of Czechoslovakia. To be squeezed between Germany and Russia demands a certain distance. Walesa, whose father died as the result of German internment, was in no mood to hug the leader of the new Germany, nor was he able to mimic Havel in making grand gestures of forgiveness; not while the Oder–Neisse line was still being questioned in and out of the Bundestag. In a certain sense, then, Walesa envied Havel the geography of his country. But chiefly he envied Havel the presidency. At a lacklustre news conference ending their mountain lunch, Walesa showed his true colours. What made Walesa think that Poland was so far ahead of Czechoslovakia in the matter of reforms? asked a Czech reporter. "It depends on your point of view," replied Walesa. "But on one thing Czechoslovakia is surely ahead – it has left Poland behind in resolving the question of president."

Walesa, then, felt he was being undervalued. The opinion polls for the first seven months of 1990 consistently showed that Mazowiecki was far more popular than Walesa. As far as Walesa and his court were concerned there was only one reason for this: Walesa was absorbing all the country's discontent with the slow pace of reform, Walesa was being blamed by workers and farmers for all the sacrifices being demanded of them. Walesa was losing popularity because he was supporting the government, because he had invested Solidarity's authority in an austerity government. There was a logical flaw in this reasoning. Why were people not blaming Mazowiecki for his government's sluggishness? Ah, said Walesa's men, that is because Mazowiecki controls television and can steer the popular mood. Walesa has become a scapegoat, forced to defend the indefensible. Walesa did not react as fiercely as his courtiers to the opinion polls. He was more upset by the way that other opinion-makers seemed to be following the tune played by Mazowiecki. It was not just Havel and von Weizsaecker. Henry Kissinger dropped in and warned Walesa against splitting Solidarity into Warsaw and Gdansk factions. The Western press, which had barely uttered a critical word about Walesa since 1981, now started to complain about the way he was rocking the boat, comparing him unfavourably with, of course, Havel. To Walesa this was beginning to smack of conspiracy. At sessions of the Citizens Committees, which were being refined by Najder into election-fighting machines, Walesa began to snarl about "eggheads", the arrogance of the intelligentsia which refused to listen to the rumbling misery of the workers. "He needed this anger," says one close Walesa associate, "to over-come the phobia of power. Although he was ravenous for power, he was also somewhat scared of it." For a decade Solidarity had been reassuring people that it did not want full power; it wanted only to monitor how it was exercised, to share responsibility for the interests of the workers and look after the social welfare of the nation. This plea was never very credible, even when the Polish authorities enjoyed the backing of several Soviet army tank divisions, but it was a necessary part of the credo and Walesa's appeal was precisely his reluctance to scramble for a ministerial post. The 1989 elections and Walesa's skilful coalition-broking had begun to change that perception. For the first time, Walesa was regarded as being in the game for himself.

Daniel Passent, writing in *Polityka*, blew away some of the fog surrounding Walesa's ambitions. "If anyone wants to believe these assurances about abstaining from power," said Passent (21 April), "that is up to them but with every passing day Solidarity activists take over new nomenklatura posts, I include ones in internal affairs and the army, I think that these promises are best forgotten ... In keeping with the old principle 'the Whole Power to the Soviets', Walesa is reaching for the third apex of the Parliament–Government–Presidency triangle not yet controlled by Solidarity, a triangle that will become even more monopolised after the likely success of Solidarity Civic Committees in local elections. So setting their sights on the presidential palace signifies not only the rejection of the old assurance about aspirations to power but the completion of Solidarity's hold on power." Passent was right about the political drift but wrong in assuming that Solidarity could ever again be regarded as a monolith. And he missed the important human point: that Walesa was not dissembling when he would blurt out to interviewers that he did not want power, he was being forced into it. Walesa wanted power, yes, but it was an immense psychological leap for him. The Solidarity leadership election that spring showed how vulnerable Walesa felt when he put himself up for election. The fury he was generating within himself and his Gdansk base was a way of fuelling himself for the election and for power. As he told Western reporters there would have to be a "war at the top" in order to prevent trouble at the grass roots, a metaphorical war to stave off a physical civil strife. A secret meeting in Gdansk, at Bishop Goclowski's residence, had brought Walesa together with many of his opponents including Alexander Hall, Adam Michnik and Piotr Nowina-Konopka. Their argument was that Walesa was indeed the natural candidate for president, but not yet. Walesa should wait until the following spring, maybe 1991, before breaking open the presidential contest.

Walesa scented conspiracy again; Mazowiecki's supporters were merely buying time to build up their leader as a presidential candidate. Walesa therefore had to justify the urgency of his ambition. First that meant dramatising the plight of the workers – who had the potential to scuttle economic reform – and then to drive a wedge between the workers and the intellectuals in government. If he could demonstrate that the government no longer spoke the same language as the workers then he would talk himself into a job. That was a shrewd enough plan. It would allow him to fight for the presidency without a concrete programme; Walesa would simply declare himself to be at the disposal of the workers, to be their spokesman, an arbiter at a time when the market revolution was sweeping aside the people on the shopfloor. And such a campaign would also give Walesa time to convince himself, to master his power-phobia.

Yet Walesa was barely mentioned in the press accounts of the strike settlement. And Mazowiecki was not exactly brimming with praise for Walesa. If Walesa had a role in the Solidarity-state, it was to put out fires. He had done so but there was a deafening silence from Warsaw. "I was told that the strike would have collapsed anyway," said an angry Walesa (*Gazeta Wyborcza*, 20 June 1990). "No understanding. They said I intervened to

235

satisfy my ambitions and said I benefited while the others lost their ambition. The strike would not have ended because there was a whole staff of people working there to make sure it did not end. The most important thing was that the railwaymen did not emerge from the strike morally defeated. Who (in Warsaw) understands that?"

Walesa had a point. The shock-therapy team of Leszek Balcerowicz, working to a blueprint worked out with Harvard professor Jeffrey Sachs and enthusiastically approved by the International Monetary Fund, were working in a cocoon. Certain assumptions were being made about the level of tolerance of state sector workers but nobody was actually talking to them. Walesa understood that a strike was more than a straightforward transaction along the lines of: workers demand money, management refuses, strike hurts factory budget, bargaining and finally a settlement is reached, everybody goes home. Strikes express a sense of frustration and are thus part of a psychological process; the workers demand attention, reassurance and credible promises of continuing interest; taking these elements into account was more important than the level of the wage rise in ending a strike. Walesa grasped and applied these principles, Mazowiecki's team did not. Of the Mazowiecki cabinet, only Jacek Kuron had the knack of listening to workers and seeing beyond their immediate demands. But Kuron was absorbed in the vast task of creating a comprehensive social welfare system.

Walesa stressed that his mission was not to break the alliance between workers and intellectuals – the axis that had converted a strike wave into a social movement, that was the very essence of Solidarity – but to make the intellectual élite more responsive to workers. Sometimes this sounded plausible. Sometimes it appeared to be mere bluff. Walesa's Civic Committee, meeting after the Solidarity chief had proclaimed a "war at the top", allowed him to put the case for more rapid change. It was a tense session. Mazowiecki decided not to attend. And since Najder was doing his best to separate the Civic Committees from the Solidarity parliamentary group under Geremek, the knives were out. Still, Walesa kept control of the session. "If there is calm at the top, there is a war at the rank-and-file level. Hence I encourage you to fight." But the fight should, he said, be over a concept of democracy. Two governing philosophies had emerged since the Solidarity takeover in the summer of 1989. "The first understanding of democracy is that politicians steer the ship home through dangerous waters. Yet even the best helmsman can lose control. The waters are deep and still, but once they become rough all hell will break out." That was the line being followed by the Mazowiecki team, he said. "Various decelerating mechanisms are being used – no matter what you say, this is manipulation. Of course anarchy should not be allowed but we must allow diverse ideas – conflicts and public debates on the president, premier and ministers – not to scare people but to motivate them." His audience listened patiently until Walesa started to draw parallels between the Jaruzelski regime (which had jailed many of those present) and the Mazowiecki team. "Martial law introduced torpor and the present concept is doing the same." What then was Walesa proposing instead of the evolutionary change? "The second perception of democracy – the one I opt for – is to allow spontaneous action and see the benefits that can be gained by spontaneous moves, obviously within the framework of strong legislation. This demands public unrest, not calm." This was the voice of Walesa as a revolutionary. It was articulate, and radical at a time when the new Solidarity establishment was more concerned with consolidating its power. The consensus among the new political class was that Walesa was rocking the boat, that the power-seeking Kaczynski twins and perhaps a broader rightist grouping were behind Walesa, and that the revolution was almost complete. In time, following an agreed schedule, parliament and president would be freely elected. There was however no rush since Poland first had to swallow some extremely bitter economic medicine; some semi-authoritarian structures could be kept for that transitional period. This was the view propagated in and widely accepted by the West. Even the US embassy had begun to see Walesa as a rogue element. After the May Civic Committee session, however, there was no denying that Walesa was offering an alternative to Mazowiecki, not merely criticism from the sidelines. It was thus no longer sufficient to try to silence him, or draw him into some kind of consultative arrangement: he had to be fought, whether he was aiming for the presidency or not. That is how a conceptual debate about the future of the Solidarity revolution ended up as a personal and often vindictive battle.

Walesa struck first with that most potent of modern revolutionary weapons, the fax. The local elections had been duly won by Solidarity Civic Committees and Walesa was keen to bring his own supporters onto the Civic Committees and use their skills to win a presidential election on his behalf. Najder had convinced Walesa that the Committees were too supportive of Mazowiecki and too intimately linked with Solidarity deputies in parliament. They were thus slowing down the revolution rather than accelerating it – and under their present leadership they could easily be turned against Walesa. The first step then was to sack the Secretary of the Civic

Committees, an old KOR ally of Walesa's, the physicist Henryk Wujec. A brief correspondence followed.

Walesa to Wujec:

Gdansk, 1 June 1990

Henryk, the elections are over and so it is a good time to make the necessary organisational changes in the [Civic] Committee. As you know, as I see it, the Civic Committee should adopt a broader political formula. It cannot be base either of the government or of the OKP.

This point of view has prompted me to take the painful decision to recall you from the position of the [Committee's] Secretary. It was a difficult decision to make as I am aware of the fine, responsible job you have done. I trust that as a politician you will understand my motives as well as the necessity of this decision.

Please hand over all matters to Mr Zdzislaw Najder.

I thank you once again for your disinterested effort and I wish you success in your further dedicated work on behalf of Poland.

Lech Walesa

Wujec to Walesa:

Warsaw, 1 June 1990

Dear Lech, thank you for your wishes. You see, while being so overworked, you probably forgot that I was elected Secretary to Lech Walesa's Civic Committee by the Civic Committee itself, and that only this Committee can recall me from this position.

Needless to say, I am ready to resign the moment the Civic Committee recalls me.

Henryk Wujec

Walesa to Wujec:

Gdansk, 1 June 1990

Deputy Henryk Wujec, consider yourself recalled.

Lech Walesa

On the same day, Walesa decided to sack his friend Adam Michnik from the editorship of *Gazeta Wyborcza*. The reasons were complex. *Gazeta* had become an extremely popular and politically influential paper. Its philosophy was broadly that of the social democrats – the "lay left" – in KOR and its political preference was firmly for Mazowiecki. Jaroslaw Kaczynski pointed

238

out to Walesa that only his newspaper, the far less influential *Tygodnik Solidarnosc*, was giving Walesa's point of view. In gearing up for the presidential contest, Walesa should try to neutralise *Gazeta*. But there was more at stake. Walesa was trying to safeguard his role as standard-bearer of the Solidarity tradition. *He* was the revolution, not Michnik or Mazowiecki, and therefore only *he* could determine who should use the Solidarity emblem. *Gazeta Wyborcza* had been printing the 1988 strike slogan – "No Freedom without Solidarity", in the characteristic ink-blob script – on its masthead. Walesa argued that gave the impression that Michnik's paper was speaking for Solidarity. It was not. Only Walesa could speak for Solidarity. To outsiders it seemed a ridiculous, trivial quarrel. But it was an important part of the divorce proceedings within Solidarity; it was natural in an emotional break-up to argue over who owned what, who had brought most to the marriage. It was not however a pretty sight.

Walesa to Michnik:

Adam,

Since we are friends we should not find it difficult to resolve the problems which have arisen in connection with your paper. I see that I have to do two things, namely:
– dismiss you from the post of *Gazeta Wyborcza*'s editor-in-chief. (Since it was I who appointed you, I believe I have the right to dismiss you);
– deprive *Gazeta Wyborcza* of the right to use Solidarity's emblem.

I have been forced to make such a decision, and I would like to do this on friendly terms. Could you therefore advise me about the form in which I should do so?

L.W.

Gdansk, 1 June 1990

Michnik refused and waited for the temporary madness to pass from Walesa. Three days later another fax-missile landed from Gdansk.

Adam,

Before the elections of 4 June 1989, I appointed you the editor-in-chief of *Gazeta Wyborcza*. A lot has happened in the meantime. The Agora Ltd company was founded and became your paper's publisher. In this situation, the nomination you received from me is no longer valid. You should therefore receive the new nomination from the Publisher.

We should also consider if a paper published by a private company can use Solidarity's emblem.

Lech Walesa
Gdansk, 4 June 1990

Michnik to Walesa:

Lech,

You know that I have always been honest with you. It will be the same this time.

More has happened than can be judged from your letter. As the leader of Solidarity, the mass movement of Polish democracy, you are slowly changing into an Emperor sending successively to your friends the following instructions: "Feel dismissed."

I consider your letter to Henryk Wujec a political mistake, and, above all, a moral mistake. I want to ask you, as a friend, to revoke that bad and unwise decision.

I simply consider your statement that you "feel ashamed for the government" as harmful for Poland. Please set aside the emotions and ask yourself what *you* would think had I said such things about a government which you yourself were heading.

I agree with you. It should be the paper's staff and not the Solidarity chairman who ought to decide about who should be *Gazeta Wyborcza*'s editor-in-chief. After receiving your letter, I handed in my resignation to the editorial board and it was turned down.

Naturally, I am ready to consider with you, as happened many times in the past, all matters of importance for Poland. You know why for the past ten years I have felt attached to the Solidarity emblem. I think I have never betrayed it.

Adam Michnik
Warsaw, 4 June 1990

It soon emerged that Walesa had no authority to sack either Wujec or Michnik. *Gazeta Wyborcza* was the property not of Solidarity but of a joint stock company, its profits were being ploughed back into the paper. Wujec was elected by the Civic Committee and could only be dismissed by it. Walesa, when reminded of this, replied: "He got elected because I proposed him. After all, the Civic Committee meets at Lech Walesa's invitation, and I sign those invitations every time." (*GW*, 20 June 1990). What was at issue then was the paternity of the revolution. Wieslaw Wladyka (*Polityka*, 30 June) observed about Walesa: "His attitude towards Mazowiecki is like

240

a father's towards a son who disappointed him." The sense of paternity probably shaped his rivalry with Havel – who was the true father of the 1989 revolutions? – and certainly fed his resentment of the Solidarity deputies in parliament. He told them that they had only been elected on the Solidarity ticket because they were photographed together with the legendary chairman. It is, as Walesa's critics were quick to point out, a short step from declaring oneself to be the Father of the Revolution and assuming the powers of a dictator. In one short year Walesa the national hero was being compared in Warsaw salons with Castro and Peron. Walesa shrugged off the criticism. Ever since the birth of Solidarity he had been accused of dictatorial tendencies. The same people, though, accused him of being a demagogue and a populist. Somehow these various labels did not quite match the man. His skill is to swim against the mood of a crowd and turn it around. "The most important moment in August 1980 was when Borusewicz, Gwiazda and others democratically decided that the shipyard should thank the advisers Mazowiecki and Geremek and they should then be sent back to Warsaw. To this I said 'no' and this is how my dictatorship began. If I had not played autocratically, Mr Mazowiecki would still be writing for *Wiez* magazine, and Geremek would not be Geremek . . . those elements helped to build Solidarity. But undemocratically it offended democracy." (*GW*, 20 June). The problem was not so much that Walesa demanded uncritical trust in his intuition, that he bent the rules, that he would always play a hunch rather than trust a majority decision. It was rather that the political system itself was so poorly formed, that there were no institutional checks on the powers that he was claiming. In the middle of 1990, Senator Janusz Ziolkowski could justifiably claim: "We are not any kind of parliamentary democracy, there is not even a clear division between legislative and executive authority because increasing numbers of deputies and senators hold government jobs. We work at gunpoint because everything has to be changed, yet practically all the bills stem from the government."

It was in fact the Mazowiecki government that was a quasi-dictatorship, albeit benign. Walesa, with the backing of a political party – the Kaczynskis' Centre Alliance – represented an opposition and it did not know how to deal with it. For a year, the Mazowiecki team had appropriated the Thatcher slogan "There Is No Alternative". Andrzej Celinski, the sociologist adviser to Walesa in 1981 who had become a senator, put the dilemma crisply enough during an unusually self-critical conference ("Sociologists caught in the cogwheels of power"). "A politician achieves his goal when he captures as many decision-making centres as possible. But in Poland there is no

241

network of interests that would tie him to his voters, there is no need to account for the captured centres. Individual politicians do not have to pay their obligations. And this sets us apart from other countries – and it is what the present authorities have in common with the previous." Walesa's reaching for power and his abrupt manner certainly raised fears that Walesa on the political throne would be a whimsical, unpredictable semi-dictatorial leader. But he was still some way from the presidency, and ordinary Poles knew enough about Walesa to make an informed choice at a free election. It was the people already in power who were to some degree mimicking the Communists.

Walesa argued, and argues still, that it was in the long-term interests of Polish democracy to destroy Solidarity and thus create the germ of a party system. If you wield a hammer you cannot be choosy about your methods. The main thing is to warn people what you are going to do, explain your actions and then strike firmly. But it was not in Walesa's nature to protect innocent bystanders from the flying shards. When Walesa convened a session of his Citizens Committee on 24 June, it became shockingly clear to ordinary Poles that the Solidarity leader was not a very nice man. One could argue for many hours or years about what constitutes authoritarian rule or an authoritarian personality, but Poles have a very precise understanding of what constitutes "personal culture", the moral calibre of a politician. Walesa did not emerge well from that long Sunday afternoon in the lecture hall of Warsaw university.

Walesa began with a naked attack on Jerzy Turowicz, the 80-year-old editor of the independent Catholic weekly *Tygodnik Powszechny*. Turowicz, close to the Pope, had been a stalwart champion of the Church and human rights for many decades and a cluster of bright, essentially Christian democrat intellectuals had grouped around his Cracow newspaper. He was a friend of Mazowiecki's and had formed a group to protect the government. Walesa was bitter and turned on the old man. "Mr Turowicz, you said it was necessary to protect Tadeusz Mazowiecki's government. Let me reply: this government is protected with words but not with actions . . . it is not a Poland which I wanted to build. Mr Turowicz, Poland is waiting to hear what you have against Walesa and democracy . . ." Turowicz, stumbling because of a combination of nerves and old age, said he was not aiming at Walesa.

"The restoration of political parties after 45 years of totalitarianism is a slow process. I do not see how we can artificially speed up political pluralism." As far as Walesa was concerned, the damage had been done. In Poland, old professors are treated with great, even exaggerated, respect and Turowicz was much more than a retired academic or journalist: he was at the core of Christian Solidarity, one of the key threads that connected the Solidarity revolution with the 1968 student rebellion, with the liberals who resisted Communist anti-Semitism, with the movement to revise the constitution and make it less slavishly pro-Soviet. Walesa broke something in Solidarity at that moment. Snatches of the discussion show how far the movement had plunged.

WALESA: Any plan to dissolve the Civic Committee is tantamount to high treason, a crime committed on a living organism.
WUJEC: I would rather not disturb Lech in purging the Committee. Let me present my resignation.
HALINA BORTNOWSKA (*who helped the Pope to draft* Laborem Exercens): We must vote on this resignation. Wujec was elected by the Committee. Let democracy be democracy and not demagogy.
WIKTOR WOROSZYLSKI: I would like to ask if the support for Walesa's presidential campaign was intended to develop the concept of imposing dictatorship on Poland.
WALESA: If the right wing gains the upper hand in Poland, I will declare myself in favour of the left . . .
ANDRZEJ WIELOWIEYSKI: We have managed to achieve so much during these ten months because the majority has felt that the country is changing according to a new morality and that people enjoying moral prestige are acting together. Walesa is making a flanking attack and thus ruining public hopes.
WALESA: You have accused me of sowing unrest. Prove it.
WIELOWIEYSKI *then began to read out the results of public opinion polls.*
WALESA: Break the thermometer and you will have no fever.
ALEXANDER HALL: The election campaign seems to have started already and it is too early for that. We still have to proceed together. I respect Lech Walesa but I do not think that he is a good presidential candidate.
WALESA: I don't think Hall is a good minister.

And the former Solidarity heroes argued on through the afternoon and evening. Walesa drew loud applause since the structure of the Committee was already being changed by Najder. There were supporters of Walesa, including the economist Stefan Kurowski and the essayist Stefan Kisielewski. Walesa was not isolated at the session, but he had crossed an invisible frontier. His verbal assault on Turowicz had reduced some of the shrewdest figures in the Solidarity revolution to the level of a mob. Even Michnik, probably the wittiest of the Solidarity inner circle, lost control. Accused of trying to let the Communists in through the back door, he burst out: "If I am a crypto-Communist, then you are a swine."

It had been obvious for some time that the Pope was worried. The *nobility* of Solidarity formed an important building-block in his philosophy of labour. Work, he had written, was supposed to serve man and not the other way round. Man could not be enslaved in that way, rather he had to discover the dignity of work and through that dignity pay tribute to God. Solidarity, in its early form – powerful steel, car and shipyard workers striking on behalf of doctors and nurses, teachers and pensioners, the strong with the weak – was an object lesson in how a Christian social movement could defeat atheistic Communism. And now Solidarity was involved in what seemed to be its terminal struggle. Acting on instructions from Rome, the Papal Nuncio tried to bring Walesa and Mazowiecki together again at a crowded diplomatic reception at the Nuncio's residence on Aleja Szucha. Rumour had it that the Vatican secretary of state, Agostino Casaroli, had written a letter passing on the Pope's dismay at Walesa's behaviour. Certainly the Nuncio spent 45 minutes closeted with Walesa before the reception began. It was a conventional party with ambassadors guzzling canapés from silver platters and bishops on their best behaviour.

Walesa entered the high-ceilinged ballroom from the Nuncio's study and placed himself in a corner far away from Mazowiecki. Piotr Nowina-Konopka and one of Mazowiecki's closest friends, Jacek Ambroziak, scurried between the two men trying to bring them together. Mazowiecki was showing an unusually intense interest in the probing chatter of a minor-league ambassador; Walesa was mainly silent, exchanging brisk words with his assistant Krzyzstof Pusz. Eventually the two key figures in the Solidarity revolution were pulled into a conversation.

MAZOWIECKI: Ah, Mr Lech, did you receive my cabled greetings on your name day?
WALESA: No.

Both men then wheeled away and struck up conversation with diplomats. When they left the party they hugged each other but to at least one onlooker, "it was more of a collision than an embrace".

There was no escaping the fact, however, that the Church was becoming deeply involved in keeping the Solidarity establishment together. The

Gdansk bishop Tadeusz Goclowski, in particular, was regularly in contact with the Primate and the Vatican on the political feud. All the energy that the Church had once drawn on to bring the Communist reformers together with the Solidarity opposition was now being turned on Solidarity itself. In the old days secret meetings between Communist ministers and the still illegal union could be held in monasteries, church basements and convents. The same principles were now being applied to Mazowiecki and Walesa, who were persuaded to hold six hours of talks in a monastery outside Warsaw in July. The meeting merely confirmed each man's prejudices. Walesa was convinced that Mazowiecki was trying to manipulate him and keep him away from the presidency: Mazowiecki told friends later that Walesa's personality had changed, that he was now completely in the grip of the Kaczynski twins.

But the Church, and specifically the Pope, kept on trying; rarely had the Pontiff interfered quite so actively in domestic politics. Walesa realised that the Primate regarded the row in Solidarity as "the Walesa problem". The Episcopate, especially its secretary Archbishop Bronislaw Dabrowski, was close to Mazowiecki and took over the "Warsaw" view of the power-struggle. Goclowski tried to redress the balance but the inner circle around Glemp clung to the idea that Walesa was a rather pliable character, not, admittedly, a simple worker out of his depth but a transitional figure. The main line of defence for Walesa was to play on the Church's lingering fears about the leftist dissidents like Jacek Kuron who were an important component of the Mazowiecki team. Priests, even senior clerics, could be heard making suspicious remarks about the "Christian" Mazowiecki government being subverted by the "Jews" in and around the cabinet. There were indeed several politicians of Jewish origin in the Warsaw power circle since they had also been at the hub of KOR and the dissident movement. Bronislaw Geremek was head of the Solidarity parliamentary caucus. Jan Litynski was Kuron's right-hand man at the Ministry of Labour, Adam Michnik (despite Walesa's efforts to dislodge him) was still running the influential *Gazeta Wyborcza*. Kurski heard Walesa thinking aloud as they flew to Warsaw for a meeting with Casaroli. "Lech was opening large piles of letters with a kitchen knife and saying: 'I trusted my friends the Jews and they made a fool of me. And I have been warned so many times not to trust Jews, not to surround myself with them, not to listen to their advice! I would always reply: these people are my friends. And now what? That was the last time I let myself be outmanoeuvred like that.'" Kurski and Bishop Goclowski listened to this soliloquy and nervously tried to talk him out of it. To

Kurski at least it was proof positive that Walesa, if not exactly anti-Semitic, had at least a rather crude understanding of how Catholics and Jews should live together. Obviously Geremek, Michnik and Litynski felt as Polish as the Catholic Walesa; like him they were Polish "Patriots", True Poles – all the usual fuzzy terms for non-Jews engaged in Polish politics. Kurski remembers the scene. "Walesa was saying, 'Even when I was a child I was warned by my family to watch out for Jews.' He was saying it all in a very convincing way – it was hard to say when he was just joking and when he really believed his own nonsense. Unlike the rest of us, he was really enjoying himself." Kurski may well have missed the point. Yes, Walesa was teasing them, trying to shock them. But he was also rehearsing his line before meeting the Warsaw clergy.

In 1980 Alojzy Orszulik, episcopal spokesman and adviser to the Primate, had warned Solidarity against listening to dissidents from KOR, suggesting that they might not have Poland's true interests at heart. The anti-Semitism was there then, only just below the surface. By 1990, Orszulik and the inner circle around Glemp were still in place and still nursing the same prejudices. Walesa understood this and was willing to play the anti-Semitic card to sway the Church behind him rather than Mazowiecki. His diatribe in the plane that had so shocked Kurski was not the rambling of a bigot. He seems to have been saying that his family – certainly his stepfather – the workers in 1968, the Church in 1980, had all told him to be on guard against Jews. He had ignored advice. Did he sack Geremek as a strike adviser? On the contrary, he protected him. And so it would be again. But if the Church's anti-Semitism could be exploited for political gain, if election rallies brandished anti-Semitic banners – well, where was the harm? Their view was not his. In short, Walesa's record is not that of a rabid anti-Semite, but neither does it suggest a particularly nice person.

To mark the tenth birthday of Solidarity, the Pope saw Walesa on 27 August. Again, Walesa said later that it was an occasion to recharge his spiritual batteries. In fact the Pope was tougher on Walesa than usual and urged Walesa to keep Solidarity together. The Pope had a better grasp of Walesa's political game than Glemp; he could see that Solidarity had only a limited future and that its division did not automatically mean anarchy. But the language barrier between the Pope and his countryman was never more apparent than in this session.

Walesa talked about the need for pluralism, but in woolly terms. The Pope by contrast used Polish words with great precision. What did Walesa mean by "pluralism", where would it lead? How could it be expressed?

How was it constrained? Walesa grasped the general message: he should try one more time for a reconciliation with Mazowiecki. Walesa knew that the friction was now too acute for that but he had in effect been ordered to go through the motions. The obvious occasion was the anniversary of the signing of the Gdansk accords on 31 August, the day when an out-of-touch government had caved in to the workers. Indeed when the ministers trooped into the shipyards to address the workers, they looked almost as frightened as Jagielski had in 1980. The truth was that the Solidarity élite felt more at home in Strasbourg and Brussels than in a factory; shock-therapy economics is always difficult to justify to heavy industrial workers, but for a government that drew its legitimacy from a workers' movement it was nigh impossible. Nobody was actually pelted with eggs – the workers were too conscious of the occasion for that – but the balance of advantage was definitely with Walesa. The meeting with Mazowiecki was held at Goclowski's residence before Walesa was due to appear at the yards. It was a tense, abrasive session. Walesa said he was determined to seek the presidency. If Mazowiecki did not run against him then he could retain the prime minister's job. As far as Walesa was concerned that was a big concession. It flew against all his instincts and the advice of the Kaczynski twins, who had after all developed a programme of "acceleration". At every opportunity Mazowiecki was being painted as an obstacle to change and to keep him on would send the wrong signals. But this was Walesa's way of showing his respect for the advice of the Pope; Walesa as president, Mazowiecki as premier would have been a difficult partnership but it would have preserved something of the Solidarity ethic. Mazowiecki, however, was not interested in the Walesa idea. He had fought too hard for his independence – his first speech as premier had stressed his determination not to be a marionette of any kind – and he knew too much about Walesa's personality to take the risk. Instead Mazowiecki suggested that a mutually acceptable third candidate be found to be Polish president. That would allow Mazowiecki to continue and would give Walesa a sense of having influenced events. Walesa thought the suggestion foolish and said as much. There was little sense in replacing one impotent and embarrassing president with an equally impotent, but less embarrassing Solidarity candidate. The president had to have the power to talk to, persuade and lead the people since the prime minister plainly had no time to do this; that was how Walesa phrased his thoughts and the result was that both men left the bishop's residence feeling bruised. Walesa was more convinced than ever that he had to run for president – and that Mazowiecki believed him incapable of the job. Mazowiecki could see that his

247

dream of a long-term reforming government was doomed unless he took over the presidency himself. It was not a position he wanted, yet his options were rapidly shrinking.

Walesa had been approached in July by two dedicated market liberals from Gdansk, Jan Krzyzstof Bielecki and Janusz Lewandowski. They offered their support for Walesa's presidency if they were given the chance of implementing their programme. The liberals – mainly Gdansk-based economists who saw Margaret Thatcher as their intellectual beacon – were convinced that Walesa's slogan of acceleration could be applied to economic policy by a much more resolute approach to privatisation. Walesa had politely brushed off this advance in July: he regarded it as premature since no formal presidential campaign had been launched. Now he thought about the encounter again. Mazowiecki was stubborn. There was a strong probability that he would resign as premier if Walesa won the presidency. Walesa would need a self-confident, but at the same time dependent prime minister if he wanted to make a serious impact. Bielecki, Lewandowski and the other liberals – who had been on the fringes of the Gdansk underground during martial law and who thus possessed adequate Solidarity credentials – filled a need. The chief criticism of Walesa from the Warsaw Solidarity élite was that he did not really know what he wanted to do; he merely wanted change for change's sake. Personal ambition had taken him over. The liberals had a well-developed economic blueprint, one moreover that seemed (at the time) to have worked successfully in Britain. Walesa began to think of himself as Poland's Thatcher, the strong central authority needed during the destabilising rush for the market.

And by 31 August 1990 there was little real choice but to run for president. Jaroslaw Kaczynski put the matter crisply enough. "What were his options then? Walesa could either become president – and therefore everybody aware of the situation should have tried to help him be the best, the most responsible president. Or . . .? There was no other option. Walesa, left outside the system, could have destabilised the social situation at any moment he chose . . ." Strangely Kaczynski, Walesa's ally in the presidential campaign, argues from the point of view of Walesa being a danger if left to his own devices rather than a natural president. "Let's imagine all the social unrest concentrated around Walesa not as a president but as a popular leader. It might have been enough for him to make, say, one speech to make everything collapse. Then he would have become president but according to different rules, elevated by a popular uprising. That would have been dangerous because he'd be out of any democratic control."

The Church hierarchy made one further attempt to bring the Walesa and Mazowiecki camps together. Glemp invited 24 politicians to his residence on Miodowa (Honey) Street for tea and biscuits. The idea was to explore all the possible permutations, and put some group pressure on Walesa. Sensing that the tea party would end up as a collective attempt to persuade him to withdraw from the presidential contest, Walesa issued a statement at noon formally declaring his intention to run for head of state. That, as Walesa intended, shook up the tea drinkers when they met in the afternoon. Six formal speeches were planned to open the session and five of them had to rewrite their words at the last moment. Yet again, Walesa had created his own agenda. But the announcement did clear the air and it focused attention again on General Jaruzelski, one of the participants at Glemp's talks. It was all very well Walesa throwing his hat in the ring but there already was a president and although he had let it be known that he was willing to step down a few years before his allotted span, General Jaruzelski had barely been consulted in the long hot political summer. The Kaczynski brothers had button-holed the general's right-hand man Jozef Czyrek and told him that the general should start to think in terms of resigning. Then, the general's first response had been to worry about the army – to ensure that the new defence minister and command would be broadly accepted (by the army itself, by Poles, by Moscow). Jaruzelski had been quiet during his months in office, allowing reforms to go ahead unobstructed. That was because he understood the big constitutional limitations on his post. The one area where the president could make an impact, where he could seriously destabilise the country, was the army, since the head of state was also, formally, supreme commander. Jaruzelski was nervous about a purge in the army should Walesa become president. There was even the possibility of an anticipatory coup should Walesa look set to win the presidency. The general was probably being over-timid; he had lost touch with much of the middle-ranking officer corps, youngish men in their forties, who did not view Walesa as a particular threat and who indeed discreetly welcomed the chance of shedding some of the military dead wood that had stayed in place since martial law.

Despite Jaruzelski's apprehensions, a short-order calendar of transition was agreed. The presidential elections – a nationwide poll for the first time – would be held in the late autumn. If there was no outright winner at the end of November, a second round would be held in early December and by the end of the year a new president could be sworn in. Parliamentary elections would be held in 1991 (the assumption was spring) and a new

249

constitution defining the relative power of president, parliament and government would be drawn up, probably by May 1991. The race was on, but Walesa was the only one wearing running shoes. Mazowiecki was still brooding about his candidacy. The opinion polls showed him still ahead of Walesa and he had the built-in advantage of office, including control of the militantly pro-Mazowiecki state television. Most of his cabinet – Alexander Hall being the noisiest – were urging him to run. But Mazowiecki was a man who always balanced risk and gain with the precision of a pharmacist preparing a prescription. After all, what if he lost? The Kaczynski twins would move in, the Balcerowicz economic programme would be ripped up and a year of remarkable progress would be squandered. Nonsense! exclaimed his aides. Walesa is a clod, will trip himself up. Walesa is the past and the Poles are shrewd enough to grasp the fact. Mazowiecki continued to agonise, however, and the most able of his aides began to realise that it was going to be very difficult to sell their boss. Could he win against Walesa? Could anybody?

"Selling Tadeusz was like trying to run a Hamlet for president campaign," confessed one of the Mazowiecki election team. Even the campaign manager, the personable young journalist Henryk Wozniakowski, had to admit "the prime minister is not a media animal by nature". In front of the camera Mazowiecki tended to mumble and qualify his sentences. Interviewers despaired. It was almost impossible to extract from him a sharp-edged sentence or sentiment. He obviously believed powerfully in his government's mission, was fiercely loyal to his cabinet (refusing to drop some obvious liabilities), he was honest, slow, dependable; in short, not the kind of person who won elections. Yet his year in government had notched up some solid achievements and seemed on the brink of many more. The Balcerowicz programme, fully operational since January, had already ended hyperinflation. The easing of foreign trade restrictions had opened Poland up to a flood of imported goods. In early 1989 a Polish parent recalled having been reprimanded by his daughter's class teacher for putting a banana in her lunch-pack. Bananas were a luxury and as such a source of social friction in the class. But by the summer of 1990 banana-skins were spilling out of the granite litter-bins on Warsaw's Marszalkowska Street. Driven in small refrigerated vans from Berlin, traders were selling the fruit at reasonable prices on every street corner. Nor did the miracle stop at bananas. Western clothes imports were beginning to give Poles high street choices similar to those available to the English or the Germans. Personal computers (and cheap pirated software) were being snapped up. The zloty, almost as worthless as the Weimar Mark a year earlier, was now of real value. The queues that used to snake outside every shop had almost disappeared, travel abroad was restricted not by the Communist secret police but by Western reluctance to issue tourist visas. And the economic turnaround was not solely due to import and price liberalisation; a trade surplus of close to $3 billion was predicted for the end of 1990. In foreign policy Mazowiecki had won an explicit promise from Chancellor Kohl that the German–Polish border would be formally recognised.

These achievements translated into high popularity-poll ratings for Mazowiecki. But the sampling for his government as a whole was not so strong, and Balcerowicz in particular was viewed as something of a cold-blooded villain. Perceptions were changing. In 1989 there had been a general consensus that Mazowiecki was a wise choice and his brand of cautiously managed political reform could, with economic shock therapy, be regarded as the best formula for stability. Indeed Poland, a troublespot for so long, seemed to have become an oasis of calm compared to the upheaval in Germany and the accelerating disintegration of the Soviet Union. By the autumn of 1990 Poles had started to want more from their government. The financial sacrifices were hurting and the new time-scale was beginning to sink in. Industrial production had slumped by over 20 per cent, the unemployment system was in its infancy yet the number on the dole was rising fast and looked set to reach 1.2 million by the end of the year. Balcerowicz was saying that the recession might soon bottom out; other economists were complaining that the strict monetarist policies, not accompanied by an industrial recovery programme, would merely deepen the recession. Even Balcerowicz's advisers had to admit that Poland could not hope to reach the living standards of, say, Greece for at least a decade. Those who had viewed Balcerowicz as a quick-fix, a short cut to the market, now felt betrayed. In state factories, wages were being nailed down by a special tax known as Popiwek. Managers who awarded pay rises not justified by productivity would have to pay hefty taxes. Private companies on the other hand were exempt from Popiwek. The idea, apart from restraining wage inflation, was to encourage a drift from the state into the private sector. In the long term this and other strategies were quite successful. By 1992 Poland could boast that 30 per cent of output was produced privately. But to workers trapped in their state factories it appeared that the Mazow-iecki government was sentencing them to a kind of penal servitude. Poles working in the private sector were getting rich quick and starting to flash their wealth while the former aristocrats of the working class – the miners, the shipyard workers, the steel-men and the people on the car assembly lines – were condemned to a sudden near-poverty. The values established over the previous four decades had been turned upside-down in less than a year. On the whole, the workers understood why but they wanted at least recognition of their sacrifice from the Solidarity government and an offer of faster political change. There had of course been political changes – the censor's office had been abolished and the state publishing monopolies had been breached, for example. But that benefited merely the intelligentsia and the new rich; cinema tickets were out of the financial reach of many worker households. Others were unhappy too. Farmers who had been demanding a free market for their produce for decades suddenly found they were unable to sell at high prices; moreover their suppliers were charging Western-style prices. Imported food was becoming cheaper than Polish-grown produce. And the banks were charging enormous interest rates on the normal winter loans that kept farming households alive until the harvest was gathered. The consumer revolution had only trickled through to the countryside. The village shop had been privatised but there was still only one; the shopkeeper promptly put up the prices. Pensioners in towns and villages were also feeling the pinch; Kuron was trying to put their pensions onto a sensible, systematic basis, but the reality was that the hyperinflation of 1989 had wiped out their savings and made daily survival very difficult.

Each of Mazowiecki's achievements was therefore shadowed by a real grievance. The Kaczynski twins knew how to channel this discontent into election support for Walesa. When Mazowiecki eventually declared himself for the presidency there were six candidates. Mazowiecki was assured, so it seemed, of the vote of the Warsaw intellectuals. Peasants' leader Roman Bartoszcze would pick up a chunk of the countryside, the ultra-nationalist Leszek Moczulski would gain mainly the votes of his own Confederation for an Independent Poland (KPN), the Canadian émigré Stanislaw Tyminski might mop up a few fringe votes, Wlodzimierz Cimosiewicz of the ex-Communist Party would win the support of any virulent anti-Solidarity constituency. Jaroslaw Kaczynski warned Walesa that the arithmetic might deny him outright victory in the first round. Walesa shrugged off the advice but his earlier boasts that he would pick up seventy or eighty per cent of the vote gave way to more modest – though still confident – assessments. The Kaczynskis, like almost every political analyst, had misjudged the situation but they had correctly gauged that Walesa's support would come from the right wing of Solidarity. Mazowiecki had three cardinal weaknesses – all of which seemed to identify him with Communism or soft-left liberalism – that Walesa could exploit at rallies. The first, plainly, was that Mazowiecki was the product of the Round Table agreement. Since the Communist Party had dissolved itself, the agreement was no longer valid and so Mazowiecki too had scant claim to legitimacy. Secondly, his policy of drawing a "thick line" under the past had in effect protected many Communists. The martial law experience had not been properly digested, even by historians. Was it wrong, or was it not? The bookstalls were full of memoirs – dictated to friendly journalists, edited and published within three months – of former Communist bigwigs. They jostled for attention with sensational revelations about the Katyn murders, Stalin's crimes, the long catalogue of what *They* did to *Us*. The journalist Andrzej Krzysztof Wroblewski calls this phenomenon "porno-Stalinism" and there was indeed something prurient about it. But it had also awakened old anger and raised the question of why Jaruzelski and others had not been brought to trial. Finally, in the absence of a managerial class, many ex-Communist dictators appeared to be buying into their old, now privatised companies and converting their defunct political power into wealth.

The Mazowiecki government was not moving against this trend and this allowed the Walesa election team to hint at conspiracy; was the Mazowiecki government in some way compromised; had it struck one, or a series of deals with Communists since the Round Table? What was the true price of stability and how long would it last? Those were the themes of the Walesa campaign as devised by the Kaczynskis. Whether Walesa personally believed that Mazowiecki was a crypto-Communist was another matter. In interviews Walesa threw heavy punches at Mazowiecki, accusing him of being essentially anti-democratic. "Mazowiecki, who is supposed to be such a great democrat, used police to throw strikers out of the Agriculture Ministry. I'm not saying who was right. I'm just noting the method and the danger. If a weak Mazowiecki today throws them out what will he do when he is powerful? He will use more force. I never resorted to force." (*Newsweek*, 19 November 1990). Yet his punches glided past the issue of "crypto-Communism". Perhaps because if Mazowiecki was guilty of striking bargains with the Communists, then so too was Walesa – Walesa is well aware that he is deeply vulnerable on this matter, said one former Walesa enthusiast whose relationship later turned sour. Walesa grasped though that his core constituency for the election was right-wing and that he was obliged to cater for their prejudices. Many rightist groupings were emerging and setting up proper party structures. In the countryside there were virtually no leftist groups. Even the PSL, once the loyal ally of the Communists, was now being run by God-fearing sons of farmers. In the towns the various pre-war nationalist strands were surfacing again as embryo parties. The NOP (Polish National Rebirth) and the PSN (Polish National Party) – led by the slightly unhinged Boleslaw Tejkowski – were trying to continue the tradition of the pre-war Endecja, the pre-war National Democratic movement. Endecja's radical right-wing anti-Semitic ideology had permeated the political life of Poland between the wars. Now the PSN were marginal to the political game, but provided a useful banner for the various gangs of skinheads who had taken to beating up African and other foreign students in the high-rise estates of Wroclaw and Nowa Huta. Like the more peaceful National Party they drew their inspiration from the thinker Roman Dmowski who, in the 1920s and 1930s, had argued that nations were spiritual entities with distinct personalities. Implicit in this vision was the idea of ethnic purity; the Dmowski philosophy was anti-Jewish, anti- any ethnic minority. A Jew or an ethnic German would never be regarded as a Pole.

A second nationalist strand drew on the writings and example of Josef Pilsudski, the formidable Polish leader of the inter-war years. His nationalism was ready to accept other political forces and ethnic groups. But Pilsudskites also wanted to build a Greater Poland. Pilsudski had expanded Poland's frontiers into Ukraine, Belorussia and Lithuania. While that did not coincide with Walesa's plans, he did see in Pilsudski a handy model as a leader who stood above party politics.

Yet another thread that ran through the right wing was that of the clericalist parties. The most important was the Christian National Union (ZChN), led by the lawyer Wieslaw Chrzanowski who had advised Walesa in 1980 and who helped to draft the Solidarity statutes. How close were these parties to the popular mood? Judging by the results of the October 1991 elections they could command considerable backing. The Confederation for an Independent Poland, which carried the flame for Pilsudski, and ZChN both captured about ten per cent of the vote. The Centre Alliance of Jaroslaw Kaczynski, which shared many of the clericalist and nationalist values, also picked up around ten per cent. It was thus political common sense for Walesa to curry the support of these groups. He was always a natural leader of the frustrated and the inarticulate. That too was the basic constituency of the right-wing groups. And so a marriage of convenience was arranged. The effect could be seen immediately at Walesa's election rallies. Skinheads were often present and rare indeed was the rally when they did not beat up a heckler. A shrill questioner would often ask why the Jew-Bolsheviks were still in power, why Walesa did not take an axe to them. Walesa's appearance at the rally outside the Warsaw steelworks, kicking off his campaign in the capital, was typical of the new style. Walesa presented no programme. "My programme is your programme." On the fringes of the meeting somebody was being beaten quite badly by self-appointed vigilantes. The routine anti-Semitic question was fielded but Walesa merely dodged it, did not slap it down. Throughout the two-hour rally – during which Walesa mainly made unscripted pronouncements about the state of the economy and nation – there was a sense that Walesa, the skilled crowd politician, was not wholly in control. His anger was not theirs. Mazowiecki, still striving to be fair, summed up the mood. "I don't know whether they [the Walesa camp] promote anti-Semitism, but I do see that people who create such an atmosphere have rallied around him. This is like releasing demons from a bottle – it's very harmful. Sometimes Walesa distances himself from this, but the atmosphere persists." Mazowiecki felt this personally. His election posters were defaced every night; the graffiti-warriors gave his photograph a hooked nose and, lest anyone missed the message, daubed stars of David on the flysheet. At one rally a middle-aged woman tearfully tried to prove – with the help of an old newspaper clipping from Plock – that the prime minister was not Jewish, that he had been baptised a Catholic and that the local bishop had known the family. Bishop Orszulik also announced that he had found Mazowiecki's baptismal certificate. Walesa, instead of calling a halt to this absurd and distasteful campaigning, merely repeated his old folk-wisdom: that he was a Pole and proud of it and that had he been a Jew he would be proud of that too – so why should Jews hide their Jewishness? Walesa was in fact trying to span every nationalist current. In front of a crowd, he was a Dmowskite; in front of the television camera he was a Pilsudskite. Indeed the camera was usually angled to take in a small statue of Pilsudski on his trusty chestnut war-horse.

None of this helped to clarify what kind of national leader he would be if elected president. Adam Michnik, though, was certain about it: a politician capable of stirring up old ghosts was a liability. In a formidable piece of polemic Michnik made the case against Walesa. Entitled "Why I Will Not Vote for Lech Walesa", it painted a picture of an unpredictable and fumbling man who could not be trusted with the leadership of Poland.

Perhaps because they shared Michnik's doubts, many Poles did not vote for Walesa. But they also shunned Mazowiecki. The time for heroes had passed, or was slipping away. Instead people were beginning to think in Messianic terms: only a saviour capable of miracles could drag Poland out

255

of its hole. Piotr Kwiatkowski noticed something strange in his computer printouts about two weeks before the election. His CBOS sampling institute had predicted a two-horse race for months, but suddenly there was a blip on the screen. His returns were showing a surge of support for Stanislaw Tyminski, a slight bespectacled figure with the charisma and charm of a customs clerk. When Kwiatkowski first registered the Tyminski phenomenon it seemed like a statistical hiccup, the kind of support that would melt on polling day. A few days before the poll Kwiatkowski shrugged: "This is not going away, these people are determined to vote for him." Kwiatkowski was right. There was a Third Poland, a world apart from the Solidarity and Communist supporters, and nobody had noticed it. Walesa, who had been warning about the monopoly of Solidarity power and urging its break-up, had done his sums wrong; his political instinct had let him down badly.

Poland was a country of almost 40 million. At Solidarity's peak, in 1980–88, some ten million claimed to belong to the union while two million were Communist Party members. That left a lot of uncommitted people, especially as a number of Poles contrived to belong simultaneously to the Party and to Solidarity. By 1990 the ten million had shrunk to two million, and the Party had dissolved itself. It was natural then that millions of Poles would search for another candidate that had neither Solidarity nor Party affiliations, that was not part of the Solidarity old-boy network. In Tyminski they found their man, a millionaire who had seemed to drop from outer space to rescue Planet Poland. Mazowiecki too was rattled by the emergence of Tyminski. His rather haughty personal philosophy was that the election decision had to be made on the basis of the tested commitment to the common Solidarity cause. The choice could thus only be between Walesa and himself; Tyminski was a man without a biography. Or rather, it was so odd and eclectic that the Solidarity campaign managers could not take it seriously.

Tyminski had emigrated from Poland in 1969 first to Sweden, then to Canada where he eventually set up a small electronics company. He also established the Libertarian Party – an anti-taxation, anti-welfare, pro-individual liberty pressure group – which claimed about 3,000 members. During his period of exile in the West Tyminski spread his business to Peru. In an Indian settlement near Iquitos he had set up a cable television station and managed a restaurant. There he also married his second wife, Graciella, a fine-boned Peruvian woman who sat uncomprehendingly through her husband's many election rallies. Those were the undisputed facts. But a bit of digging by the Polish press raised some disturbing questions. Where did Tyminski's fortune really come from? The Canadian company, though consistently profitable, was hardly in the big league, turning in a before-tax profit of some 250,000 dollars. The Polish press also tracked down a report by a Peruvian parliamentary commission which claimed that Tyminski's cable network had been pirating Brazilian, Colombian, Venezuelan and North American programmes. Tyminski denied the charge and said *Gazeta Wyborcza* was muck-raking on behalf of Mazowiecki. But then the Interior Ministry revealed that Tyminski had entered Poland during the martial law years some six times – with visas picked up at the Polish consulate in Libya. Tyminski denied every having been to Libya and said there must be another Stanislaw Tyminski around. The newspaper *Zycie Warszawy* dug up Tyminski's army records and found that he had been exempted because of mental illness. The medical report cited behavioural disturbances and personality shifts. (It had been a common enough ruse to dodge army service by engaging a sympathetic psychiatrist. And, as one commentator put it, to be slightly mad was part of the political condition; to seek power in a country as chaotic as Poland went beyond healthy ambition into the realms of mental sickness.) Still, it made people read Tyminski's testament more closely. He had written, and published at his own expense, a book entitled *Holy Dogs*. "In order to connect all people with Polish blood in their veins, to give them a common spirit, one has to find a common goal close to their hearts and heads, independent of their personal convictions. One such goal that can unite Poles throughout the world is WAR." All key words in the book are set in capital letters in case the reader is tempted to skip. In order to work calmly for Polish recovery, wrote Tyminski, the country needs weapons. "The most effective weapon for Poland would be an intelligent missile of medium range with a nuclear warhead equivalent to one megatonne." Plainly, if Tyminski won the presidency Poland would become an interesting place. His appeal was that of all businessmen-turned politicians – Ross Perot, Milan Panic in rump Yugoslavia. He seemed to have clean political hands, and had concentrated his energy on becoming rich. Now he was about to show the electorate how they too could become rich and forget about political squabbles. A vote for Tyminski was a vote to forget history.

That was the reason for the voting on 25 November 1990. Walesa was first with just over 39 per cent of the votes, a long way short of the fifty per cent he needed for an outright victory. Tyminski was a clear second with 23 per cent, three per cent ahead of Mazowiecki. Tyminski was jubilant. Looking much younger than his 42 years, Tyminski could not conceal his excitement. He had knocked out Mazowiecki and now he was going for Walesa. "I expected these results and I'm really happy ... I hope that in the second ballot I will have better relations with the press and that there will be no lies and forgeries, that we will spend more time on the future than the past." The time for chortling at Tyminski had passed. The Solidarity establishment – both the Mazowiecki and the Walesa camps – agreed that Tyminski was a real threat, the possible vehicle for a counter-revolution. Walesa refused to appear at his campaign headquarters on election night. The loyal Kaczynski told reporters that Walesa was too offended by his failure to win at the first hurdle. A more likely explanation is that Walesa's plans had been thrown into confusion and he needed to think. He had prepared statements in case he won outright and for the eventuality that he would win narrowly ahead of Mazowiecki. In either case he would have made a conciliatory speech inviting Mazowiecki to cooperate in putting Solidarity together again. Instead, he had to gear up for another fortnight of fighting, he would have to bargain with Mazowiecki for his voters and above all he would have to focus very precisely on Tyminski's weaknesses to encourage the many Poles who might not bother to vote at all on 9 December. At Mazowiecki's campaign headquarters many of his team were in tears. They were in no mood to switch their votes to Walesa and save Poland from Tyminski; their feeling was rather that Walesa had created the mess and should now clear it up himself.

Michnik's analysis was the accepted wisdom of the government and the Mazowiecki camp. "Tyminski's success was the rout of reason and has brought shame on us all. If Walesa capitalised on his own myth and the frustration of part of the old Solidarity camp, Tyminski exploited the frustration of the people who did not identify with Solidarity. The mixture of these two frustrations produced the defeat of the Mazowiecki government. It might be said that Stanislaw Tyminski is a caricature-like byproduct of the political style Walesa presented at his rallies. 'Every one of you can be president,' he used to say. If every one, why not Stan Tyminski?" A CBOS analysis of the results showed that Tyminski had high support in Silesia, especially in coal-mining regions, that he was favoured by small-town dwellers, very young people (39 per cent of his supporters were under 24 years of age), by those who longed for a return of the welfare state, who rejected liberalism in the economy but not in social morals (Tyminski had come out in favour of legal abortion). Polling showed that Tyminski was considered nice (by 27 per cent compared to 19 per cent for Walesa), much less unpredictable than Walesa and as the candidate most likely to drag

Poland out of recession. These are typical "third candidate" results; Ross Perot attracted similar opinions in the US presidential contest of 1992. Still, for the die-hard Solidarity men Tyminski's constituency was entirely baffling. After the first round of balloting, Jaroslaw Kaczynski went to Malbork, a small town in the north of Poland. During a school visit he was shouted at by pupils: "They said – 'You claim it is all rubbish but we trust Tyminski, we want him as our president because he at least can promise that things will get better.' " The teachers whispered to him that the pupils were influenced by their parents, many of whom were working at the nearby army garrison. "I was watching these youngsters and I felt helpless. They were aggressive in a typical Communist style, accusing us of being a new nomenklatura, sneering at what we had done. As for the teachers, they were all for Mazowiecki – they even said they would not go to the run-off voting because it was morally impossible to cast a vote for Walesa. A total disaster." Kaczynski's one consolation was that the loudest of the teenage protesters were in fact too young to vote.

Mazowiecki and his government resigned the day after the votes had been counted. One could argue for months about the true meaning of the presidential elections but one thing could not be denied: the consensus support for the Mazowiecki government had been shattered. Walesa still claimed that one option, perhaps even the most desirable one, was that Mazowiecki should stay in power until early parliamentary elections tested how much backing there was for the Balcerowicz shock-therapy programme. In the meantime not only Mazowiecki but also Balcerowicz could stay in place, making only minor adjustments to the economic programme. But this idea was doomed, as Walesa well knew; Mazowiecki would never agree to serve under him. Walesa therefore kept his future plans vague. He needed Mazowiecki's followers on his side not only to beat Tyminski but also to give him a full pack of cards when he took over the presidency. If Mazowiecki supporters – in Western terms a blend of social democrats, Christian democrats and market liberals – withdrew from the political process, Walesa would become entirely dependent on the nationalists (Chrzanowski) and opportunist (Kaczynski) right-wing that had so enthusiastically supported his election campaign. It was time therefore to make some kind of peace with Mazowiecki.

On the Wednesday after the election Walesa rang Mazowiecki and Geremek and determined two things: there was still a depth of bitterness about Walesa's campaign, and there was a general agreement that Solidarity had to act as if it was intact for one last time to ward off Tyminski. That evening a session of the Solidarity campaign caucus was summoned by Geremek to consider two resolutions. The first, pushed through by Walesa's supporters, called on deputies to vote for him in the run-off. The second, drawn up by members supporting Mazowiecki, stated that it was the basic patriotic duty of all Poles to prevent Tyminski from becoming president. Simply, the Mazowiecki loyalists could not stomach signing a resolution that helped Walesa. Michnik resigned from the caucus because of its "horribly fawning attitude" to Walesa. In his fiery, stammered speech he said he would rather chop off his hand than vote for Tyminski – but he was also rejecting Walesa. Moreover, Walesa as the leader of the victorious side in the Solidarity war should talk to the leader of the losing side, Mazowiecki, not as emperor to subject, or boss to adviser, but as leader to leader. The next day parliament, infected with the general air of panic, refused Mazowiecki's resignation until his government gave a full report on its activities over the past year. That ensured at least a measure of stability during the last days of the presidential elections. But there was little doubt in anyone's mind that Mazowiecki was indeed finished; although he would later emerge as a competent opposition party leader (and later still as a UN special rapporteur on Yugoslav war crimes), he was burnt out. He was a private man, a man who cared about dignity and also a rational thinker; he had been overwhelmed by public quarrels, by the dirtiness of elections and the passion of partisan politics.

There was some reason to fear that Tyminski might make life difficult for Walesa. The raw election figures gave Walesa an almost 17 per cent lead and in the run-off all Walesa had to achieve was a simple majority. But if most of the Mazowiecki followers did not vote on 9 December, if the ten per cent who had chosen the Communist candidate plumped for Tyminski and if he could also pick up some of the six per cent that had gone to the farmers candidate, above all if Tyminski could mobilise the non-voters in the first round, then the Canadian Pole would stay in serious contention. For Tyminski everything depended on being able to set off a snowball of support. For Walesa it was a matter of changing style. To engage Tyminski directly would merely legitimise him. Walesa was to strike a statesmanlike role, to act as if he already had the presidency in the bag, while behind the scenes he had to mobilise the full forces of the Solidarity establishment.

The turning-point came on the weekend of 1–2 December. Tyminski had withdrawn from a television appearance on 29 November, demanding that the whole format of the programme be changed. Although Tyminski was mocked and accused of cowardice he was right to be suspicious of state television. Coverage of Tyminski had been laced with some very *ad hominem* attacks, including distinctly suspect claims that he had beaten his first wife. Tyminski's supporters regarded television in much the same way as they watched it during the Communist years – as a propaganda tool that automatically told the reverse of the truth. Critical programmes thus did not inflict much damage on Tyminski as far as his core constituency was concerned. But he was vulnerable in a head-on television duel with Walesa. Tyminski, after two decades away from Poland, spoke Polish in a rather wooden manner. He was at his most effective when using short crisp sentences, but his nature was to go on at length. The longer he talked the less coherent he became. He was like the perfectly sensible people who sidle up in bars and who present perfectly reasonable and reasoned solutions to the wars in the Balkans, to the problem of taxation and the public transport system – and who then suddenly veer off in a discourse about UFOs, Zionist conspiracies and men from Mars. Tyminski always seemed only a step away from Mars and his minders knew it, heading off a television appearance until it could no longer be avoided.

Walesa was well briefed before their joint appearance at a televised conference on the Saturday night. The rules were that both politicians had to field questions from the gathered journalists and should avoid direct confrontation. Walesa knew how to bend such rules. When Tyminski started to answer questions, Walesa would ostentatiously roll his eyeballs and suppress a giggling fit. He could also simulate outrage. In front of the cameras Tyminski repeated threats that he had made only at rallies: that he had compromising information on Walesa's past. The implication was either that Walesa had been collaborating with the Communists, or that he had been having love affairs. Pointing at a shiny black leather attaché-case at his feet Tyminski set the tone of the conference.

"I have a lot of material and I have it here and some of it is very serious and of a personal nature," said Tyminski.

"I demand that you publish these documents, that you show them right now!" snapped Walesa.

"Perhaps we can talk privately about it," answered Tyminski, looking Walesa in the eyes for the first time.

"No," barked Walesa, appearing to be genuinely angry. "If you accuse me like this, then show me the documents – open the briefcase!"

The briefcase stayed closed throughout the last week of the campaign. Was Tyminski bluffing? It had emerged in the campaign that several former secret-police colonels were on his national and regional election staffs and his main speechwriter, Roman Samsel, was a former journalist for the

Communist organ *Trybuna Ludu*. Samsel and other campaign organisers had connections that ran deep into the police and army establishment. It was thus conceivable that they had got hold of photocopied secret-police documents on Walesa. (One such file, which gave Walesa the police codename Bolek, was later to be used by ministers in the Olszewski government of 1992 to show that Walesa had collaborated with the secret police in the early 1970s. The dossier was written off as a crude forgery but it might well have been Tyminski's unused trump card.) In any case Walesa used the presence of so many police agents on Tyminski's team to warn that the businessman was a front for displaced Communists. Tyminski, who had previously denied having agents in his circle, told the television audience that he had employed the ex-policemen as an act of charity, "like Jesus when he invited Judas to become a member of his group". He saw nothing shameful about using secret policemen. "If someone cooperates with someone outside our staff, it's not my problem."

Most of the Polish audience watching television at home disagreed. By the end of the weekend Walesa's support had jumped to 58 per cent, Tyminski's had edged up to only 30 per cent. That Sunday the bishops issued their most obvious partisan statement in years, telling believers to opt for the candidate with Solidarity roots. And Mazowiecki, after a week of hesitation, issued a statement that accused Walesa of unleashing "a wave of demagoguery and easy promises" but which concluded: "In the face of the extreme irresponsibility which may endanger Poland, my opinion is that one has to vote for Lech Walesa." It would be difficult to find a more grudging endorsement, but the message was plain: Mazowiecki supporters should not stay at home sulking. Their absence from the polls might just put Tyminski in power, and that would be intolerable.

There was little surprise then when Walesa eventually won with a comfortable margin. Gdansk celebrated all night, bursts of *"Sto Lat, Sto Lat"* – May He Live a Hundred Years – gusting out of the windows in Zaspa, Nowy Port, in Oliwa, in the centre and the suburbs of the great Baltic port. A television report abandoned any pretence of objectivity and lampooned Tyminski while hailing Walesa in the manner of Caesar. Wojciech Reszczynski, a lean young television reporter who in an earlier era would have been busily penning an Ode of Victory and Joy, breathlessly commented as Walesa and Danuta drank their champagne. But elsewhere in Poland the mood was more restrained; it was the sourest of victories. The crowning of Walesa should have been the culmination of decades of struggle, the capping of the revolution. Walesa's second volume of autobiography is called in

English *The Struggle and the Triumph*, and ends with his election to the presidency. But what kind of triumph was it? Communism had been destroyed, but so too had Solidarity which had once embodied all that was noble about the fight for independence. Walesa's presidency was about to begin, but so too was the post-Solidarity era.

CHAPTER FOURTEEN

The president and his chauffeur

For seven months or so before the presidential elections there had been half-jesting chatter in Gdansk about what would happen when the Boss became president. The road to Warsaw would be widened into a multi-lane highway, ambassadors would have to be accredited to the shipyards, the heroes of the Gdansk underground (and almost everyone regarded himself as such) would become courtiers. Gdansk would be chic, the *de facto* capital. It touched everybody, the shopgirls in Grunwaldzka Street, the bank managers, the schoolchildren: the port had been brought closer to the centre of the world. The playful café talk about who should be Foreign Minister, who would be given which diplomatic post, stopped suddenly when Walesa won the presidency. Now it was for real and even Walesa's closest advisers, such as the Kaczynski twins, realised that they had no idea what the Boss was planning. Walesa had promised that he would never leave Gdansk, that he would commute every morning to the Belvedere Palace in Warsaw, or that he would set up his presidential team in Gdansk and rule by fax. The promise was soon broken. True, his first public visit was to the shipyards, where he invited the workers to call on him and keep in touch. The workers were happy for him, but also slightly cynical. "Leszek is one of them now"; "Are we supposed to bow or what?"; "Soon they'll call this place the Walesa shipyards"; "He'll forget us soon enough." Walesa left the yard in an armour-plated limo, accompanied by a gaggle of muscled bodyguards and flashing police sirens. The workers went back to the dry dock.

A temporary presidential residence was found in Gdansk: a finely restored pre-war villa that had belonged to the director of the shipyards in the 1930s. Walesa took two quick decisions. He sent his secretary Krzysztof Pusz to Warsaw to search for a large villa to house his family, and he demanded a list of parliamentary deputies with their home phone numbers. Walesa had no intention of staying in Gdansk; he had to show himself to

264

be a serious president. That meant ruling from the capital, and it meant finding a robust government to replace Mazowiecki. But neither mission proved simple.

Pusz and his team of house-hunters realised that the traditional residence of heads of state at the Belvedere Palace was unsuitable for Walesa. Jaruzelski had been using the place as an office but continued to live in a modest three-bedroomed house on Ikara Street, a short drive away. The palace was too small to house Walesa's family, the kitchen inadequate. It had not been renovated since the Second World War and many pieces of furniture had been mended with carefully concealed wire and string. Of course the Palace had a distinct history; previous tenants had included Czar Alexander's brother (who had had to escape disguised as a woman), Marshall Pilsudski, President Narutowicz (who was assassinated), the German governor Hans Frank and the post-war leader Boleslaw Bierut. This was not exactly a hall of fame.

Walesa could safely set up home elsewhere without seeming to flout tradition. Pusz decided that Gierek's former residence at Klarysew outside Warsaw might suit Walesa: it was big, there was plenty of fresh air for the children and with a motorcycle escort Walesa could be sped to the Belvedere in under half an hour. Danuta Walesa rejected the idea. Klarysew, she said, had been constructed for large formal receptions, not for living; the children would be uncomfortable here. Danuta also turned down the Otwock Palace where Walesa had been briefly held after martial law, and another house on Zawrat Street close to the residence of the American ambassador. By Christmas it was plain that the Walesas were in the midst of a serious row not about houses but about her future role. Danuta told Jaroslaw Kaczynski that she was determined to stay in Gdansk for the sake of her younger children. Their daughter Magda was attending a ballet school and that set a priority of sorts. Jaroslaw Kaczynski recalls the conversation with Danuta.

DANUTA: She has real talent – it would be a shame to take her away from the school.
KACZYNSKI: Mrs Walesa, these things can take nine or ten years. She'll finish one school, enter high school – it's worth moving her to Warsaw.
DANUTA: You know it may only be four or five years. Enough of this wandering about, the child is already eleven.

Danuta, in other words, had surmised that Walesa's presidential career could be relatively short, shorter than ballet school. Under the circumstances she did not see a pressing need to uproot herself from Gdansk. Lech would fly up at weekends (he took to hitching rides with a routine air-force training flight) and she would appear on the big occasions. But after a decade of politicking from home, with journalists and conspirators trudging through her living-room and with bugs planted in the bedroom wall, she was happy to distance herself from the political world. She had become accustomed to living without Lech. "I just imagine he's in prison again," she told a friend, "and if I see him now and then it's a nice surprise." Close observers of the couple had noticed a subtle change in their relationship since 1989. "Lech was talking of her with respect but more as if she were a trusted sister than a wife or physical partner," commented one aide who saw both Danuta and her husband at least three times a week. When we spoke in October 1989, Walesa had said, "Of course, I could play around with girls but I won't – my wife's too strict for that." It was a joke but a rather strained one. His irritability during the period of exile in Gdansk infected his home life; on some weekends, he barely talked to Danuta and snarled at the children, especially the boys. During the election campaign Walesa was constantly on the road and frequently asked an aide (usually Wachowski) to pass greetings on to his wife rather than do it personally. Even so Danuta was an election asset, especially in the second round when he was pitted against Tyminski and his exotic Peruvian Indian wife, Graciella, who could speak no Polish. "Will this be the Mother of Poland, *Matka Polka?*" he would ask on the hustings. The point was obvious to even the dimmest of the election crowd. Danuta, a Catholic who had borne so many children, was a natural candidate to be the wife of a Polish president. There was not much to be seen of the Polish Mother after the election, however. To make up for the blunder of excluding General Jaruzelski from the presidential inauguration, Walesa invited the outgoing president round to the Belvedere. Danuta played hostess, slightly gauche in a strange hat, but with a certain charm. Then she returned to Gdansk and Walesa settled into a bachelor existence. An official announcement stated that the Walesa brood would start school in Warsaw after the February 1991 winter break. This was amended to the new school year in September 1991. Quietly, over the ensuing months, the question was dropped. The children stayed in Gdansk; Danuta had won her case.

In Klonowa Street, a secluded carefully guarded thoroughfare a few yards from the palace, Walesa's aides found an apartment as a temporary home. He shared the flat with Mieczyslaw Wachowski and his priest-confessor

266

Father Franciszek Cybula. They had their own rooms but shared meals and watched television together. This was a decisive period in the relationship between Wachowski and Walesa. Wachowski had disappeared from public view after arguing with Walesa in 1983. Although he was the godfather of Maria Wiktoria, born during the martial law years, and was bound to the family in a dozen different ways, he did not turn up at Walesa's name-day parties. These were grand social occasions when opposition chieftains would come to pay their respects to the Solidarity leader in his apartment. Wachowski was certainly not unoccupied during those years. He set up a workshop to retread tyres, he sailed a great deal, including a trip around the world as a bosun on the *Zawisza Czarny*. He also divorced his wife. Suddenly in October 1990 he re-emerged at Walesa's side. At first he sat in the main secretarial office in Solidarity headquarters, helping to answer the telephone. But after a while he took on many of Pusz's functions. Pusz, a rugged man who liked his cognac, was overworked. He had no objection to Wachowski taking up some of the slack and did not even protest when Wachowski started to use Pusz's unofficial title "Secretary to Lech Walesa". Wachowski was a gifted office politician. Despite his patchy education and his worker's background, he had a talent for manoeuvre, the poisonous memorandum, the use of innuendo. He was behind the sacking of Walesa's two personal assistants. One, who had worked for Walesa for seven years, was fired for incompetence. The other was forced to resign after being accused of "immorality" – having an affair with one of Walesa's burly official bodyguards. The source of the information, which the secretary tearfully denied, was Wachowski. Pusz tried, unsuccessfully, to defend the women but Wachowski's judgment was trusted by Walesa. By the time that Wachowski had moved into the bachelor apartment with Walesa, Pusz had been sidelined. Wachowski, Walesa's former chauffeur, had within six months positioned himself at the right hand of the Polish president. Soon enough he would be awarded his own chauffeur.

Walesa's enemies said there could be only one explanation for the rapid rise of the driver: Wachowski must have had some compromising information on Walesa. Two theories were frequently voiced in public and in print. The first was that Wachowski was a trained secret agent who had access to Walesa's dossier and to some of his darkest secrets. There has been much hectic excavation of Wachowski's past to pin down this allegation. The best that anybody has come up with is a blank, unexplained, period in the 1970s when Wachowski might have attended a secret-police college. But the evidence for this is thin. Jaroslaw Kaczynski claimed to have found a police college photograph showing Wachowski but this quickly proved to be a case of mistaken identity. Wachowski has denied the claim but he has not tried to fill in the biographical gaps.

Anna Walentynowicz and the Gwiazdas claim that Wachowski used to procure girls for Walesa when he was Solidarity leader. Similar charges were made in an otherwise well-researched book by Pawet Rabiej and Inga Rosiewicz called *Who Are You, Mr Wachowski?*. The publishers refused to publish some passages relating to the procurement of women and secret-service connections. But some simple probing in Gdansk showed that Wachowski had a web of black-market connections and that he certainly knew his way around the red-light districts – contacts regarded as unexceptional for a taxi driver whose main pitch was around hotels frequented by Westerners. There is not much solid evidence of Wachowski's shadow life and even less to prove that Walesa had been nurturing a dark secret. Even if a fraction of the claims made against Wachowski were true, why would Walesa want to keep Wachowski at his side? Only in the crudest detective yarns are blackmailers given such a position of trust.

The most likely explanation for Wachowski's proximity to Walesa at this time was his discretion. Both Cybula, as a confessor, and Wachowski were out of the political mainstream. They owed nothing to Jaroslaw Kaczynski, or any other member of the inner political circle; they were, in Walesa's view, absolute loyalists. Walesa had embarked on a complex game which was aimed partly at cutting adrift the Kaczynski twins and their Centre Alliance party. Having initiated the process of "acceleration" and having wrongfooted the Mazowiecki team, having in effect organised Walesa's election, they now wanted to divide up the spoils. Walesa had no intention of letting this happen. He needed time and space; the Kaczynskis and their men, though they still had a limited usefulness, were scrambling for personal power and had put Walesa's interests on the back burner. Wachowski's merit was that he could sit in on countless conversations, aimed at re-positioning Walesa on the political spectrum, and say nothing. Later, in private, Walesa would think aloud, set out his tentative plans and Wachowski would be permitted to chip in. He was adept at gathering personal information about the new emerging politicians and passing it on to Walesa. It was the talent of a spy – but also of a good *chef du cabinet*. The president rarely used the morsels that Wachowski gathered but merely knowing the sexual peccadilloes or old political sins of those he was talking with gave him confidence. Wachowski had something else going for him: he was trusted by Danuta. She was reassured that Lech was living with Wachowski, whose wife she knew well, and Cybula. Both men, she was sure, would keep her husband on the right track. Alone, or in unsympathetic company, Walesa was wont to plunge into a deep depression. She understood that the presidency could isolate Walesa as much as the year of internment in Alarmowo. The enduring relationship between Danuta Walesa and Wachowski is another reason for doubting Wachowski's alleged role as a procurer.

Father Cybula's position in the very masculine ménage of Klonowa Street was not so clear. In theory he provided a channel of communication with Cardinal Glemp and even the Vatican, ensuring that the presidency would from the start be addressing the needs of *Catholic* Poles. In fact Father Cybula's contacts with the episcopate were rather flimsy. And the first reaction of the Vatican, on being presented with the protocol list for Walesa's first presidential meeting with the Pope, was to ask why an obscure parish priest had been included in an otherwise high-powered delegation. Father Cybula was the chaplain of a seaman's church, the "Star of the Sea", in Sopot but had been involved with Walesa since 1981. He had visited Walesa in internment and had been Walesa's confessor from at least that period. Cybula, like Wachowski, was not suspected of having private political ambitions; when Wachowski and Cybula manipulated others they did so purely on behalf of Walesa. The same could not be said of Father Henryk Jankowski, whose politicking and vanity had started to grate on Walesa's nerves. Cybula could be trusted to keep his silence; Jankowski loved an audience. Cybula was given his own office in the presidential palace, a set of phones and the salary of an undersecretary of state (then about $500 a month). His routine was settled soon after the move to Warsaw. He celebrated a 7.30 mass for the president in the Belvedere chapel, participated in a working breakfast with Walesa, Wachowski and other courtiers, and then took care of charity matters. Sometimes he was required to draft those of Walesa's speeches that touched on matters of faith.

The pushing and the pulling at the court of the new president was not particularly surprising. It was a feature of all political changeovers from the Clinton White House to the Yeltsin Kremlin. Early selections were made on the basis of loyalty and debts owed; there was thus a frantic competition to show one was more loyal, or others less loyal, to the president. To most ordinary Poles, the sight was distasteful. Walesa sat passively through this performance, occasionally pointing his thumb downwards but for the most part letting the games continue. As he had said at the hustings, *he* was the programme and so the best possible chancellery was the one that best projected *his* image. Since he occupied the only freely elected institution he could for a while view himself as the true voice of the Poles. It was just a matter of finding something to say.

Walesa wanted to place Jaroslaw Kaczynski as the formal head of the chancellery. Wachowski rang him and invited him to the Belvedere. "I had a slightly different idea and wanted my deputy Antoni Pietkiewicz to run the chancellery," says Kaczynski. "For myself I wanted the post of First Minister of State." That would have made Kaczynski into a kind of shadow premier. "But Walesa insisted – 'No, if you are to be the most important man, be the boss of the chancellery.' Eventually I agreed." The job had first been earmarked for Jacek Merkel, who had quite skilfully run the Walesa election campaign. He had a far more polished manner than Kaczynski and was a good organiser. But neither Wachowski nor Kaczynski liked him. Merkel was a market liberal, self-assured, an old underground hand with a web of contacts in the political class. By contrast, Kaczynski had been on the outer margins of the Gdansk underground and favoured a combination of state-steering and the market. Merkel was instead made head of a newly created National Security Council. This was an important but politically vulnerable position. Merkel and his deputy Jerzy Milewski had run much of the huge funding operation for Solidarity during martial law. They knew a great deal about secret-police infiltration of the Solidarity movement and about the corrupt underground activists who had diverted money into their own pockets. They also had dealings with Western intelligence agencies, or their front-men, who had taken considerable interest in Solidarity finances. On paper this might seem to have uniquely qualified Merkel to be the head of a National Security Council; he understood the business, could keep secrets, knew English, could think in global terms. In practice it opened him up for attack by innuendo. What kind of game had Merkel played? What kind of game was he playing now?

By March 1991 he had been levered out of his job on the spurious grounds of "exhaustion". In his place, Walesa appointed Jaroslaw's twin brother Lech Kaczynski. Merkel was bitter though not entirely surprised – Walesa had given him support then withdrawn it on a number of other occasions – and he may even have been rather relieved to get out of the hot-house atmosphere of the Belvedere Palace. Had he been confronted with any precise accusations he could have proved his innocence, or at least fought his corner. Instead the "exhausted" politician slipped quietly away to run a Solidarity bank in Gdansk. To the average Pole it seemed as if the Kaczynski twins had staged yet another successful coup; now they were running Walesa. "Actually the twins were being set up by both Wachowski and Walesa," says

270

a court insider who survived two shake-ups at the palace. "Walesa had already decided to clean out the PC [Centre Alliance] from the chancellery. First, though, he had a nominal debt to pay off. And he needed time. If people became impatient he would let the Kaczynskis take the flak and then drop them off. If they did a good job he would push them sideways into government, where they both really wanted to be anyway." Wachowski, who watched this process unfold, must have known that it could only work out in his favour. Sooner or later Walesa would need an informal "unpolitical" head of chancellery and security adviser. Wachowski groomed himself for the role. From the spring of 1991 he took it on himself to make discreet soundings in the army. Were the generals happy? What could the president do for them?

The Kaczynski brothers should have realised something was amiss when Walesa first encouraged, then scotched the chances of their candidate for the premiership. Walesa soon after his election victory issued a cryptic statement to the nation. The Poles, he said, had to work out whether they wanted to keep a semblance of the old Mazowiecki government in place and then go for early parliamentary elections; or whether they preferred an extremely new government and delayed elections. This was a confusing choice. Many Poles had voted for Walesa precisely because they disliked the Mazowiecki government, or at least its shock-therapy reforms. The second option was odd too: it would pit the new government against the old government in a way that would paralyse the legislative process. Fortunately, perhaps, Walesa had no intention of letting the Poles advise him one way or another. He had already decided that the government should continue with more or less the same policies as the Mazowiecki administration though with a more pliable premier. To abandon shock-therapy reform at this stage would frighten the International Monetary Fund, send Western creditors running for cover and send all the wrong signals to other East European states contemplating serious market reforms. Yet there was no denying that he had won the election with vague promises of change. He thus had to go through the motions of finding a prime minister who was markedly different from Mazowiecki. The Kaczynski brothers and Zdzislaw Najder (who first recommended himself as the ideal candidate) put forward the name of Jan Olszewski. Walesa did not much like Olszewski. His gentle demeanour hid great stubbornness. Walesa wanted to create a prime minister from scratch. His formal powers as president – nominating the premier, dissolving parliament if the budget was blocked, declaring a state of emergency, nominal supervision of defence and foreign policy – were limited.

271

He thus had to exercise power informally. The best way, perhaps the only way, to do this was to find a premier bonded to him by personal loyalty. Olszewski was too independent. He had a clique of friends, some, like Antoni Macierewicz and Najder, drawn from the dissident circles of the 1970s. Olszewski was also determined to gain control of economic policy. He wanted to strip Finance Minister Leszek Balcerowicz of much of his real power and balance Balcerowicz's monetarism with an active industrial policy that addressed the problem of the state factories. It was all too ambitious for Walesa. Olszewski was charged with finding a cabinet but secretly Walesa was putting together an alternative government anticipating Olszewski's failure. "Walesa was suggesting cabinet members to Olszewski that would have put him in an impossible position – he would have been surrounded by strangers," says Kaczynski. "Naturally he rejected the suggestions and gave up the mission."

Walesa pulled his rabbit out of the hat: a diffident Gdansk entrepreneur, Jan Krzysztof Bielecki was to be premier. Bielecki was a Thatcherite, a firm believer. His party, in truth little more than an economists' debating club, was called the Congress of Liberal Democrats and was based on the Baltic coast. Some party members had approached Walesa before the elections and sold him the idea of mass voucher privatisation. The future privatisation minister Janusz Lewandowski had been impressed by the speed of Walesa's conversion; there seemed to be nothing remotely socialist about him any more. "I think he would rather hang a portrait of Margaret Thatcher in his office than one of Peron," said Lewandowski in what was intended as a reassuring comment to his colleagues. Bielecki was not well known even in Gdansk. He had been the head of an economic research team in Solidarity headquarters in 1980–81 and on the night that martial law was declared had had the presence of mind to rescue a printing machine and take it to the shipyards, where it was used to run off the first underground bulletins. During the years of military rule he was unemployable because of his Solidarity connections. So he set up a private transport company (consisting of one truck) and a consultancy that linked the Gdansk opposition to more mainstream but reform-minded economists scattered among various universities and polytechnics. Walesa told me that "Bielecki was very much in the third division – but that's all right. Down there they try harder for promotion." Bielecki was certainly aware that he was not exactly on intimate terms with the president. Before the 1989 elections Walesa, "for whom I had done some work in the underground, kept asking: 'Bielecki? Which one is he?' He did not associate my name with a face." (*Tygodnik Solidarnosc*,

25 January 1990). The offer of the premiership came on the first day after Christmas when Olszewski was still trying to forge an acceptable cabinet. "We were flying together to Warsaw," recalls Bielecki. "We did not exchange a single word during the whole flight. Then we went to the Belvedere. Walesa sat down and told me he was entrusting me with the mission of forming a cabinet." In the event Bielecki turned out to be a shrewd choice. He was an affable and energetic man. Since he did not know how long his government would last – parliamentary elections were being pencilled in for spring, which would give him barely three months – he did not waste time. Rapid privatisation was made a priority. Balcerowicz stayed in place and if anything gained in importance. The Foreign Ministry, still under Krzysztof Skubiszewski, was told to press hard for a debt-forgiveness deal from the West. The Labour Ministry was given to Michal Boni, a close colleague of Jacek Kuron. The cabinet was in short not dramatically different from that of Mazowiecki's government. But its work was more focused and gave the appearance of making swifter progress.

Walesa's plan was simple enough. His constitutional powers were only dimly outlined. He had, in the absence of a new constitution, to re-invent the job and scratch together any power that he could. An interim government – one that was moreover convinced of its own limited lifespan – would find it difficult to prevent him from taking a day-to-day interest in army and foreign affairs. A contract parliament, whose composition and internal balance had been fixed in advance, could be sidestepped without giving the impression of being anti-democratic or authoritarian. The country's institutions were in limbo, and that suited Walesa as he tried to come to terms with his own institutional authority.

Once Bielecki was installed, Walesa could turn his mind to foreign affairs. His foreign policy adviser Janusz Ziolkowski knew how to present critical counsel gently. It was, he suggested, time to rebuild Walesa's image abroad. Walesa, though famously abrupt with diplomats and journalists, cared deeply about foreign opinion. Translations of the Western and Russian press were compiled and presented to him before the mid-morning coffee break even when he was merely chairman of Solidarity. At home he frequently irritated Danuta by turning the dials of his radio between the American station Radio Free Europe, and the BBC Polish service. The Western press had kept him alive as a politician during the barren martial-law years. Now Western politicians and public opinion were supposed to help him define the presidency. But first there were bridges to be rebuilt. In particular

Walesa had come out of the election campaign looking like an anti-Semitic rabble-rouser. That impression had to be corrected.

But Walesa's initial test of statesmanship came from the East. Soviet army tanks had rolled into Vilnius, the tough marine infantry were occupying strategic sites. The Lithuanian rush for independence had touched a raw nerve in the Soviet general staff. Who would protect the Russian minority in the Baltic republics, or the many army families that were garrisoned there? What was to stop an independent Lithuania inviting NATO to set up a base to replace the Soviet army and navy? From the perspective of the barrack-room, Lithuanian independence was a direct threat to Russian security. Walesa understood the anxiety of the Russians. There were after all 200,000 Poles in Lithuania. Walesa had pledged to be president of all Poles – and that presumably included the minority in Lithuania, the 200,000 in Belorussia (later Belarus) and the 300,000 in Ukraine. The *Ostpolitik* of the Mazowiecki government had struck a reasonable balance, trying to maintain normal relations with Gorbachev's Kremlin while also negotiating bilateral friendship treaties with its immediate neighbours.

That was, however, a rather tentative policy and it was soon thrown awry by the crackdown in Lithuania. Walesa had to improvise a policy. Was he to condemn Gorbachev for the bloodiness in Lithuania, should he pursue a narrow line concentrating on the safety and the rights of the Polish minority? Should he urge restraint on Vilnius, throw his support wholly behind independence, or just keep his nose out of the whole matter? The issue was of course complicated by history. For four centuries Poland had a personal, and then a state, union with the Grand Duchy of Lithuania. There was deep suspicion in Vilnius about a president who kept a small statue of Pilsudski in his office. Did Walesa have ambitions to restore Polish influence in Lithuania? Moscow was Big Brother, but what kind of brother was Poland?

Walesa reacted well. He backed Lithuanian independence and said that its eventual break with Moscow was inevitable: "Lithuania must have freedom – and it will have it. It is merely a question of timing and price" (*Zycie Warszawy*, 18 January 1991). He disagreed however with the tactics of Vytautas Landsbergis, which he said amounted neither to civil disobedience nor outright rebellion, neither fish nor fowl. "I would have acted differently. Had I decided to use peaceful methods I would have done so consistently. Had I chosen open struggle I would have waged it differently." This rather patronising tone irritated Landsbergis, as vain and as prickly a leader as Walesa himself. But there was little he could do about it because Walesa *was* helping. He had made clear for example that Warsaw would shelter a

274

Lithuanian government-in-exile should the axe fall. Senior Lithuanian officials were already criss-crossing the border, using Warsaw airport to fly to Western capitals and using the snug Napoleon Inn as a base for daily news briefings. On 16 January Vaclav Havel rang Walesa from Prague and proposed a joint Central European declaration condemning Gorbachev and the use of force.

"We have to send a clear signal now, Lech. Lithuania sets a precedent. What happens there could happen elsewhere," said Havel in his usual cigarette-stained, gruff tones.

"Well, Mr Vaclav," replied Walesa, "if need be we will talk and align our positions – if it comes to the worst – but if it doesn't we shouldn't set about scaring the bear. Making the bear angry may just play into its paws. The Russians would be able to blame us, say that we were stirring things up in Vilnius. That wouldn't be good for Vilnius or for us."

Perhaps because of the crackly line, perhaps because of the on-line translation, but more likely because of Walesa's disjointed telephone manner, Havel was bewildered by the conversation. For him it was important to establish a principle: that force should not be deployed against any country seeking independence. That was the great lesson of Prague 1968 and was a significant measuring-rod of Gorbachev's behaviour. However Walesa – as he later told the Solidarity caucus in parliament – was acutely aware of the 59 Soviet divisions that were still strung along Poland's borders, as well as the troops stationed in Poland. In 1991 what Walesa – and indeed all of Central Europe – had most to fear was a militarisation of Soviet politics. The great retreat from empire was under way: thousands of officers, deprived of comfortable billets, were beginning to worry about their future welfare and their present mission. Walesa, who had survived the many invasion scares of 1980–81, understood the psychological and political upheaval in Russia better than Havel; there was always more than one way of expressing moral outrage.

Walesa steered Poland through the Lithuanian crisis because he understood the Soviet mentality, he knew how Politburos worked, how scared and confused collective decision-makers became when confronted with popular protest. His experience not only of martial law and August 1980, but also of the shootings in December 1970, had equipped him with the necessary political vocabulary. It did not, however, provide him with a coherent *Ostpolitik*, a frame of reference for the future. Both he and the Foreign Ministry should have been nudged into serious thought by Lithuania. Instead it was shrugged off as a crisis successfully weathered. And the National

Security Council, rather than being geared up for a perpetual crisis in the East, became a political toy. Walesa turned his attention westwards.

Both Havel and Walesa were aware of the tradition that newly appointed Soviet bloc leaders make their initial foreign trip to Moscow, to kiss the ring in the Kremlin. Havel broke with this practice by making Germany his first destination as statesman. The gesture, much appreciated in Bonn, recognised the new alignment of power in Central Europe – Prague would become as dependent on Germany as it had once been on the Soviet Union – but it drew scorn from the Poles, and indeed some Czechs. Walesa played his cards differently: he visited the Pope. Afterwards he declared, as he had after previous audiences, "My batteries have been recharged." The weekly *Wprost* extended the metaphor – indeed, galloped away with it (10 February 1991): "There used to be a time when the batteries were taken to Moscow by the supreme authorities but now there is an alternating current and a situation in which the electrolyte coalesces . . . The Czechs recharge their batteries in Bonn, the Hungarians in Vienna, the former East Germans have got a dynamo, the Bulgarians still can't tell the positive from the negative pole while the Romanians keep finding that someone has pilfered the acid again. The Polish president travels to the Pope in search of biocurrents."

The Pope was broadly supportive of Walesa, though he was aware that various political groupings were emerging, many of them closer to Catholic teaching than the president. He approved Walesa's handling of the Lithuanian crisis; Walesa could play an important part in the new Vatican *Ostpolitik* that aimed at reviving and fortifying the traditions of Catholic politics in Lithuania and Ukraine, and even at competing against the Orthodox Church for new believers in Russia itself. The time was fast approaching when the Soviet Union would be confronted with the question: after Communism, what? The Vatican wanted to be ready with an answer. To Vatican officials it was somewhat disappointing that the new Polish president could not present a strict anti-abortion bill as a present for the Pope. The Sejm, the contract parliament, was resisting the histrionics of militant Catholic deputies like Jan Lopuszanski who managed to equate abortion-on-demand with Communism. Opinion polls showed that most Poles favoured some tightening of the rules but not the Draconian penalties – jail for women who terminated their pregnancies, for the doctors and for any accessories – advocated by Lopuszanski.

The consensus in the chancellery that spring was that Walesa was doing well. Some trips to the West – there was no rush to travel East – would help reconstruct Walesa's image at home. In marketing terms the aim was to make the transition from rough-edged union leader to wise leader of all Poles. Walesa's inclination was to bring the ex-Communists into the political game and demonstrate his readiness to stand on a left as well as a right leg. The Kaczynski twins, Slawomir Siwek (in charge of relations with parliament) and others at the Walesa court warned him against any such move; he should instead demonstrate his qualities of national leadership by gaining international plaudits. That is why every destination – France, Britain, the US among them – was chosen for its sympathetic government and public; Walesa needed a few easy publicity gains before embarking on serious business at home.

The United States was an obvious pitstop. Recalling his enthusiastic reception by Congress after the fall of Communism, Walesa felt sure he would be given a hero's welcome again. To make doubly sure Chicago, with its dense population of ethnic Poles, was put on the schedule. Diplomats had already found a rabbit for George Bush to pull out of his hat. To reward Walesa for keeping Leszek Balcerowicz and his policies in place, the president would announce a 70 per cent write-off of Poland's official debt to the US. Money would be earmarked for advice to US investors in Eastern Europe and some import tariffs would be reduced. The US set an example for other Paris Club governments who were not particularly keen to write off Polish debts. But it was not an altogether smooth trip. He had come prepared for some criticism about anti-Semitism and he had worked out a form of words for two scheduled meetings with Jewish representatives. "I'd do everything to prevent attacks of anti-Semitism ever happening again," he told an audience of 200 rabbis and other Jewish delegates. He would, he said, set up a special council for combating anti-Semitism. The council was indeed established, but after an early flurry of activity it settled into a quiet backwater, ignored and underfunded. In a session with Holocaust survivors in Los Angeles Walesa admitted that he had been loose-tongued on the subject of Polish Jews: "I did in the past give cause to be accused of anti-Semitism and I never want to repeat that. I'm not an anti-Semite – more to the point I believe a real Catholic cannot come out against the Jewish people." Those were the correct, and apparently sincere, words, but still the issue refused to disappear. Walesa began to grasp how badly his image had been dented abroad by the election campaign. He tried to bluster his way through a session of the American Press Club. Yes, he said, he loathed anti-Semitism. But then in a great tangle of words he came out with: "Poland is safe because it has one religion. If we had to cope with more than one religion, we'd have many problems. But we cannot rule that out because after the downfall of Communism there are plenty of lunatics..." What did that mean? The US reporters were baffled. The original Polish was even more turgid than the translation. In the context of anti-Semitism, was he saying that Poles and Jews living together were bound to rub each other up the wrong way, and so a single religion was preferable? Or was he (as Walesa's apologists subsequently claimed) predicting the problems of multi-ethnic post-Communist societies like Yugoslavia? Bigot or prophet?

Walesa had never really thought through a position on Polish Jewry; it did not seem important. He knew the Pope's teachings on Catholics and Jews but he also retained his primitive Popowo prejudices. Many Polish priests, even on at least one occasion the Primate of Poland himself, lurched from Wojtyla's high-minded prescriptions into silly, sometimes poisonous talk about the Jewish-steered American press that was stirring up sentiment against Poland.

Partly persuaded by Czeslaw Bielecki, an architect and former underground publisher of Jewish origin, Walesa started to identify his more obvious prejudices and cut them loose. By the time Walesa travelled to Israel in May his position was far better defined. He would acknowledge that Poland had displayed anti-Semitic attitudes – though obviously nothing to compare with the bloody crimes of the Germans – and he would ask forgiveness. Then he would argue that Poland had changed, had capacity for further change and that he himself would ensure that anti-Semitism was marginalised. That was the thrust of his speech to the Knesset, a text that was hectically re-written in the plane in an attempt to strike the right note. It still failed to please many Jews, though, who waved placards about Jewish blood and Polish shame. "It would have been better," commented the newspaper *Ha'aretz* (21 May 1991), "had we been a little less generous and not given the guest the mistaken impression that everything had been forgotten." Walesa found it difficult to live down his old anti-Semitic asides and many Israelis were not convinced by his apparent conversion to a model of tolerance. But he had faced the problem with candour and some courage; the difference between the US and the Israel trips showed that he had an ability to learn the techniques of statesmanship.

The repackaging of Walesa as a politician extended to his style of dress. Before the presidential elections Walesa's aides had approached a menswear designer from the state fashion house Moda Polska and asked her to run up a set of presidential outfits to replace the shiny, tight Sunday suits that comprised his current wardrobe. Krysdyna Wasylkowska stitched some double-breasted suits, sports jackets and a Chesterfield coat, all amply cut to disguise Walesa's widening girth. She devised a colour-matching chart and Walesa had it pinned to the door of his bedroom wardrobe. Danuta had always told him how to dress – not, admittedly, a difficult task given his limited wardrobe – but since they lived apart he had to make do with occasional advice from Wachowski. Walesa's courtiers were determined that the Boss should shed his proletarian image before embarking on any major diplomacy abroad. Italian and German clothes were brought in. A new hairstyle that seemed to expand Walesa's forehead was devised and the rapidly greying moustache was trimmed back.

But Walesa's harsh contours did not disappear. If left without a script on foreign trips he often resorted to his old nervous patter, charming enough when he was a union chairman but jarring in a statesman. His nights at Windsor Castle, he told reporters during his visit to Britain in April 1991, were sleepless. "The bed was so big I couldn't find my wife." He envied Britain her queen, he said. "Nations like these need a mother. The Queen is such a mother. Poland misses a mother." Walesa was certainly missing his mother; he told a relative in the first weeks of the presidency that he had not felt so adrift since his move from the countryside to the city. There was so much to learn and somehow, in the midst of contradictory advice, he had to hang on to his old values, his simple, robust views of morality and fairness. Once he had admired Edward Gierek as the paterfamilias of the Poles. Now he had slipped into that role, and it was beginning to chafe.

CHAPTER FIFTEEN

Historical games

The year 1992 was to be a difficult one. Poland was in a state of clinical shock. The uprooting of Communism, the dislocation of the economy, the upheaval of everyday life; the revolution was exhausting. Most polls agreed that people still wanted change but that they wanted to see the benefits more quickly. They were not in a bloodthirsty mood, did not want to string up the Reds, but neither did they want to see the former Communists flourish as private businessmen. The passion of revolution gave way to unfocused, knotted social anger and listlessness. A dozen private grammar schools had opened up in Warsaw alone – new opportunities for the new middle class. But the schools were perceived as an affront to those left behind, a mockery of the underfunded and overcrowded classrooms in state schools. Fat, chromed cars crawled around the capital, nightclubs throbbed, women started to advertise massage services. Yet the factories, the productive heart of the country, were as broken down as ever. The privatising draftsmen from the West came and went, offering technically perfect share schemes or costly chunks of textbook advice.

Women were the first victims of the revolution. They were the easiest to sack, shamefully under-protected by Solidarity. If they were lucky they were employed again at lower wages or on a part-time basis. Most stayed at home. State kindergartens were shutting down or desperately seeking private sponsors. Factory crèches were a thing of the past, of socialism. While the queues had disappeared – apart from critical points such as the US embassy and hospital corridors – the time saved had not translated into a better standard of living. "It had been exciting like a children's party," recalled a sociologist who abandoned her time-consuming honorary job as a legislative adviser to Solidarity to take up a more lucrative post with a Western company. "You know, balloons and fizzy drinks and sweets and lots of jumping up and down. Then came the tears and the arguments and the people being sick on the carpet."

Walesa took to playing billiards. Downstairs in the Belvedere P⸳lace there was a full-scale table. It was a game new to Walesa, though not to Wachowski, and he liked it. Walesa had good eye–hand coordination. As a teenager he had won a prize in a local archery contest. In the army he was classified as a marksman. Ping-pong remained a favourite pastime at the palace but Walesa's accumulated flab was slowing him down. Snooker was altogether more gentle and more intellectually demanding. There was something in the tactical play – boxing in the opponent or sending him flying into an alien corner, the careful potting – that was akin to the pre-party politics that was his lot in 1991. But he was beginning to grasp that more was required of him. He could carry on dividing and ruling and perhaps extract some kind of political philosophy of control out of his undoubted talent for destruction. To do so, though, required finding new enemies – the Gwiazdas and Rulewskis of 1980, the Jerzy Urbans and secret agents of the martial law years, Tadeusz Mazowiecki and the Warsaw clique of 1990 – and then splitting and snookering them. The presidential brief had to be broader. Walesa had to think in different terms. It was no longer enough to broker coalitions. He had to create a sense of independent statehood.

A prominent senator, a proud man who had been very close to Walesa in 1980, came to tea at the palace. Walesa was in playful, or at least competitive mood and soon abandoned any pretence at formality. He proposed snooker. The senator cried off, claiming a sprained wrist. Walesa then leaned forward, suddenly very earnest: "Tell me, you know history, did Pilsudski play snooker?" Walesa was on the search for a model. He had consciously adopted a pose of Pilsudski's for one of his election posters, but that was as far as matters went. The official line from the Belvedere was: Pilsudski was an authority in his own time but his experiences could not be applied to the present, temporary situation (Drzycimski, 20 June 1991). Yet the parallels between the two leaders of independent Poland, the Second and Third Republics, were striking. Even the political environment bore some comparison. In 1918 too there was a "war at the top". Charges of treason, corruption and collaboration with the occupying power flew thick and fast. Governments, flimsy coalitions, had an average lifespan of seven months. The first president, Gabriel Narutowicz, was elected by a Sejm that had come together as a result of a political contract. Jaruzelski, unlike Narutowicz, was not assassinated, but he was quickly swept aside. The Sejm in post-1918 Poland split into twenty caucuses and the tone of parliamentary debate deteriorated rapidly. The peasants' parties were at each other's throats. Communist deputies were regarded as malodorous – Pilsudski once ordered the police to drag Communist deputies out of their seats. There were serious attempts to stabilise the currency and contain public borrowing. But despite some successes Wladyslaw Grabski – like Leszek Balcerowicz in 1989–91 – was unable to supply the complete economic miracle demanded of him. Trade unions were staging hundreds of strikes in pursuit of better wages and working conditions. Farmers refused to pay tax and blocked the roads. Priests played a very public role (and in the 1918 regime were even elected to parliament). In 1926 Polish newspaper headlines expressed daily outrage about corruption scandals. Pilsudski said he would be able to win 300 parliamentary seats by merely using one slogan: "Beat the whores and the thieves!" Walesa won the presidential election partly by threatening to take an axe to corrupt officials: sometimes he would wave an axe for the photographers. In March 1992 67 per cent of Poles were convinced that financial corruption was on the rise and 89 per cent believed that the guilty people were being allowed to get away with it. In Pilsudski's Second Republic, the army was being purged of those officers who had served under occupying powers. In the Third Republic, there was a vocal parliamentary minority (that would briefly form the Olszewski government of 1992) arguing for a strict de-Sovietisation of the Polish army. In the 1920s, as in the 1990s, many in the political class were unable to work out who posed a bigger threat to Poland: Russia or Germany.

There are, of course, limits to such historical game-playing. Plainly, though, a modern independent Polish state, whether it emerged out of war or the breakup of empire, faced similar and recurrent problems. That Walesa should explore the idea of taking over Pilsudski as a model was thus quite natural. Pilsudski's mother (a safer bet than his wives, since he had a complicated private life) was regarded as the Mother of Poland, a role later awarded to Walesa's wife. They came from quite different backgrounds (Pilsudski was brought up in the tradition of nobility and military service) yet both were risk-takers, ambitious, with strong egos. Both shared a contempt for parliament. Perhaps nothing struck the Pilsudskite chord more powerfully than Walesa's impromptu speech at a rally in front of St Brigyda's Church in Gdansk. Walesa complained about the failure of politicians and then, referring to himself in the third person, burst out: "Walesa has failed to teach these people anything. Now I will show them how my people are fed up with their chit-chat. Who is in favour of dissolving the Sejm? Hands up please!" The crowd immediately raised their hands and chanted: "Long live the president! Get rid of the politicians!" (23 June 1991). By 1993, in the run-up to another set of parliamentary elections, Walesa had gone a significant step further and had taken over Pilsudski's idea of a Non-Party Bloc for Cooperation with the Government (BBWR). Pilsudski formed the Bloc before the 1928 elections. It grouped left-wing politicians, landowners and peasants, trade unionists and capitalists; they came together because they wanted to share in Pilsudski's personal power. There was no programme worth the name. Instead the coalition was based on a negative premise: that parliamentary rule should be limited, that parties should have no influence on government and that executive authority should be enhanced. Walesa's Bloc – using the same acronym – corralled free-marketeers and state interventionists, trade unionists and businessmen. "I divided important Polish issues into four sectors: employers, employees, farmers and people involved in self-government. The population should know today which group its candidate for deputy will belong to, and what problems he will deal with in the future Sejm." Forming such a coalition came easily to Walesa. The Citizens Committees were just such crude alliances. They had been broken up precisely to make way for a proper multi-party structure. By 1993 Walesa, unable to handle the complexities of party management, was galloping back to 1928. There was only one point to Walesa's BBWR: to boost his power at the expense of parliament. The headquarters of BBWR were set up temporarily in a closed-down kindergarten. The school urinals, built for four-year-olds, defeated the likes of Andrzej Olechowski, the 6ft 3in economic mastermind of BBWR. That was the first, and as it turned out, one of the least messy challenges awaiting Walesa's non-party party.

Both Pilsudski and Walesa had been political exiles – Pilsudski for years in Sulejowek outside Warsaw, Walesa for critical months in Gdansk – and they showed the pent-up resentments of the immarginated politician. They were fuelled by a sense of having been cheated; the cheats were the intellectuals, the "élite", party hacks, the small-minded and the high-minded. A specific form of energy was generated by this feeling of exclusion. It was energy appropriate for combat but difficult to reconcile with careful sustained rule. Pilsudski, operating in the authoritarian climate of the 1920s and the 1930s, was able to expend some of that energy. By contrast Walesa, frustrated by democratic process, was becoming sour. "I'm not Pilsudski. I'm not going to run around with a gun in my hand," he promised shipyard workers during a visit in June. But he said it wistfully. And he did little to dispel the idea that whatever model he should unearth from history – books on Charles de Gaulle had appeared on the bookshelves of his two-room apartment within the palace – he was inclined to dress up as a benign dictator. Where was the publicly stated commitment to parliament, to an independently run television, to strong responsible government? At best Walesa dodged these matters, at worst he and his staff tried to undermine anything that could sap his power or block his purposes.

Walesa was capable of learning, though, from Pilsudski's mistakes. The economy had been one of the marshal's blindspots. Walesa was impressed by Balcerowicz, by the stripped-down arguments in favour of shock therapy and above all by the admiration of the West for the Polish courage in adopting the Big Bang road to the market. He liked the idea that Poland was in some way leading Central Europe. And so despite the election slogans about "acceleration" and the vague promises of a change of economic tack, Walesa was convinced that Balcerowicz should stay. That was the thinking behind an economic summit held at the Belvedere Palace in May. Walesa's council of advisers – right-wing critics like Stefan Kurowski – were there and were encouraged to rip into Balcerowicz. But the Finance Minister had shrewdly anticipated some of the criticisms and devalued the zloty on the eve of the meeting. "The enemy had suddenly lost their main target," reflected a participant at the Belvedere summit, Jerzy Baczynski, "so they fired a few salvos as a salute and a few more at their own ranks. It has not been possible to use the president's prestige against the government. By declaring full confidence in the government Walesa stripped the economic opposition of virtually any chance of political victory – yet a mere two or three weeks ago it seemed that the Balcerowicz team could not emerge from the clash unscathed" (*Polityka*, 25 May 1991). Walesa did not have any deep understandings of the issues. Indeed, after his initial speech, he showed that he was deeply bored by the discussions. Antoni Macierewicz recalled that after his ten-minute address supporting Balcerowicz, Walesa sat down, slipped off his shoes and started to rub his stockinged socks against his leg – a gesture that Walesa only makes when his mind is elsewhere.

Walesa understood that he could amass power by exploiting the ambiguity of the presidential position; there was an argument, a thin one, for direct presidential intervention in police, military and foreign affairs, but that he could never hope to run the economy from the palace. Nor was it desirable to do so. Blame for unemployment and inflation had to be put firmly on the government's doorstep, not his. "I would not support the proposals to authorise me to issue economic decrees," he told a television interviewer (1 May 1991). "Because the president does not need such decrees. It is the government that needs such decrees. It has so many problems to solve and

284

parliament does not keep pace." Despite the hip-shot at parliament, that did not sound much like Pilsudski. Even so, Walesa was determined to make a Pilsudski-like strike against parliament. He had wanted elections in May. Since a new election law would first have to be drafted and passed, that proved impossible. Walesa knew all along that he had made an unreasonable demand.

The Sejm, on the defensive, came up with a draft which proposed a largely proportional system, with only 112 of the 460 seats in parliament chosen on a first-past-the-post basis. It was the result of long consultations and reflected the fears of most groups – including all the post-Solidarity parties – that a first-past-the-post system would wipe them off the map. Walesa rejected the bill. The electoral procedures were unclear, he said, the bill discriminated against the Catholic Church (because of a ban on political activity in churches) and it limited the rights of political émigrés. The real reason was that some of his advisers had told him the bill was weighted in favour of the broad left, the ex-Communists, the left-wing of Solidarity and Mazowiecki's supporters. Did Walesa agree with his advisers? More likely he played along with them because he wanted to put parliament into *Zugzwang*. If they did not redraft and re-submit the bill within weeks, elections in October (the new date) would have to be cancelled. Three months had to pass between the ratification of a bill and its implementation. If parliament could not meet the deadline, it could be blamed for blocking democracy and would allow Walesa to rule by presidential decree. If parliament came up with a quick solution Walesa would still have accomplished a propaganda coup: parliament would have been humiliated and would be seen to be dancing to his tune. Another bonus: the Pope's pilgrimage to Poland in June was, as usual, increasing the religious fervour of the Poles. By making a stand on the rather marginal issue of political activity in churches, Walesa showed himself to be the Pope's champion. Yet the gesture did not, as anticipated, boost Walesa's popularity.

Partly this was because of the nature of the pilgrimage. The Pope, looking tired and even ill, rarely stirred the usually thin crowds. His message was no longer fervently anti-Communist but rather anti-abortion, not an issue designed to spark spontaneous applause from his youthful audiences. But chiefly, Walesa's ploy fell flat because of the suspicion that he was itching for a strong-man role. It is difficult to detect a general yearning for a Pilsudskite leadership from the opinion polls of the summer of 1991. The OBOP polling institute found one per cent of Poles willing to state that Walesa was doing a "very good job" on the domestic front. Almost 26 per cent said he was doing a rotten job, while 51 per cent described his achievements as merely "average". Walesa had fallen behind the Primate, Jacek Kuron, the Foreign Minister, Adam Michnik, and even Tadeusz Mazowiecki in social approval ratings. The fact is that the three big stabilising planks of post-Communist Poland had been smashed. The round-table philosophy which could have served as a rallying point had been shattered by the rhetoric of de-Communisation. The Solidarity pattern, the mass movement that could reach any region and almost every professional group, was broken up by the "war at the top". And the debate about abortion had taken away the Church's role as a potential peacemaker among warring factions; it had become a party to a political conflict. It was even using the inflated vocabulary of party politicians. Primate Glemp complained of the "barking mongrels" of the press. "Now that the three chief stabilising systems have been destroyed," said Adam Michnik (interview in *Prawo i Zycie*, 22 June 1991), "the political parties are fragile and so is overall democratic stability. It is easy to imagine the idea – which comes from all milieux – that a dictatorship is needed in order to protect the state order. I hear with horror the authoritarian calls for iron-handed rule."

To many it seemed as if Walesa was readying himself for action. There was his outburst to nervous Solidarity union leaders: "I will be tough if we fall into anarchy. I will use all means and force to defend our ideals of 1981." He was speaking after putting an end to an air-controllers' strike that had paralysed air traffic over Poland for twelve hours. Walesa had threatened to place the controllers under military command. "This is where the joking has to stop," he barked at the strike leaders. "You should not put the government and the president in such a situation." In the absence of solid democratic institutions, and with the Bielecki government on very thin ice, Walesa could be spurred on and on; there seemed to be no limits to what he could do. Solidarity chieftains warned him (13 June 1991) that Poland was on the brink of an uncontrolled explosion, because, as one said, "Instead of working people it is the smart-alecs and the fiddlers who profit from the reforms." Walesa replied: "Thieves will be punished, even if it has to be done by special courts. I will take back every stolen zloty and if necessary I will leave them standing in nothing but their socks." (The thieves referred to were ex-Communists.) Then Walesa added: "Organisers of strikes are also breaking the law. Strikes interfere with Poland's normal life." He might have to order the use of force to break such strikes, he warned. "I wonder whether evolution from Communism to democracy is possible or whether we need some different, tougher methods," he said.

Strikes interfering with Poland? This was the hero of the Gdansk ship-yards? Perhaps Walesa thought he was speaking with the voice of Pilsudski. In fact he reminded people more of his old opponent General Jaruzelski. Jerzy Urban, Jaruzelski's tart-tongued spokesman, gleefully seized on the parallels (*Nie*, 20 June 1991).

What exactly does President Walesa say and do?
1. In a letter to leaders of parliamentary parties he threatens to resort to radical political measures if his veto of the electoral law is overruled. General Jaruzelski made similar announcements addressed to Solidarity prior to the imposition of martial law. From now on Walesa will continue making such threats on various occasions.
2. He demands special powers for the government so that his decisions can replace laws, ignoring parliament. Premier Jaruzelski also tried to obtain special powers in the autumn of 1981.
3. Walesa proposes that trade unions be given certain powers of prosecution to combat nomenklatura-based companies and initiate special organs to persecute economic offences. This is reminiscent of old, unsuccessful methods of venting public anger through the people's inspectorate and special repressive actions that were conducted under martial law.
4. Walesa tells Solidarity leaders exactly the same thing General Jaruzelski and deputy premier Rakowski used to say in 1981: that anarchy and violation of the law would have to be answered by force, that strikes are a burden to Poland, that their organisers are responsible for breaking the law and that this will lead to the disintegration of the state. Hence the president, Walesa adds, will be compelled to use force if the reforms are endangered . . . We remember all this from 1981. Somehow Walesa does not feel ridiculous when he delivers the same speeches he used to listen to and argue with when sitting opposite Rakowski at the table.

Urban was of course arguing from his usual position of utter cynicism. In Urban's world view the actors change, but the mechanism of defending power – in the name of avoiding greater evil and protecting the state – remains unaltered. Nonetheless there was more than a grain of truth in the criticism.

It was however the August coup attempt in Moscow that brought home the fickleness of Walesa's position. He was, it emerged in a few tense panic-stricken days, neither Pilsudski nor Jaruzelski nor even Gierek. When it came to a global crisis, one that directly threatened Polish interests, he turned out to be a rather frightened man with an unsure touch. His handling of the crisis showed that the presidency as a decision-making centre had been stripped to its bare bones: Wachowski, and anybody Walesa could get on the telephone. It showed that Poland had only a threadbare *Ostpolitik*. And it demonstrated clearly that Walesa could never, by himself, become a dictator in the old manner. He had some access to the leaders of power but at critical moments did not know which one to pull and which one to push. The fact that many more mature Western leaders faced a similar dilemma was no consolation and no excuse: Walesa was supposed to be the man who shattered Communism and one of the architects of the new order in the East. He, more than, say, President Mitterrand, should have grasped how to behave.

Early on the morning of 19 August, a colonel in the Polish secret service woke up Wachowski and told him that a state of emergency had been declared in Moscow. Wachowski was the only man authorised to wake Walesa in emergencies. Within the hour the Prime Minister, the Defence Minister, the Interior Minister and a representative of the Foreign Ministry were in the palace sitting around a long table waiting for Walesa to speak. That group comprised the political core of the National Security Council. In theory, the council, which had been meeting regularly ever since Merkel was deposed as its chief, should have devised a political and operational strategy to prepare for a coup in Moscow. There had been rumours of such a military takeover for months. Yet Walesa behaved as if Poland's politicians were working from scratch, as if the coup were merely an opportunity for yet another grand improvisation. "We set up an extra constitutional body, a staff that could for example mobilise the police and the army," said Walesa (press conference, 28 August). The men drew on a makeshift Ministry of Defence document that had been drafted in 1990 in case of a Soviet attack on Poland. It was outdated and full of holes. And so these men, at one of the most critical junctures of the new Polish state, found themselves discussing details such as how to keep Polish bakeries working should there be a flood of refugees across the eastern border. The implications of the coup attempt sank in quickly though. A military anti-reform regime would have immediate effects on Poland. There were still hundreds of thousands of Soviet troops on Polish terrain. The new junta, backed by officers embittered by the enforced retreat from Eastern Europe, could try to depose the Solidarity establishment or at least strongly influence the political game. And there was no hope of support from the West; Walesa had already made plain in a visit to Brussels that Poland was not even contemplating an early application to join NATO. European Community membership was also a distant dream. There was thus a possibility that a newly aggressive, nationalistic and militarised Soviet Union would try to turn back the clock and "Finlandise" Poland.

The next morning, entering the Cabinet office, a reporter asked the pale Bielecki about the October elections. "We don't know if there will ever be any elections in Poland again," he said in a quavering voice. At the very least Poland had to reckon with a great tide of refugees from the East. A successful coup would mean, according to Polish analyses, fighting on the western peripheries of the Soviet empire; probably a violent assault on the Baltic republics; a breakdown in the food chain; financial chaos. As long as the Polish–Soviet borders were relatively open, Poland would be the first choice of refugees. Yet there were almost no preparations for such numbers. The most important deficiency was that of a coherent policy towards the Soviet Union. How important was Gorbachev's personal survival to Poland? Was Boris Yeltsin a credible successor? If Ukraine broke away – perhaps violently – from the Union, should Poland make a choice between Moscow and Kiev? As a matter of principle, was Warsaw to support a Union – albeit as a confederation – or the outright independence of individual republics? What responsibility did Poland have for the Polish minorities in Lithuania, Belorussia and Ukraine? None of these questions had been addressed by Walesa as president. Certain assumptions had been used by the Foreign Ministry in developing a practical day-by-day policy, but the concentration had been entirely on how to integrate successfully with the West. His confirmation of Stanislaw had been a sign of Walesa's indifference. Walesa's policy towards the East had been coloured entirely by the domestic political game. He had insisted for example on the withdrawal of Soviet troops and then let the matter quietly drop when there were no more votes to be squeezed out of the issue. The staff scrambled around for telephone numbers. Walesa even rang Jaruzelski to ask him to intercede with friendly Soviet army officers in Moscow. He rang Havel in Prague, Antall in Budapest. He rang local politicians with a smattering of Russian, Polish ambassadors throughout the world. He rang everybody apart from Boris Yeltsin. (It was apparently difficult to find his telephone number.) "Frankly speaking, President Walesa could have displayed much more activity," said Oleg Rumyantsev, a Russian social democrat and one of Yeltsin's closest collaborators. "And not only Walesa. Where were our friends Michnik, Geremek, Frasyniuk and Kuron? During the putsch we didn't devote that much thought to it but we are now beginning to analyse the course of events."

At last Yeltsin's number was discovered. By then the outcome was already clear: the coup had crumbled. Yeltsin told Walesa what he had already told dozens of Western politicians: that the state-of-emergency committee had been declared illegal, that the army, the KGB and the Interior Ministry in Russia were subordinated to the Russian president. The official transcript of the conversation says: "Walesa asked Yeltsin to convey his best regards and words of friendship to Gorbachev, wherever he is." A later phone conversation with Gorbachev seemed to mock Walesa's lack of determined action. (Gorbachev: "I greet you, Mr President, my dear neighbour. I would like to tell you how grateful I am to you for immediately siding with our joint course, from the very first hours . . .")

Walesa subsequently swaddled his bungled moves in an elaborate self-justification. He had acted prudently, he stressed, with restraint, like a statesman. Was that not what was required of him? A brainstorming session at the palace a week after the coup showed him that in fact he had been found wanting in many different ways. Zdzislaw Najder made the most cogent criticisms. He said that Polish foreign policy had been passive and muddled towards the East for the past two years and as a result Poland had become an object rather than a subject of international policy, a client waiting for the go-ahead from Moscow so as not to "irritate the Russian bear". Walesa grew uneasy. That was precisely his phrase. "We have always been late," said Najder, "to take only the question of Lithuanian independence. As for the coup, Polish society was not prepared for it at all. And Poland has not been looking after its countrymen in the East." Najder proposed an immediate recognition of Ukrainian independence, even without waiting for the returns of the December referendum in the Ukraine. Moreover, there was no sense in sending delegations to Moscow, he said. "We should be sending our delegations to all the individual republics which need our food rather than to Moscow once again." Najder spoke with the vehemence of a man who aspired to be foreign minister, but also with the authority of his years at Radio Free Europe. He knew, certainly far better than the Belvedere team, that Poland should completely reorientate its policy and acknowledge that the Soviet Union was no more. Walesa was still convinced that a form of Communist commonwealth would survive. In the same debate Walesa said: "What we would like to do is not the same as what we can do. The Soviet Union treats us differently than Hungary and Czechoslovakia." The phrase could have been uttered by Jaruzelski ten years earlier.

The Moscow coup was a defining moment for Walesa and for the Polish political future. For many of Walesa's right-wing admirers it was also a moment of revelation: their chief was not a revolutionary, they suddenly realised, but a slightly remodelled version of *Homo Sovieticus*. Jan Parys remembered the change in mood: "The total fear of the politicians, the silence of the government and the Belvedere, later some meaningless commonplace statements." It went much further than that. Prime Minister Bielecki had in fact had to talk Walesa out of dispatching a congratulatory telegram to Yanayev, one of the leaders of the August coup. "Walesa's reaction to the putsch was depressing," says Grzegorz Kostrzewa Zorbas, a high-ranking foreign-ministry official in charge of negotiating the Soviet troop withdrawal from Poland. "He waited for the results, was certain of the old system's final victory, was psychologically ready to accept the new, even more Finlandised relationship with Moscow. That is the only explanation for his supine, fortunately unsent cable to Yanayev . . . After the putsch there was an ideal moment for negotiating an earlier date of troop withdrawal from Poland and embarking on a new stage of Polish–Russian relations." Instead, says the diplomat, Walesa backtracked. In a conversation with Gorbachev, Walesa promised not to take advantage of the situation and humiliate the Soviet army. "Poland behaved of its own accord like a castrated mongrel because of the president. It wasted a great opportunity and made an offer of continued imperial military presence," said Kostrzewa Zorbas.

Some of Walesa's nationalist admirers refused to accept that their former hero was selling out. They looked instead for a puppet-master and found an unlikely one in the form of Mieczyslaw Wachowski. What was the nature of his power over the president? How far was he dictating policy? What were his sources of authority and information? But irrespective of whether they blamed Wachowski or Walesa, the die was cast. The nationalist right was bracing for elections and some participation in a new centre-right government alignment. Once in power they would try to correct the wrongs committed by the Belvedere court and by the president who could not shrug off his old cautious respect for Moscow and for Communist authority.

CHAPTER SIXTEEN

Black magic

A large Interior Ministry truck, escorted by two jeeps of armed troopers, drove to the paper mill in Swiec in April 1989. The commander demanded that thirty crates of secret files be destroyed immediately in the pulping machines. Soldiers stood by, smoking and cracking jokes, while the huge, loud crushing machinery ground down every one of the secret biographies. The files were from Gdansk police headquarters. The police had drawn the appropriate conclusions from the Round Table talks – it would soon be a liability to keep easily accessible information about collaborators or clandestine police operations within the Solidarity hierarchy. Three further truck-loads came that year to Swiec from the central archives of the secret police. Was Walesa's file among the pulp? Was Wachowski's file there too? If the dossiers survived, were they tampered with? Was the KGB involved?

Sadly, these questions came to dominate the Polish political scene. It was a world without certainties. For many Poles, confused by the whirligig of change, Walesa had been the last political certainty. Yes, he was a peasant, a bully, a man obsessed with power – all these things, and more. But that he was in the pay of the police, that he steered the revolution as a conscious agent of the Communist secret service: that was hard to believe. It would make a nonsense of everyone's lives. And it would make Walesa a version of Ion Iliescu, the sinister Romanian leader who with the help of the Securitate became the successor to Nicolae Ceausescu.

The spy scandal – or more precisely, the questioning of Walesa's roots and loyalties – arose from the October elections. The results were a mess, a jumble of 29 parties. As expected, Tadeusz Mazowiecki's Democratic Union party came out on top, but only just. The main parties – the Democratic Union (12.2 per cent), the ex-Communists (12.1 per cent), the pro-Communist Farmers Party (8.9 per cent), the Catholic Election Action group

292

(8.8 per cent), the Centre Alliance (8.7 per cent) and the Confederation for an Independent Poland (8.6 per cent) – hovered around the 10 per cent mark. There were a number of surprises, including the strong showing of the ex-Communists. Walesa almost certainly contributed to this success by making a televised pre-election speech attacking the Communists. The point, he was to claim later, was to mobilise the voting public. The real effect was to mobilise the pro-Communist vote. The low turnout on Poland's first fully democratic elections for half a century (barely 42 per cent of Poles turned up) probably helped to boost the Communists; pensioners, the backbone of the leftist vote, have always been the most disciplined of Polish voters. The combinational possibilities for a future government were strictly limited. In theory Walesa could have found a majority among the Christian parties, the left, the right, or the opponents of economic reform. In fact, a number of difficult personalities and awkward policy differences restricted that choice.

Nobody wanted to join an alliance with the ex-Communists, the second largest party, since that would smack of a Restoration. They first had to prove their democratic credentials – and as in Italy that was thought to be the work of generations. Without the Communists, it was difficult to piece together a liberal–left coalition. But a nationalist coalition was also a tricky prospect since it would almost inevitably mean striking up a deal with Leszek Moczulski of the Confederation for an Independent Poland. Moczulski was a veteran oppositionist, though always in competition with Solidarity, and was one of the most intractable personalities on the political scene. Only one thing could have brought Moczulski's 38 parliamentary seats into a government: the offer of the Defence Ministry. Walesa would never have approved such an appointment and no serious candidate for prime minister could consider such an offer. Moczulski, a temperate rational man in private conversation, had a strong fanatical streak; it was not difficult to imagine what he could have done as head of the army. For the Polish army was one of the key elements in the equation. It had been largely untouched by the revolution. Gentle, very gentle, reforms and cutbacks were being carried out under the stewardship of Admiral Piotr Kolodziejczyk, but Poland still had one of the strongest armies in Europe. The challenge was to convert it from a Soviet-trained force ready for an offensive war in the West, to a more democratically-minded force prepared to cope with the collapse of the Soviet Union. The condition of the army influenced many debates: how fast Poland should or could integrate with the West. The relative balance of power in Central Europe (Hungary and Czechoslovakia had puny armies), the capacity to stand up to Moscow in political quarrels, to reach separate arrangements with Ukraine, the political position vis-à-vis Kaliningrad and the Baltic states, the standing of the Soviet troops within Poland and the pace of the Soviet withdrawal from Germany – all these issues demanded intelligent handling of the army. Moczulski would plainly have been a risk. But Walesa, who had the technical post of supreme commander of the army, was scarcely more reassuring.

The army was to emerge as a key issue only after several months. Walesa's first concern was to find a line-up that would guarantee the construction of a sensible economic policy. That was difficult, if only because one plausible reading of the election results was that the consensus for shock-therapy economic reform no longer existed. Walesa chose to overlook this, claiming that almost 60 per cent of non-voters were essentially passive supporters of reform. He would be their voice – that was his constituency. The critical question was thus: should some form of modified Balcerowicz–Bielecki programme be put in place, or should there be a radical departure, a "breakthrough"? Walesa nominated Bronislaw Geremek as candidate-premier. That was largely a matter of protocol – since Geremek's Democratic Union was the largest party – and the aim was rather to clear the board to find a solution that did not necessarily include the Democratic Union or the ex-Communists. Predictably Geremek failed to put together a government. Walesa put forward Bielecki. That also foundered on the rocks of right-wing objections. Walesa, perhaps to scare politicians into agreement, hinted that he could become premier himself.

The most active blocking force was Jaroslaw Kaczynski's Centre Alliance. Having been ousted from the presidential chancellery, Kaczynski was full of resentment. His conversion from close Walesa ally, and effective election manager, to full-blown enemy of the president had taken just over a year. There was more than wounded ambition at stake; Kaczynski argued that it was Walesa who had changed, that he had cheated the electorate by promising a clean-out of Communists and a more dynamic policy. Now it seemed Walesa was searching for a puppet prime minister instead of pushing on with the revolution. Kaczynski was sure that there was one man strong enough to resist Walesa, wise enough to govern, likeable enough to hold together a disparate coalition: Jan Olszewski. Walesa had already resisted Olszewski once. In December 1990, bending to Kaczynski's pressure, Walesa had given Olszewski the mission to form a government. But from the very first moment Walesa did his best to thwart Olszewski, to the extent of faxing him a full cabinet list and insisting that all the names mentioned

294

should be accepted by Olszewski. Walesa probably thought he could trip up Olszewski, again and so gave him the brief.

Olszewski however was a doughty figure; his family came from a long Polish Socialist Party (PPS) tradition and he had begun his political career – as a law graduate, writer for the weekly *Po Prostu*, member of the dissident Crooked Circle Club – as a reform socialist. But he drew closer to the Church and by the time he became a member of the Bar in 1959, he was already launched as a human-rights campaigner. He defended Jacek Kuron in 1964, signed dissident documents, helped draft the Solidarity charter, negotiated on behalf of Solidarity, and helped to prosecute the secret police murderers of Father Jerzy Popieluszko. It was a track record that could stand comparison with almost any other Polish politician. He was a stubborn, loyal, blunt-speaking bear of a man. Walesa started to lay his booby-traps. He refused to take part in Olszewski's coalition talks and instead sent Wachowski as his plenipotentiary. It was viewed at the time as a calculated insult: "Walesa sends his chauffeur!" said one headline. Wachowski, though, was already far more than a chauffeur. He was Walesa's eyes and ears and, in this case, his incisor teeth. Wachowski, speaking for Walesa, repeatedly suggested that the president would accept an Olszewski line-up if it excluded the Centre Alliance and brought in the Democratic Union. This political manoeuvring – rejected out of hand by Olszewski – was accompanied by some below-the-belt tactics. The palace accused Kaczynski of plundering a special presidential fund while he was serving as head of the chancellery. Kaczynski denied the charge, and the timing of the "discovery" was clearly supposed to hurt Kaczynski's chances of taking part in a future government. The level of political debate was abysmal.

It was not altogether clear whether Walesa or Wachowski was responsible for this infighting. Certainly Walesa was not above making barbed references to Kaczynski and "his husband". Kaczynski was a bachelor but denied that he was homosexual – a politically wounding accusation in the context of militantly Catholic parties like the Christian National Union, whose representatives were describing Aids as a divine scourge on homosexuals and prostitutes. Much to the chagrin of Walesa, both Olszewski and Kaczynski survived. A vote for the Speaker of parliament, the Christian National Union politician Wieslaw Chrzanowski, showed that there was a shaky majority for the politics of the clerical-right. Walesa dissociated himself from Olszewski's cabinet list. Olszewski resigned. "During my meeting with the president yesterday he said he would not co-operate with the government whose composition and programme I have presented. Under the circumstances, in spite of the Sejm's support, I see no possibility for fulfilling the mission entrusted to me," Olszewski wrote to Chrzanowski (17 December 1991). Walesa immediately started to sound out an alternative premier while Kaczynski worked the parliamentary lobbies on behalf of Olszewski. The next day, the Sejm voted to reject Olszewski's resignation. The breakdown of the voting showed how flimsy was his support: 132 deputies were in favour of him stepping down, 73 abstained and 214 voted to keep Olszewski as prime minister. Even so, it was a hard knock for Walesa. He was saddled with an openly hostile government that was now rightly suspicious of any political statement by Walesa. Kaczynski publicly reminded Walesa of the example of France where Jacques Chirac, a right-wing politician, was head of a government during the first presidential term of the Socialist François Mitterrand. Walesa's style was not easily matched, though, with French cohabitation: he needed enemies, but only one at a time. He could cope with a self-willed parliament, but he needed a dependent premier for the simple reason that the powers of the Polish president were much more modest than those of the French. His political will could only be exercised through a compliant premier. Walesa was in danger again of being pushed to the margins.

Olszewski moved slowly at first, and this was no bad thing. The ministerial line-up seemed surprisingly cautious. The Foreign Minister, Krzysztof Skubiszewski, was unchanged; the Finance Minister was, initially at least, a clone of Balcerowicz; the Defence Minister, Jan Parys, was known as a thoughtful economist. Jerzy Eysmont at the planning office was to be given broad economic powers but was known as a shrewd man. Seasoned dissidents like Adam Michnik quickly spotted the weak points in the Cabinet however: Antoni Macierewicz, familiar from the *Glos* milieu in the 1970s, seemed a risky appointment at the Interior Ministry; Adam Glapinski at Foreign Trade was both self-important and accident-prone; Jerzy Kropownicki, now a devout Catholic, at the Labour Ministry, had been a rather unpleasant student functionary in the 1968 purge of the universities. The government was committed to an economic policy that took more notice of state factories and easing the rapid rise in unemployment. But modest adjustments to the Balcerowicz programme were not enough for parliament. On 5 March it rejected a declaration of principles underpinning the government's economic programme. That starkly demonstrated the fragility of the government. By hook and by crook the Olszewski team managed eventually to pass a budget that was acceptable to the IMF;

but it came at the price of weeks of intensive negotiations and a few close calls.

The chief cause of tension was not so much between parliament and premier on economic management as between premier and president on "de-Communisation" – the purging of Communists, agents or sympathisers from the old regime. Mazowiecki's government had promised to draw a "thick line" between the past and the present. That was partly intended as an act of Christian forgiveness, partly the recognition that Solidarity had to work with the old institution, and partly it was a way of keeping the peace. It was the deliberate choice of evolutionary rather than radical change. The Olszewski team wanted to repudiate that policy, not just to satisfy popular longings for some kind of reckoning with the past but also to ensure that Moscow could not at some stage activate a Fifth Column among the many ex-Communists still sitting behind important desks.

First to strike was Jan Parys. He was acquainted with military problems from his time at the planning office, and was correspondingly quick off the mark. The two deputy defence ministers, Bronislaw Komorowski and Janusz Onyszkiewicz – both connected with the Democratic Union – were dispatched and replaced by Romauld Sheremetyev and Radek Sikorski. Sheremetyev was an old colleague and later a rival to Leszek Moczulski. He shared the master's deeply antipathetic feelings towards the Soviet Union and all its works. Sikorski had claimed and been swiftly granted asylum by Britain after martial law. As a result he had dual Polish–British citizenship, an unusual position for a senior defence appointment in any country. His credentials – apart from perfect English and a useful network of contacts in the British Conservative Party – were that he had seen combat against Russian soldiers, albeit in Afghanistan as a photo-reporter. The Parys appointments said a great deal about the intentions of the Olszewski government. Sheremetyev's dislike of Russia was ideologically rooted, Sikorski's was romantic, but there was no mistaking the identity of the future enemy.

Walesa was displeased. He had expected to be consulted on the defence appointments, he did not like the forced retirement of Admiral Kolodziejczyk. But the moves were not entirely unexpected. During his trip to Britain in May 1991 a row had flared up between Lech Kaczynski, as head of the president's National Security Council, and Janusz Onyszkiewicz about who was ultimately responsible for the armed forces – president or government. Kaczynski claimed that Walesa, as supreme commander, should appoint the chief of the general staff and that the president should also have the sole right to nominate members of the National Security Council.

Onyszkiewicz said this was scratching away at government control of defence policy and left almost no role for a defence minister. Walesa had not won that battle and was determined to have another go. The Olszewski team wanted to stake out its position from the beginning.

All this was part of the normal interplay between democratic institutions, but it soon began to get out of hand. The new Defence Ministry leadership began to study the career patterns of senior Polish officers. Almost all had done a stint at staff college in the Soviet Union: plainly a broad-brush anti-Communist purge was not going to be possible in an officer corps that was 95 per cent Communist. But some colonels and generals who had been active in implementing martial law were still serving in the army; in particular the military intelligence organisation seemed to have survived virtually intact from the Communist days. That was disturbing, though not quite the dramatic threat portrayed by Parys, since it suggested a continuing web of contacts with the GRU (the Soviet Military Intelligence).

Moscow's colonial control of East European states had been exercised through six principal channels: the Party apparatus, the Interior Ministry, the army, the economic planning machine, the Foreign Ministry and direct contact between the Soviet ambassador (a kind of pro-consul) and the local political élite. By 1992 most of these lines of communication had been severed, but had been replaced by informal contacts. The Party, it emerged, had been borrowing money from the Soviet mother-party for years. Now the Party was dissolved but one of the key players in the new-look Social Democratic Party, Leszek Miller, had been deeply involved in Party financing and retained his old acquaintances in Moscow. The Interior Ministry, and in particular the SB secret police, still have a strange and enduring relationship with the KGB. When the Interior Ministry were asked to comment on first reports of Walesa's alleged police collaboration in the 1970s, the report was phrased as follows: "The Interior Ministry has information saying that the KGB is aware of collaboration activities of one of the high-ranking Polish statesmen." The KGB, in other words, was aware of something unknown to the new masters at the Polish Interior Ministry and, through its special channels, tipped off Warsaw.

It was the army connection, however, that gave Moscow its best listening-post in Warsaw. The military intelligence organisation had in the early 1980s spread its wings far beyond the usual monitoring of enemy troop formations and securing high-tech secrets. It had targeted the Solidarity opposition, especially on the Baltic coast (intelligence from the Szczecin dissident scene was highly prized), since this could plausibly be said to be a threat to the smooth military operation with the Soviet Union. In 1993 military intelligence was still in the political game. Its role was opaque and probably on the margins, but it was active nonetheless. Fear of a purge propelled senior officers from military intelligence and other generals towards the sympathetic listeners in the Belvedere Palace. Wachowski and Jerzy Milewski, head of the president's bureau for national security, gave tea and biscuits to several generals, and apparently promised promotions and encouraged dissent. Walesa was constantly wrong-footing the Defence Minister. While on a visit to Germany Walesa proposed a kind of NATO Second Division made up of Central Europeans who could not yet be promoted to the Premier League. More disturbingly, it seemed that Walesa was even ready to admit Russia into this so-called NATO *bis*. That smacked to many in, and out, of government of an attempt to reconstruct the Warsaw Pact (assumed to be the secret wish of many Polish generals). "I was in Brussels at the time Walesa made the offer," recalled Parys, "and was completely baffled. The Czechs and the Hungarians were also surprised and asked whether this NATO second league was supposed to be based on, or was to be independent of, the Prague–Budapest–Warsaw triangle. I didn't know what to tell them. Such concepts as NATO *bis* are designed to preserve a divided Europe – the very curse we want to shed." Polish embassies abroad were instructed to play down Walesa's idea and it was quietly dropped by all, apart from Walesa himself, who would occasionally drop it into conversations with world leaders – to their utter bafflement.

The most damaging comment on Walesa's military competence came from Parys in the book *Lewy Czerwcowy*. Parys met the Ukrainian defence minister Konstantin Morozov in Warsaw on 14 January. The new government was keen to shift the base of Polish *Ostpolitik* away from Walesa's Soviet-orientated strategy to a more even-handed approach. Ukraine, with plans to build a large standing army of 400,000 or more, and with a big nuclear arsenal, was obviously an important element in any new regional constellation. "When I reported on Morozov's visit to the President and mentioned the removal of nuclear weapons from Ukraine to Russia, the President suggested that Poland might benefit from the situation and improve its arsenal. Walesa said: 'Your conversation with Morozov went in a wrong direction – you should have arranged some nuclear missiles for Poland and Poland would have benefited accordingly.' Walesa returned to this subject several times afterwards." Parys claims he was terrified. "Poland would have been seen as a cheat deceiving both East and West. Even if we managed to get hold of several tactical missiles – with a range of only about five hundred kilometres – on what should we target them? Berlin or Kiev? I saw no enemies there."

Walesa's idea was irresponsible, even unhinged. None of the possible explanations show him in a good light. Was he joking? Since he repeated the suggestion several times, it seems not. Was he trying to test Parys, to see how far the Olszewski government was prepared to go in forging its new *Ostpolitik* and defence policies? But Walesa was supreme commander, Parys defence minister: this was not a conspiratorial or party-political game. Was Walesa, then, merely a military buffoon, badly advised? Walesa did not lack for military advice, from Milewski to Kolodziejczyk. The most likely explanation for Walesa's odd behaviour is that he was trying to tie the Olszewski government in knots, to lure it into making an offer for nuclear weapons and then promptly disown the idea. From mid-February 1992 the Walesa team had only one political goal in mind: to dismiss the Olszewski government. Tension crackled between Walesa and Olszewski in each of their personal meetings. By the beginning of April a showdown seemed inevitable. While the president was in Bonn at the turn of March and April, Antoni Macierewicz sacked an intelligence chief, a certain Colonel Jasik. Macierewicz, who was also deputy premier, then went to the airport to welcome Walesa back from Germany. Wachowski strode past him and hissed: "We will square things with you later for your *changes*." Two days later Macierewicz was called to the palace and Wachowski proposed a deal. The Interior Minister, he said, could continue to fire people for political reasons – providing that they could be re-employed by the president. "He tried to get me involved in protecting the Communists – he presented it as a joint game *against* them, hoping I could be fooled."

On 6 April, Jan Parys, even paler than usual, publicly accused politicians of lobbying for army support in order to undermine democracy. The "politicians" were, of course, Wachowski and Milewski and the tone of the speech was that a coup was being plotted. War had thus been declared on Walesa and his court. Olszewski was immediately put under pressure to sack Parys. Instead he sent the minister on holiday and left for the United States, where he found his hosts as confused as the Poles. Parys was sworn to secrecy during his long suspension from duty but somehow, perhaps by telepathy, more and more information about Wachowski's military machinations leaked out to a pro-Olszewski newspaper, *Nowy Swiat*.

The moral tone of the Olszewski government was becoming clear. Religious education was made compulsory in schools, an ethical code that effectively banned doctors from performing abortions was put into place, as was a new law banning foreigners from holding stock in casinos. The Cabinet, meanwhile, was crumbling. Andrzej Olechowski became the second finance minister to resign in three months and the IMF set an almost impossible budget deficit limit of 65 trillion zlotys as a condition for further negotiations. The overall impression was of Olszewski as a sorcerer's apprentice, hopelessly trying to bale out water spilled by magic, malign broomsticks. Just as Walesa had hoped, the government was losing control. Certainly it was losing the information war. Apart from *Nowy Swiat* it had no defenders in the daily press. By May Polish politics had taken on a slightly crazed feel. Either Walesa and his advisers were bad, or Parys and company were mad: there seemed to be no middle course. A fringe nationalist politician, Boleslaw Tejkowski, was referred in the same month for psychiatric examination: he had been arguing that the Pope was a Jew. The Tejkowski case raised some interesting questions of principle (when is a politician *not* clinically mad?) and he contributed in his own small way to the high-pitched buzz of mental disturbance in Warsaw politics. If Parys was not mad (and he appeared, in private, to be perfectly reasonable with only a slight tendency to fanaticism) then Wachowski was bad. But just how bad? And why?

Understanding the personality of this shadowy man had become a matter of national interest. Two years earlier Kaczynski had seen Wachowski bring Walesa his slippers. He carefully undid his boss's shoes and helped him ease his feet into soft moccasins. Now he was suspected of acting as the Rasputin at the Belvedere court. Something had plainly changed. Wachowski's toughness in eliminating Krzysztof Pusz from Walesa's inner circle was a sign of things to come. He was continually jostling for position. When the court moved from Gdansk to the presidential palace, Wachowski ensured that he was given a room in the east wing of the Belvedere. Jaroslaw Kaczynski and other members of the chancellery staff moved out of the cramped palace to offices near parliament. But Wachowski stayed put: he understood that Walesa needed personal contact, needed to butt and to challenge. The quality of advice was not as important as its immediacy. "All his life," reflects Krzysztof Wyszkowski (quoted in J. Kurski), "Walesa has lived in a milieu that was more civilised than himself. But at present he lives among thugs – cynical, unashamed of using coarse words. Mietek's [Wachowski's] task is to reduce the whole sophisticated and complex world to Walesa's level . . . Mietek and the official bodyguards are on one level. Walesa too is ready to ask a bodyguard for advice, just as he asks Mietek. Because everything seems worthless to him."

When Wachowski re-emerged in the Walesa circle in October 1990, his first move was to sit in the secretarial office and pick up telephones. The secretaries were quite charmed by his wit and flattery, and were happy to have some of the telephone pressure taken off them. But Wachowski had understood the political significance of the ante-room. Walesa could field only a few telephones. Wachowski found himself dealing with important politicians trying to lobby the future president. Unlike the secretaries he did not simply put them on hold. He heard what they had to say and decided himself whether to pass it on to Walesa. In the Belvedere, with Pusz elbowed out of the way, he had managed to position himself as Walesa's main link man with the outside world. In the evening as Walesa sat with Wachowski, Father Cybula and Drzycimski, he demanded amusement and Wachowski was ready with a few tart comments and some cruel mimicry of the day's visitors. And then the president would ask for political advice. Should the fire brigade be subject to the Interior Ministry? Walesa had no opinions on this, or on many issues but he was constantly under pressure to make decisions and was battered with interested advice from all sides. Wachowski had no political axe to grind – his was the politics of unquestioning personal loyalty. His opinion was therefore canvassed on many matters and was decisive. Walesa also trusted Wachowski's judgment of people: who to trust, who to drop? The objection to Wachowski was that such high-level and seriously regarded advice was coming from a man with a murky past, both political and personal.

There was a question mark about his military service. He was enrolled in a marine academy but did not complete the course – he was expelled in April 1972 after failing exams – and should therefore have been called up in the army. He was not. Since he did not have a medical exemption, the Wachowski critics believe there could only be one explanation: that he was signed up by the secret police. Certainly there are mysterious gaps in his official biography around the middle of the 1970s when he might well have gone on some kind of police training course. Wachowski has formally denied that he was employed by, or collaborated with the police. He is reluctant, though, to supply the kind of biographical detail needed to answer the many questions raised by his critics. His case has been helped by some sloppy research: Kaczynski was sure that he had nailed Wachowski when he was given a team photograph from the police academy. The face, however, belonged to somebody else.

Wachowski's private life has not exactly encouraged those who believe that Walesa, as leader of a Catholic country, should be surrounded only by morally upright civil servants. Wachowski, who was from a worker household, married upwards – to a blonde high-school history teacher with well-off parents. But the marriage started to go off the tracks in the mid-1970s. He drank heavily starting at breakfast time. As a taxi driver on the Baltic coast he started to mix with the black-market money traders and prostitutes in the Sopot hotels. He used regularly to drive three prostitutes to and from their work; one of the three was later murdered in strange circumstances. In 1979, however, he went on a Catholic summer camp and was converted to Christianity. He gave up hard drinking and his marriage was patched together again. More important, perhaps, his sudden conversion brought him into the milieu of Alexander Hall's Young Poland Movement. Instead of prostitutes, he started to transport dissident literature in his taxi (bought with earnings from illegal working holidays in Britain). When Walesa's first chauffeur was unmasked as a police agent, Wachowski seemed like a natural replacement.

Walesa knew of the doubts about Wachowski. Yet those very doubts became for him a kind of recommendation. The Gwiazdas, for example, had from 1981 been denouncing the new driver as "Captain" Wachowski (his notional rank in the secret police). Yet even Andrzej Gwiazda grudgingly admits there was perhaps some strategy behind Walesa's choice: "He always liked to have an agent in his circle, it was his way of saying – we're doing all this openly." If Wachowski were an agent, and even if he remained one throughout the 1980s, the fact had little practical significance now. To whom would he report? How could he damage Walesa? As for Wachowski's sleazy years, they were in the past. He was a penitent now, helping every morning at the seven o'clock Mass in the Belvedere chapel. Walesa has always been more comfortable with confessing sinners than with the saintly. Despite the fireworks of 1989–90, Walesa's politics were surprisingly close to those of Tadeusz Mazowiecki. But he could never spend more than an hour in his company; he felt awkward, as if he was being judged. Wachowski did not judge. He obeyed orders and catered to whims. Wachowski created a task for himself. Walesa, he could see, had no power base comparable to, say, the First Secretary of the old Communist Party. There were however a number of institutions that had been decapitated by the 1989 revolution and which could be given a new master. This new power network could not be openly constructed. It had to be pieced together informally, as a club of sympathisers. There was nothing intrinsically wrong with Wachowski's approach, though it drew heavily on his love – and apparent mastery – of conspiracy. The problem was rather that he had such a narrow and primitive understanding of power, as if he had studied a textbook on how to carry out a *coup d'état* in a banana republic: seize the television station, promise loot to the generals, buy the loyalty of the police, create a proletarian guard, install loyalists in all key positions.

Wachowski's priorities became clear as soon as he moved into the Belvedere. The bodyguard service, known as BOR, was his first target. BOR guards spent 24 hours a day protecting politicians. They therefore knew a great deal. Wachowski suggested that Father Cybula be the father confessor for everybody working in the palace, including the BOR bodyguards. That would ensure no secrets leaked out of the palace, and would be a useful instrument of control. The BOR guards resisted the idea but Wachowski tightened the reins in other ways. A typical incident: one day Wachowski ordered a bodyguard to pick up a piece of litter. The guard refused and there was a row. Later that week Wachowski suggested to the guard that they make up. Together they drank three or four stiff vodkas and parted friends. Wachowski then rang the commander of the guard and told him there was a drunk BOR bodyguard roaming around the palace. The guard was promptly arrested and fired. The result: BOR, a state institution, became terrified of Wachowski, in effect took its orders from him, and was moulded into a personal *gard du corps* of the president. The BOR men were supplemented by ex-secret policemen who used to follow Walesa and his wife during martial law. Partly because of Wachowski, partly because of Danuta's urgings, these familiar figures had been permanently assigned to the Walesa household. In an odd way they were regarded as more trustworthy than agents trained and assigned by the new democratic state.

Wachowski also understood the military and police mentality, the significance to career soldiers of promotion. Walesa's signature was essential for every senior promotion. This purely formal gesture was transformed into an instrument of crude power by Wachowski. He would invite clutches of generals for drinks at the government hotel and sound them out. Sometimes he would ask for explicit services – certain intelligence reports, for example – but more often than not they would talk about cars, sailing, women or drink. After a while Wachowski would ask quietly about the personal ambitions of the officer. There is no blacker magic in democratic statecraft than inducing army officers to think like politicians. Similar spells were cast on television directors, for they too treasure promotion and preference. Wachowski had good relations with the two devisers of Poland's most successful television satire, "Polish Zoo". Modelled on the British "Spitting Image" series, it lampooned the politicians of the day, though it rarely gave

304

Walesa – depicted as a lion speaking with fractured grammar – a rough ride. Danuta was upset that she was cast as a mouse, but Wachowski soon persuaded her that it was harmless fun. One of the creators of the cabaret was Marcin Zaorski. He was the brother of the television executive Janusz Zaorski, who had been appointed head of television by prime minister Bielecki. The Olszewski government, not happy with television news, put its placemen into the politically sensitive news programming section. Zaorski's position looked shaky.

Wachowski took up the cudgels. The ex-chauffeur was, like Walesa, part of the television generation of the Polish People's Republic. After the war the Communists tried to end illiteracy with a crash reading programme and channelled their propaganda through cheap tightly-controlled newspapers. But under Gierek television had become the primary propaganda organ: it was used to instruct, to conceal information, to calm down and to heat up the political atmosphere, and even occasionally to entertain. Walesa and Wachowski were skilled newspaper readers and television watchers. (Books barely figured in their lives.) They had learned from Gierek that control of television was a form of power and Wachowski at least was determined not to surrender such an important instrument. Videotapes of potentially sensitive material were taken to the palace for approval; the man in charge of the evening news desk was accustomed to last-minute cancellations or reordering of news priorities at the behest of the president. Walesa was in fact far more broad-minded than Wachowski or his other courtiers. Boleslaw Sulek's sharply observed "In Solidarity" – which showed Walesa at his coldest – was regarded as a diplomatic affront by the president's courtiers, but Walesa himself insisted that it be shown. Wachowski tried to pull a programme on political priests that featured Father Cybula: Walesa overrode him. But in the main Wachowski kept a close day-by-day watch on news and documentary coverage and did his best to influence personal decisions in television. After a fashion he won the battle. Zaorski, ousted by Olszewski, was reinstated when Olszewski was toppled. In the long run, though, Zaorski was destined to lose. There was no practical way that the president could run television. Public television was bound to fall into the fiefdom of government, and private television challenging the state monopoly was also inevitable once enough capital could be found.

There is quite a strong case for blaming every row between the president and prime minister in 1992 on Wachowski. But the relationship between Walesa and Olszewski was more complex than that. Wachowski thought in terms of naked power, and as such he was important to Walesa. But he was, and is, not everything to Walesa. Wachowski's significance was rather that he reinformed Walesa's gut feeling that the old defeated order was not all bad. It was Communism that had allowed Walesa to escape from the countryside and it was Communism that had given him his pride as a worker. It is difficult to find any recent critical comment by Walesa on Gierek or Jaruzelski. Perhaps Wachowski wanted to restore something of the informal power structure of Communism because it was the only way that Poland could be effectively governed.

Wachowski has not said this aloud – he says little – but it can be deduced from his actions. Walesa, on the other hand, had a sentimental rather than an instrumental attachment to Communism. He *missed* the Soviet Union. That did not make him however a KGB agent. Olszewski started from quite a different point: it was time to stop being submissive to (or sentimental about) Soviet interests and to define and to assert Polish national interests. For the first time in over 50 years Poland was in a position to dictate some conditions to Moscow, and in Olszewski's view it should not have ducked the opportunity. But that also meant putting an end to the myth that Communists at home had been rendered harmless and could safely be reintegrated into the governing system. These were differences of the most fundamental kind, and they emerged most clearly in the wrangle over the Polish–Russian friendship treaty. Macierewicz recalls visiting the palace at the end of April and finding Wachowski settled deep in an armchair reading out fragments of the draft treaty to Walesa, Father Cybula and Drzczymski. "Wachowski was simply dictating the contents of the document – telling what he wanted included and what was supposed to be left out. The president, listening all the time, seemed a bit nervous and hesitant . . . I got the impression that Walesa was as if having second thoughts about it but Wachowski was determined: 'No, it was to be like this and like that.' "

Macierewicz may well have grasped the wrong end of the stick. One of Wachowski's functions was to read aloud, slowly, important bills. Walesa absorbed information better that way. In general many of the conspiratorial views of Walesa are based either on an incomplete understanding of the Belvedere court, or a failure to understand Walesa's sense of humour. Kaczynski, at the time of the August coup in Moscow, waddled up to Walesa and expressed his suspicions about Wachowski. "Yes, I know he's an agent – but what can I do?" replied Walesa. "I just have to promote him." Kaczynski, excited, noted down the conversation, told all of his friends and took it as proof positive that Wachowski was a spy. In fact, say those close to the president, Walesa was pulling Kaczynski's leg; he was a man utterly without humour.

Even so, something did go amiss with the Polish–Russian treaty. The Olszewski government was barely consulted on its form or content. There had been early drafts prepared by the Foreign Ministry but the August coup attempt forced a complete rephrasing and re-ordering of priorities. In the frenzy of the October elections, the months of uncertainty over who would govern Poland, the initiative slipped into the hands of the president. It was a flawed treaty in many ways but the most obvious shortcoming was Article 7A, which provided for the setting up of Polish–Russian joint ventures on the army bases vacated by the Red Army. This not only smacked of corruption, it also gave Russian army officers a formal right to stay in Poland and retain their hold on huge swathes of Polish land. Soviet units had already been exploiting their bases by selling off cheap petrol, importing and exporting goods brought in by Soviet military transport planes. There was only a fuzzy idea about what was intended by these joint ventures, but what if they began to use Polish territory to sell surplus Russian arms to the world? The whole point of the Olszewski government's policy – and Walesa's promises before the presidential election – was to get the Russians out, not to find ways of keeping them in. A Russian presence, half commercial, half military, would certainly set back Warsaw's attempts to join NATO. Radek Sikorski had been trying to interest Western armies in using former Soviet and Polish training grounds for military exercises. That proposal was not exactly helped by the new treaty. Walesa and his delegation travelled to Moscow and hugged Yeltsin, but in Warsaw there was panic. The prime minister's office had only just managed to get hold of the final draft. An urgent cable was sent to the Polish embassy in Moscow: delete Article 7A. The reference to joint ventures was scrubbed at the last minute. Walesa was furious. He had lost face in, of all places, Russia.

The Olszewski team was now convinced that to make a genuinely clean break with the past – a pre-condition for a more assertive foreign policy – it had to release the names of those who had co-operated with the Communist secret police in the 1970s and 1980s. Since Macierewicz knew of a file codenamed Bolek – describing a worker in the W4 department of the Lenin shipyards who informed for two, or perhaps six, years in the 1970s – he was sure that he could box Walesa into a corner. The Bolek file unquestionably referred to Walesa. The only question was whether the file itself was a total forgery. Macierewicz had no doubts. "I have not come across a case of a registered secret agent that had nothing at all to do with reality.

One can fictitiously extend or shorten the period of collaboration, but one cannot create it out of nothing." According to the leaks from the Bolek file, Walesa collaborated between 1970 and 1975 and the documents in the dossier gave the impression that he was re-activated in 1980–82. Walesa had already admitted in his memoirs that after interrogation in the early 1970s he signed two official protocols. Yet to present him, on the basis of these signatures, as a fully-fledged police collaborator required enormous confidence in the veracity of the Bolek dossier.

Macierewicz, after barely five months in office, was no great expert on police archives. Despite his assurances, there was no good reason why the Bolek file could not have been fabricated in its entirety. That would have been an almost impossible exercise for all the 62 leading politicians suspected of collaboration. But for one man, the key figure of Walesa, an elaborate forgery would have been worthwhile. The files on the suspected politicians, including Walesa, were dug out by investigators during the Mazowiecki and Bielecki governments. But it was decided then to do nothing about them.

The Czech process of *Lustracja* had opened up wounds, split the post-dissident establishment and in the end had not given a definitive verdict on who collaborated and who did not. As in Poland many sensitive files have been destroyed, while others have been faked. In particular there was confusion over whether files referred to a target – someone who was supposed to be recruited – or to an active informer. Some dissidents called in for interrogation consciously collaborated, with the aim of misleading the secret police and protecting colleagues. All this confusion, of purpose and of organisation, indicated that the files should not be introduced into the political game.

Macierewicz persuaded the few doubters in the Cabinet, however, that this was the wrong approach. He did so in an almost evangelical way: Poland had to be ruled on the basis of truth. There was a direct link, he claimed, between truth-telling and sovereignty. But there was something more bloodthirsty about the whole process. "It was as if Macierewicz saw himself as Caesar," said a member of the Democratic Union who admitted that he was on Macierewicz's list. "He wanted to see parliament's gladiators fight to the finish." The list was not entirely self-serving. It did include the names of Wieslaw Chrzanowski, Speaker of parliament and, like Maciere-wicz, a member of the Christian National Union. On 29 May Macierewicz visited the palace and told the president that he was determined to release the list or at least hand it over to parliament. The same resolution the previous day had authorised the release of information about SB collaborators between 1945 and 1990. The Sejm had not reckoned with Macierewicz's speed nor the way that he would present the facts. Walesa only half believed that the government would go ahead. If deputies were pressed to resign for past collaboration then he too would be pushed towards the brink. There would be a kind of creeping takeover: dozens of parliamentary by-elections when compromised deputies stood down, and no president – or at least one who was politically crippled.

On 3 June a heavily guarded convoy took sealed copies of Macierewicz's list to the Sejm. The lists were distributed to the chairman of the parliamentary caucuses and to the speakers of Sejm and senate. Each envelope contained the name of the suspected deputy, with birth dates, pseudonyms, photocopied signature and, usually, the period in which he or she was supposed to have collaborated with the secret police. This was not the "full information" that was supposed to be offered under the 28 May parliamentary resolution. It was poison administered by the teaspoon. Many deputies were furious. Jerzy Osiatynski of the Democratic Union glanced into his file précis – and promptly found evidence that he was mentioned only because he had *refused* to co-operate with the secret police. Another deputy, Antoni Furtak, from a farmers' party, bumped into Macierewicz in the corridors of parliament and almost beat him up. "What you have done is a lie, you've slandered me, insulted me after years of working for the opposition!" Furtak, like many others, said his signature agreeing to spy for the police was a crude forgery. Kuron was almost incoherent with rage. He was not on the list but had known some of those mentioned for 30 years, had served in prison with them. "Macierewicz is sick," he bellowed.

Walesa received the copy of his edited file – the actual dossier, if not the genuine article, was in a safe in police headquarters in Rakowiecka Street – at eight o'clock on the morning of 4 June. According to some reports he began to draft a public letter acknowledging that he had signed "three or four" police interrogation protocols but pleading for understanding of all those caught in the Communist web of the 1970s. A few phone calls later he changed his mind and scrapped the draft. The sentiment in the Sejm had become so hostile to the Olszewski government that there was no need to embarrass himself or go to the brink of resignation. He could topple the government.

He was helped in particular by KPN. Leszek Moczulski, the KPN leader, was on the blacklist. Some days earlier members of the Olszewski government had encouraged KPN politicians to lever out Moczulski because of his alleged history of collaboration. KPN under a new leader would then be free to join the Olszewski coalition. The party refused to play along, and a sense of resentment made it determined to join in any attempt to get rid of the Olszewski government. The news that Chrzanowski, a man who had spent years in Communist jails, was on the list fuelled suspicions that at least one sub-plot involved Macierewicz's ambitions to take over the leadership of the Christian National Union. Walesa issued a motion calling for the dismissal of the government. At 9.15 p.m. Walesa slipped into the wooden presidential throne in the parliamentary gallery. At one point the deputy Kazimierz Switon, who had founded the first free trade union movement in Silesia long before unions were set up in Gdansk, shouted from his seat that Walesa was an agent and was on the blacklist. The debate was broadcast live and it was the first time that many Poles had heard the accusation spoken openly. But the mood of parliament was definitely against Olszewski. Later Walesa was to set out his interpretation of the affair (Radio Zet, 19 June): "It would have become necessary to elect a new temporary president through the Sejm and the Senate. The best solution would have been Olszewski as president, Macierewicz as prime minister, Parys as defence minister, Najder as foreign minister." In short, a putsch. That was certainly the gloss put on it by many deputies that night. As the debate wound up, Walesa's face was red with glee. The voting figures came up on the scoreboard and Walesa clapped and laughed until the tears rolled down his cheeks. He had destroyed another government! The date was 4 June, exactly three years since Solidarity's victory in East Europe's first free elections.

A case of amnesia

At the beginning of December 1993 Walesa received a group of school-children at the Belvedere Palace. Prompted by a teacher, recorded by a radio reporter, the president set out the highlights of his daily routine. "Well, kids, I get up at 5.30 a.m. – that's very early, I know, but it's important to get up early. Then I go to Mass – Father Cybula, that's him over there, he says it – and I have breakfast of milk soup. It tastes very good and you should all eat it. Then I go for a twenty-minute walk, as my doctor has ordered, and Minister Wachowski usually goes round the gardens with me. Well, the morning passes meeting ambassadors and heads of state and suchlike. But then there's lunch, which is very good. Fish, mushrooms, good meat, always very good. Then it's a nap and a stint on the exercise bike with Minister Wachowski. In the afternoon I have to sign documents. That's not easy because I have to read them all first. At last dinner comes and I can go to my room and do crossword puzzles . . ."

Walesa obviously caricatured his day, but even allowing for some self-mockery he could not conceal the emptiness of his life in the palace. Most courtiers reckoned that Walesa's marriage had become little more than a matter of form by 1994. Danuta stayed in Gdansk and even for state visits requiring the presence of a "first lady" she would fly down only for a few hours. The children quickly sensed the drift in the marriage and a few of the boys swerved out of control. Bogdan, the oldest (born 1970), was acutely shy and seemed to his Gdansk friends to be living in a dream world, devoid of ambition or achievement. He failed examination after examination but his father protected him as surely as Gierek had shielded his sons. When Bogdan made his girlfriend pregnant, the wedding was quickly organised, a 135-square-metre apartment was bought in Gdansk, and he was given a Toyota. Bogdan's younger brother Slawomir was given a Daihatsu by his father, which he promptly crashed. The car ran onto the pavement and struck a woman pedestrian. When Danuta and Slawomir visited the woman in hospital, Slawomir sat without saying a word. Lech Walesa bought a wheelchair and had his bodyguards deliver it to the unfortunate woman. Slawomir continued to get into drunken scrapes. Although he was a poorly paid electrician, Slawomir was given a generous enough allowance to spend his weekends in the pricey nightclubs of Gdansk. Przemyslaw, born in 1974, was also in and out of the Gdansk clubs. When he was too drunk to drive his VW Golf he would order the bodyguards to take him and his friends home, or to the next dive, publicly cursing them if they demurred. Walesa describes the emotional, thin-skinned Przemyslaw as "my best son, a boy with a big heart". In April 1994 a local prosecutor started investigating charges that Przemyslaw had hit a policeman in the face. Few of these antics were ever reported in the Polish press.

Not all the Walesa children were running wild. Jaroslaw (born 1976) was a conscientious schoolboy. And the fortunes of Magda, who made a successful ballet début in Warsaw, seemed to bring Walesa and his wife a little closer. The overall impression, though, was that Walesa was compensating for his long absences from home by throwing money at the children. Danuta began to understand that she should not raise the children's problems on the telephone with Walesa; he would simply blurt out: "For God's sake, they're grown-up!"; or "I've got a crisis with Russia on my hands and you bother me with this!"

Wachowski, for years one of the bridges between Walesa and his wife, no longer mediated. Some of the public distrust of Wachowski had been taken on board by Danuta. And it was becoming clear that Wachowski could be the confidant of the president, or his wife, but not of both. Wachowski concentrated on becoming the master-courtier. He understood that to make himself indispensable to Walesa he had merely to state, with apparent sincerity, his willingness to withdraw and leave Walesa alone. "Lech, you don't need me to do this . . . Mr President [in the company of others], if you think otherwise, then please say so . . . You know, you can get rid of me just like that, with a snap of the fingers . . ." That was the refrain overheard in the palace. Walesa had in fact given serious thought to getting rid of Wachowski. He had retained him because to do otherwise would have been a huge concession to his critics, a tacit admission even that Wachowski was a former agent, a compromised man. By 1994 these tactical considerations were no longer paramount. Walesa had arrived at a more subtle analysis of his chief courtier. Yes, perhaps Wachowski was unsavoury; but bad men could do good things, just as good men could do bad. Years of opposition under the Communists had taught him as much and Wachowski was nothing if not the product of the morally grey Communist years. Even if Wachowski had been an agent in the old days, he now had a new life and a new significance. If he stayed loyal and discreet, and continued to learn, Wachowski's job was secure. Outside the court Wachowski could be dangerous since he was above all defender of the myth of Walesa. Criticism aimed at Walesa was sponged up by Wachowski; he was the Great Deflector. And he helped to camouflage the essential hollowness of the Belvedere; for Walesa had indeed become a ruler without clothes, draped in the imaginary ermine of office.

Behind Walesa's study in the Belvedere Palace there is a small corridor leading to a shower room. One day Walesa heard the telephone ringing on his desk and burst into the room, dripping water on the carpet. His secretary entered at that moment, bringing him his afternoon tea and biscuits. She gawped at the wet, hairy figure. "What's the matter?" he barked. "Have you never seen a naked president before?" By toppling the Olszewski government Walesa had kept a small fig-leaf over his political nakedness. But he was very vulnerable. His courtiers had come up with the idea of parrying the Bolek file with a dossier codenamed "Cigarette Lighter" on one of Olszewski's closest associates. That brought Walesa no protection at all; "Cigarette Lighter" became an irrelevance as soon as the Olszewski cabinet fell. Walesa decided to go instead for controlled self-exposure.

Walesa wrote to Adam Strzembosz, president of the Supreme Court, asking him to select and assess all documents that might relate to his clandestine collaboration. Strzembosz turned him down. For a start there were several draft screening bills under consideration in parliament but none of them entrusted the job to the Supreme Court. Screening, said the lawyer, could not be carried out on the individual request of a senior politician. To have a legal basis, such screening had to apply equally to all politicians, and had to endow the screener with sufficient power to call in expert witnesses to assess the likelihood of forgery. Walesa, in other words, was told to wait his turn. Although he feigned anger, this was the precise response that Walesa wanted. Kazimierz Woycicki of *Zycie Warszawy* (2 February 1993) summed up the situation: "Even if a special act of parliament is passed, it will not be possible – given that dozens of SB files on Walesa have been destroyed – to confirm or deny collaboration charges. Therefore Walesa will have to remain 'presumed innocent'. And his opponents who repeat the claims about his SB past will themselves have to produce evidence that the man who beat the Communists was their agent at the same time."

313

The Strzembosz decision bought time for Walesa, yet deep into 1993 he was having to explain his actions. During a visit to the Gdansk shipyards (26 February 1993) Walesa complained that the shipyard workers who had known him for years were keeping silent on the issue of whether he cooperated with the police. "Where are my friends of 1970? This is disgusting! There is talk that I must have been an agent to be that courageous!" In the yards there were very few veterans from the December 1970 riots and even those who were employed there had only a dim memory of Walesa's role. If Walesa said he had been a hero at the time – well then, he was a hero. The workers gave Walesa the benefit of the doubt, but they did so coolly; by 1993 not even his old workmates were ready to put their necks on the block for him. The historical point, made by both Walesa and his supporters, was that dissidents in an authoritarian regime naturally exposed themselves to compromise. Most oppositionists had signed something, if only the interrogation protocols. Others had signed vows of loyalty to the Polish state that, taken at face value, were little more than a patriotic commitment to Poland. Removed from this context, slipped into a police dossier along with a faked receipt for money received from one spymaster or another, the loyalty oath could be viewed as altogether more sinister. Only those of little importance in the opposition movement, or so in tune with the regime that they attracted no attention, only they were spared the bullying of the secret police. Walesa, as a young worker with a family, knew the limits of defiance. A general screening law could redress some of the balance lost over the past year by showing clearly the level of exposure of almost every leading member of the opposition. Walesa had another valid point to make: the level of political dialogue in Poland had to be dragged out of the mud. The dirty tricks were almost as cruel as under the Communists. Indeed, the dirtiness went beyond mere political rhetoric. The displaced Olszewski team started to complain about mysterious incidents: a firebomb attack on Olszewski's offices, the loosening of the brakes of Jan Parys's car. By making the secret police the centre of the political debate Polish politicians found that more and more shady ex-police agents were being brought into play. Offices were being bugged, deputies manipulated. Push the secret agent issue aside, Walesa could plausibly argue, and the focus of debate could again shift to the condition of the national economy.

Walesa however had not addressed all of the problems raised by the Olszewski government. It was not just the question-mark over his past. Many institutional issues were at the heart of the war between Olszewski and Walesa, yet the president believed that the toppling of the government had removed the need to come up with an answer. Even Adam Michnik, no fan of Olszewski's Cabinet, admitted that the government's complaints were not merely the product of "heat-oppressed brains". "Given the wavering and unstable situation in all the countries of our region, the emergence of former patterns of old nomenklatura in a rejuvenated form cannot be ruled out . . . they may well be contemplating ways to reach out for power again." The president was not only ignoring such important threats, his court was also "clamouring for more powers, even though they have never said what reform programme they propose to implement in the exercise of those powers". And, added Michnik (*Gazeta Wyborcza*, 6–7 June 1992), "I am not at all convinced that Jaroslaw Kaczynski's repeated allegations of informal ties between some Belvedere officials and some senior army officers are merely the product of his fertile imagination."

Eighteen months later, Walesa had still not addressed the suspicions nor clarified his ambitions. On the contrary Walesa – with the active assistance of both Wachowski and Jerzy Milewski – had started to establish a national guard that would answer only to his office. The plan was to raise a force of 50,000 that would supplement the police and be capable of putting down serious riots, smashing through road blocks erected by unruly farmers, protecting the palace from big demonstrations – Walesa had already been bombarded by overripe pears as he tried to calm a crowd of coalminers inside the palace courtyard – and helping to protect the frontiers from asylum-seekers on their way to Germany. The basis of the force would be the 12,000 Vistula units who had previously come under the command of the Interior Ministry. These units would not only be expanded but also equipped with light trucks, armoured cars and mortars. On paper the proposal did not seem unreasonable. The army, after all, was being quickly trimmed back in line with East–West troop reduction accords and a shrinking budget. The ordinary police were in the middle of a big overhaul and were unable to keep up with the rise in crime. The troops assigned to cope with civil unrest were the former ZOMO – the force that had been deployed so often in the 1980s against Solidarity demonstrators – and these were not, in Walesa's opinion, sufficient. But his critics saw the plan as a clear move towards grabbing power. He had fought and won the battle for the army. Now the president wanted to grab the command of the Vistula troops from the Interior Ministry.

The Vistula troops had been built up by Gomulka to make the Party more resistant to tensions within the army, a counterbalance to the generals who were in large part subservient to Moscow. Walesa's aim was similarly to provide a check to the army, but command was also supposed to give him an important instrument in domestic politics. "It is obvious that someone assumes that it may become necessary to pacify striking factories or mass demonstrations – even if it involves bloodshed," said Jan Parys (*Lewy Czerwcowy*). "The troops involve the president and his authority in numerous conflicts. They change his role from that of an arbitrator, or the leader of a whole nation, to that of a defender of the government's policies, of someone who will do the Interior Minister's job as far as quenching riots is concerned." Certainly Parys had reason to be alarmed about the proposed choice for the commander of the new national guard – General Marek Toczek, who had been thrown out of the army by Parys himself. Why, asked deputies, could the new force not be subject to parliament rather than the president? The answer was obvious, though: Walesa, frustrated by his limited ability to act in domestic politics, was preparing for the time when he had to declare a state of emergency. The same logic propelled him towards the formation of the BBWR, the non-party bloc for reform. It was a structure founded on personal loyalty to the president that could stay intact and give Walesa a platform if parties had to be suspended. The president was not so much reaching for dictatorial powers as preparing for what he regarded as the inevitable failure of parliament and the paralysis of the governing process. And if the government tried to use the army against him (and for a while the Belvedere genuinely thought that the Olszewski team was planning such a step) then he would no longer be the Naked President.

Walesa's other priority was to find a non-confrontational prime minister. His first candidate was a farmer politician, Waldemar Pawlak. Everything about him – his age (34), his politics (Reform Socialist Peasants Party) and even his high reedy voice – suggested that he would be a pushover for Walesa. Newspapers began to write of a new worker–peasant state. But it was not to be – not yet. Pawlak had none of the sophisticated bargaining skills needed to put together a coalition. There was scarcely a party left that had not been wounded or at least grazed by the shootout at the Sejm. At last a survivor was found; Hanna Suchocka, an academic lawyer from Poznan, whose stiff hairspray, firm gaze and commitment to tight budgets quickly earned her the label of Iron Lady of the East. She was drawn from the Democratic Union Party but was sufficiently hostile to liberal abortion laws to appeal to the right-wing Christian National Union. Her market economics were sound and encouraged Jan Krzysztof Bielecki's Congress of Liberal Democrats. Throw in a farmers party, stir to taste, and a shaky but internationally credible government was the result. Skubiszewski remained

Foreign Minister, ex-prime minister Bielecki became Minister for European Affairs, Jerzy Osiatynski took up finance, Janusz Lewandowski privatisation, the highly-strung Christian Nationalist Henryk Goryszewski became deputy prime minister, Janusz Onyszkiewicz took over defence with the brief of calming down and simultaneously modernising the army, Jacek Kuron took over the Labour Ministry again. These were all familiar faces. For Walesa it was a reassuring line-up. But the return of so many ex-ministers was not merely a matter of presidential convenience. The options had gravely narrowed over the past three years.

Suddenly it was plain that Solidarity did not represent a bottomless barrel of talent. The Polish élite, not unlike the political class in Prague and Budapest, was in a crisis of competence. Most of the politically ambitious ex-dissidents were not up to ministerial work. A shrewd political scientist, Wojciech Lamentowicz, depicted the weakness of the Solidarity class, both those with revolutionary credentials and those who came from a more reformist background. "People with radical temperament may have been caught in the trap of double nihilism: the more determined they were in rejecting the old laws and institutions, the less likely they are to respect the new laws and institutions and to consider the limits of their power. The rejection of the old rules − perceived as a condensed evil − gives birth to the rejection of one's own rules. Bolsheviks were once trapped like this: in the name of shaping an altruistic man they constructed a system combining absolute freedom of the authorities with a total lack of freedom for the people." Reformists, on the other hand, were liable to instrumentalise the law. "That is because of the various purposes that law is supposed to serve in a time of transition. It must be an instrument of change (for example speeding the way for privatisation) but at the same time every power élite wants the law to defend its power . . . reformists must stay in power in order to continue reforms. But in the very act of protecting their power they became less efficient in reforming the country" (*Tygodnik Solidarnosc*, 7 February 1992).

Walesa, or perhaps his adviser, the constitutional lawyer Lech Falandysz, had worked out that the relationship of the political élite to the law was crucial. One did not need a sophisticated brain, only a political one, to see that the revolution would not be complete until its principles had been codified. Mazowiecki, Walesa would say, was chosen because he would not startle the horses in Moscow; Bielecki because the revolution demanded someone with economic competence; Olszewski because he was a lawyer − and, at last, Suchocka because she too was a trained lawyer. This was a typical piece of historical revisionism by Walesa. He had not, of course, wanted Olszewski at all and had the opportunity arisen to replace him with a dustman or a gardener he would undoubtedly have done so, claiming after a month or two that the revolution was simply crying out for a dustman to sweep away the Communist debris, or a gardener to prune the tree of democracy. Still, the sound academic qualifications of Suchocka impressed him. There was much to be said for a cool legal expert (rather than a combative defence attorney like Olszewski) who could clearly set out and work within the constitutional boundaries. The bluff, bearded Aleksander Malachowski, from the left liberal section of Solidarity, certainly echoed Walesa's thoughts when he talked about the "cult of incompetence" in the political class. "The former Sejm was led by a sexologist, with oncologists and other doctors acting as his deputies. They were all nice, valuable men but the Sejm is a factory of the law. The situation has now improved with a serious professor of law as Speaker, and a lawyer as his deputy. But what about the parliamentary commissions? With Party membership and not academic qualifications viewed as a decisive factor, most commissions have ended up dominated by incompetent men" (*Gazeta Wyborcza*, 3 January 1992). The same charge could naturally be levelled against any of the mature Western democracies, including Britain and the United States. But Malachowski, like Walesa, saw the problem from the revolutionary perspective. "If people are planning to strike this year, to boo outside the Belvedere, they should bear in mind that it's a waste of time to talk with the authorities about specific issues. What good can farmers' protests achieve when nobody in the government understands the problems of agriculture?"

Walesa saw all this, and addressed the problems much as Robespierre would have done: the people were not worthy of the revolution, *his* revolution. Parliaments let him down, and so too did governments; they were second-leaguers, dwarves, opportunists, also-rans. Those were the kind of phrases bandied about at the Belvedere court. That was more than the arrogance of the power-broker. It reflected a certain degree of truth. Not only the competence, but also the personal moral integrity of deputies was often suspect. A woman plunged out of a deputy's window, and later told stories of sex parties. A KPN deputy, blind drunk at the wheel of a car, threatened policemen; another barged to the front of a queue and abused shop managers. One senior deputy used his authority to put pressure on a young lover of his teenage daughter: the daughter eloped and the deputy set the full police machinery in operation to arrest the man as a "kidnapper". The average backbench deputy knew that, as long as the unpredictable

Walesa had the power to dissolve parliament, their political future was at best uncertain. As a result they made haste to accumulate fortunes, to back shaky business ventures, to find ways of exploiting their inside knowledge. The Polish parliament in 1993 was not a pretty sight. The government line-up had usually skimmed the cream of the political class. Once a justice or a foreign trade minister faltered it was never easy to replace him.

Yet the most profound problem of the Polish élite lay not so much in its lack of expertise – a correctable deficit – as in the absence of a coherent Solidarity ideology. The Communist system grew from mythological roots. Faith in the class struggle, Party infallibility, the almost holy quality attached to its supreme decision-making bodies, the myths of the Radiant Future: these were the illusions that sustained the post-war political class and to some degree motivated younger generations. The new political class, indeed even the former Communists, rejected the Communist icons. A vacuum opened up. "Without a coherent mythology it will be hard to be either a director or an actor on the political stage," reflected the psychologist Professor Jozef Kozielecki. Indeed the new post-Communist politicians did not even have a common language. The old Communists have their New-speak. The post-Communists, having exposed the banality and manipulative intent of the Politburocratic idiom, should have moved on, and reclaimed the use of words, searched for meaning. The new age demanded a new language. That was Walesa's duty: to define with honest speech the political culture of the post-Communist world.

Focusing exclusively on personal power, inhibited by his upbringing and his ambition, Walesa failed to pull Poland out of the rubble of the old order. The office of president demanded a Pole capable of integrating society. Walesa, however, remained a vain man bearing grudges, a man of conflict. By June 1993 he had moved into a position of complete ambiguity. In the old days this had seemed to be a tactical device, a way of avoiding the mantraps dug by the secret police or by opposition rivals. But a decade later it was plain that Walesa did not stand for anything very palpable. "Three days of the week he supports the government, three days of the week he opposes it, and on the seventh day he rests," quipped Alexander Kwasniewski, head of the former Communists, who emerged the victors in the September 1993 parliamentary elections. That was the sum of it. Walesa supported the Suchocka government with the faintest of praise – and simul-taneously gave some backing to teachers and hospital workers who were striking over pay. At one point he met a group of Solidarity unionists in the palace, to discuss his future non-party party, while outside another

Solidarity group burned Walesa's portrait and chanted that he was a traitor. Was he inside, or outside the palace? For or against the power of the crowd?

Solidarity decided to invite Walesa to attend their 1993 congress on the final day, a crowning gesture from their legendary leader. No thank you, said Walesa. "My road and that of Solidarity are drifting apart," he told television (*Panorama*, 28 June). "I would not like to belong to a union like that . . . the current Solidarity is not my Solidarity any more." Certainly Solidarity had changed as an organisation – by 1993 it could command barely half the support of the Communist unions – but until that moment it had been assumed that there was still a Solidarity ethos, a code of political behaviour that loosely connected all those with dissident roots, including Walesa. Suddenly Poles realised that the ethos too had gone. There was no longer any reason not to vote for Communists again.

The Communists indeed came to power. Through much of Central and Eastern Europe in 1993–94 the tide seemed to flow in favour of the Left. By mid-1994, a colour-shaded map would have revealed big blobs of pink and red. Former Communists made up the largest groups in the Bulgarian and Ukrainian parliaments. In Slovakia they seemed poised to win the next election. In Serbia and Romania the Communists had never really gone away, barely pausing to change their ties and socks before ruling under a nationalist banner. In Lithuania a former Communist boss, Algirdas Brazauskas, had taken over as president. In Hungary's general elections in September 1993, the former Communists captured an absolute majority in parliament. There was no simple, uniform explanation for this trend. Naturally there was disillusion about the long haul of reform. Yet it would be a misreading of popular moods to view the leftward shift as a blanket rejection of the market. Different discontents seemed to be bubbling in the cauldron: about the way that privatisation was benefiting only a very narrow circle, about inflation and the erosion of savings and pensions, about budget cuts and the neglect of the "social interest". Social and professional groupings had started to splinter. Teachers, for example, were squabbling over wages and scarce resources. Hospital directors, once patriarchal figures who used their substantial political clout on behalf of every employee, were sacking orderlies, closing down departments, speaking for doctors rather than for nurses. Differential pay rates, competition from the private sector, fear of unemployment, the lack of clearly identifiable political patrons, the marginal status of trade unions – all this propelled the peoples of the East towards the Left and the dimly remembered security of the centrally planned society.

There was, too, an urge to be more competently governed. In Poland the triumphalism of the Church, supported and even encouraged by the Olszewski government, irritated many in the emerging new middle class. Priests had begun to demand that their religious education lessons – in fact the Catholic catechism – be placed in the middle of the daily school schedule to make it more difficult for children to opt out. The tough abortion law, which made doctors vulnerable to prison sentences (and private blackmail) for terminating pregnancies, had caused much ill-feeling, not only in the medical profession. Some employers started to demand baptismal certificates from job applicants. An unseemly scramble for the restitution of Church property was under way. Prime Minister Suchocka's deputy, the Christian Nationalist Henryk Goryszewski, probably contributed more than anybody to the victory of the former Communists in September 1993 with comments like "It's not important whether Poland is poor or rich – the important thing is that it be Catholic", and "The director of the state company should end his day with a prayer and the statement 'My products cost too much'." All this contributed to a popular feeling that the government was abdicating from its normal responsibilities. It could not control the economy, it had aggravated the army and the police (though the Suchocka government had in fact done its best to calm down the mood); and it was abandoning key elements of educational, health and social policy to the Church. The score was clear: the government did not really know what it was doing. The former Communists, by contrast, were professional politicians who were evidently prepared to take responsibility for their actions. They were not saints, but neither did they pretend to be; it was enough that they were modest, hard-working and avoided public feuding. Even though they had emerged from the rubble of the shattered and discredited Communist Party, they really did appear to have changed: for the most part, bright polite young men (and even a few women) who had nothing in common with their thuggish memoir-writing forebears.

The two men to emerge most clearly from the September 1993 election were Waldemar Pawlak and "Olek" Kwasniewski. Pawlak had matured as a politician in the year since he was last considered prime-ministerial material. Then his chief asset had been his naivety, his willingness to be pushed around the board by Walesa. Now he was the leader of a party that had put most of its squabbles behind it and commanded 132 seats in parliament (compared to the Communists' 171 and the 16 won by Walesa's BBWR).

The election result had shown Pawlak's party quite starkly that they had to stick to and not disavow their history as a left-leaning protector of farmers. Pawlak convinced his party that their victory was his: he was identified in the Polish village as an honest clean-cut chap who could be both Catholic and vaguely leftist. He was probably correct in this assessment. The party's policies were largely indistinguishable from those of the other peasant groupings defined by suspicion of the European Union and a willingness to capitalise on the seasonal discontent of the farmers and (an increasingly important factor) their wives. Pawlak was one of the few politicians to visit the countryside with any regularity and he knew that reform had barely licked the mud tracks and grimy smallholdings of rural Poland. His strength came from this knowledge, the intimate sense of what his constituency could bear. It certainly did not come from his charisma. The tart-tongued commentator Slawomir Majman said Pawlak deserved some kind of award for negative charisma: "I strained my mind to remember what this silent and invisible politician said during the election campaign. Finally, with difficulty, I found his policy statement on dieting: 'In Poland we don't have to eat veal, we can do with pork chops – and our girls will manage to enrich our menus.' In Poland when you take on only important issues like this one, you have no trouble becoming prime minister."

The former Communists, though the largest party in parliament and the new coalition, were sensible enough to realise that they should not force on Walesa a candidate for prime minister. Rather the undisputed party leader, Kwasniewski, decided to stay in the background and pull strings. Kwasniewski had lost over ten kilos of flab before the election, conforming not to Pawlak's menu but to a strict no-meat, no-alcohol and no-mistress regime. Add to that Kwasniewski's regular bouts on the tennis court and disco-hopping with a pretty, financially successful real-estate-agent wife, and it was clear to Poles that the new Communist-run government was going to be somewhat different from the grey team of General Jaruzelski. Kwasniewski and Jaruzelski had only one thing in common: they both broke their promises. Having won votes with a pledge to water down the strict monetarism of earlier Solidarity governments and shift the balance again in the direction of the socially weak, the new government promptly set out a programme that was, if anything, even more deeply committed to budget-cutting and strenuous market reforms than that of Hanna Suchocka. This came as a relief to Western creditors.

Walesa was bemused by the newly self-assertive Pawlak and the lurking Kwasniewski. For years he had been calling for a "left leg" to balance the right in Polish politics. Now as the result of the elections, a new election law and, some would say, his own unhappy game playing, the right leg was lame and the left looked as if it might score a few goals. Walesa feigned horror. "A strange lapse of historical memory," said the shrewd Democratic Union's Alexander Smolar about the Communist victory; in public, at least, Walesa was inclined to agree. On paper the election was a formidable blow to Walesa: his own presidential party only just scraped more than five per cent of the vote, freezing it out of any government calculations, while Solidarity the union-cum-party failed to win any seats at all, a real snub for its historical patron. Yet Walesa found he had fallen into a familiar and even comfortable slot: he was once again pitted against a Communist government, allowing him to draw on his own historic myth. Since the turnout had been low and the peasant-Communist government represented only 35.8 per cent of the total vote, Walesa could claim to be the voice of the silent majority. Since the two parties formed a stable coalition he did not have to juggle as desperately as before. And since the Communists were understandably reluctant to assert themselves, Walesa could move in forcefully. Pawlak's anti-reformist farmers could be played off against Kwasniewski's free-marketeering socialists, who had already earned the nickname of Red Liberals. Walesa's placemen were installed in the three most sensitive ministries: Andrzej Olechowski took over at foreign, Admiral Piotr Kolodziejczyk at defence, Andrzej Milczanowski at interior. Walesa's grip on three critical offices of state was stronger than ever. Walesa argued that the West's nervousness about the resurgence of the left in Poland gave him virtual carte blanche in these three ministries and the vague phrasing in the constitution, entrusting him with the security of the country, legitimised the move. After all, even the Poles would balk at the idea of a Communist sitting again in Rakowiecka Street, deciding what to do with the old secret-police dossiers and compiling new ones. "I am the guarantee that these files will never again be used in a political game," Walesa told an interviewer, "They are in safe hands." Safe, at any rate, for Walesa.

The first trial of strength came over the budget and the appointment of a finance minister. Walesa turned down two candidates and seemed to put much at risk in terms of smooth relations between Warsaw and the Western creditor states. Walesa's real target was not the two hapless ministers – both quite adequate candidates with budget-balancing skills – but Kwasniewski. In a long strategy talk with Wachowski and two other advisers, Walesa had been persuaded that Kwasniewski could be a serious rival for the presidency in 1995. Walesa had no doubt that he wanted to run again despite opinion polls that showed his popularity rating had dropped to three per cent. In December 1993 a poll conducted by Demoskop showed that only one in four Poles accepted Walesa and only one per cent approved of his policies. Building Kwasniewski into a Communist threat would accelerate personnel changes within the defeated right-wing parties, make them more sympathetic to Walesa, and swing their votes behind him in November 1995. That was the calculation in the Belvedere Palace. There were at least two ways that the strategy could backfire. First Kwasniewski, a canny politician, was leaving his presidential ambitions open for as long as possible; Walesa was tilting at windmills. Second, the right-wing parties were as determined in their opposition to Walesa as they were to Kwasniewski. Jaroslaw Kaczynski of the Centre Alliance, and former Walesa ally, put it clearly enough: "Walesa has been propping up the old regime, has strengthened the left and drawn the security service into the political debate. There is not the slightest question of support for Walesa not only because of the above reasons but also because he has no chance of being re-elected."

None of this mattered to Walesa though; he was taking real pleasure in the positioning game. By the middle of 1994 he was again courting the Solidarity union that he had so firmly, and so recently disavowed. Restless workers chanting Solidarity slogans and marching on the cabinet offices, pushing against police cordons and yelling about price rises – that was well-charted terrain for Walesa, the agitator-turned-president. Indeed, the panorama of Polish politics suddenly seemed remarkably similar to that of a previous era. On one side there was a hostile, edgy Russia; on the other a lukewarm West, which might yet again surrender Central European interests for the sake of a friendly Russia. The revolution, some argued, had come full circle.

That was not quite the case. Poland, whoever is in charge, is a captive of geography and the resulting geo-politics. Its room for manoeuvre was, and will always be, restricted. And history constantly chews at the ankles of modern Polish politicians. But as Walesa approached the end of his first tenure as president, it was plain that something had changed: the mood was sour. Wyspianski's riotous *Wesele* – the great allegorical work on the Polish political condition – had portrayed the liberation of Poland as a kind of magical transformation. But five years after the Central European revolutions that magic had disappeared, and the liberation of Poland had moved from poetry to prose.

Chronology

992–1025	Reign of Boleslaw the Brave.
1202–27	Reign of Leszek the White.
1279–88	Reign of Leszek the Black.
1576–86	Reign of Stefan Batory, prince of Transylvania.
1674–96	Reign of Jan Sobieski.
1791	Constitution drawn up establishing constitutional monarchy and permanent army; religious freedom guaranteed.
1794	Tadeusz Kosciuszko leads unsuccessful attempt to recapture land lost in first and second partitions of Poland. Third partition follows, between Russia, Austria and Prussia; loss of statehood.
1797–1815	Polish legions serve Napoleon.
1815	Congress of Vienna creates Kingdom of Poland under Russian control.
1830	Unsuccessful November uprising against Russian rule.
1848	Unsuccessful uprising against Prussia and Austria.
1863	Unsuccessful January uprising against Russia.
1918	Independent Polish state created.
1919–20	Polish–Soviet war; Poles recapture part of eastern territories under command of Jozef Pilsudski.
1926	Pilsudski leads coup. Constitution suspended, opposition suppressed until new government is formed and new constitution passed in 1931.
1939	23 April: Molotov and von Ribbentrop sign alliance with secret protocol agreeing a partition of Poland.
	1 September: Germany attacks Poland.
	17 September: Russia attacks Poland from the east.
	5 October: Polish army surrenders. Government in exile is formed. Polish units later fight on all major fronts including Battle of Britain, Norway, D-Day.
1940	Soviet NKVD squads murder 4,000 Polish officers in Katyn Forest.

1941–45	Jews forced into ghettos in Polish cities. Concentration camps set up, many of them in Poland.
1943	Warsaw ghetto uprising brutally suppressed.
1944	Warsaw uprising led by Home Army; Warsaw set ablaze.
1945	Yalta (February) and Potsdam (July) agreements. Political interest of Soviet Union in Central Europe acknowledged; Moscow-backed provisional government in Poland accepted on condition there are free elections.
1953–56	Cardinal Stefan Wyszynski held prisoner.
1956	October: Bread and Freedom riots in Poznan. 74 killed when workers try to storm Party buildings.
1968	March: Student protests. Anti-Semitic (and anti-Church, anti-liberal) campaign stirred up by the Party. Most workers refuse to join the students.
1970	December: Food price increases before Christmas trigger riots in Gdansk and elsewhere along the Baltic coast. Troops shoot on workers.
1976	New round of price increases sparks protests. Strikes at Radom – where Party offices are set on fire – and Ursus. Workers badly beaten by police.
	September: Intellectuals, including Jacek Kuron, set up Committee for the Defence of Workers (KOR) to defend persecuted workers, gather information, collect legal aid.
1978	Idea of free trade unions launched in Katowice.
1979	First Polish pilgrimage of Polish Pope, John Paul II.
1980	August: Strikes in Gdansk, led by Walesa, and elsewhere on the Baltic coast press for free trade unions, higher wages. Government caves in, agrees to key demands in Gdansk accord (31 August), Szczecin (30 August) and Jastrzebie (4 September).
	November: Independent trade union, the first in Soviet bloc, legally registered under the name Solidarity.
1981	March: Bydgoszcz sit-in strike leads to violent clashes with police and brings Solidarity to the brink of a general strike.
	13 September: Martial law is declared by prime minister and Party chief General Wojciech Jaruzelski. At least 5,000 oppositionists are interned without trial. Communications cut. Military courts replace civil courts. Transport, food distribution, factories put under direct army command.
1982	April: The Temporary Coordinating Committee links the various regional chieftains of the Solidarity underground resistance.
	October: Solidarity formally declared illegal, ending immediate hopes of a negotiated settlement with Jaruzelski regime.
	November: Brezhnev dies; Walesa released from internment.

1983	June: Pope's second Polish pilgrimage.
	July: Martial law formally lifted. Strict civil laws stay in place. Walesa meets underground leadership.
	October: Walesa wins Nobel Peace Prize.
1984	19 October: Solidarity sympathiser Father Jerzy Popieluszko murdered by secret-police agents.
1985	March: Gorbachev appointed General Secretary of the Communist Party of the Soviet Union.
	June: Trial of Wladyslaw Frasyniuk, Bogdan Lis, Adam Michnik.
1986	September: Amnesty of almost all political prisoners.
1987	Pope's third pilgrimage to Poland.
1988	May: Strike at Gdansk shipyards.
	August: Walesa and Interior Minister Kiszczak agree to Round Table talks after second round of strikes.
	30 November: Television duel between Walesa and official union leader Alfred Miodowicz.
1989	6 February–April: Round Table talks.
	7 April: Solidarity declared legal again.
	June: Semi-free elections. Solidarity wins full quota of 35 per cent in Sejm and 99 out of 100 seats in the freely elected senate.
	24 August: Tadeusz Mazowiecki appointed prime minister.
1990	January: First stage of Balcerowicz plan to control inflation and privatise the economy is introduced.
	April: Solidarity's second national congress.
	December: Walesa freely elected president of Poland.
1991	January: Jan Krzysztof Bielecki forms second Solidarity government.
	October: First free parliamentary elections; 29 parties represented in parliament.
	November: Walesa proposes "small constitution" to give himself greater executive powers; battle with parliament begins.
1992	January: Jan Olszewski leads a centre-right government.
	June: After months of struggle with Walesa, Olszewski government is toppled over secret files scandal.
	July: Poznan lawyer Hanna Suchocka forms fourth Solidarity government, a coalition of social liberals, free marketeers, farmers and Catholic activists.
1993	After months of only tepid support from Walesa, Suchocka government falls. Loses vote of no confidence because key ministers locked in lavatory.
	September: elections. Former Communists emerge as strongest party in parliament. They form government with Peasants Party under premiership of Waldemar Pawlak.

1994   Spring: Walesa opposes two nominees for finance minister and holds up budget, threatens to topple government. More than one million workers take part in protests against social spending cuts. Walesa prepares for presidential re-election in 1995.

Bibliography

Two of the Polish books listed – the second volume of Walesa's autobiography and Jaroslaw Kurski's *Wodz* – have been translated in English. I have relied however on the Polish original; my translation may differ from those published in the West.

ADAMSKI, Wladyslaw, *et al.*: *Polacy 80: Wyniki Badan Ankietowych*, Warsaw, Polska Academia Nauk, 1981

ANDRZEJEWSKI, Jakub: *Kor od Zewnatrz*, London, Aneks No. 34, 1984

ARENDT, Hannah: *On Revolution*, London, Penguin, 1973

ASCHERSON, Neal: *The Polish August*, London, Allen Lane, 1981

ASH, Timothy Garton: *The Polish Revolution*, London, Granta, 1983

BADKOWSKI, Lech: *Zapis*, 17, London, 1981

BERLIN, Isaiah: *Russian Thinkers*, London, Hogarth Press, 1991

BUJAK, Zbigniew: *Przepraszam za Solidarnosc*, Warsaw, BGW, 1991

CHECINSKI, Michael: *Poland: Nationalism, Communism, Anti-Semitism*, New York, Karz-Cohl, 1983

Collective work: *The Book of Lech Walesa.* First edition, London, Penguin, 1982. Second edition, Gdansk, Wydawnictwo Morskie, 1990

DAVIES, Norman: *God's Playground: A History of Poland*, Oxford, Clarendon Press, 1981

DROZDEK, Michal: *Istota Sporu Centrum Kontra Road*, Warsaw, Spojrzenia, 1990

DUBINSKI, Krzysztof: *Magdalenka: Transakcja Epoki. Notatki Z Poufnych Spotkan Kiszczak-Walesa*, Warsaw, Sylwa, 1990

FLORCZYK, Andrzej: *Kto Nie Lubi Lecha*, Warsaw, Wydawnictwo Andrzej Bonarski, 1990

GABRYEL, Piotr and JACKOWSKI, Karol: *Jablon i Jablko*, Koscian, Story, 1990

GACH, Zbigniew: *Antybohater*, Wroclaw, FOPRESS Agency, 1991

GIELZYNSKI, Wojciech and STEFANSKI, Lech: *Gdansk-Sierpnia '80*, Warsaw, Ksiazka i Wiedza, 1981

GIEREK, Edward: *Edward Gierek Replika*, Warsaw, BGW, 1990

GWIAZDA, Andrzej: *Gwiazda Miales Racje*, Sopot, ZP Sopot, 1990

GROCKI, Michal: *Konfidenci sa Wsrod Nas*, Warsaw, Editions Spotkania, 1993

HOLZER, Jerzy: *Solidarnosc 1980–81*, Paris, Instytut Literacki, 1984

KACZYNSKI, Jaroslaw: *Odwrotna Strona Medalu*, Warsaw, MOST, 1991

KARPINSKI, Jakub: *Countdown*, New York, Karz-Cohl, 1982

KISZCZAK, Czeslaw: *General Kiszczak Mowi . . . Prawie Wszystko*, Warsaw, BGW, 1991

KOLAKOWSKI, Leszek: *Czy Diabel Moze Byc Zbawiony i 27 Innych Kazan*, London, Aneks, 1982

KURSKI, Jacek and SEMKA, Piotr: *Lewy Czerwcowy*, Warsaw, Editions Spotkania, 1993

KURSKI, Jaroslaw: *Wodz*, Warsaw, Pomost, 1991

LIPSKI, Jan Jozef: *Kor: A History of the Workers' Defence Committee in Poland 1976–1981*, Berkeley, University of California Press, 1985

MICEWSKI, Andrzej: *Cardinal Wyszynski: A Biography*, San Diego, Harcourt Brace Jovanovich, 1984

OST, David: *Solidarity and the Politics of Anti-Politics*, Philadelphia, Temple University Press, 1990

POZOGA, Wladyslaw: *Wojciech Jaruzelski Tego Nigdy Nie Powie*, Warsaw Reporter, 1992

PULS 48, Warsaw–London, January-February, 1991

RAINA, Peter: *Poland 1981: Towards Socialist Renewal*, London, Allen and Unwin, 1985

RAKOWSKI, Mieczyslaw: *Jak to sie Stalo*, Warsaw, BGW, 1991

RABIEJ, Pawel and ROSINSKA, Inga: *Kim Pan Jest, Panie Wachowski?*, Warsaw, BGW, 1993

SINGER, Daniel: *The Road to Gdansk*, New York, Monthly Review Press, 1982

STANISZKIS, Jadwiga: *Poland's Self-Limiting Revolution*, Princeton, Princeton University Press, 1984

SMOLENSKI, Pawel and GIELZYNSKI, Wojciech: *Robotnicy '88*, London, Aneks 1989

WALESA, Lech: *A Path of Hope*, London, Collins Harvill, 1987

WALESA, Lech (with RYBICKI, Aram): *Droga do Wolnosci*, Warsaw, Editions Spotkania, 1991

Notes

The idea of revolution is discussed by Hannah Arendt, *On Revolution* (pp. 43ff of the Penguin 1990 edition)

CHAPTER ONE

pages 8–10: Author interviews Popowo and family, March 1992. First volume of Walesa's autobiography (*A Path of Hope*, Collins Harvill, 1987) describes his family in the first chapter but gives no detail on his parental relationships
page 11: Volker Elis Pilgrim, *Muttersöhne*, Rowohlt, 1989
page 15: See also *The Revolutionary Personality*, E. Victor Wolfenstein, Princeton University Press, 1971
page 17: "sticks and stones" – author interviews Plock

CHAPTER TWO

page 22: The rebuilding of Gdansk is well described in *Poland's Western and Northern Territories*, F. E. Ian Hamilton (OUP, 1975)
page 23: Author interview Father Jankowski, Jan. 1992
pages 27–28: Walesa devotes only two pages to the events of March 1968
pages 28–29: Published accounts of Danuta Walesa's background include *Wprost*, 11 Oct. 1992; *Kobieta i Zycie*, Jan. 1991; *Poznaniak*, 22 March, 1992

CHAPTER THREE

page 32: Author interviews Andrzej Gwiazda, Jan. 1992
page 33: *Countdown*, Jakub Karpinski, 1982, pp. 157ff
pages 36–8: The best English-language accounts of 1970–76 are in "The People's Polish Republic" chapter of *God's Playground*, Vol. 2, 1982, by Norman Davies, and in *Polish August* by Neal Ascherson, 1982

331

page 39: Author interviews Jerzy Borowczak, Feb. 1992

CHAPTER FOUR

pages 43–4: Author interview Andrzej Gwiazda and Joanna Duda-Gwiazda, Jan. 1992
page 45: Author interview Edmund Szczesiak, Feb. 1992
page 52: More fully treated in *The Priest Who Had to Die*, by Roger Boyes and John Moody, Gollancz, 1985
page 52: Author interview Jerzy Borowczak, Feb. 1992

CHAPTER FIVE

page 53: The life of Anna Walentynowicz is eloquently described in Hanna Krall's *Unschuldig für den Rest des Lebens*, Neue Kritik Verlag, 1983
page 54: The best narrative account of 1980 strikes is still Timothy Garton Ash's *The Polish Revolution*, Granta, 1991. An interesting analytical account is contained in David Ost's *Solidarity: The Politics of Anti-politics*, 1990. The most vivid description in Polish is *Gdansk-Sierpnia '80* by Wojciech Gielzynski and Lech Stefanski (KiW, 1981)
page 68: Author interview Tadeusz Wozniak, Feb. 1992
page 74: Author interview Wojciech Lamentowicz, May 1992

CHAPTER SIX

page 86: Ewa Berberyusz, *Tygodnik Powszechny*, Dec. 1980
page 93: Author interview Gwiazda, Jan. 1992
page 96: He was deeply tired; Danuta had just suffered a miscarriage.
page 96: Isaiah Berlin, *Russian Thinkers*, Penguin, 1978, pp. 22ff
page 97: see Walesa's *A Path of Hope*

CHAPTER SEVEN

page 105: Author interview Stefan Kisielewski, April 1992
page 108: More on the strange character of Adam Pietruszka in *The Priest Who Had to Die*
page 110: Author interview Jankowski, Jan. 1992
page 113: Agent quoted in General Kiszczak, *Mowi . . .* , BGW, 1991, pp. 152–3
page 118: Author interview Borowczak, Feb. 1992
pages 119–20: General Kiszczak, *Mowi . . .*

CHAPTER EIGHT

page 131: Author's notes from papal trip
page 137: I am grateful for the notes and insights of the late Stein Savik of Norway's *Aftenpostn*

CHAPTER NINE

pages 139–42: See the memoirs of General Pozoga (details in Bibliography)
page 145: Walesa's second volume of memoirs, *Droga do Wolnosci*

CHAPTER TEN

page 149: Rifkind was apparently influenced by a *Times* editorial urging the gesture
page 151: A full account of Glemp meeting and Popieluszko philosophy is contained in *The Priest Who Had to Die*
pages 158–9: Author interview Borowczak, Feb. 1992
page 160: Author interview Wojciech Gielzynski. Best account of the new worker mood can be found in his and Smolenski's *Robotnicy '88*, Aneks, 1989
page 164: Walesa's second volume of memoirs, *Droga do Wolnosci*, deals with this

CHAPTER ELEVEN

page 173: The memoirs of Bronislaw Geremek
page 174: See Mieczyslaw Rakowski's *Jak to sie Stalo*
page 178: *Magdalenka: Transakcja Epoki*, Krzysztof Dubinski. See also Krzysztof Leski's *Cos Rzecz o Okkraglym Stolc*, Warsaw, 1989; and Konstanty Gebert's *Mebel*, Aneks, 1989
page 181: General Kiszczak, *Mowi* . . .
page 189: Jaroslaw Kaczynski's *Odwrotna Strona Medalu*, MOST, 1991
page 190: Author interview Jacek Kuron, June 1992
page 193: Kaczynski, *Odwrotna*

CHAPTER TWELVE

page 210: Walesa quotes from author interview, Oct. 1989
page 214: See Hannah Arendt on worker councils in *On Revolution*, p. 249
page 216: Kaczynski, *Zycie Warszawy*, 7–8 April 1990
page 219: Author interview Szczesiak, Feb. 1992
pages 219–20: Jaroslaw Kurski's account of the episode and this short, but

critical period of Walesa's life is excellent. His observations are a model for all disgruntled courtiers.

page 223: *Ekha Planety*, 27 Dec. 1989

page 224: *Rzeczpospolita*, 3 April 1990

CHAPTER THIRTEEN

page 232: Kaczynski in *Odwrotna Strona Medalu*

page 235: *Gazeta Wyborcza*, 20 June 1990

page 240: Ibid.

page 240: *Polityka*, 30 June 1990

page 243: Author's recording

page 244: Nuncio story related by Kurski, confirmed by ambassador present at the exchange

page 253: Andrzej K. Wroblewski supplied one of several useful accounts

page 253: *Newsweek*, 19 Nov. 1990

page 254: Dmowski–Pilsudski duel discussed at length in Norman Davies, *In the Heart of Europe*, OUP, 1984

pages 257–8: Author notes on Tyminski campaign trail

CHAPTER FOURTEEN

page 265: Kaczynski on Danuta conversation in *Odwrotna Strona*, p. 130

page 268: *Who Are You, Mr Wachowski?* by Rabiej and Rosiewicz

page 272: Bielecki in *Tygodnik Solidarnosc*, 25 Jan. 1990

page 274: "Lithuania Must Have Freedom" in *Zycie Warszawy*, 18 Jan. 1991

page 276: Battery quote from *Wprost*, 10 Feb. 1991

page 278: *Ha'aretz*, 21 May 1991

CHAPTER FIFTEEN

page 284: All Parys and Macieriewicz quotes from *Lewy Czerwcowy*

EPILOGUE

page 313: Woycicki quote from *Zycie Warszawy*, 2 Feb. 1993

page 315: Michnik, *Gazeta Wyborcza*, 6–7 June 1992

page 316: Parys quote from *Lewy Czerwcowy*

page 317: Lamentowicz, *Tygodnik Solidarnosc*, 7 Feb. 1992

page 320: Walesa quote from the *Panorama* programme, Warsaw, 28 June 1993

INDEX

Other than in the entry under his name Lech Walesa is referred to as W.

341